Between the Devil and the Deep Blue Sea

"The Idle 'Prentice turn'd away, and sent to sea," engraving by William Hogarth, from the series "Industry and Idleness," 1747.

BETWEEN THE DEVIL AND THE DEEP BLUE SEA

MERCHANT SEAMEN, PIRATES, AND THE ANGLO-AMERICAN MARITIME WORLD, 1700–1750

Marcus Rediker
University of Pittsburgh

CAMBRIDGE
UNIVERSITY PRESS

CAMBRIDGE UNIVERSITY PRESS
Cambridge, New York, Melbourne, Madrid, Cape Town, Singapore, São Paulo, Delhi

Cambridge University Press
32 Avenue of the Americas, New York, NY 10013-2473, USA

www.cambridge.org
Information on this title: www.cambridge.org/9780521303422

First published 1987
First paperback edition 1989
12th printing 2007

Printed in the United States of America

A catalog record for this publication is available from the British Library.

Library of Congress Cataloging in Publication Data

ISBN 978-0-521-30342-2 hardback
ISBN 978-0-521-37983-0 paperback

To my mother, Faye Ponder
and to the memory of my father,
Buford C. Rediker

CONTENTS

vii

ILLUSTRATIONS

ix

ACKNOWLEDGMENTS

It is a great joy to thank the many people who, over the past ten years, have helped, directly and indirectly, to make this book. I would like to thank the staffs at the Public Record Office of Great Britain, at Kew Gardens, and especially at Chancery Lane for their tireless efforts in retrieving the huge, dusty collections of documents produced by the High Court of Admiralty. Similar thanks go to the many helpful people I encountered at the British Library, the National Maritime Museum, the Bodleian Library, the India Office Library, the Historical Society of Pennsylvania, the Virginia State Library, the Federal Records Center (Bayonne, New Jersey), and the Library of Congress. The librarians at Van Pelt Library at the University of Pennsylvania, where this book originated amid research on a doctoral dissertation, were unfailingly polite and helpful. I would also like to express my gratitude to the Department of History at the University of Pennsylvania, the Philadelphia Center for Early American Studies, and the Department of History at Georgetown University, who in various and generous ways made my research and writing possible.

My first personal thanks are reserved for my undergraduate mentor, Alan V. Briceland of Virginia Commonwealth University, who showed me how important the historian's work can be. I also wish to thank my advisor in graduate study at the University of Pennsylvania, Richard S. Dunn, whose scholarly example, wide-ranging knowledge, and good counsel have been invaluable. Michael Zuckerman has challenged, provoked, and encouraged me for years; his unruly brilliance has shaped this study in ways so numerous and subtle that I can no longer

count – or even see – them. I am grateful to Richard R. Bee-
man, Drew Gilpin Faust, and Walter M. Licht, who helped to
make my years at Penn an intellectual pleasure. I am pleased to
acknowledge the help of a host of fine scholars whom I happily
claim as friends: Craig Becker, Christopher Hill, Joanna Innes,
David Jaffee, Ken Morgan, Robert K. Schaeffer, Amy Dru
Stanley, Richard Stites, Daniel F. Vickers, and Steven Zdatny. I
would like to acknowledge the irreplaceable assistance of Leslie
S. Rowland and Alfred F. Young, two gifted historians who
have freely given both enthusiasm and insight to this project.
Special gratitude goes to friend and fellow-creature Peter Linebaugh, with whom I have exchanged views and materials on
the eighteenth century (and much else) for years. His comradely help is present in the following pages in the very ways in
which many of the historical problems are seen. Nancy Hewitt,
Dan Schiller, Susan Davis, and this project go way back together, to long nights at Walsh's Tavern on 43rd Street in West
Philadelphia. To my good fortune, all three have continued to
help, despite having been scattered to different corners of the
country. Nancy in particular has made a singular contribution
to the pages that follow.

I have enjoyed working with and getting to know Frank
Smith of Cambridge University Press. I have appreciated both
the interest and the fine editorial touch he has brought to bear
upon this study. My thanks to Helen Greenberg, who copy-
edited the manuscript with skill and precision. Portions of
Chapter 6 appeared as " 'Under the Banner of King Death':
The Social World of Anglo-American Pirates, 1716 to 1726," in
the *William and Mary Quarterly*, 3rd ser., 38 (1981), and are
reproduced here with thanks to the *Quarterly* and its superb
editor, Michael McGiffert.

Finally, I wish to thank my parents, Walt and Faye Ponder,
and my brother, Shayne Rediker, whose warmth and wisdom
helped to sustain me through many years of study. My greatest
thanks go to my wife, Wendy Z. Goldman, who has helped me
more than anyone else. She has enriched this book, and my
life, with her unbounded imagination, adventurous spirit, and
hard-headed genius.

ABBREVIATIONS

ADM	Admiralty Papers, PRO, London.
AHR	*American Historical Review.*
Barlow's Journal	*Barlow's Journal of his Life at Sea in King's Ships, East & West Indiamen, & Other Merchantmen from 1659 to 1703,* ed. Basil Lubbock (London, 1934).
BL	British Library, London.
CO	Colonial Office Papers, PRO, London.
EHR	*Economic History Review,* 2d series.
HCA	High Court of Admiralty Papers, PRO, London.
JEH	*Journal of Economic History.*
LC	Library of Congress, Washington, D.C.
MASS ADM	Records of the Court of Admiralty of the Province of Massachusetts Bay, 1718–47, Manuscript Division, LC.
P&P	*Past and Present.*
PRO	Public Record Office, London.
SC ADM	Minutes of the Vice-Admiralty Court of Charleston, South Carolina, 1716–63, Manuscript Division, LC.
VMHB	*Virginia Magazine of History and Biography.*
WMQ	*William and Mary Quarterly,* 3d series.

INTRODUCTION

The winds blew "most dreadfully" and the sea crackled like a "continuous flame." Whitecapped waves slapped the bobbing ship and, in the words of a trembling witness, "foamed upon our deck ready to tear us to pieces." The cargo below deck shifted and tumbled, water casks rolled from side to side, and cables screeched in the pulleys and tackles: "What a terrible cry the people gave, expecting to go every minute." The *Dove*, bound from Topsham, England, to Virginia, carrying manufactured goods and passengers, was no match for the violence of the elements, which quickly flipped the frail vessel onto its side. Two seamen armed with axes went on deck "to cut away the top mast, then the ship righted." But the *Dove*'s troubles were far from over. (See Figure 1.)

To lower the ship's center of gravity, lessen resistance to the whipping winds, and hence reduce the risk of capsizing, two of the *Dove*'s best seamen went aloft "to cut away the fore top mast and the ropes that held the bowsprit." As they hacked at the foretop, a monstrous wave hit the forward part of the ship, snapping the foremast as though it was a thin twig and carrying both it and one of the sailors "close by the board" and into the sea. The other seaman was crushed between the mast and the side of the ship. The man swept into the churning sea had taken the precaution of tying a rope to his leg; as a result, he finally "got in safe but had drunk so much salt water, and worked himself so that he was not able to stir."

Figure 1. English ships in a storm, by Willem Van de Velde II. Seamen work amid tattered sails, broken masts, and frayed, tangled rigging in a desperate effort to lessen the ships' resistance to the wind.

Meanwhile the masts that had been cut away or broken remained entangled with the ship's rigging, and a third seaman struggled to sever the connecting ropes to let the masts "go clear." But he soon returned to the hold clutching his mangled arm; he had "almost cut off his left hand" as he tried to free the dangling masts. The sea, meanwhile, continued to swell and rage. "The head of the ship" was "all under water," and the sea, according to passenger John Fontaine, was "foaming amongst us upon deck." With every dip of the rolling seas the entangled masts slammed against the side of the vessel, "thumping the ship to that degree that we expected every minute the masts would come through." The *Dove*'s most experienced seamen now lay disabled, "grieving that they could not help themselves" but encouraging the others as best they could. "We were surrounded by nothing but death and horror within and without," concluded Fontaine.[1]

The omnipotence of the elements and the fragility of human life marked the consciousness of every early-eighteenth-century seaman. Many a seaman "was wakened by a most horrible din, occasioned by the play of the gun carriages . . . , the cracking of cabins, the howling of the winds through the shrouds, the confused noise of the ship's crew, . . . and the clacking of the chain pumps." Francis Rogers in 1704 stood in terror before a lightning storm: "the sky seemed all on fire and [all around] were such swift darting rays of lightning, flying in long bright vains, with inexpressible fury as was very frightful."[2] At such times the air smelled "very much of Sulpher," as "every sea that broke sparkled like Lightning." Crashing thunder, "soe Sevear as if it would Split our Ship in Two," was sometimes loud enough to make the seamen "for some time Deaf." Seaman Jack Cremer described a storm in which everyone aboard shook "at each clap" and each looked upon the rest "as if Ghosts."[3] In such storms,

[1] *The Journal of James Fontaine: An Irish Huguenot Son in Spain and Virginia, 1710–1719*, ed. Edward Porter Alexander (Charlottesville, Va., 1972), 49–50. Fontaine's account has been slightly embellished with details from accounts of other severe storms. See, for example, William Dampier, "A New Voyage round the World," in Dampier, ed., *A Collection of Voyages* (London, 1729), 543.
[2] Tobias Smollett, *Roderick Random* (1748; reprint London, 1927), 165; "The Journal of Francis Rogers," in *Three Sea Journals of Stuart Times*, ed. Bruce Ingram (London, 1936), 189.
[3] Dampier, "New Voyage," 131, 414; *Ramblin' Jack: The Journal of Captain John Cremer*, ed. R. Reynall Bellamy (London, 1936), 216; Anonymous, "Voyage

the winds shrieked in the shrouds, so that "you could not hear a man speak, although he bawled in your ear as loud as he could." Other natural perils included the doldrums, in which a ship might eerily sit for days upon a sea as "smooth and bright as a looking glass." Waterspouts could erupt at any moment to overturn and sink a vessel. All too often, as sailor Ned Coxere noted, "death" appeared "before us, and where our graves were like to be if sudden means were not used."[4]

The crew and passengers aboard the *Dove* were lucky, as were Francis Rogers, Ramblin' Jack Cremer, and Ned Coxere. They survived; they lived to tell their chilling tales. Many others did not. The bed of the Atlantic is littered with the unmarked graves of the unlucky, with the rotting hulks of many wooden ships that were swallowed up, often without a trace. "Sea men are . . . to be numbred neither with the living nor the dead," explained a minister familiar with the dangers of life at sea; sailors' "lives [hang] continually in suspense before them." In their daily work, mused another cleric, seamen "border upon the Confines of Death and Eternity, every moment."[5] The perils at the edge of eternity haunted the eighteenth-century deep-sea sailor as he plied the forbidding oceans of the globe in small, brittle wooden vessels. The awesome dangers of the deep constituted one of the central facts of his life.

Indeed, the life-and-death drama of seafaring has given rise to a "romance of the sea" that has long, and in many ways rightly, dominated maritime history. There is something deeply stirring about the image of agile, determined seamen scuttling up and down a ship's mast in foamy, rolling seas, battling the winds, the waves, and the odds to eke out a living. Such an image commands attention, respect, even awe, particularly in a nation like the United States, bred on frontier heroes and the adventurous, sometimes vicious conquest of nature.[6]

---

to Guinea, Antego, Bay of Campeachy, Cuba, Barbadoes, &c., 1714–1723," BL, Add. Ms. 39946, f. 1.

[4] "Journal of Francis Rogers," 145; Dampier, "New Voyage," 452; William Falconer, *An Universal Dictionary of the Marine* (London, 1769; reprint New York, 1970), 60–61; *Adventures by Sea of Edward Coxere*, ed. E. H. W. Meyerstein (New York, 1946), 55.

[5] John Flavel, *Navigation Spiritualized: Or, A New Compass for Sea-Men* (Boston, 1726), i; Anonymous, *Mariner's Divine Mate* (Boston, 1715), 6.

[6] Richard Slotkin, *Regeneration Through Violence: The Mythology of the American Frontier, 1600–1800* (Middletown, Conn., 1973).

American maritime imagery owes much to Samuel Eliot Morison, Boston patrician, admiral, patriot, romantic, and Harvard historian.[7] Professor Morison's sailors went to sea brimming with enchantment. They were "adventure-loving youth," plow boys with "wanderlust" who longed "for a sea-change from grubbing stumps and splitting staves." Or, more poetically: "When gray November days succeeded the splendor of Indian summer, the clang of wild geese overhead summoned the spirit of youth to wealth and adventure."[8] Morison's seafarer was not so different from Herman Melville's Ishmael in *Moby Dick,* who fled to sea to escape "a damp, drizzly November in [his] soul," to hurtle after adventure and to inspect the self in a personal quest for truth and knowledge.[9] Morison's lad was perhaps a bit more materialistic and a bit less philosophical. But both were variations on the romantic theme.

Such images had small relevance to the lives of Anglo-American sailors in the first half of the eighteenth century, and consequently have small presence in this study. Courage and adventure – as demonstrated, for example, aboard the *Dove* – abound in the pages that follow, but wanderlust and romantic introspection receive but sparing mention. The early eighteenth century was, after all, a preromantic era, although something of the romantic obsession of the sea was emerging in the accounts of voyages around the world and in novels like *Robinson Crusoe.* It is important to remember that the sailors of Morison and Melville belong (if anywhere) to the nineteenth century.

The romantic image of seafaring has tended to obscure important features of life at sea in the eighteenth century. It has, for example, misrepresented the motives of the men who cast their lot with the sea. As Jesse Lemisch observed of Morison's vision of maritime life, "The presence . . . of fugitives and floaters, powerless in a tough environment, makes *wanderlust* appear an ironic parody of the motives which made at least some men go to sea."[10] Further, romantic maritime historians

---

[7] Wilcomb E. Washburn, "Samuel Eliot Morison, Historian," *WMQ* 36 (1979), 325–52.

[8] Samuel Eliot Morison, *The Maritime History of Massachusetts Bay, 1783–1860* (Boston, 1921), 16.

[9] Herman Melville, *Moby Dick* (New York, 1967).

[10] Jesse Lemisch, "Jack Tar in the Streets: Merchant Seamen in the Politics of Revolutionary America," *WMQ* 25 (1968), 377.

have tended to see the seaman's quest, like Ishmael's, largely in individual and national terms.[11] Yet the struggles against nature, like the many conflicts among men, were, at bottom, co-operative and collective undertakings. And these confrontations, like so much of maritime life, were deeply informed by the international character of both maritime work and the workers themselves. The romantic perspective has thus misrepresented or omitted vital segments of the seaman's experience.

The romantic image has distorted the reality of life at sea by concentrating on the struggle of man and nature to the exclusion of other aspects of maritime life, notably the jarring confrontation of man against man. A full understanding of life at sea requires a broader social approach, one that takes into account the crewmen of the *Dove* as they wrangled with their merchant-shipowner over wages; Jack Cremer as he regularly thwarted his captains by deserting their ships; and Ned Coxere as he matched wits with royal officials by seeking to escape impressment. The seaman's dilemma went beyond the menacing, seemingly boundless forces of nature he confronted. The tar was caught between the devil and the deep blue sea: On one side stood his captain, who was backed by the merchant and royal official, and who held near-dictatorial powers that served a capitalist system rapidly covering the globe; on the other side stood the relentlessly dangerous natural world. Many important ideas and practices emerged in the social zone between the man-made and natural dangers that governed the seaman's life.

The eighteenth-century deep-sea sailor is still by and large an unknown man. Gary Nash has noted, for example, that all of the early American northern seaports had hundreds of free unskilled workers, including seamen, but that such men "are perhaps the most elusive social group in early American history because they moved from port to port with greater frequency than other urban dwellers, shifted occupations, died young, and, as the poorest members of the free white community, least often left behind traces of their lives on the tax lists or in land or probate records."[12] Nonetheless, "[t]o ignore this group of

---

[11] Washburn, "Samuel Eliot Morison," 341, comments on Morison's emphasis on the individual.

[12] Gary B. Nash, *The Urban Crucible: Social Change, Political Consciousness, and the Origins of the American Revolution* (Cambridge, Mass., 1979), 16.

struggling, disease-prone, ill-paid laboring men is to dismiss from consideration those without whose lives the wheels of maritime commerce could not have turned."[13] Nash's comments are equally appropriate for eighteenth-century England, where seamen played a major role but in whose history they have been largely invisible.[14] In this study I have attempted to recover the experiences of the common seaman in the first half of the eighteenth century, to continue and extend the path-breaking work of Jesse Lemisch, and to do so in the spirit of "history from the bottom up."[15] Although I have necessarily treated the merchants, maritime captains, lesser officers, and royal officials who shaped the seaman's life, the emphasis throughout is on Jack Tar himself – his hopes, fears, aspirations, defeats, and victories. I hope that my findings and speculations will encourage further research on the elusive but important workers who inhabited a wooden world.

In emphasizing the collective nature of maritime life, this book is part of a larger current effort to transform "labor history" into "working-class history." The new history, in the words of Gregory S. Kealey, "ceases to be simply a category of political economy, a problem of industrial relations, a canon of saintly working-class leaders, a chronicle of local unions or a chronology of militant strike actions. Instead it becomes part of the history of society. Workers are no longer seen as isolated figures engaged only in trade unions, strikes, and radical politics; instead they are studied in a totality that includes their cultural background and social relations, as well as their institutional membership and economic and political behaviour."[16]

My main intention has been to study the collective self-activity of maritime workers; to ask, with Eugene D. Genovese, Herbert G. Gutman, and others, not "what was done to these work-

---

[13] Ibid., 64.
[14] Two recent and very good books, Robert W. Malcolmson's *Life and Labour in England, 1700–1780* (New York, 1981) and John Rule's *The Experience of Labour in Eighteenth-Century English Industry* (New York, 1981), illustrate the point by saying very little about seamen.
[15] Jesse Lemisch, "The American Revolution Seen from the Bottom Up," in Barton Bernstein, ed., *Towards a New Past: Dissenting Essays in American History* (New York, 1968), 3–45.
[16] Gregory S. Kealey, "Labour and Working Class History in Canada: Prospects in the 1980s," *Labour/Le Travailleur* 7 (1981), 69.

ing people?" but rather "what did these working people do for themselves and how did they do it?"[17] I have therefore given special attention to the efforts made by seafaring workers to free themselves from harsh conditions and exploitation. Seamen devised various tactics of resistance and forms of self-organization. Needless to say, such tactics and innovations have rarely been studied in the older maritime historiography. There have been few investigations of the areas and the ways in which the interests and values of shipowners, merchants, and captains diverged from those of the "ship's people." The failure to explore the full range of the activities of seamen – and to study them on their own terms – has obscured many of the critical features of maritime culture.

William Weeden, a nineteenth-century historian of early New England, wrote that "[i]f we could look into the living of these hardy mariners in their dingy cabins, it would be history indeed."[18] This study takes up Weeden's challenge but emphasizes Jack's life at sea – in the damp, dark hold of the vessel, on the decks, aloft among the sails – and only secondarily his life in his "dingy cabin" in port. The effort has required an approach that draws not only on recent scholarship in working-class history but also on work in social, economic, cultural, and political history. I have also borrowed from other disciplines, notably linguistics, sociology, economics, anthropology, and especially ethnography. The interdisciplinary approach proceeds from the belief that the history of seafaring people can and must be more than a chronicle of admirals, captains, and military battles at sea: It must be made to speak to larger historical problems and processes. The seaman's international life and labor require an international history, linking the pasts of Britain and America to broad intercultural histories of continental Europe, the Mediterranean, Africa, and the East and West Indies. Jack Tar challenges us to adopt his almost nomadic mobility and to follow him from port to port around the globe. His interna-

---

[17] Eugene D. Genovese, "American Slaves and Their History," in his *In Red and Black: Marxian Explorations in Southern and Afro-American History* (New York, 1971), 106; Herbert G. Gutman, *Work, Culture, and Society in Industrializing America* (New York, 1976).

[18] Quoted in Nash, *Urban Crucible*, 64.

tional existence beckons us to transcend the often artificial barriers of regional-national history.

Trade linked the world's regions and nations, and the eighteenth century – "the century of trade" – was especially important in the growth of commerce. The century of trade was necessarily the century of the growth of the maritime working class, a fact that provides compelling reasons for studying seamen between 1700 and 1750.[19] This period witnessed the maturation of the British shipping industry as well as a remarkable expansion of the American merchant marine. Britain's maritime hegemony was taking shape, the structure of the empire was fixed and durable, and the international market chain was becoming more orderly. A strong measure of stability came to the commerce of the North Atlantic. Sailoring settled into a relatively routine, lifelong occupation for ever larger numbers of wage workers. Indeed, seamen were one of the earliest and most numerous groups of free wage laborers in the British and American economies. Their experiences pointed in many ways toward the Industrial Revolution.

In accordance with the imperial and international organization of the eighteenth-century maritime labor market, I have concentrated here upon Anglo-American seamen, the transatlantic sailors who were subjects of the British crown. Early-eighteenth-century seamen, whether formally residents of Bristol, Port Royal, Glasgow, Boston, London, New York, Liverpool, or Philadelphia, were part of the same maritime culture and society, and must therefore be studied within a framework that situates them within both the British Empire and the larger world.

This study is organized topically. It begins with a survey of the seaman's world circa 1740, which tours the major ports of the British North Atlantic, describes the commodities piled on the docks and quays, and details those aspects of political economy and history that shaped the seaman's life. Chapter 2 discusses the organization and experience of work at sea. Chapter 3 considers the "wage" in free wage labor and analyzes wage

---

[19] See Karl Marx, "The German Ideology," in Marx and Frederick Engels, *Selected Works* (Moscow, 1969), vol. I, 59–60; Edgar Gold, *Maritime Transport: The Evolution of International Marine Policy and Shipping Law* (Lexington, Mass., 1981), 51, 61, 62.

rates and negotiations. Chapter 4 examines culture and community at sea, and Chapter 5 explores maritime authority and labor discipline. Chapter 6 investigates the social world of piracy, suggesting the ways in which it embodied features of the larger culture of maritime labor. The Conclusion returns to a more general level of analysis, relating the seaman's experience to the process of social change and working-class development in America and England.

Throughout the text, original spelling has been retained in all quotations, and *sic* is employed only where the meaning may be unclear. All dates are rendered by the Old Style Julian calendar, except those from January 1 to March 25, which appear according to the New Style Gregorian calendar.

In reconstructing the social and cultural life of the early-eighteenth-century common seaman, I have sought both to tell a story and to write a history. I hope that general readers as well as specialists will find the effort of interest. Following Tobias Smollett, one of the earliest writers concerned with the plight of the seaman, I have also sought to inspire "that generous indignation which ought to animate the reader against the sordid and vicious disposition of the world."[20] As we shall see in abundant, sometimes gruesome detail, the jolly tar did indeed live in a world fully possessed of a "sordid and vicious" side. His creative survival in it is the subject of this book.

[20] Smollett, *Roderick Random*, 5.

1

THE SEAMAN AS MAN OF THE WORLD

A Tour of the North Atlantic, c. 1740

In an age when most men and women in England and America lived in small, clustered local communities, the early-eighteenth-century sailor inhabited a world huge, boundless, and international. The seaman sailed the seven seas; he explored the edges of the earth. He toiled among a diverse and globally experienced body of workingmen, whose labors linked the continents and cultures of Europe, Africa, Asia, and North and South America. Thus the seaman's world consisted of the North Atlantic and beyond. He sailed from London to Europe, the Mediterranean, and the East Indies. He made his way to Bristol and Liverpool; his slave ships voyaged to the coast of Africa; he ventured to Glasgow, the Chesapeake, and Charleston in Carolina. He skimmed the bright blue waters of the Caribbean and passed northward to Boston, New York, and Philadelphia, the budding metropolises of a hopeful New World. The seaman was central to the changing history and political economy of the North Atlantic world.[1]

By 1740 Jack Tar was a man of distinctive appearance, easily recognized as a man of the sea by his contemporaries. Sir

[1] This chapter is indebted to the arguments, old and new, about the transition from feudalism to capitalism in the West. See Rodney Hilton, ed., *The Transition from Feudalism to Capitalism* (London, 1976); Maurice Dobb, *Studies in the Development of Capitalism* (New York, 1947); Immanuel Wallerstein, *The Modern World-System: Capitalist Agriculture and the Origins of the European World-Economy in the Sixteenth Century* (New York, 1976) and *The Modern World-System II: Mercantilism and the Consolidation of the European World-Economy, 1600–1750* (New York, 1980); Perry Anderson, *Lineages of the Absolutist State* (London, 1974); Robert Brenner, "Agrarian Class Structure and Economic Development in Pre-Industrial Europe," *P&P* 70 (1976), 30–75.

John Fielding, observing seamen across a chasm of class and culture, explained in 1776: "When one goes to Rotherhithe or Wapping, which places [in London] are chiefly inhabited by sailors, but that somewhat of the same language is spoken, a man would be apt to suspect himself in another country. Their manner of living, speaking, acting, dressing and behaving are so peculiar to themselves. Yet with all, they are perhaps the bravest and boldest fellows in the world." Ned Ward once came across a "knot of jolly, rough-hewn" seafaring men "who looked as if they'd been hammered into an uncouth shape upon Vulcan's Anvil; whose iron sides, and metal-coloured faces seemed to dare all weathers, spit fire at the frigid zone, and bid death defiance."[2]

Most of the seaman's "peculiarities" resulted from the nature and setting of his work. The seaman had an unmistakable way of talking that included technical terms, unusual syntax, distinctive pronunciation, and a generous portion of swearing and cursing. He also had his own way of walking. Sailors, as Ward pointed out, tended to "swing their Corps like a Pendulum, and believe it the most upright, steady Motion." Their gait gave balance on pitching, rolling decks. "They are sure to walk firm, where all other Creatures tumble," admitted Ward.[3]

The seaman was also distinguished readily by the dress that covered his sturdy frame. He wore wide, baggy breeches, cut a few inches above the ankle and often made of a heavy, rough red nap. The breeches were tarred as a protection against the cold, numbing wetness. He frequently wore a checked shirt of blue and white linen, a blue or gray "fearnought" jacket, gray stockings, and a Monmouth cap. Some of his apparel he might well have made for himself, so deft was he with needle and thread after years of mending sails at sea. Always making clever use of commonplaces, the seaman used bits of hardened cheese or "ye Joints of ye Back-Bone" of a shark as buttons on a jacket.[4]

---

[2] Fielding quoted in Hugh Phillips, *The Thames about 1750* (London, 1951), 28; Ned Ward, *The London Spy: The Vanities and Vices of the Town Exposed to View*, ed. Arthur L. Hayward (1698; reprint London, 1927), 268.

[3] Ned Ward, *The Wooden World Dissected: In the Character of a Ship of War* (1708; reprint London, 1756), 4. On maritime language, see Chapter 4 of this book.

[4] "Voyage to Guinea, Antego, Bay of Campeachy, Cuba, Barbadoes &c., 1714–1723," BL, Add. Ms. 39946, f. 6. See also Christopher Lloyd, *The*

Jack Tar's body often gave away his line of work. The tattoo, then as now, often adorned his forearm. "The Jerusalem Cross" and other popular designs were made by "pricking the Skin, and rubbing in a Pigment," either ink or, more often, gunpowder. Seafaring left other, unwanted distinguishing marks. Prolonged exposure to the sun and its intensified reflection off the water gave him a tanned or reddened – "metal coloured" – and prematurely wrinkled look. Roderick Random's uncle, seaman Tom Bowling, had a face that "had withstood the most obstinate assaults of the weather." Heavy cargo often scarred or disfigured Jack Tar's hands. Thus the sailor was in many ways a marked man, much to the delight of the press gangs that combed the port towns in search of seamen to serve the crown.[5]

Most seamen had gone to sea in their late teens or early twenties. The average common tar in the first half of the eighteenth century was twenty-seven years old. The ship's lesser officers tended to be in their late twenties, and captains and

Footnote 4 (*cont.*):

British Seaman, 1200–1860: A Social Survey (Rutherford, N.J., 1970), 235; "Introduction" by Captain Alfred Dewar in *The Voyages and Travels of Captain Nathaniel Uring*, ed. Dewar (1726; reprint London, 1928), xxix; Arthur Pierce Middleton, *Tobacco Coast: A Maritime History of Chesapeake Bay in the Colonial Period* (Newport News, Va., 1953), 283; *Adventures by Sea of Edward Coxere*, ed. E. H. W. Meyerstein (New York, 1946), 111; R. Campbell, *The London Tradesman* (London, 1747), 324.

[5] William Dampier, "A New Voyage round the World" in Dampier, ed., *A Collection of Voyages* (London, 1729), 514; J. R. Hutchinson, *The Press-Gang Afloat and Ashore* (New York, 1914), 173; Ward, *Wooden World*, 74; Tobias Smollett, *Roderick Random* (1748; reprint London, 1927), 16. For a later period, see the excellent article by Ira Dye, "Early American Merchant Seafarers," *Proceedings of the American Philosophical Society* 120 (1976), 353–7; Dye notes the frequent scarring of seamen's hands. For a general history of tattoos, see Albert Parry, *Tattoo: Secrets of a Strange Art* (New York, 1933). The quotations about tattooing are from Ward, *London Spy*, 268, 269. Richard Pares, in a fine article, "The Manning of the Royal Navy in the West Indies, 1702–1763," correctly observed that during the eighteenth century the "distinction between seamen and landmen was probably less marked in America than in Europe" [*Royal Historical Society Transactions* 20 (1937), 44–5]. The availability of land retarded the development of wage labor and a landless working class in the North American colonies. Yet there were, of course, many English seamen present in American port towns; moreover, the distinctive seafaring culture was quickly finding a place in the colonies. See Gary B. Nash, *The Urban Crucible: Social Change, Political Consciousness, and the Origins of the American Revolution* (Cambridge, Mass., 1979), 16, 64, and Jesse Lemisch, "Jack Tar Versus John Bull: The Role of New York's Merchant Seamen in Precipitating the Revolution," Ph.D. diss., Yale University, 1962.

mates in their early thirties. These men would have called any one of the major ports "home," though many had been born elsewhere. Some were younger sons of yeomen and poor farmers, men who had migrated to the cities in search of work and finally found it on the docks. Some, perhaps, had been dispossessed of land by enclosure. Others had been picked up by press gangs, and once forced to acquire the skills of maritime labor in the Royal Navy, decided to work as merchant seamen. Still others were rural folk who had been drawn to the sea by the lure of high wages during wartime.[6]

Economic necessity pushed many to the water's edge. Seamen's proverbs often suggested a lack of choice in their occupation. "Those who would go to sea for pleasure would go to hell for pastime," one maxim had it. Or, inveighed another, "whosoever putteth his child to get his living at sea had better a great deal bind him prentice to a hangman." A group of landmen told sailor Matthew Bishop that "they took the Sea to be fit only for those who could not get Bread by Land." The rigors of a seaman's life, likened to hell and measured against popular hatred of the hangman, were widely known and not often freely chosen.[7]

Yet there were brighter motivations that coexisted with the darker, and these were richly illustrated in the life of a late-seventeenth-century sailor, Edward Barlow. Born in Prestwich, England, to a family of poor, struggling farmers, Barlow and his brothers had no chance to be apprenticed to the better crafts "by reason [that] the tradesmen would not take us without money or unless we would serve eight or nine years," an unreasonably long term. Barlow could have become an agricultural laborer but sneered, "I never had any great mind to country work, as ploughing and sowing and making of hay and reaping, nor also of winter work, as hedging and ditching and thrashing and dunging amongst cattle, and suchlike Drudgery." Young Barlow had instead a mind to travel. He had always loved "to hear our neighbors and other people tell of their travels and of strange things in other countries." At the

---

[6] Very little is known about the social origins of seamen. But see Ralph Davis, *The Rise of the English Shipping Industry in the Seventeenth and Eighteenth Centuries* (London, 1962), 153. For data on the ages of seamen, see Appendix A.

[7] Charles Napier Robinson, *The British Tar in Fact and Fiction* (London, 1911), 353; *Barlow's Journal*, 90; *The Life and Adventures of Matthew Bishop* (London, 1744), 61.

age of seventeen he cast his lot with the sea, looking back over his shoulder at provincial village life with the contempt of the worldly: "Some of them [his neighbors] would not venture a day's journey from out of the [sight of the] smoke of their chimneys or the taste of their mother's milk, not even upon the condition that they might eat and drink of as good cheer as the best nobleman of the land, but they would rather stay at home and eat a little brown crust and a little whey." Edward Barlow became a sailor, though he hardly fared like a nobleman, and many were the times when he bitterly lamented his decision to pursue the seaman's calling.[8] (See Figure 2.)

The reasons men sailed the waves in the early modern period were best summed up by the late historian Ralph Davis: "To see the world, to get a good rate of pay, to get a good job of some sort at any price, to do what father did – these were the motives of those who went to sea; perhaps some went willy-nilly, drunk or unconscious, as the crimp made up the required crew as best he could." Almost all working people knew, by way of family, friends, or relatives, the hardships the seaman faced: His was, as a sea song said, "a damned hard life, full of toil and strife."[9]

A contemporary of Edward Barlow, a man by the name of Sir William Petty, was developing a completely different perspective on seafaring, one concerned not with the sailor's need for sustenance or the quality of the life itself, but rather with the place of the seaman in the imperial scheme of things, in the rapidly unfolding system of international capitalism. Petty was a key figure in the development of political arithmetic, the seventeenth- and early-eighteenth-century forebear of political economy and statistics. Political arithmetic was an early effort to analyze capitalism as a system, to calculate the direction and magnitude of social and economic forces, and to plot a course for the accumulation of capital and the extension of national power in a turbulent, expanding economic universe. Political arithmeticians had two main preoccupations: the "wealth of the kingdom," especially its social distribution, and the balance and terms of trade, especially foreign trade. Apparently they did not grasp, or did not care to grasp, the connec-

---

[8] *Barlow's Journal*, 15, 21, 31, 163. See also *Adventures by Sea of Edward Coxere*, 15.
[9] Davis, *English Shipping*, 153.

Figure 2. The *Wentworth,* 1701, as drawn by seaman Edward Barlow. Barlow was unusual among maritime artists in peopling his ships with sailors.

tion between the increasing wealth of the few and the increasing poverty of the many, but to some extent they understood that commercial supremacy helped to produce predominance in manufacturing and industry.[10]

[10] Sir William Petty, "Political Arithmetic" in *The Economic Writings of Sir William Petty,* ed. Charles Henry Hull (Cambridge, 1899), 259–60; Charles Henry Wilson, *England's Apprenticeship, 1603–1763* (London, 1965); 226; Joyce Appleby, *Economic Thought and Ideology in Seventeenth-Century England* (Princeton, N.J., 1979), 83, 144. Karl Marx, who considered Petty's treatment of the origin and computation of surplus value to be "somewhat confused," admitted that in "the grappling with ideas[,] striking passages can be found here and there." See *Theories of Surplus Value* (Moscow, 1963), vol. I, 354–63, quotation on 355.

In Petty's grand and abstract view, seamen were "the very Pillars" of the English nation and empire, and not only in their role as naval defenders. "The Labour of Seamen, and the Freight of Ships," Petty explained, "is always of the nature of an Exported Commodity, the overplus whereof, above what is Imported, brings home money." Sailors, in this early formulation of the labor theory of value, were the source of an "overplus," a surplus value central to the international accumulation of capital. Barlow's lack of money and desire to see the world were transformed, through maritime labor, into Petty's accumulation of capital and imperial domination of the world. Petty elaborated in theory what Barlow experienced in practice. The seaman's labor was a commodity to be sold on an open market like any other.[11] Labor had not always been organized in this manner.

Beneath the seemingly neutral and impersonal language of Petty's political arithmetic lay the harsh realities that attended England's long, slow, uneven, and bloody transition from feudalism to capitalism. Since the capitalist mode of production ultimately requires the sale and purchase of labor power in a market through the medium of the wage, a major imperative of early modern capitalist development was the simultaneous dispossession of large numbers of small property holders and the consolidation and centralization of newly available property in the hands of a minority. This was the process of "primitive accumulation." The many, "suddenly and forcibly torn from their means of subsistence," were hurled on the labor market, "as free, unprotected, and rightless proletarians"; there they had no alternative but to sell their labor power to make a living.[12]

In England the major sources of dispossession were the disbanding of feudal retainers, the dissolution of feudal monasteries, changes in agricultural methods, foreclosure by debt, and probably best known of all, enclosure. Wealthy landowners enclosed their lands and extinguished the common rights that lessened dependence on wage labor. One major part of a complex popular response to enclosure was captured in verse:

---

[11] Petty, "Political Arithmetic," 259–60, 276, 280–3, 292, 304.
[12] Karl Marx, *Capital: A Critique of Political Economy*, trans. Ben Fowkes (New York, 1977), 876; Dobb, *Studies*, 7.

They hang the man and flog the woman
Who steals the goose from off the Common;
But let the greater criminal loose
Who steals the Common from the goose.[13]

"They" – the English ruling class – preferred to turn the land over to capitalist small farmers and to evict the "undisciplined." Those evicted, the "seething mobility," remained in rural areas as agricultural wage laborers or tramped to the cities and found their way into crime, casual labor, the lower trades, and the army, navy, or merchant shipping industry. These tenants and laborers, freed from the lord of the manor, were not yet subject to the disciplinary gaze of the factory master. They rambled about as masterless men and women, and they symbolized the radical changes wrought by capital. The integument of rural culture had been gashed, and new independent actors, free to find a job and free to starve if they couldn't, traipsed the countryside trying to keep body and soul together.[14]

Dispossession was only one part of the process of primitive accumulation. What was lost by the many had to be consolidated by the few. Consolidation proceeded along three basic lines. First was the centralization of agricultural production. The size of farms and estates increased steadily from 1550 to 1750, as did agricultural productivity. At the end of the seventeenth century only some 60 percent of the English population remained in agricultural production, and by 1750 wage labor had become a basic component of both urban and rural economies.[15]

[13] Quoted in Robert W. Malcolmson, *Life and Labour in England, 1700–1780* (New York, 1982), 128. See also his discussion of enclosure (140–4, 127–9) and that of Dobb (*Studies*, 224, 227, 242).

[14] Wallerstein, *Modern World System*, 165; Christopher Hill, *The World Turned Upside Down: Radical Ideas in the English Revolution* (New York, 1972), 44; Peter Clark, "Migration in England during the late Seventeenth and early Eighteenth Centuries," *P&P* 83 (1979), 57–90. The summary offered here of the transition from feudalism to capitalism is necessarily oversimplified. The movement from peasant to proletarian was for some English men and women quick and wrenching; for many others, surely a majority, it was a protracted and phased process. The transition was not as sharp as my brief summary may imply.

[15] Dobb, *Studies*, 185; D. C. Coleman, *The Economy of England, 1450–1750* (Oxford, 1977), 124; B. A. Holderness, *Pre-Industrial England: Economy and Society, 1500–1750* (London, 1976), 60–1, 203, 228; Brenner, "Agrarian

Manufacturing was a second domain for the consolidation of economic power. Shipbuilding, mining, and other enterprises expanded, and, even more crucial, manufacturing moved into rural areas. In regions where small producers were powerful enough to forestall enclosure, where the centralization of agricultural production moved at a slower pace, or where population grew most quickly, people clung to the land even when unable to wring a living from it. Merchants established the putting-out system in this context of rural underemployment, extending the hand of the urban capitalist into the new areas of production and new parts of the English countryside. The process of dispossession was incremental and often led to intermediate arrangements in which households combined work on common or private lands with work for wages.

Neither the putting-out system nor export agriculture could have developed apart from the third major area in which economic power was concentrated: international trade and the new colonial system.[16] England earnestly took to the seas in the second half of the sixteenth century, particularly with the cod and herring fisheries and the coal-carrying trade. But the rise to deep-sea supremacy began with the founding of the Russia Company (1553), the Eastland Company (1578), the Levant Company (1581), the East India Company (1600), and, considerably later, the Royal Adventurers into Africa (1660), soon to

Footnote 15 (*cont.*)
Class Structure," 63, 65; Peter Mathias, "The Social Structure in the Eighteenth Century: A Calculation by Joseph Massie," in *The Transformation of England: Essays in the Social and Economic History of England in the Eighteenth Century* (New York, 1979), 178.

[16] Brenner, "Agrarian Class Structure," 75; Dobb, *Studies*, 151, 230; Hans Medick, "The Proto-Industrial Family Economy: The Structural Function of Household and Family during the Transition from Peasant Society to Industrial Capitalism," *Social History* 3 (1978), 297; John Merrington, "Town and Country in the Transition to Capitalism," in Hilton, *Transition*, 190; George Lefebvre, "Some Observations," in Hilton, *Transition*, 122–7. The starting point for the growing body of studies of proto-industrialization is Franklin Mendels, "Proto-Industrialization: The First Phase in the Industrialization Process," *JEH* 32 (1972), 241–61, but see also D. C. Coleman, "Proto-Industrialization: A Concept Too Many," *EHR* 36 (1983), 435–48. Some of the links between the different processes of consolidation are discussed in E. J. Hobsbawm, "The General Crisis of the European Economy in the Seventeenth Century, II," *Crisis in Europe, 1560–1660*, ed. Trevor Aston (New York, 1965), 37–9. See also R. Millward, "The Emergence of Wage Labor in Early Modern England," *Explorations in Economic History* 18 (1981), 21–39.

become the Royal African Company. Apart from the all-important commerce in slaves, the chartered companies traded in luxury goods, seeking to "buy cheap and sell dear" and to exploit price differentials between widely separated markets and spheres of production.[17]

Cries of opposition to the trading monopolies mounted in the early seventeenth century. Advocates of freer trade, excluded from the lucrative commerce in luxuries, sought profits elsewhere and, logically enough, turned to the prospering trades with America. Since these newer routes were organized around bulk goods – largely tobacco and sugar – the new merchants were forced to mobilize huge amounts of labor to move their commodities on a regular basis. Labor-intensive shipping, already characteristic of the northern European trades, grew at the pace of expanding production, and increasingly at the pace of the exploitation of slave labor, in the New World.[18]

Between these English merchants and their dizzying dreams of wealth stood a formidable adversary, the Dutch, who as the "principal carriers" of early transatlantic trade sat upon the summit of the international capitalist economy. But England's new men of trade had decided that the seas should be theirs, and in 1651, having employed their new wealth and standing to move into parliamentary circles, they fired the "opening gun" in what would prove to be a bitter, protracted struggle with Holland for maritime supremacy.[19] Hoping at once to cripple the Dutch trade and to reduce the privileges of English monopolies, they pushed for the Navigation Act of 1651. No goods were to be brought into England but by English ships,

---

[17] Lloyd, *British Seaman*, 28; Davis, *English Shipping*, 5; Colin A. Palmer, *Human Cargoes: The British Slave Trade to Spanish America, 1700–1739* (Urbana, Ill., 1981), 5; Merrington, "Town and Country," 177; Dobb, *Studies*, 89, 109–20, 198–9.

[18] Dobb, *Studies*, 167, 193, 219; Robert Brenner, "The Social Basis of English Commercial Expansion, 1550–1650," *JEH* 32 (1972), 375, 378, 381, 382, 384. See also Wilson, *England's Apprenticeship*, 271.

[19] J. H. Parry, "Transport and Trade Routes," *The Cambridge Economic History of Europe*, vol. 4: *The Economy of Expanding Europe in the Sixteenth and Seventeenth Centuries*, ed. E. E. Rich and C. H. Wilson (Cambridge, 1967), 204, 205; Appleby, *Economic Thought*, 73; Davis, *English Shipping*, 12; Wallerstein, *Modern World System II*, 38, 75; Charles M. Andrews, *The Colonial Period in American History* (New Haven, Conn., 1938), vol. 4, 32; Brenner, "Social Basis," 384.

manned by English sailors, and no foreign vessels were to carry English coastal trade.[20]

Legislative action was soon matched by military confrontation; the contest for trade and empire turned bloody. English rulers fought three wars against Holland in the third quarter of the seventeenth century: in 1652–4, 1665–7, and 1672–4. Meanwhile, parliamentary initiatives continued. Additional Navigation Acts were passed in 1660, 1663, and 1673, each more detailed than the first and more concerned with the increasingly important trades with the New World. Certain commodities – those most central to bulk shipping such as sugar, tobacco, indigo, rice, cacao, molasses, and naval stores – were "enumerated": English carriers were strictly to monopolize their movement.[21] With the passage of the Navigation Act of 1696 and the Board of Trade it established, the English state enlarged its role in the direction of commerce, seeking to tighten imperial controls by regulating and rationalizing trade. These efforts simultaneously helped to defeat the Dutch and to launch England's "Commercial Revolution." The new colonial system, with its captive and quickly growing group of producers and consumers, helped to triple English shipping tonnage in the last half of the seventeenth century.[22]

The assault upon the Dutch was part of a broader pattern, for trade itself in the early modern period was regarded by many as "part of international conflict," a "mild form of war." Cannon-heavy gunboats, aggression, and war were central to international trade and the growth of the new colonial system.

[20] L. A. Harper, *The English Navigation Acts: A Seventeenth Century Experiment in Social Engineering* (New York, 1939), 49, 34; Dobb, *Studies*, 174; Andrew, *Colonial Period*, vol. 4, 37; Appleby, *Economic Thought*, 103.

[21] Lloyd, *British Seaman*, 83; Peter Kemp, *The British Sailor: A Social History of the Lower Deck* (London, 1970), 38; Davis, *English Shipping*, 49; Violet Barbour, "Dutch and English Merchant Shipping in the Seventeenth Century," *Essays in Economic History*, ed. E. M. Carus-Wilson (London, 1954), vol. 1, 233; Andrews, *Colonial Period*, vol. 4, 64; Harper, *Navigation Laws*, 239, 253; Wallerstein, *Modern World System II*, 236.

[22] Wallerstein, *Modern World System II*, 269; Carl Ubbelohde, *The Vice-Admiralty Courts and the American Revolution* (Chapel Hill, N.C., 1960), 15; Andrews, *Colonial Period*, vol. 4, 294, 296; Ian K. Steele, *Politics of Colonial Policy: The Board of Trade in Colonial Administration, 1696–1720* (Oxford, 1968), 17, 31–46; Ruth Bourne, *Queen Anne's Navy in the West Indies* (New Haven, Conn., 1939), 15; David, *English Shipping*, 20; Harper, *Navigation Laws*, 376, 358. On shipping tonnage, see Appendix B.

Seeking ever-larger portions of international markets, English merchants led their nation into an "age of trade wars" that lasted for more than a century, roughly from 1651 to 1763. They battled the Dutch until 1689 and thereafter grappled with the French for commercial supremacy. The early modern English merchant, the pivotal figure in the consolidation of power during the early rise of capitalism, understood that the militant, not the meek, would inherit the earth.[23]

English trade routes constituted the arteries of the imperial body between 1650 and 1750. They unified distant parts of the globe, different markets, and distinct modes of production. They joined local, regional, national, and international economies. They linked hunters, farmers, planters, merchants, craftsmen, workers in putting-out industries, free wage laborers, state officials, and slaves. They organized the flow of commodities and the movements of labor. These pulsing routes, stretching from one port city to the next, were the most elementary material structures of the empire, indeed of the entire world economy. (See map.)

The life-pumping heart of the system was London, a quarter of whose population in the early eighteenth century was in some manner bound up with commerce.[24] V. S. Pritchett once observed that "the very name London has tonnage in it."[25] Phonetics in this case reflect history, for in the early modern period London throve on the tonnage of ships. Britain's maritime power and the city's eminence expanded together. London soon contained perhaps the greatest concentration of capital on earth. It was the home of the greatest fortunes; it was the

---

[23] Coleman, *Economy of England*, 132; J. H. Parry, *Trade and Dominion: The European Overseas Empires in the Eighteenth Century* (New York, 1971), 12; Wilson, *England's Apprenticeship*, 184, 376. See also Harper, *Navigation Laws*, 9, and the comment by Coleman: "Because of the slow or limited growth in aggregate income in a given market area, merchants could not normally hope for significant increases in sales save by capturing more of the market from their rivals" (*Economy of England*, 131). For discussions of commerce as war, see Carlo Cipolla, *Guns, Sails, and Empires: Technological Innovation and the Early Phases of European Expansion, 1400–1700* (New York, 1965), and Fernand Braudel, *Capitalism and Material Life, 1400–1800* (New York, 1973), 289, 300.

[24] Davis, *English Shipping*, 390; Wilson, *England's Apprenticeship*, 171.

[25] V. S. Pritchett, *London Perceived* (New York, 1962), 5.

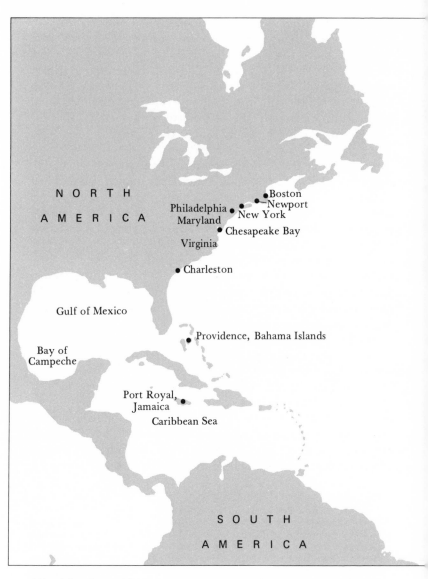

The Atlantic world.

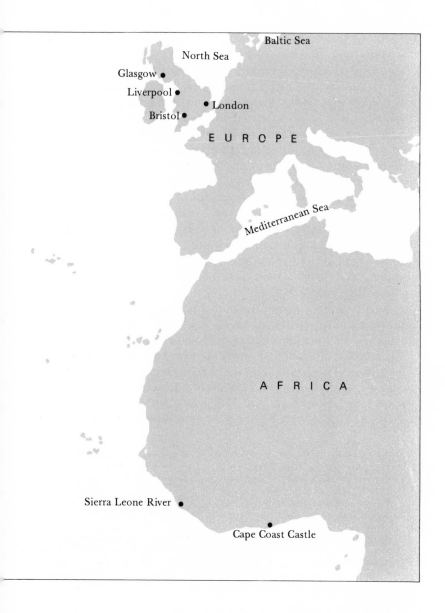

home of those whom Defoe called "universal merchants," the world's most internationally minded traders; it was the home of the English state.[26] London was the point of intersection between national and international markets, between domestic and foreign trades. It was the great entrepôt, boasting an extraordinary range of items imported and exported.[27] It accommodated both the English customs service and a labyrinthine underworld of smugglers who siphoned off 8 percent (or more) of the city's trade during the course of the eighteenth century.[28] Favored by an extensive division of labor, a broad manufacturing base, and a wide range of available commodities, London merchants controlled huge shares of trade to Europe, Africa, North America, and the Caribbean. The city necessarily contained what was probably the largest seafaring community in the world. By 1702–3 more than 12,000 Londoners worked in the international trades, and several thousand more labored on voyages that ranged the coasts of England.[29]

Jack Tar lived in the East End of the city. He and his brother seamen populated the parishes of Stepney, Whitechapel, and Aldgate, the neighborhoods of Spitalfields, the Minories, St. Katharine's, Shadwell, Ratcliff, Limehouse, Rotherhithe, and Wapping. The latter two faced each other across the Thames and, as suggested by Sir John Fielding, were widely known as sailors' neighborhoods. On Wapping's side of the river stood Execution Dock (see Figure 3), where pirates, mutineers, and

[26] Daniel Defoe, *A Tour through the Whole Island of Great Britain*, ed. Pat Rogers (1724–6; reprint New York, 1971), 541; Coleman, *Economy of England*, 140–4; D. A. Farnie, "The Commercial Empire of the Atlantic, 1607–1783," *EHR* 15 (1962), 214.

[27] Wilson, *England's Apprenticeship*, 37–8; T. S. Willan, *The English Coasting Trade, 1600–1750* (Manchester, 1938), 189; Holderness, *Pre-Industrial England*, 141, 142.

[28] Elizabeth Everlynola Hoon, *The Organization of the English Customs Service, 1696–1786* (New York, 1938), 92; C. Ernest Fayle, *A Short History of the World's Shipping Industry* (London, 1933), 215; Neville Williams, *Contraband Cargo: Seven Centuries of Smuggling* (London, 1959), 101, 105. Williams notes the readiness of the London mob to come to the assistance of a smuggler hemmed in by customs officials.

[29] Davis, *English Shipping*, 270; James A. Rawley, *The Transatlantic Slave Trade: A History* (New York, 1981), 233. On the number of seamen, see the London customs report, "An Account of the English Ships with the Number of Men cleared . . . by ye Officers of the Customs House, between the 1 December 1702 and 1 December 1703," BL, Add. Ms. 5459, f. 104.

Figure 3. A pirate is hanged at Execution Dock in Wapping. British authorities punished maritime criminals in London's largest seafaring neighborhood in the hope that the spectacle of terror would have a broad social effect.

Figure 4. A view of the Thames at Wapping, the seamen's neighborhood in the East End of London. Sailors and dock workers cooperate in the lading and unlading of cargo.

other seafaring men were "launched into eternity"; on Rother-hithe's side lay the Angel Pub, where in the late seventeenth century Hanging Judge Jeffries had sat to gaze across the river as his condemned were "turned off." Sailors, it seemed, often found themselves on the wrong side of the law, or at least that was the grisly impression conveyed by the blackened, decaying, crow-shredded corpses of seamen that hung on gibbets up and down the river.[30]

Jack Tar most likely lived in Wapping among the narrow-fronted, two-story houses of wood and Flemish wall, many of which by the 1740s were in a state of decay. Families and individual boarders, longtimers and transients filled the modest dwellings that crowded the serpentine streets, narrow lanes, and back alleys and clustered around the sometimes rowdy music houses, the small shops, markets, workshops, and ale-houses.[31] Jack and his friends were especially fond of alehouse cheer. Whether in search of spirits, food, rest, a short pipe full of tobacco, or a game of cards, dice, or ten-bones, or just the latest information on shipping, satisfaction could usually be found in these establishments "run by the poor for the poor."[32] Jack also counted on the pubs, gin shops, and taverns to keep himself informed of the activities of the spirit, the crimp, and the naval lieutenant who led the press gang, three shrewd and ruthless characters who took a deep if not always honest interest in the sailor's affairs.[33] (See Figure 4.)

Jack had heard the terror-fraught tales of one of the greatest disasters in the history of the London seafaring community. At 11:00 P.M. on November 26, 1703, "began ye most violent storme of winde . . . yt ever was known in England," the Great Storm that visited hurricanelike destruction upon London's maritime industries and their workers.[34] An estimated 6,000

---

[30] Information of William Galloway, HCA 1/55 (1725), f. 57; Phillips, *The Thames*, 24.

[31] M. J. Power, "East London Housing in the Seventeenth Century," *Crisis and Order in English Towns, 1500–1700: Essays in Urban History*, ed. Peter Clark and Paul Slack (Toronto, 1972), 243–7, 249–50, 253, 257.

[32] Peter Clark, "The Alehouse and the Alternative Society," *Puritans and Revolutionaries: Essays in Seventeenth-Century History Presented to Christopher Hill*, ed. Donald Pennington and Keith Thomas (Oxford, 1978), 48, 49, 53, 60, 63.

[33] *Barlow's Journal*, 27, 90.

[34] "An Account of the Great Storm, 1703," Stowe Manuscript 713, BL, f. 1b.

seamen were lost to the raging elements; 15 men-of-war and 300 merchant vessels were sunk. Gusts of wind destroyed or set fire to 400 windmills, blew down more than 19,000 trees in Kent alone, and toppled 2,000 chimneys and 800 houses.[35] Edward Barlow, amid the flotsam of masts, yards, and sails drifting by him down river the next day, thought the storm a "warning of God's anger" about the growing materialism of the age and the ways in which "All commanders and masters [of ships] are grown up with pride and oppression and tyranny."[36]

As Jack Tar sailed westward along the Thames, he observed open fields, windmills, and buildings of all kinds. Londoners had rebuilt large parts of the city after an earlier calamity, the Great Fire of 1666. Jack passed Blackfriars Stairs, where the jailbirds from Newgate prison – a friend or two more than likely among them – boarded vessels for transportation to America as indentured servants. He passed the Milford Lane wharves, home of the Perry Gang, one of the biggest bands of smugglers in a city well known for what sailors called "trading by stealth." He passed other vessels from which bargemen jeeringly cast the ritual insults known as "River Wit." Soon he arrived at "the Pool," a narrow area between the Tower and London Bridge that contained a forest of ship masts and a massive cluster of two to three thousand vessels of all nations. Seamen, stevedores, and watermen, creating a great clamor, unloaded cargo of all descriptions onto hoys, prams, lighters, and barges. This was the hub of London's maritime activity, its center of "wealth and commerce."[37]

Vessels of all varieties – ships, brigs, and schooners, to name but a few – clogged the Pool. Merchants bustled from ship to ship, pausing to watch with satisfaction as dock workers and seamen lowered the last bale of cargo into the vessel's full belly or to argue furiously with shipbuilders over the costs or pace of slowly completed repairs. Captains and customs officials haggled, cursed, and winked at each other. Butchers, vivid in their

---

[35] Ibid.; Defoe, *Tour*, 137, 138; *Barlow's Journal*, 553n.
[36] *Barlow's Journal*, 553.
[37] Defoe, *Tour*, 306, 296, 312, 317; Phillips, *The Thames*, 25–6, 78, 32; Dampier, "New Voyage," 308; Cesar de Saussure, *A Foreign View of England in the Reigns of George I & George II*, ed. Madame Van Muyden (London, 1902), 66–95; Ward, *London Spy*, 117.

bloody aprons, stocked the merchant craft with salt beef and pork, while hawkers and peddlers tendered their wares along the stone and log wharves. Slaves, servants, and day laborers toiled under the sharp gaze of overseers, lifting from ship's hold to shore's warehouse the commodities of the world. The workers who handled these goods intercepted some of them along the way. "Mudlarks" tipped over the light vessels used to transfer goods from ships to the docks, then returned at late-night low tide to claim their take from the riverbed. On the vessels, on the quays, or in the nearby pubs and taverns, seamen quizzed merchant captains about destinations and wages, just as they asked each other about the sturdiness of a particular vessel or the character of her captain. The whole area around the Pool smelled of tar.[38]

Not far from the Pool stood several imposing buildings that housed state and private agencies whose activities shaped the sailor's life. In the Customs House the state used the Act for Preventing Frauds and Regulating Abuses in the Plantation Trade of 1696 to search, seize, and tax vessels and to extract its share of trading surpluses. Enlarged and renovated in the late 1710s and early 1720s, the Customs House embodied in more ways than one what Defoe called "stateliness."[39] Other nearby institutions included the Excise Office, whose police force of several thousand battled smugglers; the Bank of England,

---

[38] Phillips, *The Thames*, 39; Defoe, *Tour*, 318.

[39] Defoe, *Tour*, 312; Hoon, *English Customs Service*, 290, 52–88; Joseph Doty, *The British Admiralty as a Factor in Colonial Administration* (Philadelphia, 1930), 13, 14, 16–17. See also "An Act for Preventing Frauds and Regulating Abuses in the Plantation Trade" (7 and 8 William III, c. 22, 1696) in Sir Thomas Parker, *The Laws of Shipping and Insurance, with a Digest of Adjudged Cases* (London, 1775), republished in *British Maritime Cases* (Abingdon, Oxfordshire, 1978), 25–6. Other initiatives were taken against illicit trade in 1718, 1733, 1736, and 1746. See also Harper, *Navigation Laws*, 135, 142; Williams, *Contraband Cargo*, 105, 86, 94, 114, 108, 112; Andrews, *Colonial Period*, vol. 4, 210; idem. "Colonial Commerce," *AHR* 20 (1914), 49; Bourne, *Queen Anne's Navy*, 15; Patrick Crowhurst, *The Defense of British Trade, 1689–1815* (Folkestone, Kent, 1977), 61. As Peter Linebaugh has written of the Thames, "The division between legitimate and criminal [customs] transactions was never clear at any level. Purloining, bribery, fraud, collusion, embezzlement, wage payment, perquisite, the purchase, the sale, the pay-off, and the blind eye took forms which were barely separable as part of the daily traffic of the river" ("Socking: Tobacco Porters, the Hogshead, and Excise," *The London Hanged: Crime and Civil Society in the Eighteenth Century* [forthcoming]).

whose capital and credit financed so much foreign trade; and the Royal Exchange Assurance and London Assurance Society, which insured against "all hazard by sea" – as long as it pertained to the property of merchants and not the lives of seamen. On Leadenhall Street sat the offices of the East India Company, "a corporation of men with long heads and deep purses"; between Broad and Threadneedle streets lay those of the South Sea Company; and nearby, those of the now nearly defunct Royal African Company. Jack Tar and his brothers past and present had sailed the ships of these companies.[40]

Farther up the Thames Jack passed Billingsgate Dock, where 500 to 700 coal-carrying "cats," "hags," and "flys," as seamen called them, lay at anchor. He sailed by royal and private shipyards where gangs of laborers stretched lumber around the curved ribbing of a ship's hull. He saw wet and dry docks full of vessels either lame or rotten. He noted the endless array of retail warehouses that supplied shipbuilders with naval stores. On his left, as he proceeded up river, just across from the House of Commons, his eyes fell upon Marshalsea prison, whose inmates always seemed to include a good many sailors sent there by the Admiralty Court that met at the Old Bailey. Daniel Defoe had noted that "[t]here are in London, notwithstanding we are a nation of liberty, more private and public prisons, and houses of confinement, than in any city of Europe, perhaps as many as in all the capital cities of Europe put together." Jack knew these places of confinement well enough – from the inside – to doubt such a proud pronouncement about the "nation of liberty."[41]

Not far from the river in the West End of London was the Admiralty Office, built in the late seventeenth century to handle the increasingly complicated and important affairs of the Royal Navy. The navy had by 1740 become the longest and strongest arm of state power. It had grown dramatically over

---

[40] Defoe, *Tour*, 310, 312, 306, 309, 311; Fayle, *Short History*, 193; Barry Supple, *The Royal Exchange Assurance: A History of British Insurance, 1720–1970* (Cambridge, 1970), 11; A. H. John, "The London Assurance Company and the Marine Insurance Market of the Eighteenth Century," *Economica* 25 (1958), 126–41; Ward, *London Spy*, 14 (quotation about the East India Company).

[41] Defoe, *Tour*, 316, 317, 321 (quotation), 330. See also Arthur L. Hayward, ed., *Lives of the Most Remarkable Criminals* (1735; reprint New York, 1927), 35.

the previous century, acquired stability through the organizational reforms of Samuel Pepys, and met the challenges of war against Holland, Spain, and France. This expansion of the navy and of state power had, however, created problems. A stronger navy required more maritime labor, yet the low pay and mean working conditions in the king's service made seamen none too willing to serve. Increasingly the impressment of maritime workers, planned and organized by the Admiralty Office, did the job where a free labor market could not.[42] Impressment was crucial to the making of a maritime working class.

As Jack Tar returned down river, the passing view of London's layout along the Thames provided an image of the city's social and economic order. Beginning in the far western reaches, in Westminster, and sailing down to the York Buildings, Jack beheld the greatest material symbols of England's aristocracy. From the York Buildings to the Temple he gazed at the quarters and offices of the city's business and professional elite. The area between the Temple and the Tower was that of commerce, where traders large and small engaged in the arts of buying and selling. From the Tower down to Limehouse, Jack saw his own people, the working class and particularly the maritime laborers of London.[43] Finally he arrived at Gravesend, "the last town of the River of Thams," where all London vessels departed for all parts of the globe. To one seaman, Gravesend was "a right name as every body of Sailors knows," it being where "many Never returne again."[44] Sailors uncertain of their fates disembarked for "strange places"; in so doing, they served aristocrats concerned with state and imperial power, a bourgeoisie earnestly engaged in the accumulation of capital, and small traders in search of a decent competency. Many kinds of power and interest depended upon the London seaman who watched Gravesend disappear into the distance as his vessel rode out to sea.

---

[42] Defoe, *Tour*, 327, 335; Wallerstein, *Modern World System II*, 248, 249; Lloyd, *British Seaman*, 100; Kemp, *British Sailor*, 41; Bourne, *Queen Anne's Navy*, 264; Parry, *Trade and Dominion*, 203; Leslie Gardiner, *The British Admiralty* (Edinburgh, 1968), 104.

[43] Phillips, *The Thames*, 119.

[44] *Ramblin' Jack: The Journal of Captain John Cremer*, ed. R. Reynall Bellamy (London, 1936), 74, 94. See also Defoe, *Tour*, 137.

Whether England and its colonies were at war was the single most powerful determinant of the seaman's life in the early modern era. Between 1650 and 1750 England engaged in six major wars: the three Dutch wars mentioned earlier; the War of the League of Augsburg (King William's War), 1689–97; the War of the Spanish Succession (Queen Anne's War), 1702–13; and the War of Jenkins' Ear, 1739–42, which expanded into the War of the Austrian Succession (King George's War), 1740–8. The simultaneous mobilization of the Royal Navy and of enormous privateering forces generated furious competition for the skills and strength of Jack Tar. Wages in the merchant service increased sharply during wartime, not only as compensation for the possibility of attack, seizure, and incarceration by the enemy but also as compensation for the possibility of attack, seizure, and incarceration by Jack's own government through impressment.[45]

Wartime offered the seaman substantially higher wages, prize money, greater choice of destination and captain, and looser, less violent discipline. But it also created grave perils that threatened at any moment to annihilate the benefits. Many of these perils resulted from what Edward Barlow called the "evil custom" of impressment. Many a seaman lost "his chest and clothes and several months pay." Many others lost their lives to disease and battle. Enemy actions, especially those undertaken by foreign privateers, were sources of eternal worry to seamen, since they often resulted in the loss of pay, personal effects, and liberty. Seamen felt a deep ambivalence about the gambles of wartime. They might be lucky and win; they might lose it all.[46]

London in 1740 was a dangerous place for Jack Tar. War had just been declared against Spain, and press gangs snooped about the city looking for likely seafaring men. The navy itself was an even more dangerous place, not least because of the typhus epidemic raging through the royal fleet.[47] During

45 Lloyd, *British Seaman*, 137; Davis, *English Shipping*, 325. See also Parry, *Trade and Dominion*, 217: "Navies not only absorbed men, they destroyed them, and that not only – not even mainly in battle, but by disease. Like the ships, the men in them rotted."

46 *Barlow's Journal*, 95. See Chapter 3 of this book on wages.

47 Daniel Baugh, *British Naval Administration in the Age of Walpole* (Princeton, N.J., 1965), 179.

Queen Anne's reign, seamen had entered the navy like men "dragged to execution." And that is precisely what naval service amounted to for untold thousands, since almost half of all of those pressed in the seventeenth and eighteenth centuries died at sea. Those lucky enough to stay alive often went unpaid. Some commanders, in an effort to prevent desertion, held the wages of their crews in arrears for three, four, or up to six and a half years.[48] The state's demand for maritime labor and the seaman's refusal to be the supply produced something of a civil war over maritime muscle and skill. Press gangs boarded incoming vessels to the sound of "the slashing of Cutlashes," by which they knew that the "verry Rugged Stout Sailors" aboard were unwilling to serve the king and willing to risk a limb to prove it.[49] The tactics of resistance varied widely. Seamen waged portside riots; turned over press boats full of "recruits"; inflicted upon themselves disabilities, such as burning a wound with vitriol to make it look like scurvy; and feigned every manner of paralysis, idiocy, and fits. Without a good disguise, seamen "could not walk the streets without danger, nor sleep in safety."[50]

For a time, matters were a little easier for sailors in America. In 1708 their own many-sided resistance combined with the

---

[48] Hutchinson, *Press Gang*, 28 (quotation), 44. See J. S. Bromley, ed., *The Manning of the Royal Navy: Selected Public Documents, 1693–1873* (London, 1974), xxvi–ii. See also Lloyd, *British Seaman*, 44 and chaps. 6–9 for an excellent discussion of impressment in its many dimensions.

[49] Examination of John White, HCA 1/54 (1718), f. 85; Information of Randolph Barber, HCA 1/54 (1718), ff. 76–7; Francis Nicholson to Matthew Teate, CO 5/1314 (1704), ff. 288–9.

[50] *Adventures by Sea of Edward Coxere*, 36, 27, 34; Hutchinson, *Press Gang*, 304. Peter Kemp has written: "Until the start of the major wars of the eighteenth century, the press had never bitten deeply into the overall fabric of [English] national life." Further, the harsh new means of procuring labor was met by resistance, which was in turn countered by new forms of discipline. The grisly spectacle of "flogging round the fleet" – whipping a sailor to death in view of the men of an entire squadron of vessels – was implemented in 1698 and reached a pinnacle during the War of Austrian Succession. "Running the gauntlet" also grew to prominence during this period. See Kemp, *British Sailor*, 99, 88, 90, 116, and G. Hinchliffe, "Impressment of Seamen during the War of Spanish Succession," *Mariner's Mirror* 53 (1967), 137–142. For a pioneering analysis of the tactics of resistance to impressment, see Jesse Lemisch, "Jack Tar versus John Bull," and idem, "Jack Tar in the Streets: Merchant Seamen in the Politics of Revolutionary America," *WMQ* 25 (1968), 381–400.

pressures of entrepreneurs in privateering and trade to secure the "Sixth of Anne," an act that made it illegal to impress anyone in the colonies other than naval deserters. Impressment continued nevertheless, especially after 1739, when
war broke out, and even more intensively after 1746, when
the Sixth of Anne was repealed for the continental colonies.
Though Parliament could repeal the law, it could not repeal
the seaman's belief that impressment violated his rights as
guaranteed by the Magna Carta. Impressment, as Jesse Lemisch has convincingly shown, was an ever-present concern to
Jack Tar.[51]

War also affected the merchants in England and America
who hired Jack Tar, and at first sight its dominant impact
would seem to have been negative. War was the chief source of
instability for trade. International networks of communication
and transportation were disrupted; the costs of maritime insurance rose as shipping risks increased; impressment of workers
diminished the merchant's supply of labor. French and Spanish
privateers harassed and seized vast numbers of English and
American vessels. Trade to certain ports, depending upon the
alliances and theaters of war, contracted; some ports suffered
depressions. Investors in the merchant shipping industry sustained many losses, some of them crippling.[52]

Yet the losses of wartime were not distributed evenly within
the mercantile community. Wars created tangible benefits for
many. They were, after all, often undertaken to capture new
territory and markets. The War of the Spanish Succession, for
example, resulted in England's possession of a heftier share of

[51] Dora Mae Clark, "The Impressment of Seamen in the American Colonies,"
Essays in Colonial History Presented to Charles McLean Andrews by his Students
(New Haven, Conn., 1931), 207, 209, 214, 218–19; Lemisch, "Jack Tar
versus John Bull," 47; John Dennis, *An Essay on the Navy* (London, 1702), 46;
John Oglethorpe, "The Sailor's Advocate" (1728), in Bromley, *Manning the
Royal Navy*, 72.

[52] T. S. Ashton, *Economic Fluctuation in England, 1700–1800* (London, 1959),
56; Holderness, *Pre-Industrial England*, 5; Paul G. E. Clemens, "The Rise of
Liverpool, 1665–1700," *EHR* 29 (1976), 215; Davis, *English Shipping*, 316–
17; J. S. Bromley, "The French Privateering War, 1702–1713," *Historical
Essays, 1600–1750, Presented to David Ogg*, ed. H. E. Bell and R. L. Ollard
(London, 1963), 229; Donald F. Chard, "The Impact of French Privateering
on New England, 1689–1713," *American Neptune* 35 (1975), 154; Crowhurst,
Defense of British Trade, 19.

the Spanish-American market.[53] Other merchants found bonanzas in war contracts, privateering, and illegal trade. During periods of conflict, the terms of trade tended to shift to England's advantage. English merchants usually ended international struggles with more vessel tonnage than they had possessed previously, because their privateering campaigns normally produced overall gains.[54]

Perhaps the most important effect of war lay in its tendency to centralize economic power within the merchant shipping industry, strengthening the most powerful parts of the merchantry. Despite the dangers of war, the great majority of ships completed their voyages safely; the ships that sailed, though fewer in number, toted fuller cargoes. To offset higher insurance rates and higher wages, merchants charged proportionally higher freight rates. They often made greater profits. Those traders with enough capital to withstand short-term losses gained the most. "War," Gary Nash has written, "vastly increased the risks of overseas trade and those who could not sustain the loss of one, two, or even more ships to enemy marauders on the high seas were driven from the field." Such dangers loomed largest, of course, for the smaller shippers. Thus wartime commerce helped to concentrate wealth in the hands of the merchant capitalists who already occupied positions of wealth and power. In so doing, it contributed to the growth of social and economic inequality in eighteenth-century England and America. The very concentration of power in the hands of merchants made the sailor's lot even more difficult.[55]

---

[53] Ashton, *Economic Fluctuations*, 68; Nash, *Urban Crucible*, 56, 65; Bourne, *Queen Anne's Navy*, 13, 282; Curtis Nettels, "England and the Spanish American Trade, 1680–1715," *Journal of Modern History* 3 (1931), 32; Parry, *Trade and Dominion*, 110; Williams, *Contraband Cargo*, 143; Richard Pares, *War and Trade in the West Indies, 1739–1763* (Oxford, 1936), 126; George H. Nelson, "Contraband Trade Under the Asiento, 1730–1739," *AHR* 51 (1945), 55; Harold V. W. Temperley, "The Causes of the War of Jenkins' Ear," *Royal Historical Society Transactions* ser. 3, 3 (1909), 197; Wallerstein, *Modern World System II*, 256; Wilson, *England's Apprenticeship*, 280–1.

[54] A. H. John, "War and the English Economy, 1700–1763," *EHR* 7 (1955), 339, 333, 343–4; Harper, *Navigation Laws*, 369.

[55] Davis, *English Shipping*, 318, 329, 320, 41; Nash, *Urban Crucible*, 56 (quotation). See Nash's superb chapter, "The Seaport Economies in an Era of War," 54–75, as well as 165, 257, 55, 65. See also Bernard and Lotte Bailyn, *Massachusetts Shipping, 1697–1714: A Statistical Study* (Cambridge, Mass., 1959), 63; Ashton, *Economic Fluctuations*, 64, 60.

London merchants hired Jack Tar to serve the thriving trades they drove with almost every part of Europe. Jack and his mates bore the merchants' goods to Dunkerque, Calais, St. Malo, Brest, and Bordeaux, in France, to Rotterdam and Amsterdam in Holland, and to the northeastern ports of Bremen, Hamburg, and Bergen. These trades with nearby Europe were less reliable than other routes because they were so consistently plagued by international rivalry and hostility. Some merchants felt that Englishmen should not trade with an enemy; others preferred profits to ideology and continued to move their goods by smuggling.

The northern European trades included the ports of Gottenburg (Goteborg) and Stockholm in Sweden, Copenhagen in Denmark, Riga in Livonia (later Latvia), St. Petersburg in Russia, and Oslo in Norway. These trades, long dominated by the Dutch, handled bulky commodities: wine, salt, fish, grain, timber, naval stores, lead, tin, iron, copper, coal, corn, and woolens. Such goods were the lifeblood of shipping. Their movement required merchants to mobilize sizable amounts of maritime labor. The regularity of such commerce and the experience that accrued to the merchants who organized it were crucial to increases in the productivity of maritime labor. Favorable man/ton ratios and quick turnaround times in port had been achieved in the northern European trades by the late seventeenth century. A healthy portion of such efficiency originated in the smaller ports of Yarmouth, Hull, Bideford, Falmouth, Deptford, Sunderland, and Topsham. On the whole, trade with northern and nearby Europe expanded significantly between 1650 and 1750, but not at a rate as high as the overall pace of English commercial growth.[56]

English trade with the Mediterranean and southern Europe was well established by 1600, and covered a diverse array of ports and countries. English vessels carried wares to Lisbon, Madeira, Seville, Malaga, Cádiz, the Canary Islands, Leghorn (Livorno), Genoa, and Zante (Zakinthos), to name but a few of the trading destinations. (See Figure 5.) This commerce, though on a smaller scale than that of northern Europe, was also

[56] Barbour, "Dutch and English Shipping," 230; Davis, *English Shipping*, 179, 204; Parry, *Trade and Dominion*, 214 and idem, "Transport and Trade Routes," 204–5.

dominated by staples: oil, wine, cheese, and fish. By 1700, however, English trade with the Mediterranean had begun to decline and continued to do so until 1770. The dried fish shipped to southern Europe were caught by English and North American vessels off the coast of Newfoundland and New England. This trade in fish was more central to the Atlantic economy in the seventeenth century, when the fisheries were regarded as "nurseries" for deep-sea sailors, than in the eighteenth. Relatively few seamen beyond the small coastal communities of Massachusetts, Canada, and England worked as fishermen.[57]

Thousands of seamen worked in the European trades. The voyages, especially those to northern and nearby Europe, were short and predictable, usually lasting only a few months. The danger to health and well-being was as minimal as deep-sea sailing permitted, since the nearest port, provisions, and repairs were never half an ocean away. Sailors sometimes refused voyages to the Baltic ports if they were offered late in the year, fearing a freeze-up that would strand them for a long northerly winter. But on the whole, the short, swift voyages were quite popular. After all, there was much to see and do. The European port cities offered seamen everything from the grandest entertainment to the artifacts of the progress of Western civilization.[58]

Trade to the Mediterranean was more worrisome, because round-trip voyages lasted longer (six to nine months) and featured the threat of Algerian pirates, the famed and feared "Sallie Rovers." Captain Nathaniel Uring reported in 1712 that his "people" had "terrible Apprehensions of being made slaves" by these raiders. And scores of tars were indeed seized and enslaved by the Algerians and "those unreasonable barbarians," the Turks. The lucky seamen were ransomed; many of the others perished. Yet most sailors must have been aware that the danger of such capture was receding during the course of the eighteenth century. Such knowledge left them more peace of

---

[57] Davis, *English Shipping*, 232; Harper, *Navigation Laws*, 354; Wilson, *England's Apprenticeship*, 38. On the New World fisheries, see the fine study by Daniel F. Vickers, "Maritime Labor in Colonial Massachusetts: A Case Study of the Essex County Cod Fishery and the Whaling Industry in Nantucket," Ph.D. diss., Princeton University, 1981.

[58] Row v. Sheldon, HCA 24/133 (1720); *Barlow's Journal*, 164.

Figure 5. English merchantmen in a Mediterranean harbor, by Willem Van de Velde II. One of the vessels fires its cannon, perhaps in celebration or merriment.

mind to contemplate the visual beauties of the Mediterranean, such as the "Four Chimneys of Hell," the volcanoes that soared above the Lipari islands off the coast of Sicily.[59]

Commerce with the East Indies, though also organized from London, was in many ways the very antithesis of that with Europe. Handled by a monopoly, the East India Company, rather than a welter of private traders, this trade dealt almost exclusively in luxury, not bulk, goods, chiefly calico, silk, porcelain, tea, and metalwares, items whose enormous value produced exorbitant profits. The volume of the East India trade, in contrast to its value, was never great. But the length and demands of the voyages to the East, which lasted upward of two years and traversed dangerous waters, required mammoth vessels of 300 to 500 tons and extremely heavy manning. The East India Company consequently employed more seamen than any of the other luxury trades of the early modern era.[60]

Following the Portuguese and the Dutch to the East Indies, the English established trading posts at Surat (1612), Madras (1639), Bombay (1665), and Calcutta (1690), but for some time remained largely dependent upon the political goodwill of the leaders of the Mughal Empire. In the 1680s English merchants initiated limited exchange with China, whose leaders after long supplication agreed to trade with the "red-haired barbarians," but only on their own terms, which included a massive transfer of silver from English to Chinese coffers. The East India Company, in exchange for its silver, brought home among many other items tea, which became a favorite English drink in the eighteenth century.[61]

Voyages to the East Indies were, above all else, grueling. Seemingly endless confinement on the ship tried the patience,

---

[59] *Voyages and Travels of Captain Nathaniel Uring,* 180. For the diary of a New England seaman who was captured by the rovers, see *The Narrative of Joshua Gee, 1680–1687* (Hartford, Conn., 1943). See also *Barlow's Journal,* 55–8.

[60] Davis, *English Shipping,* 257–66. The early history of the East India Company can be followed in K. N. Chaudhuri, *The English East India Company: The Study of an Early Joint-Stock Company, 1600–1640* (New York, 1965). A general overview is offered by Ramkrishna Mukherjee, *The Rise and Fall of the East India Company: A Sociological Appraisal* (New York, 1974).

[61] Eric Wolf, *Europe and the People without History* (Berkeley, 1982), 240, 252. For the best recent overview of the trade in the East, see K. N. Chaudhuri, *Trade and Civilization in the Indian Ocean: An Economic History from the Rise of Islam to 1750* (Cambridge, 1985).

nerves, and health of everyone, from captain to cabin boy. The risk of death on such a long voyage ran high. Most sailors showed more than a trace of scurvy by the time they were halfway down the African coast. In Indian ports, which tars considered unhealthy, seamen sought their salvation in heavy drinking, which of course made matters worse. The seaman's lot was not aided by the organization of the East India Company as a monopoly controlled by "commercial aristocrats."[62] Wages were rigidly controlled, opportunities for desertion were limited, and the company's concern for its employees was legendarily meager.[63] And on top of all this lay the problem of being an imperial intruder. One wonders how many seamen shared the doubts of Edward Barlow, who, during a voyage to the East Indies in 1690, pondered the morality of empire: "But for nations to come and plant themselves in islands and countries by force, and build forts and raise laws, and force the people to customs against the true natures and people of the said places without their consent, how this will stand with the law of God and the religion we profess, let the world judge." An array of misgivings and difficulties made East India vessels hothouses of mutiny and rebellion in the 1690s.[64]

Yet there were, to be sure, some advantages to laboring in the East India trade. During wartime some seamen deliberately signed on for long voyages in order to dodge the press. A few chose the distant Indies as a way of imposing fiscal discipline on themselves, hoping to have saved a good bit of money by the time they returned to London. The East India Company also offered a pay system that must have appealed to seamen

[62] Crowhurst, *Defense of British Trade*, 208, 224, 218; "The Journal of Francis Rogers," *Three Sea Journals of Stuart Times*, ed. Bruce Ingram (London, 1936), 188. J. H. Parry notes that the value of citrus in treating scurvy was well known in the seventeenth century. For many commanders, however, the value of lemons exceeded that of their sailors' lives: The failure to treat scurvy was "due to culpable meanness or negligence, . . . not to ignorance" (*Trade and Dominion*, 219).

[63] A few seamen did desert and join the Indian navy. See Dampier, "New Voyage," 507.

[64] *Barlow's Journal*, 401, 445. For a vivid example of mutiny in the East India trade, see "An Account of the Discovery of an Horrid Plot and Conspiracy on board the Ship *Antelope*," CO 323/3, ff. 92–3. Much can be learned about the East India trade from Robert C. Ritchie's fine new book, *Captain Kidd and the War against the Pirates* (Cambridge, Mass., 1986).

with families. It supplied two months' advance pay before departure and permitted a designated representative to collect wages in London at regular intervals during the voyage, providing vital support for dependents in the seafarer's absence. Probably the most attractive feature of the trade to the East was the "privilege" accorded each seaman: a small allotment of cargo space in which he could ship, freight free, a few items for "private trading." It was a prized and important part of his wage.[65]

Seamen's journals and diaries make it clear that the grandest thing about an East India voyage was the trip home, particularly the stop-off at the island of St. Helena, 1,150 miles off the southwestern coast of Africa. St. Helena was a "general rendezvous for our English shipping homeward bound from India," noted Francis Rogers, and "is reckoned one of the most healthful places in the world." Many men "just [nearly] dead with the scurvy and other diseases . . . when carried ashore here, recover to a miracle, rarely any dying though never so ill when brought ashore."[66] A seaman who believed he had been poisoned by a prostitute in India told his doctor that if he "could keep him alive until we got to St. Helena, he strongly fancied that wholesome island would recover him." The island seemed seldom to fail the seeker of miracles. It offered good arrack wine, fine fishing, medicinal herbs, a clean breeze, and fresh fruit and food.[67] William Dampier observed that seamen so sick that they had to be carried ashore in their hammocks were within a week "able to leap and dance." The festivities at St. Helena were joyous, and many a tar took a sweetheart. A big part of the celebration no doubt came from the seaman's very survival of one of the most trying routes of early modern seafaring.[68]

By 1740 London had lost a considerable share of its trading eminence to the western ports of Bristol, Liverpool, and Glasgow. Whereas in 1702 London had handled 43 per-

---

[65] Parry, *Trade and Dominion*, 64. On wages, see Chapter 3 of this book.
[66] "Journal of Francis Rogers," 191, 192; *Barlow's Journal*, 198.
[67] "Journal of Francis Rogers," 190, 192; *Barlow's Journal*, 193; Dampier, "New Voyage," 548.
[68] Dampier, "New Voyage," 548.

cent of all English trade, that figure by 1751 had shrunk to 28 percent; outport tonnage increased to 72 percent of the total.[69] The rise of the western ports was accompanied by a swift increase in trade with the New World, in which they took a leading part. Two material advantages aided the ascent of the western ports. Their location tended to shield them from the depredations of enemy privateers during wartime, and their distance from the customs control of London permitted their merchants to smuggle goods with equal ease and elation. Successful smuggling meant in many cases a threefold increase in profits, and "trading by stealth" became a key to the accumulation of capital in the outports.[70]

The merchant seaman sailing toward Bristol in 1740, up the Avon River, would have seen a lowly-situated city that edged up the side of a hill: "the greatest, the richest, and the best port of trade in Great Britain, London only excepted" lay before him. The city held a population of roughly 50,000, "tightly packed together." Depending on the time of the year, the seaman would have seen as many as a thousand or more vessels, "their masts as thick as they can stand by one another," clustered at Kingroad and Hungroad on the Avon or at the quays a few miles upriver at the center of the harbor. In midtown stood the Tolsey, the overcrowded center of trade and exchange, where, it was said, merchants counted their money on ancient bronze tables. "Sumptuous mansions, luxurious living, liveried menials, were the produce of the wealth made from the sufferings and groans of the slaves bought and sold by the Bristol merchant"; so wrote a local annalist during the reign of Queen Anne. Slave traders and other merchants, recognizing Bristol's strategic location and operating with an "entire independency" of London, gave instructions for the transshipment of goods, routing them inland in "a very great trade" that ran southward to Southampton and northward to the banks of the Trent. Small traders meandered through Bris-

---

[69] Wilson, *England's Apprenticeship*, 271, 276; Holderness, *Pre-Industrial England*, 138–9.

[70] Davis, *English Shipping*, 27; Rawley, *Transatlantic Slave Trade*, 179; Clemens, "Rise of Liverpool," 214; T. C. Barker, "Smuggling in the Eighteenth Century: The Evidence of the Scottish Tobacco Trade," *VMHB* 62 (1954), 399, 398; Price, "Economic Fluctuation and Growth of American Port Towns in the Eighteenth Century," *Perspectives in American History* 8 (1974), 167.

tol, between buildings "close and thronged," drawing their goods on "geehoes" – "sleds, or sledges without wheels."[71]

Most of Bristol's 2,000 or so sailors lived in the central part of the city or else a few miles down river where many ships, especially the larger ones, docked. In either place a seaman found a room for a sevennight or so, as well as cheap food and drink. The pickpocket and the crimp, notorious in these parts, in turn found him. The former hoped to catch the unsuspecting seaman flush with money after a recently completed voyage; the latter, after that money had gone who knows where, so that the tar's labor could be sold to an outward-bound merchant captain. Many a drunk or indebted sailor found himself aboard a slave ship he might have preferred to avoid. The voyages that brought fame, wealth, and hand servants to Bristol masters and merchants more often brought illness and death to their sailors; mortality rates, for seamen as for slaves, ran hideously high. The merchant who gave the captain a bounty for every slave delivered alive in the New World offered no such reward for a sailor still living at voyage's end.[72]

Liverpool profited even more handsomely from the sailor's labor that carried commodities to the "coast of Guinea" to be exchanged for human cargoes. The slave trade, the tobacco trade to Virginia and Maryland, and the European trades had produced abrupt expansion in Liverpool, including an impressive increase in "wealth, people, business, and buildings," all of which would have been evident to the seaman's eye in 1740. Fine new stone and brick buildings lined the clean and spacious

---

[71] Defoe, *Tour*, 361, 362, 523, 363, 705. Quotations on the "packed" population and the masts in the harbor are by Alexander Pope and can be found in William Hunt, *Bristol* (London, 1895), 175, 176. The unidentified Bristol annalist is quoted in Peter Fryer, *Staying Power: The History of Black People in Britain* (London, 1984), 477. For more information on Bristol, see *The Journeys of Celia Fiennes*, ed. Christopher Morris (London, 1947), 237–8; Penelope Corfield, *The Impact of English Towns, 1700–1800* (Oxford, 1982), 41; Bryan Little, *The City and the County of Bristol: A Study in Atlantic Civilization* (London, 1954), 154–5; W. E. Minchinton, "Bristol – Metropolis of the West in the Eighteenth Century," *The Early Modern Town*, ed. Peter Clark (London, 1976), 297–313.

[72] Jonathan Press, *The Merchant Seamen of Bristol, 1747–1789* (Bristol, 1976), 3, 4, 11; Rawley, *Transatlantic Slave Trade*, 179; Fryer, *Staying Power*, 19 (quotation); F. O. Shyllon, *Black Slaves in Britain* (London, 1974), 4, 5; Robert Stein, "Mortality in the Eighteenth-Century French Slave Trade," *Journal of African History* 21 (1980), 39.

streets. Particularly conspicuous were the mighty dwellings of merchants, many of whose bricks, later abolitionists would note, were forged in the burning miseries of the slave trade. By 1740 Liverpool merchants had begun to dominate this trade, seizing the lead from Bristol. Liverpool's population had increased from a mere 4,000 in 1680 to a bustling 30,000 only sixty years later. The Mersey River, swelling to a full two miles wide at high tide, provided the city with a "noble harbor" able "to ride a thousand sail of ships at once." But the flatness of the shoreline had in 1715 prompted Liverpool merchants to build an enormous wet dock at the eastern end of town. Only a few years later, the growth of trade required them to expand their Exchange, built of "gray stone" and adorned with arches and twelve massive columns.[73]

Liverpool's wharves stood stacked with cases of leather goods, linens, glass, metalwares, and refined sugar. Most of the men who loaded the goods lived in cramped basement dwellings amid workshops and warehouses along the Mersey, on the southern edge of the city. This area swarmed with workers who lived off the city's commerce and with commercial sharks, like crimps, who lived off the city's workers. As Liverpool merchants expanded their reach to Africa to supply the colonial labor market, Liverpool crimps tightened their grip on the seaman and the domestic maritime labor market. Crimps specialized in trapping sailors in debt. Some seamen, particularly those who drank heavily, unwittingly assisted them in their "recruitment," especially when they returned from voyages to Africa in debt, a circumstance that customarily gave their master an option on their labor for the next passage to that part of the world.[74]

Although Bristol and Liverpool dominated the slave trade in 1740, they had not sent the first English ships and men to

[73] Defoe, *Tour*, 541, 391, 392, 543, 706, 542, 543, 715. See also Clemens, "Rise of Liverpool," 211–222; *Journeys of Celia Fiennes*, 183–4; François Vigier, *Change and Apathy: Liverpool and Manchester during the Industrial Revolution* (Cambridge, Mass., 1970), 48; Corfield, *Impact of English Towns*, 39, 47; Fryer, *Staying Power*, 477.

[74] Rawley, *Transatlantic Slave Trade*, 259; Paul Edwards and James Walvin, *Black Personalities in the Era of the Slave Trade* (Baton Rouge, La., 1983), 32; F. O. Shyllon, *Black People in Britain, 1555–1833* (London, 1977), 49; Fryer, *Staying Power*, 19, 56–8, 75.

probe the African coast. English trade to West Africa originated from Plymouth and London in the mid-sixteenth century. The commerce took on larger dimensions in 1660 when
the king chartered the Royal Adventurers into Africa. A dozen
years later the crown granted exclusive rights to "black ivory"
to a new joint stock company, the Royal African Company.
Never shortsighted, except perhaps with regard to the possibility and direction of change, the English government granted
the Royal African Company a monopoly that still has nearly
700 years to run.[75] With some unwanted assistance from Dutch
interlopers, the Royal African Company began to supply the
West Indies with ever larger numbers of slaves. But the company soon felt the political pressure applied at home by traders
who fought the privileges of the chartered companies. In 1698
the company's monopoly was partially lifted; fourteen years
later it was completely rescinded. England became the first European nation to entrust the valuable African commerce to free
trade. Soon the outport traders, mostly from Bristol and Liverpool, rushed in, picking up initially the markets not served by
the Royal African Company. By the 1740s they had made
Great Britain the world's leader in carrying human cargoes.
Merchant captain William Snelgrave reported that only 33 English vessels ventured to Africa in 1712, the last year of the
Royal African Company's favored position, but by 1726 the
number had ballooned to more than 200.[76]

To secure the more than 2 million slaves torn from African
villages in the course of the eighteenth century, English merchants stocked their vessels with textiles, iron, copper, brass,

[75] Rawley, *Transatlantic Slave Trade*, 151; Palmer, *Human Cargoes*, 5. See also
K. G. Davies, *The Royal African Company* (New York, 1970), 1–46.
[76] Davies, *Royal African Company*, 344–9; Rawley, *Transatlantic Slave Trade*,
149–50, 162, 190, 164; Herbert Klein, *The Middle Passage: Comparative
Studies in the Atlantic Slave Trade* (Princeton, N.J., 1978), xviii; William Snelgrave, *A New Account of Some Parts of Guinea and the Slave Trade* (1734;
reprint London, 1971), introduction. Joseph E. Inikori, "The Slave Trade
and the Atlantic Economies, 1451–1870," *The African Slave Trade from the
Fifteenth to the Nineteenth Centuries* (Paris, 1979), 57, and Rawley, *Transatlantic
Slave Trade*, 424, have recently suggested that the figures offered by Philip
D. Curtin in *The Atlantic Slave Trade: A Census* (Madison, Wis., 1969) are too
low. But see the effective critique of Inikori and Rawley offered by Paul E.
Lovejoy, "The Volume of the Atlantic Slave Trade: A Synthesis," *Journal of
African History* 23 (1982), 473–501.

spirits, knives, glass, firearms, and other, mostly manufactured goods.[77] They concentrated their trading efforts on a narrow strip of coastland in West Africa, early in the century on the Slave Coast, including the Bight of Benin and its major port, Whidah. Farther east, the Gold Coast had long been a center of the traffic in slaves. Here the English made many of their deals through Johnny Kabes of Komenda, an entrepreneur who possessed a private army and cleverly pitted Dutch against English traders as he arranged exchanges with the royalty of the Asante Kingdom. English merchants established their greatest "factory" at Cape Coast Castle, just west of Accra on the Gold Coast. A stout fort with brick walls fourteen feet thick, rimmed by cannon, sat heavily on a sandy shore at the edge of densely wooded hills. (See Figure 6.) But by the 1740s, the merchants' gaze was turning toward the Windward Coast and the port of Calabar. As they expanded the area and scale of their African operations, these merchants required a steadily growing number of maritime workers.[78]

Seamen disliked the African trade more than any other, and their reasons are not difficult to discern. First among them was health. The African coast was deadly to English and American seamen who visited it. Malaria, yellow fever, scurvy, and dysentary were common; there were many fevers and complaints believed to be "caus'd by the Change of the Climate."[79] The summer months on the African coast were particularly dangerous. Calabar, like the rest of the region, was considered by sailors to be "a very unhealthful place."[80] A seaman's saying summed up the attitude:

---

[77] Rawley estimates the number at 2,014,700 (*Transatlantic Slave Trade*, 165). See also Wolf, *Europe and the People without History*, 218; Davies, *Royal African Company*, 45.

[78] Lovejoy, "Volume of the Atlantic Slave Trade," 499–500; Wolf, *Europe and the People without History*, 200–1, 205, 216; Snelgrave, *New Account*, introduction, 2; William Smith, *A New Voyage to Guinea* . . . (1744; reprint London, 1967), 2; *Voyages and Travels of Captain Nathaniel Uring*, 22–47, 91–7; Davies, *Royal African Company*, 240–1, 281; James Houston, *Some New and Accurate Observations . . . of the Coast of Guinea* (London, 1725), 15; Eveline C. Martin, "The English Establishments on the Gold Coast in the Second Half of the Eighteenth Century," *Royal Historical Society Transactions* ser. 4, 5 (1922), 167–208.

[79] Houston, *New and Accurate Observations*, 56 (quotation), 6.

[80] Arnold v. Ransom, HCA 24/129 (1706); K. G. Davies, "The Living and the Dead: White Mortality in West Africa, 1684–1732," *Race and Slavery in the Western Hemisphere: Quantitative Studies*, ed. Stanley L. Engerman and Eugene D. Genovese (Princeton, N.J., 1975), 88, 94–5.

Figure 6. A view of Cape Coast Castle on the west coast of Africa. This was one of the largest British "factories," where the slave trade was organized. The castle is flanked on the right by an African town, many of whose residents were involved in the trade.

> Beware and take care
> Of the Bight of Benin;
> For one that comes out,
> There are forty go in.[81]

The actual mortality rate for seamen, no matter how frightening it must have seemed, was not as severe as this piece of popular wisdom insisted. But Anglo-American seamen died in roughly the same horrendous proportions, and occasionally in even greater ones, as did the slaves themselves.[82] During the

---

[81] Quoted in Rawley, *Transatlantic Slave Trade*, 286. See also Davies, *Royal African Company*, 230.

[82] Klein argues that crew mortality was often greater than that among slaves (*Middle Passage*, 197). See also Palmer, *Human Cargoes*, 54; Jay Coughtry, *The Notorious Triangle: Rhode Island and the African Slave Trade, 1700–1807* (Philadelphia, 1981), 63, 105; Davies, "The Living and the Dead," 83. Curtin discusses the death of seamen as part of the "social cost" of the slave trade (*Atlantic Slave Trade*, 282–6). Other historians who have noted the extraordinary death rates among seamen include Michael Craton, *Sinews of Empire: A Short History of British Slavery* (Garden City, N.Y., 1974), 97–8; Roger Anstey,

daylight hours of the *Florida*'s voyage from the African coast to Antigua in 1714, the seamen tossed overboard the corpses of four to five Africans daily, 120 of 360 slaves (33 percent) in all. At night, in order to disguise their own declining numbers, they flung the bodies of their brother tars into the blue: 8 of 20, or 40 percent, were lost, and this figure does not include those who died before the vessel reached the coast of Africa. Seamen generally hated sailing in the "Torrid Zones" between the tropics, and they rightly regarded Africa as the most torrid zone in the world.[83]

The problems of health faced by the seamen were multiplied by the process of procuring a cargo of slaves, which often proved long, complicated, and tedious. In order to prevent mutinies by slaves, merchant captains drew their cargoes from scattered locations and different linguistic groups. "The means used by those who trade to Guinea, to keep the Negroes quiet," explained David Simson in the late seventeenth century, "is to choose them from severall parts of ye Country, of different Languages; so that they find they cannot act joyntly, when they are not in a Capacity of Consulting one an other, and this they can not doe, in soe farr as they understand not one an other."[84] For seamen, such divide-and-conquer tactics sometimes produced agonizingly long stays in a contrary climate, usually four months or longer. Though custom had it that sailors were entitled to a free ride home after a six-month wait on the coast, many merchants undoubtedly took the attitude of those who in 1721 told the men of the *Gambia Castle* that "they should stay till they rotted." Some tars who found themselves in such circumstances stayed, rotted, and perished. Others resisted.

The Atlantic Slave Trade and British Abolition, 1760–1810 (Atlantic Highlands, N.J., 1975), 26, 31; Johannes Postma, "Mortality in the Dutch Slave Trade, 1675–1795," *The Uncommon Market: Essays in the Economic History of the Atlantic Slave Trade* (New York, 1979), 260; Herbert S. Klein and Stanley L. Engerman, "A Note on Mortality in the French Slave Trade in the Eighteenth Century," *The Uncommon Market*, 263, 266. Stein, "Mortality in the Eighteenth-Century French Slave Trade," 35–42, offers the most sophisticated and detailed treatment of the problem of crew mortality.

[83] "Voyage to Guinea," Add. Ms. 39946, ff. 5, 6, 7; Babb v. Chalkley, HCA 24/127 (1701); *Voyages and Travels of Captain Nathaniel Uring*, 47–8; Ward, *Wooden World*, 68 (quotation).

[84] "Richard Simsons Voyage to the Straits of Magellan & S. Seas in the year 1689," Sloane Manuscript 86, BL, f. 87.

Those on board the *Gambia Castle,* led by George Lowther and John Massie, mutinied, turned pirate, and renamed their vessel the *Delivery.*[85]

Seamen were not the only ones to mutiny. The ever-present specter of uprising among the Africans was another haunting feature of the trade in human flesh. Seamen off the coast around 1740 would have heard tales of many bloody slave mutinies: the *Eagle Galley* in 1704; the *Henry* in 1721; the *Elizabeth* in the same year; and the *Ferrar Galley,* on which 300 slaves, "so many Negroes of one Town Language," rose up and killed their captain, were brutally subdued, then mutinied twice more before the ship reached Jamaica. Jamaican sugar planters discovered that they wanted no part of this "cargo."[86] These stories of bloodletting must have made many a seaman opt for another branch of deep-sea commerce. Edward Barlow, despite the fact that he never sailed to Africa, knew about desperate uprisings by slaves who "live under so much torture and hardship that rather than endure it they will run any hazard, for they are very hard worked."[87]

Dalby Thomas, a veteran of the slave trade, cautioned the Royal African Company in 1707 that its captains and mates, and presumably every sailor too, "must neither have dainty fingers nor dainty noses, [and] few men are fit for those voy-

---

[85] Petition of John Massey and George Lowther, CO 28/17 (July 22, 1721), f. 198. See also *The Tryals of Captain John Rackam and other Pirates* (Jamaica, 1721), 28. For more information on Lowther and his men, see Chapters 5 and 6 of this book. K. G. Davies has shown that of the 110 men who refused to mutiny and desert with Lowther, 71.8 percent were dead within a year ("The Living and the Dead," 91–2). For the period 1791–8, Herbert Klein estimates that the average wait on the African coast was 114 days (*Middle Passage,* 157). Robert Stein suggests that prior to 1756, the average stay on the coast for French vessels was 135 days ("Mortality in the Eighteenth-Century French Slave Trade," 37). Jay Coughtry estimates that stays of three to four months on the coast were typical and that serious unrest among the crew frequently developed during the layover (*The Notorious Triangle,* 63, 105). K. G. Davies says that stays of 120 days were typical (*Royal African Company,* 186, 217). The ominous significance of this finding becomes apparent in light of Davies's estimate that "[o]ne [white] man in three died in the first four months in Africa, more than three men in five in their first year" ("The Living and the Dead," 93).

[86] Snelgrave, *New Account,* 185–90, 187 (quotation). Rawley notes that there are 155 documented mutinies in the history of the slave trade (*Transatlantic Slave Trade,* 299). The actual figure is probably double or triple that number.

[87] *Barlow's Journal,* 314.

ages but them that are bred up to it. It is a filthy voyage as well
as a laborious [one]."[88] Seamen's filthy and laborious work
often involved some "clandestine trading" on their own accounts, which padded their wages. It took the experience of
several voyages – or being "bred up" to the trade – to manage
even this, so complex were African trading practices.[89] Seamen
also discovered that one of their greatest weapons, that of desertion, was largely ineffective in Africa – which is why merchants could tell them to sit and rot. There was simply nowhere
to go. The Royal African Company or others who served the
trade ran the English settlements, and deserters could expect to
find no favors there. Merchants reduced the room for maneuver further by manning their ships heavily, using twenty to
thirty seamen on a 200-ton "floating prison" – not only to act as
guards against rebellion but also to safeguard against the mortality that afflicted the ten- to eleven-month voyages.[90] Seamen
in the slave trade, themselves the captors of slaves, were at the
same time the captives of their own merchants and captains.

The third major western port in 1740, along with Bristol and Liverpool, was Glasgow, well known for its flourishing
trade with the American colonies and particularly for its role in
the shipment of tobacco from Virginia and Maryland. Glasgow
sat on a hill sloping down the north side of the Clyde River. Its
docks were laden with crates and boxes of manufactured
goods – woolens, linens, gloves, various wares – and with con-
tainers of processed sugar and distilled molasses from the
nearby Glasgow or Leith "sugar-houses." A line or two of hopeful but apprehensive indentured servants boarded a vessel
bound for Chesapeake plantations, there to produce the very
sotweed that Glasgow merchants would route back across the

---

[88] Quoted in Palmer, *Human Cargoes*, 47.
[89] Patrick v. Smith, HCA 24/138 (1733). The Royal African Company banned
"private trading" by seamen (Davies, *Royal African Company*, 258).
[90] Klein, *Middle Passage*, 166; Davis, *English Shipping*, 204–93; Press, *Merchant
Seamen of Bristol*, 9; Ian K. Steele, "Harmony and Competition: Aspects of
English and Colonial Shipping in the Barbados Trade at the End of the
Seventeenth Century," unpublished manuscript, 1980, 23. Between 1691
and 1713 the average Royal African Company ship was of 186 tons. Davies
also notes the lack of opportunity to leave the company's ships (*Royal African
Company*, 370, and "The Living and the Dead," 88).

North Atlantic and eventually to Europe. The seaman who walked from the docks to midtown would have seen the city's fine stone houses "even and uniform in height," some fronted by Doric columns. In the center of this city of almost 18,000 sat the ancient market on Bell Street, the university on High Street where a young moral philosopher named Adam Smith studied, and a grand cathedral topped by a "handsome spire."[91]

Many seamen were employed by Glasgow's "tobacco lords," who in their "red cloaks, satin suits, powdered wigs, three-cornered hats and gold-topped canes" met regularly at Merchants' Hall near Stockwell Bridge. Beneath a steeple 200 feet high, they discussed common concerns: trade, manufacturing, and the family ties that underlay much of their concentrated power.[92] Another interest was their great and proven dexterity in smuggling. In 1726 Daniel Defoe could answer charges of foul play against Glasgow merchants only by challenging those who were not guilty of such practices to cast the first stone. The tobacco lords' success, licit and illicit, translated into newly built mansions on aptly named Virginia Street, along Argyll Street, or on St. Enoch's Square.[93]

Fewer seamen lived in Glasgow than in London, Bristol, or Liverpool, but those who did congregated in the oldest central districts of the city, off High, Saltmarket, and Bridgegate streets, or else down the Clyde at Port Glasgow or Greenock. They lived in poor, ramshackle buildings amid dunghills, middens, and the cast-off by-products of a host of small waterside industries.[94]

A vessel that departed Glasgow for the Chesapeake carried a hold full of manufactured goods and fifteen to twenty seamen who anticipated a round trip of six to nine months. Catching

[91] Defoe, *Tour*, 606, 607, 605, 610; Andrew Gibb, *Glasgow: The Making of a City* (London, 1983), 59, 74; C. A. Oakley, *The Second City* (London, 1946), 27; James Cleland, *The Rise and Progress of the City of Glasgow* (Glasgow, 1820), 88–9, 107, 194.

[92] David Daiches, *Glasgow* (London, 1977), 51.

[93] Oakley, *Second City*, 21; Daiches, *Glasgow*, 51–2; Gibb, *Glasgow*, 65; T. M. Divine, *The Tobacco Lords: A Study of the Tobacco Merchants of Glasgow and Their Trading Activities, c. 1740–1790* (Edinburgh, 1975), 3, 4, 11, 36; Defoe, *Tour*, 610. The best recent work on tobacco smuggling is R. C. Nash, "The English and Scottish Tobacco Trades in the Seventeenth and Eighteenth Centuries: Legal and Illegal Trade," *EHR* 35 (1982), 354–72.

[94] Gibb, *Glasgow*, 44, 51, 68, 69, 74.

the northern trade winds that swept the ship into the beautiful and intricate waterways of Chesapeake Bay, some sailors in the tobacco trade arrived at their destination after a relatively quick and comfortable passage. Those few who had first stopped off in Africa to pick up a coffle of slaves reached Virginia and Maryland after a tense, arduous, and death-infested voyage. The survivors were no doubt happy to come to "a very plentifull Country where provisions and victuals are very reasonable."[95] On the other hand, they were none too pleased that the system of marketing tobacco along the Chesapeake's countless inlets and waterways required them to fetch and load cumbersome hogsheads that weighed 500 pounds and more. The warehousing of tobacco, encouraged by legislation of 1730 in Virginia, improved matters somewhat by reducing the amount of river work demanded of seamen. Nevertheless, the absence of both sizable towns and a substantial free labor force (that might have included stevedores) continued to make for more and harder work for Jack Tar in the Chesapeake.[96]

Yet these same circumstances also created a few advantages for the seaman. The undeveloped wage labor system and the small number of seamen in the Chesapeake made for a scarcity of free workers and sometimes for high wages. The dispersed setting of the work in the tidewater region made it easy for the seaman to desert one vessel, find another in search of willing workers, and sign on for more money. Desertion plagued Virginia authorities throughout the eighteenth century. Seamen "straggled" all over the countryside, sometimes briefly taking work on the plantations or among the "poor People" of the area, at other times hiding out at places such as the Rose and Crown Tavern near Cartwright's on the Elizabeth River, where they could expect to hear the latest about wages, usage, and destinations.[97] (See Figure 7.)

---

[95] Parker v. Boucher, HCA 24/132 (1719); "A List of Ships Bound to Virginia and Maryland," CO 1/68 (1690), f. 23; *Voyages and Travels of Captain Nathaniel Uring,* 229.

[96] Middleton, *Tobacco Coast,* 282, 283.

[97] *Voyages and Travels of Captain Nathaniel Uring,* 5; Deposition of James Baker, CO 5/1306 (1692); "Miscellaneous Colonial Documents," *VMHB* 16 (1908), 76; Middleton, *Tobacco Coast,* 266. The 845 ordinaries and keepers of taverns and grog shops among Maryland's population in 1746 no doubt served many a sailor. See Alexander Hamilton, *Gentleman's Progress: The Itinerarium*

Figure 7. The class relations of tobacco. At the left, a seaman sits on a hogshead, smoking a pipe, drinking punch, and looking on as an African slave haggles with a Virginia planter over sotweed.

The seaman packed his ship with the "Indian's Revenge," the tobacco introduced to Europeans by the natives of the New World. Tars also stowed the furs and timber extracted from Virginia's rich interior. Most of the seamen who loaded these goods were English and Scottish, as were the capital, credit, and ships involved in the trade. After 1710, when the Chesapeake planters began a full-scale conversion to slave labor, tobacco production increased and 3,000 to 4,000 seamen were mobilized for the trade each year.[98]

Seamen sailed to the picturesque port of Charleston either directly from England or increasingly by way of Africa, whence they transported the laborers who developed and transformed the Carolina economy. As they approached Charleston, incom-

of Dr. Alexander Hamilton, ed. Carl Bridenbaugh (Chapel Hill, N.C., 1948), 206. On desertion in Virginia, see Alexander Spotswood to Council of Trade and Plantations, CO 5/1363 (March 6, 1710), f. 294; see also CO 5/1344; CO 5/1305, ff. 30–5; ADM 1/1827.

[98] Rawley, *Transatlantic Slave Trade,* 400, 402–4; Farnie, "Commercial Empire," 206; F. C. Huntley, "The Seaborne Trade of Virginia in the Mid-Eighteenth Century: Port Hampton," *VMHB* 59 (1951), 297. See also Robert Dinwiddie, "A Computation of the Value and Trade of the British Empire of America" CO 323/10 (1740), ff. 185–92; Klein, *Middle Passage,* 134; Price, "Economic Function," 162–3.

Figure 8. A view of Charleston, South Carolina, before 1739. Several large ships, most of them owned by British merchants, lie offshore.

ing vessels passed Fort Johnson, built in 1704 on the northeast point of James Island, and sailed into the "very commodious Harbour" situated "on a Point very convenient for Trade, being seated between two pleasant and navigable Rivers." Estuarial rivers, rising from inland blackwater swamps, flowed into Charleston, by buildings of brick, cypress, and yellow pine, many of them three stories high and adorned with balconies and piazzas, that elegantly faced the waterside and greeted the visitor who approached by sea. (See Figure 8.) Middle Bridge was the busiest wharf in this town of 7,000. It was surrounded on the dockside by the town courthouse, the merchants' exchange, the customs house, the Old Market, and an array of shops and warehouses; on the waterside were bunched canoes, boats, and piraguas that themselves made up a "floating market." Ships entering Charleston harbor were emptied of Africans dead and alive, as well as sugar, molasses, rum, and a variety of manufactured goods. They were soon filled with naval stores, deerskins, timber, and, most importantly, barrels of indigo and rice. Most of this produce was destined for Europe, though some went to the West Indies. Charleston, dominated by slave owners, possessed no autonomous mercantile community. Indeed, in 1740 South Carolinians owned only 25 seagoing vessels of their own, and therefore relied upon English-owned craft – 200 per year – to serve their trade. Charleston functioned more as a "shipping point" than as a genuine commercial center.[99]

Seamen had their likes and dislikes about sailing to Charles-

[99] John Lawson, *A New Voyage to Carolina* (1709; reprint Chapel Hill, 1967), 8 (quotation), 9–11; Rawley, *Transatlantic Slave Trade*, 411; Price, "Economic Function," 162–3; Dinwiddie, "A Computation," 185–92; *Voyages and Travels of Captain Nathaniel Uring*, 229 (quotation); *The Centennial of Incorporation of Charleston, South Carolina* (Charleston, 1884), 56–7, 87, 153; on the "floating markets," Governor James Glen, 1751, quoted in Leila Sellers, *Charleston Business on the Eve of the American Revolution* (Chapel Hill, N.C., 1934), 5, 16; George C. Rogers, *Charleston in the Age of the Pinckneys* (Norman, Okla., 1969), 8, 56, 69; Frederick P. Bowes, *The Culture of Early Charleston* (Chapel Hill, N.C., 1942), 8; Carl Bridenbaugh, *Cities in the Wilderness: The First Century of Urban Life in America, 1625–1742* (London, 1938), 177, 332, 327. For Charleston's economic development, see Converse D. Clowse, *Economic Beginnings in Colonial South Carolina* (Columbia, S.C., 1971), and idem, *Measuring Charleston's Overseas Commerce, 1717–1767: Statistics from the Port's Naval Lists* (Washington, D.C., 1981).

ton. Some regarded it as an "unhealthy place," or so said Nathaniel Uring in 1718. But there was a vice-admiralty court in Charleston where tars could bring claims against their masters when necessary. They could even sue collectively. And perhaps most important of all, Judges Nicholas Trott, William Blakeway, and Maurice Lewis issued a ruling in their favor from time to time. Moreover, in Charleston, English merchant captains were just plentiful enough, and seamen themselves just scarce enough, that desertion often held the promise of a heavy purse and plentiful rum as wages for the "run home" to London.[100]

In December 1718, a gallows was erected in Providence, the capital of the Bahama Islands in the West Indies, to accommodate a mass hanging. The nooses were prepared for the necks of nine pirates. The infamous freebooter flag flew overhead, its grinning skull looking beyond its crossbones and down upon the place of execution. Woodes Rogers – governor, captain general, and vice-admiralty judge of the islands – sat among other gentlemen awaiting the spectacle. A small crowd milled about. It was composed of seamen and pirates who, prior to Rogers's arrival earlier in the year, had used the Bahamas as a base of operations. One hundred soldiers escorted the condemned men to the gallows. The malefactors were charged with "Mutiny, Felony, Piracy." Daniel Macarty and Phineas Bunce had led an uprising that overthrew Captain William Greenaway's command aboard the *Lancaster*. "[C]rying up a Pyrate's Life to be the only Life for a Man of any Spirit," Macarty and Bunce had gone "upon the account." They and their crew had "reflected on the King and the Government" in an uncomplimentary and decidedly undeferential way. And they had captured and plundered several vessels. But now the end had come.

Macarty "ascended the Stage, with as much Agility and in a Dress of a Prize-Fighter." He "wore long blue ribbons at his Neck, Wrists, Knees, and Cap." Not to be outdone, William Lewis, "a hardy Pyrate" and fighter, was brilliantly adorned with red ribbons. The spectators crowded "as near to the foot

[100] *Voyages and Travels of Captain Nathaniel Uring*, 229–30; SC ADM.

of the gallows, as the Marshall's Guard would suffer them."
James Bendall's last words were that he "wish'd he had begun
the Life sooner, for he thought it a pleasant one, meaning that
of a Pyrate." John Augur, perhaps hopeful of a last-minute
reprieve, drank a small glass of wine "with wishes for the Success of the Bahama Islands & the Governour." Macarty said
that he "knew the time when there was many brave fellows on
the Island that would not suffer him to dye like a dog," but he
acknowledged to the crowd that now there was "too much
power over their heads" for them to "attempt any Thing in his
Favour." James Morris expressed a simple wish, that he "might
have been a greater Plague to these Islands." Lewis "scorn'd to
shew any Fear to dye but heartily desired Liquors enough to
drink with his fellow sufferers on the Stage, and with the
Standers by." After brief exhortations and the singing of
psalms, "the hangman fastned the Cords as dextrously as if he
had been a Servitour at Tybourne." As the nine men prepared
to draw their last breaths, the governor solemnly extended the
royal hand of mercy, not to the health-drinking Augur but
rather to George Rounsivil, a young man whose neck was apparently saved by connections in England. The necks of the un-
chosen and the unconnected remained in the noose. The butts
holding up the gallows, "having Ropes about them, were hauld
away, upon which the stage fell and the Eight swang off." Piracy had come to a symbolic end on the island that had once
served as its greatest rendezvous.[101] It was one battle among
many.

Piracy had been a part of the English involvement in the
West Indies since the sixteenth century, when fierce Elizabe-
than sea dogs, epitomized by Sir Francis Drake, marauded the
Spanish Main, seeking in one deft move both to singe the Span-
iard's beard and to line their own pockets with gold and silver.
From this and other armed confrontations came the phrase "no
peace beyond the line." For some people these words expressed

[101] Captain Charles Johnson [Daniel Defoe], *A General History of the Pyrates,* ed.
Manuel Schonhorn (1724, 1728; reprint Columbia, S.C., 1972), 624–59,
642, 645, 628, 659, 647, 656, 659; "The Tryal and Condemnation of Ten
Persons for Piracy at New Providence," CO 23/1 (1718), ff. 76, 81, 82, 81.
See also Woodes Rogers to Council of Trade and Plantations, Oct. 31, 1718,
ff. 16–29.

the horror and discomfort of life at the edge of the world; for others, like pirates, the saying constituted a refusal to permit state officials, residing comfortably in London, to tell them whom they were and were not permitted to attack.[102] Buccaneering, usually associated with the dazzling exploits of Henry Morgan, was a source of substantial wealth during the early years of English settlement in the "Cribey Islands." Morgan and his raiders based themselves in Jamaica after England seized the island from Spain in 1655, and managed over the next sixteen years to sack eighteen cities, four towns, and thirty-five villages in New Spain.[103] They turned an overextended empire to their own purposes and raked in the booty.

English settlers in the West Indies had begun in the 1620s to produce tobacco, indigo, and spices, but then came the momentous transition of the 1640s to the cultivation of sugar. The West Indian planter class began to import slaves in massive numbers to produce the labor-intensive crop, thereby transforming the social structure of the region. The production of sugar quickly became one of the greatest sources of wealth and one of the highest priorities in both the British Empire and the world. Sugar was king. The triangular trade among Great Britain, Africa, and the West Indies had emerged. Manufactures, slaves, and sugar circulated around the Atlantic.[104]

By 1740 sugar brought 400 to 500 vessels and thousands of Anglo-American seamen yearly to the British Caribbean, to Barbados, Antigua, Nevis, St. Kitts, Montserrat, and Jamaica. Coming from the northeast and skimming along with the trade winds – which was "undoubtedly the pleasantest sailing

[102] This and the following three paragraphs are indebted to Carl and Roberta Bridenbaugh, *No Peace Beyond the Line, 1642–1690* (New York, 1972), and especially to Richard S. Dunn, *Sugar and Slaves: The Rise of the Planter Class in the English West Indies, 1624–1713* (New York, 1972). As late as 1716, pirates in the Caribbean announced that "they never consented to the Articles of Peace with the French and the Spaniards" (*Boston News-Letter*, May 21–8, 1716).

[103] Dudley Pope, *The Buccaneer King: The Biography of Sir Henry Morgan* (New York, 1978); *Barlow's Journal*, 137; C. H. Haring, *The Buccaneers in the West Indies in the XVII Century* (1910; reprint Hamden, Conn., 1966), 267; Wallerstein, *Modern World System II*, 159–61; Parry, *Trade and Dominion*, 18–25.

[104] Farnie, "Commercial Empire," 206; Richard Pares, "The Economic Factors in the History of Empire," *Essays in Economic History* (London, 1954), vol. 1, 422; idem, *War and Trade*, 141.

in the world" – or sailing westward from Africa, English vessels entered a region known for its heat, hurricanes, sea breezes, and thick nightly dew.[105] Many seamen cruised to Jamaica, the largest and busiest British colony, and in particular to Port Royal, once known as "the wickedest city in the west," a place full of "a most Ungodly debauched people." To Ned Ward, Jamaica was the "Receptacle of Vagabonds, the Sanctuary of Bankrupts, and a Close-Stool for the Purges of our Prisons. As Sickly as an Hospital, as Dangerous as the Plague, as Hot as Hell, and as Wicked as the Devil." As if due to wrathful divine intervention, Port Royal tumbled to the bottom of the sea in an earthquake of 1692, leaving an estimated 2,000 dead, whose corpses floated amid the city's crumbled and submerged ruins. The city began to be rebuilt but was destroyed again in 1701, this time by fire.[106] But Port Royal remained a favorite among seamen, and by 1705 the city boasted 400 to 500 houses. It was, according to Francis Rogers, "soon as wicked, I believe, as ever." The unruly reputation of Port Royal drove merchants away. Their largest vessels docked at Chocolate Hole and others went to Kingston, where merchants felt their cargoes were safer. But a great many merchant seamen, naval sailors, privateersmen, and pirates continued to gravitate to Port Royal.[107]

There they converged on the rowdy punch-houses and brothels so full of "Lewd dissolute fellows" that the press gang could not often do its work of body snatching without a fight and at times a bloody defeat. Betty Ware's was a popular spot where a seaman might find anything from fellowship to duels with cutlasses, swords, pistols, or light muskets. Such places were remarkable, at least to some, for the "swearing, obscene, masculine talk and behaviour" of their women, who sported

---

[105] "Journal of Francis Rogers," 149, 227–8; Ward, *Wooden World*, 68; Dinwiddie, "A Computation."

[106] "An Account of ye Earthquake at Port Royal in Jamaica" (1692), BL, Harleian Manuscript 6922; Letter of W. J. Dickinson, August 13, 1692, *Dering Correspondence*, vol. 5, BL, Stowe Manuscript 747; Michael Pawson and David Buisseret, *Port Royal, Jamaica* (Oxford, 1975), 120; Ned Ward, "A Trip to Jamaica: With a True Character of the People and the Island" (1698), in *Five Travel Scripts Commonly Attributed to Ned Ward* (New York, 1933), 13.

[107] "Journal of Francis Rogers," 226; Pawson and Buisseret, *Port Royal*, 119; *Voyages and Travels of Captain Nathaniel Uring*, 247.

names like "*Unconscionable Nan, Salt Beef Peg, Buttock-de-Clink Jenny,* etc." Port Royal seems to have been a favorite place of the seafaring men drawn to Jamaica by sugar.[108]

But if no sugar was available (and this was not uncommon), captains and their crews sailed westward for another twelve to fourteen days to the Bay of Campeche, west of the Yucatan peninsula, where since the 1660s former pirates and seamen had been battling the Spanish, hunting wild cattle, and cutting logwood (used for dies) that they sold to merchant captains in search of cargoes. The "Baymen," as they were known, were "sturdy, strong Fellows" notorious for their marksmanship, three- to four-day drinking bouts, and communal sharing of food and property. They had even drawn up a "short compendium of Laws" that contained "no Capital punishments." Although sailors enjoyed merriment with the logwood cutters, sometimes even enough to sign on to chop wood themselves for a while, they were also edgy about passages to the bay because of the constant danger of ambush by the Spanish.[109]

Although sugar was central to English trade in the Caribbean, smuggling was also crucial. Illicit trade with Spain boomed, allowing English merchants to profit not only from slave labor on British islands but also from the labor of Indians and Africans enslaved on Spanish haciendas and plantations. Together, sugar and smuggling guaranteed the lofty position of the West Indies in the English imperial scheme through the end of the eighteenth century.[110]

The West Indies, to the eighteenth-century seaman as to those who had settled the islands in the previous century, represented something of a gamble, a venture "beyond the line." Smollett called Jamaica "that fatal island," and so it was. Mor-

[108] Edward Vernon to Josiah Burchett, October 28, 1719, BL, Add. Ms. 40811, f. 26; "Journal of Francis Rogers," 229, 226; Pawson and Buisseret, *Port Royal,* 199; Ward, "Trip to Jamaica," 16.

[109] "Voyage to Guinea," f. 10; Pawson and Buisseret, *Port Royal,* 70; William Dampier, "Mr. Dampier's Voyage to the Bay of Campeachy," in his *A Collection of Voyages,* 9, 18, 44, 53, 54, 83; Dampier, "New Voyage," 242, 241; *Voyages and Travels of Captain Nathaniel Uring,* 242; Haring, *Buccaneers,* 209; Murdo J. MacLeod, *Spanish Central America: A Socioeconomic History* (Berkeley, 1973), 361–2; Warren v. Searle, HCA 24/127 (1702); Godwyn v. Mantlark, HCA 24/127 (1700).

[110] Haring, *Buccaneers,* 111, 32, 209–10; Wallerstein, *Modern World System II,* 158, 160, 161; Parry, *Trade and Dominion,* 93; MacLeod, *Spanish Central America,* 362, 385.

tality rates for sailors ran high, especially for the "unseasoned" who had never made a prior voyage. Extraordinary dangers of shipwreck lurked among the Caribbean's shoals and shifting sands. Hurricanes and tempests had to be dodged between midsummer and fall. The close proximity of English, French, Spanish, and Dutch colonies made the Caribbean "the cockpit of war" and increased the seaman's chances of death in battle or capture by a man-of-war or privateer.[111]

Yet the seaman who took courage in hand and placed the bet beyond the line often found himself a winner. Smugglers and privateersmen frequently made good money, as did pirates if they could avoid hanging in chains on Gallows Point in Port Royal. The dominance of slavery and the weakness of free labor throughout the West Indies made for relatively high wages. Desertion was a ready option. And finally, as Nathaniel Uring pointed out, seamen reaped still other advantages in the Caribbean: "the Seamen in Jamaica, being chiefly employed in Sloops, either in Privateering or Trading on the Coast of [New] Spain, are unwilling to sail in Ships, because there is more Work, and loath to go to Europe, for fear of being imprest into the Publick Service." Less work and freedom from the press were no small recommendations for the West Indies. The islands may have represented a gamble, but there were some prized chips in the pot.[112]

The eighteenth century witnessed the emergence of North American ports, particularly Boston, New York, and Philadelphia, as major commercial centers within the empire. In the previous century, shipping from these ports – or better, seafaring villages – was not deeply engaged in the transatlantic trades, but rather shuttled colonial products to the West Indies. By 1740, ships from American shores had begun to call upon more distant ports in Europe and Africa; simultaneously they were carrying an even greater volume and variety of commodities to the Caribbean. Greater numbers of British ships visited colonial ports. North American merchants also started to sink their capital into the dicey business of privateering. As a result

[111] Smollett, *Roderick Random*, 208; Dunn, *Sugar and Slaves*, chap. 1; *Barlow's Journal*, 332; Parry, *Trade and Dominion*, 45 (quotation).

[112] *Voyages and Travels of Captain Nathaniel Uring*, 165.

of these developments, a minimum of 20 to 25 percent of the adult male inhabitants of Boston, New York, and Philadelphia worked in the maritime sector – trade or fishing – throughout the eighteenth century. Sailors maintained a prominent, if not always orderly, presence in each city.[113]

A vessel coming into Boston in 1740 passed the port's lighthouse twelve miles out, then the imposing Castle William three miles below the city. "When a snow, brig, sloop, or schooner appears out at sea," reported Dr. Alexander Hamilton, "they hoist a pinnacle upon the flag staff in the Castle, if a ship, they display a flag."[114] The castle made Boston "better fortified against an enimy than any port in North America." It had a strong battery of heavy cannon, a regular and vigilant watch day and night, and its own "cannon proof" fortifications.[115] The incoming vessel, once cleared, eased through a narrow passage "not above 160 foot wide . . . at high water" and into a "large & Comodious" harbor, which was deep enough to permit the ship to come all the way to the wharves and to "lye moor'd . . . in great Safty."[116] (See Figure 9.) Long Wharf, built in 1713, ran "from the bottom of King Street" more than a quarter of a mile into the water, though Bostonians liked to brag that it was fully half a mile long.[117] Here seamen and dock workers discharged cargoes "into Warehouses Errected upon the Northside" of the wharf "without the help of Boats, Lighters, &c.," which was "a Great Ease to the People."[118] A sizable portion of these "people" were black. Probably the better part of Boston's slave population – itself 8 percent of the city's 16,400 in 1742 – worked around the docks.

Laborers black and white unloaded manufactured goods from England, rum, sugar, and molasses from the West Indies, and bread and flour from the port of Philadelphia. Into the

[113] Nash, *Urban Crucible*, 54; Price, "Economic Function," 136–7. See also James G. Lydon, *Pirates, Privateers, and Profits* (Upper Saddle River, N.J., 1970); Carl E. Swanson, "American Privateering and Imperial Warfare, 1739–1748," *WMQ* 42 (1985), 357–82.

[114] Hamilton, *Gentleman's Progress*, 107.

[115] Ibid., 145, 142; James Birket, *Some Cursory Remarks Made by James Birket in his Voyage to North America, 1750–1751* (New Haven, Conn., 1916), 19.

[116] Hamilton, *Gentleman's Progress*, 145; Birket, *Cursory Remarks*, 23.

[117] Hamilton, *Gentleman's Progress*, 107; Birket, *Cursory Remarks*, 23, 73.

[118] Birket, *Cursory Remarks*, 23; Hamilton, *Gentleman's Progress*, 107, 234; *Voyages and Travels of Captain Nathaniel Uring*, 77–8.

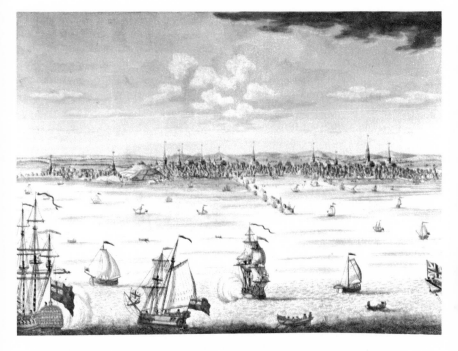

Figure 9. A view of Boston, c. 1735. Long Wharf extends from the shoreline more than a quarter of a mile into the harbor. Small vessels, built and owned by New Englanders, dot the harbor.

emptied vessels went furs, provisions, whale products, livestock, naval stores, turpentine, timber, and manufactured items for delivery to Europe, Africa, and the Caribbean. Boston's relatively unproductive agricultural hinterland and the city's consequent need to transship so many commodities produced a complex range of entrepôt activities. The outbreak of the War of Jenkins' Ear in 1739, however, meant that dockers were not loading nearly as much dried fish – "poor jack," it was called – as usual, because Boston's merchants had lost their lucrative Spanish market.[119]

[119] Bridenbaugh, *Cities in the Wilderness*, 333; Birket, *Cursory Remarks*, 23; Hamilton, *Gentleman's Progress*, 145; Gary M. Walton, "Trade Routes, Ownership Proportions, and American Colonial Shipping Characteristics," *Les Routes de L'Atlantique: Travaux du neuvième Colloque International d'Histoire*

The city's merchants met daily, near the Statehouse on Henry Street, between 11 A.M. and 1 P.M. to discuss such problems. They talked business at Samuel Wethered's Tavern, at the corner of Kilby and King streets, or at The Crown by Long Wharf, and they did so with great success. New Englanders owned more than 1,500 vessels by 1740, and many of these merchant-shipowners had already developed "that subtilty and acuteness so peculiar to a New England genius" for trade. They had "Acquired opulent fortunes" and "Great Reputation." They inhabited "very stately, well built, convenient Houses," recently constructed to proclaim their eminence.[120] Seamen commented upon the "sly, crafty, tricking, designing sort of People" they met in Boston, and none doubted that the city's big merchants were the slyest and craftiest of them all.[121] Ned Ward found that "Whosoever believes a *New England Saint,* shall be sure to be Cheated: and he that knows how to deal with their Traders, may deal with the Devil and fear no Craft." Mercantile guile was gradually reshaping the Puritan way of life: "It is not by half such a flagrant sin to cheat and cozen one's neighbor as it is to ride about for pleasure on the sabbath day or to neglect going to church and singing of psalms." George Whitefield may have had the great merchants in mind when in 1741 he noted the excessive "pride of life" in Boston.[122]

Boston itself probably made a favorable impression on seamen with its well-paved streets, its small but elegant buildings, and its solidly constructed vessels from its own energetic shipyards. The supply and variety of good-quality oak, however,

Footnote 119 (*cont.*):

Maritime (Paris, 1967), 492, 485–8; William I. Davisson and Lawrence J. Bradley, "New York Maritime Trade: Ship Voyage Patterns, 1715–1765," *New York Historical Society Quarterly* 55 (1971), 314–17; Rawley, *Transatlantic Slave Trade,* 388, 398.

[120] Bridenbaugh, *Cities in the Wilderness,* 428; Hamilton, *Gentleman's Progress,* 109, 197; Birket, *Cursory Remarks,* 24, 20–1. See also Dinwiddie, "A Computation," and *Voyages and Travels of Captain Nathaniel Uring,* 77.

[121] *Voyages and Travels of Captain Nathaniel Uring,* 80; Birket, *Cursory Remarks,* 24.

[122] Ned Ward, "A Trip to New England, with a Character of the Country and People, both English and Indians" (1699), in *Five Travel Scripts,* 7; Hamilton, *Gentleman's Progress,* 145–6; *George Whitefield's Journals* (Guildford and London, 1960), 473.

was dwindling; the woods around the city had been "very much Cut down and destroy'd."[123] Earlier in the century Jack Cremer had professed that he "never saw a begger or a poor man" in Boston, but he could not have made that claim in the 1740s. The wars against France had created disabled veterans, widows, poverty, and dependence. Seamen and their families, among others, often suffered.[124] Boston's poor, many of whom worked in maritime commerce, crowded together in tiny wooden two-family houses by the wharves. The laboring poor, seamen included, knew that Boston had seen better times.

Like Charleston, Boston had its own vice-admiralty court. Sailors knew that vice-admiralty Judge John Menzies wasn't so bad as judges went. He usually gave seamen who sued for "wages and liberation" their due and proper pay, but rarely did he release them from a captain's grasp. Menzies had even ruled that ship masters were not allowed to draw blood when administering discipline, but then again he never objected when a commander gave a crew member a zealous drubbing for cursing and swearing.[125]

Boston was considered a good town for "frolicking," not least because of its "well rigged" young women – though an amorous seaman had to be careful even in this once-holy city, lest such women "give you a doase of Something to remember them *by*."[126] Music houses offered dancing and entertainment, both welcome diversions, and thankfully so, since seamen often spent long stretches in port while their captains, plagued by Boston's lack of an agricultural staple, searched high and low for a full cargo. Good times were to be found at the Dog and Pot near Bartlett's wharf or at the Widow Day's Crown Tavern by Clarke's wharf. However he passed the time, the sailor had to be wary or else find himself in the Queen Street prison or the Fort Hill poorhouse. Puritans, even as late as the 1740s,

[123] Birket, *Cursory Remarks*, 24, 21.
[124] *Ramblin' Jack*, 113; Nash, *Urban Crucible*, 21.
[125] Webber v. Clarke, MASS ADM (1723), ff. 133–4; Hooper v. Harris, MASS ADM (1725), f. 197; Lawler v. Forest, MASS ADM (1725), f. 198; Pitcher v. Lawrence, MASS ADM (1731), ff. 100–01; Bridenbaugh, *Cities in the Wilderness*, 147, 392–4.
[126] *Ramblin' Jack*, 111.

never cared too much for outsiders, least of all those without property and families.[127]

Near Boston lay the small but dynamic port of Newport, Rhode Island, where sailors found fine wharves and a roadstead close to the sea. Docking at Peleg Sanford's or Clark's on the Cove and making their way through the small dramshops, warehouses, boarding houses, and streets that "still resembled a barnyard," seamen explored the town notorious for its slave trade, privateering, and smuggling. Newport's merchants traded with the logwood cutters at Campeche, the Dutch in Surinam and Curačao, and other Caribbean colonies. The legality of their ventures never concerned them overmuch. Newport's customs officials and naval officers dared not "exercise their office for fear of the fury and unruliness" of a threatening mob, but they received sufficient gifts and bribes – always cheaper than customs fees – to make the dare unlikely in the first place. A small town with only one main street and 6,200 people in 1742, Newport prospered as a provincial port.[128]

The port of New York, taking advantage of its superior harbor and rich surrounding farmlands, experienced swift growth as a commercial center in the early eighteenth century, particularly after 1720. The seaman who sailed into this town of more than 10,000 in the 1740s found himself in a buzzing entrepôt. On the sound eastside wharves – "logs of wood upon a stone foundation" – where deep waters made docking easy and convenient, laborers loaded furs, horses, lumber, beef, pork, flour, bread, butter, and cheese into English and American vessels usually bound for Europe or the West Indies. New York merchants also dispatched vessels to the Bay of Campeche for logwood, which they then remitted to Europe in exchange for dry goods. These latter, and many other items, were in turn transshipped to outlying regions, especially Albany, a center of the fur trade with the Mohawks and other native American tribes.

---

[127] Mackie v. Powell, MASS ADM, f. 129 (1732); Thomas Prince, *Vade Mecum for America* (Boston, 1731), 215; Vickers, "Maritime Labor," 11–12, 16–18; Bridenbaugh, *Cities in the Wilderness*, 429.

[128] Lynn Withey, *Urban Growth in Colonial Rhode Island: Newport and Providence in the Eighteenth Century* (Albany, N.Y., 1984), chap. 2; Hamilton, *Gentleman's Progress*, 102, 156; Birket, *Cursory Remarks*, 30, 29; Coughtry, *Notorious Triangle*, 34; Price, "Economic Function," 149–50; Bridenbaugh, *Cities in the Wilderness*, 323, 173 (quotation), 272, 303, 326.

During the 1740s, New York and its seamen became deeply involved in the global trades. More and more vessels bound for the coast of Africa departed New York harbor, and hordes of plunder-hungry privateers set sail in search of wartime enemies. New York's enterprising merchants and vice-admiralty Judge Lewis Morris, Jr., had helped to make the city the privateering capital of the American colonies by the 1740s.[129] (See Figure 10.)

Seamen found in New York a city "built close upon the [East] River," many of whose 2,000 houses were constructed "after the Dutch manner, with the gable ends toward the street."[130] The cobblestoned streets around the harbor were "very Irregular & Crooked & many of 'em much too narrow," though fairly well paved.[131] Along these crowded streets sat coffee houses and pubs, as well as the seaman's favorite haunts: John Mackleman's Blue Anchor on the Dock, the Long-Room, the Bunch of Grapes, and Ebenezer Grant's Sign of the Dog's Head in the Porridge Pot. Nearby was City Hall, a place visited by many a sailor, not out of civic pride or curiosity but because New York's jail was located in the basement.[132] Nearby, Fort George used a battery of fifty-six cannons to protect the city, the residence of Governor George Clarke, and a Church of England chapel. In 1742 the fort bore the scars of struggle, not against Spanish or French enemies, but rather from the elite's enemies within, the slaves and poor whites who rebelled during the difficult winter of 1741. The rebels had burned large parts of the castle, which now lay in ruins. The body of the mutiny's ringleader, John Hughson, dangled in chains in the harbor. Several seamen had fought in the ranks of the rebels.[133]

---

[129] *The Journal of John Fontaine: An Irish Huguenot Son in Spain and Virginia, 1710–1719*, ed. Edward Porter Alexander (Charlottesville, Va., 1972), 115; Hamilton, *Gentleman's Progress*, 44; Birket, *Cursory Remarks*, 43; Rawley, *Transatlantic Slave Trade*, 387–8; James G. Lydon, "New York and the Slave Trade, 1700–1774," *WMQ* 35 (1978), 375–94; idem, *Pirates, Privateers, and Profits*, chap. 1; Swanson, "American Privateering," 366; Price, "Economic Function," 140, 149, 143, 145, 158, 152; Bridenbaugh, *Cities in the Wilderness*, 303.

[130] *Journal of John Fontaine*, 115; Birket, *Cursory Remarks*, 44, 67.

[131] Birket, *Cursory Remarks*, 44; Hamilton, *Gentleman's Progress*, 44.

[132] Lemisch, "Jack Tar versus John Bull," 63, 59; *Journal of John Fontaine*, 114; Bridenbaugh, *Cities in the Wilderness*, 426–8.

[133] Hamilton, *Gentleman's Progress*, 46; Daniel Horsmanden, *The New York Conspiracy*, ed. Thomas J. Davis (1744; reprint Boston, 1971). See also Davis's

Figure 10. A view of Fort George and the city of New York, c. 1735. Fort George, designed to protect the city from enemies without, was attacked from within by slaves and free workers in 1741.

Concourse between black and white workers was not unusual in this "very rich" city. In 1746 slaves made up more than one-fifth of New York's population, and the majority of slave men were employed in the maritime and commercial sectors of the economy. Slaves toiled alongside unskilled white workers as teamsters, wagoners, dockers, stockmen, ropewalkers, and cartmen.[134] New York also offered many entertainments to this mixed group of workingmen, including gaming houses and cockpits. Although many slaves lived with their wealthy masters along Queen and Dock streets on the East River waterfront, most other workers, including a majority of seamen, lived in

Footnote 133 (*cont.*):
more recent work, *Rumor of Revolt: The "Great Negro Plot" in Colonial New York* (New York, 1985).
[134] Hamilton, *Gentleman's Progress*, 88; Nash, *Urban Crucible*, 107; Thomas J. Archdeacon, *New York City, 1664–1710: Conquest and Change* (Ithaca, N.Y., 1976), 83–94.

the east ward north of Wall Street in crowded, multifamily dwellings.[135]

Philadelphia was the newest of America's major ports. It too had developed quickly in the early eighteenth century and by the 1740s had become "a great and flourishing place" with a population of 13,000. Organizing the shipment of goods to and from a marvelously productive hinterland, Philadelphia's merchants sent provisions – pork, beef, fowl, flour, bread, "all English grains" – to the West Indies and goods such as iron, timber, flax, and hemp to England and Europe. The city's most important export was wheat; lesser items included hams, apples, sheep, hoops, staves, and hogsheads. Philadelphia traders were probably foremost among those who excelled, according to Dr. Alexander Hamilton, "in the science of chicane" and who "will tell a lye with a sanctified, solemn face."[136] These Front Street nabobs traveled in fancy hackney coaches from their red brick mansions to mercantile centers such as London Coffee House on Water Street, near Carpenter's Wharf. They conducted lively trades with Lisbon, the Madeira Islands, France and its colonies, and, increasingly, Africa. They also organized the importation of both slaves and a massive number of indentured servants. On any given day, a shipload of relieved but ocean-weary laborers might have been on sale in a "cattle-market," where their muscles were squeezed and their docility carefully judged by prospective masters. Those not purchased were taken in gangs by "soul drivers" to be peddled in the back country.[137]

Another common sight to seamen in Philadelphia in the 1740s was the impressive array of newly fitted privateers, those "Warr Castles, and Flying Engines of Destruction" that would beckon their labors.[138] Shipwrights and carpenters turned out

---

[135] Bridenbaugh, *Cities in the Wilderness*, 305, 308.

[136] Hamilton, *Gentleman's Progress*, 183, 28; Bridenbaugh, *Cities in the Wilderness*, 303.

[137] Price, "Economic Function," 140, 149, 143, 145, 158, 152; Walton, "Trade Routes," 492, 485–8; Hamilton, *Gentleman's Progress*, 29, 244; Birket, *Cursory Remarks*, 64–5; *Journal of John Fontaine*, 118–19; Richard B. Morris, *Government and Labor in Early America* (New York, 1946), 368; Abbott E. Smith, *Colonists in Bondage: White Servitude and Convict Labor in America, 1607–1776* (New York, 1947), 221; Bridenbaugh, *Cities in the Wilderness*, 254, 354, 416, 430.

[138] "The Journal of William Black, 1744" *Pennsylvania Magazine of History and Biography* 1 (1877), 244, 247, 248 (quotation); Hamilton, *Gentleman's Progress*, 21, 25.

these private men-of-war at a pace never quite rapid enough to satisfy the merchants who ordered them. If a seaman wanted any sign of his potential success in this line of work he might have found it at a dockside auction of a privateer's prize and its goods. Merchants gathered around in a bidding frenzy; the judge of the vice-admiralty made sure that he and the king received their proper shares. In 1744 a seaman dreaming of a share of his own could have joined "a parcell of roaring sailors" who led a parade 4,000 strong, complete with flags, drums, and a "scraping negroe fiddle," to inaugurate Philadelphia's privateering effort and the war against France.[139]

Jack Tar probably considered Philadelphia a congenial place. The city, after all, had much to recommend it: a regular, well-ordered layout; a set of sumptuous markets, allowed by many to be "the best of its bigness in the known World, and undoubtedly the largest in America"; enormous fairs each May and November; the "best sort" of street lamps; and 2,000 houses, "the greatest part of them Brick and three Stories high."[140] The city also featured deep-water wharves for effortless docking and a wide river of entry, the Delaware, for easy maneuvering. (See Figure 11.) Philadelphia offered a number of coffee shops and taverns, but "publick gay diversions" were a little more scarce than sailors would have liked. Music and dancing, two of the seaman's most fancied pastimes, were not easily to be found, perhaps because Quaker merchants and city fathers preferred a sober and "strenuous" concern for business and an austere style of life. But by the 1740s Quaker influence had faded; now Philadelphia's polyglot population consisted of English, Scottish, Irish, Germans, and Africans, and among the city's welter of religious folk were Catholics, Presbyterians, Methodists, "Newlightmen," and Jews. Ten percent of the city's residents were of African descent. As non-Quaker elements proliferated, popular entertainments such as bull baiting and cockfighting grew in popularity. Groggeries like the "low Tip-

---

[139] "Journal of William Black," 247–8, 42, 44; Hamilton, *Gentleman's Progress*, 25, 42; Bridenbaugh, *Cities in the Wilderness*, 193, 348.

[140] "Journal of William Black," 405 (quotation), 18, 21, 192–3; Birket, *Cursory Remarks*, 676 (quotation), 63, 69, 67; *Whitefield's Journals*, 387; *Journal of John Fontaine*, 118–19; Prince, *Vade Mecum*, 194; Samuel Curwen, "Journal of a Journey from Salem to Philadelphia in 1755," *Essex Institute Historical Collections* 52 (1916), 79.

Figure 11. A view of Philadelphia across the Delaware River, c. 1735. The City of Brotherly Love was at this time North America's most prosperous port.

pling house" kept by laborer Richard Hillyard also began to increase in number. As the city grew more complex, so did its institutional base: almshouses, infirmaries, hospitals, a prison, the city jail, and workhouses. Jack had probably spent time in one or another of these.[141]

In all of the North American ports, just as in London, Bristol, Liverpool, Glasgow, and throughout the British West Indies, smuggling was an important economic activity. Indeed, smuggling remained central to the circulation of commodities and workers throughout the eighteenth century. The Anglo-American merchant-smuggler was a key figure in the rise of "free trade." Jean Baptiste Labat merely expressed popular wisdom when he noted that "the English know as much about the business of contraband as any people in the world."[142] Smuggling and long-distance trade rose together as the English state, beginning in the early sixteenth century, attempted to impose a systematic customs service. A leading expert on illicit trade argues that in the early modern period smugglers accounted "for at least one half of English overseas trade." The seventeenth century witnessed great advances in the organization and techniques of smuggling. Elaborate social networks developed, and ships with shallow draughts and hidden cavities were specially built. Many coastal communities depended entirely upon illicit trade for their livelihood.[143]

Smugglers moved almost every major commodity: tobacco, wool, tea, rum, brandy, wine, rice, molasses, slaves, logwood. If London, Bristol, Liverpool, Glasgow, Boston, New York, and Philadelphia were the key centers of the "customed" trade of the North Atlantic, then all of these, plus Cork, Newport, Port Royal, and the Isle of Man were the nodes of the uncustomed trades. These ports all teemed with illegal traders and goods. Between 1680 and 1780, the golden century of smuggling, countless men and women in England and America "regularly

[141] Hamilton, *Gentleman's Progress*, 405, 18, 20, 22 (quotation), 193 (quotation), 20; Birket, *Cursory Remarks*, 64, 66; Nash, *Urban Crucible*, 64, 109, 127, 140; Bridenbaugh, *Cities in the Wilderness*, 327, 384, 394, 395, 430 (quotation), 438, 268.

[142] Jean Baptiste Labat, *The Memoirs of Père Labat, 1693–1705* (London, 1931), 120. I would like to thank Robert K. Schaeffer for his insights into the relationship between smuggling and free trade.

[143] Williams, *Contraband Cargo*, 28.

drank smuggled tea, regularly smoked smuggled tobacco, and never tasted brandy or rum and never owned a silk handkerchief that had passed through customs." Smuggling had broad public support, and it provided berths for many a sailor.[144]

During the eighteenth century, the North Atlantic ports were, as Gary B. Nash has shown, the "crucibles" of a nascent capitalist social and economic order. Western cities and Western capitalism advanced hand in hand, and the Atlantic ports were crucial to the process of development. Cities, as Fernand Braudel has pointed out, "organized industry and the guilds; they invented long-distance trade, bills of exchange, the first forms of trading companies and accountancy. They also quickly became the scenes of class struggles."[145] Urban class relations featured the merchant in his silken finery alongside the sailor in his rough simplicity. The merchant's mansion sometimes stood beside the sailor's shanty. The city bred such contrasts, and indeed it throve on them. The replication of urban social relations around the rim of the Atlantic indicated systemic social and economic change and created the material foundation of Atlantic empires.

The merchants in these hubs of international trade moved commodities across geopolitical boundaries, supplying wholesale and retail merchants, who were the linchpins of regional and local economies.[146] The capitalization of their trading enterprises, judged by the standards of what was to come in the nineteenth and twentieth centuries, remained modest. Yet by earlier standards, the overseas trades of the eighteenth century required exceptional concentrations of capital, which were sometimes individual but more often the creation of small partnerships of two to ten merchants. The pooling of resources

[144] Ibid., 138–41, 93 (quotation). See also Alfred Rive, "A Short History of Tobacco Smuggling," *Economic History* 1 (1926–9), 558; G. D. Ramsey, "The Smugglers' Trade: A Neglected Aspect of English Commercial Development," *Royal Historical Society Transactions* ser. 5, 2 (1952), 131–57. It would be safe – and conservative – to estimate that the trade of the empire exceeded customs accounts by 15 to 20 percent. See Marcus Rediker, "Society and Culture among Anglo-American Deep Sea Sailors, 1700–1750," Ph.D. diss., University of Pennsylvania, 1982, 38–9.

[145] Nash, *Urban Crucible*, vii–viii; Fernand Braudel, *The Structures of Everyday Life: The Limits of the Possible*, trans. Sian Reynolds (New York, 1981), 512.

[146] Price, "Economic Function," 138–9, 173.

was not just a hedge against risk but often a necessity, since many of the transatlantic trades – especially in sugar, tobacco, rice, and slaves – were capital intensive. Between £2,000 and £10,000 were frequently required to finance one voyage.[147] Essential to the success of the international merchants were the maritime workers, who created much of the value of the merchants' commodities by transporting them from one market to another. Thus we return to Sir William Petty and Edward Barlow, and to their different perspectives on seafaring.

Mr. Petty: Throughout the eighteenth century, the trade network, itself a "machinery for capital formation," grew in size, complexity, and predictability.[148] Freight rates dropped steadily between 1675 and 1775, especially after 1713. Meanwhile, insurance rates, beginning in 1635, consistently fell up to 1850 and after.[149] Piracy was largely eliminated by 1726, and once this "inefficiency of production" had been removed, the productivity of maritime labor increased dramatically. Merchant vessels began to carry little or no cannon, and the gunner and his mates were removed from the ship's manifest. Piracy had been "an obstacle to technical diffusion" and hence to the accumulation of capital.[150] But with freebooters no longer a threat, crew sizes were reduced even further, since the disarming of the merchantmen permitted the introduction into transatlantic trades of Dutch-style ships that required fewer hands to carry more cargo. Turnaround time in port also diminished as the production and distribution of goods for shipment became better organized and more methodical. One-way voyages that carried ballast in one or

[147] Holderness, *Pre-Industrial England*, 132; Pares, "Economic Factors," 423; Wilson, *England's Apprenticeship*, 271; Coughtry, *Notorious Triangle*, 45; Rawley, *Transatlantic Slave Trade*, 183–4, 176; Jacob Price, *Capital and Credit in British Overseas Trade: The View from the Chesapeake, 1700–1776* (Cambridge, Mass., 1980), 3, 24–5, 38; Bailyn and Bailyn, *Massachusetts Shipping*, 35.

[148] Parry, *Trade and Dominion*, 283.

[149] Davis, *English Shipping*, 195, 376; James F. Shepherd and Gary M. Walton, *Shipping, Maritime Trade, and the Economic Development of Colonial North America* (Cambridge, 1972), 60.

[150] Parry, "Transport and Trade Routes," 212; Douglas C. North, "Sources of Productivity Change in Ocean Shipping, 1600–1850," *Journal of Political Economy* 76 (1968), 953–70; Gary M. Walton, "Sources of Productivity Change in American Colonial Shipping," *EHR* 2 (1967), 67–78; Steele, "Harmony and Competition," 27; Shepherd and Walton, *Shipping, Maritime Trade*, 81.

more passages were common in the seventeenth century but by 1750 had decreased significantly. Moreover, the vice-admiralty court system attempted to "rationalize" the labor supply by mediating conflicts between capital and labor.[151] In sum, the capital risks associated with deep-sea shipping diminished. Trade settled into more or less regular channels, became a less speculative business, and produced more predictable returns on investment. The international market chain became more orderly. British naval power protected and reinforced all of these gains. England's maritime hegemony, fully established by 1763, was the ultimate result.[152] It represented a great victory for political arithmetic.

A central part of the victory, in fact a necessary precondition, was, in Mr. Petty's words, the constitution of "the Labour of seamen" as a "commodity." As merchant capitalists sought to maximize profits, they came to realize that this goal was inextricably intertwined with that of creating, organizing, and disciplining their "labor force." They confronted demographic trends as well as political events that limited the availability of maritime labor. They also faced the resistance of the laborers themselves. Gradually the seaman's labor became a "thing," a commodity, to be calculated into an equation with other things: capital, land, markets, other commodities.

Edward Barlow: There is a seamy underside to Petty's dispassionate language of political arithmetic. The merchant's ideal of increased work and productivity usually meant increased exploitation of seamen. Creating, organizing, and disciplining the "labor force" frequently meant dispossession and the sting of the lash. Capital gained at the expense of lower wages. Reduced capital risks sometimes increased the material and physical risks of maritime laborers. The elimination of piracy entailed ruthless suppression of popular challenges to merchants' property. The Royal Navy made the seas safer for commerce, but only by violently subjecting the seaman to involuntary labor. The international market chain became more orderly, but at the price of an always precarious and often fatal situation for the seaman whose muscle closed the links of the chain. Barlow

[151] Davis, *English Shipping*, 185, 188.
[152] Ibid., 72, 376; Walton, "Trade Routes," 476; Parry, *Trade and Dominion*, 206, 213; North, "Productivity Change," 960; Fayle, *Short History*, 198.

saw "strange things in other countries," but not without nagging fears that English merchants were making them stranger, more grotesque. The victory for political arithmetic materialized in the "pride and oppression and tyranny" of the masters who commanded Barlow's vessels. Petty's heaven was all too often Barlow's hell.

All of these matters—work, wages, culture, authority, and piracy—will be treated at length in the chapters that follow. Special emphasis will be given to the ways in which the seaman resisted his lot as a commodity. For now it is important to note that the accumulation of capital through international trade required the creation of an international working class. In the early modern period the ship was "an extraordinary forcing house of internationalism."[153] Thus Mr. Barlow's history, like Mr. Petty's, is an international one. And it is quintessentially a collective one. The ways in which he and his brother tars responded to Mr. Petty are analyzed in the chapters ahead, as are the counterresponses of Petty and the merchant capitalists he aimed to help. For the continuing dialogues between Petty and Barlow, like the histories they each helped to make, are connected in precisely the same manner as are capital and wage labor.[154]

---

[153] Peter Linebaugh, "All the Atlantic Mountains Shook," *Labour/Le Travailleur* 10 (1982), 87–121.
[154] Karl Marx, "Wage Labor and Capital," in Marx and Frederick Engels, *Selected Works* (Moscow, 1969), vol. 1, 162.

2

THE SEAMAN AS COLLECTIVE WORKER

The Labor Process at Sea

Seamen were one of the largest and most important groups of free wage laborers in the international market economy of the eighteenth century. As Eric Hobsbawm has noted, "the creation of a large and expanding market for goods and a large and available free labor force go together, two aspects of the same process."[1] Hobsbawm calls attention to the relationship between the growth of commercial markets and the growth of a working class, and implicitly to the ways in which labor processes, markets, and experiences were transformed or created during the drive of early capitalist development.[2]

The seaman occupied a pivotal position in the creation of international markets and a waged working class, as well as in the worldwide concentration and organization of capital and labor. During the early modern period, merchant capitalists were organizing themselves, markets, and a working class in

---

[1] Eric Hobsbawm, "The General Crisis of the European Economy in the 17th Century," *P&P* 5 (1954), 40.

[2] Six studies have been especially useful in the conceptualization of this chapter: Ralph Davis, *The Rise of the English Shipping Industry in the Seventeenth and Eighteenth Centuries* (London, 1962); J. H. Parry, *Trade and Dominion: The European Overseas Empires in the Eighteenth Century* (New York, 1971); Christopher Lloyd, *The British Seaman, 1200–1860: A Social Survey* (Rutherford, N.J., 1970); Immanuel Wallerstein, *The Modern World-System II: Mercantilism and the Consolidation of the European World-Economy, 1600–1750* (New York, 1980). Special mention goes to Peter Linebaugh's "All the Atlantic Mountains Shook," *Labour/Le Travailleur* 10 (1982), 87–121, and to Jesse Lemisch's "Jack Tar in the Streets: Merchant Seamen in the Politics of Revolutionary America," *WMQ* 25 (1968), 371–407, the study that cleared the way for this and many other histories of working people in early America.

increasingly transatlantic and international ways.[3] As capital came to be concentrated in merchant shipping, masses of workers, numbering 25,000 to 40,000 at any one time between 1700 and 1750, were in turn concentrated in this vibrant branch of industry. The huge numbers of workers mobilized for shipboard labor were placed in relatively new relationships to capital – as free and fully waged laborers – and to each other: Seamen were, by their experiences in the maritime labor market and labor process, among the first collective laborers. In historical terms, the new collective worker did not possess traditional craft skills, did not own any means of production such as land or tools (and therefore depended completely upon a wage), and labored among a large number of like-situated people. The collective worker, exemplified by the seaman, was the proletarian of the period of "manufacture," and would, of course, become a dominant formal type of laborer with the advent of industrial capitalism.

Maritime workers in the early modern period, by linking the producers and consumers of the world through their labors in international markets, were thus central to the accumulation of riches on a scale previously unimagined. At the same time, they were crucial to the emergence of new relations between capital and labor. In this chapter we shall study the organization of maritime labor and some of the challenges to it. After some opening remarks on the maritime labor market, we shall investigate the labor process at sea between 1700 and 1750, examining the ship as a work environment with its own complex division and organization of labor and technology. We shall then turn to the struggles over the labor process, working conditions, and the control of the workplace, the ways in which seamen resisted the capitalist organization of production or deflected it toward other purposes of their own. The chapter concludes with observations on the relationships among mari-

---

[3] C. L. R. James, Grace C. Lee, and Pierre Chaulieu, *Facing Reality* (Detroit, 1974): "Marx discerned in capital accumulation two laws, twin themes of the same movement, the law of the concentration and centralization of capital and the law of the socialization of labor" (103). Further, "The more capital succeeds in organizing itself, the more it is forced to organize the working class" (115).

time work, the rise of North Atlantic capitalism, and the nature of social relations among sailors.[4]

The maritime labor market took shape amid the buzz and hustle of the seaports that handled the commerce of the North Atlantic. The labor market was international in character, and this was a fact of first importance, as shown in the work lives of John Young and Edward Coxere. Young, apparently seized by British authorities from a French privateer during the War of the Spanish Succession and quickly charged with treason, tried to explain to the High Court of Admiralty how the vicissitudes of an international work experience had gotten him into his present predicament. He proceeded to outline where his worldwide labors had taken him. Born in Spitalfields, he went to sea at "14 or 15 years of Age," apprenticed to a Captain John Hunter. During the next twelve years he traveled from London to Barbados and Jamaica, sailed and fought aboard three West Indian privateers, went "sugar-droghing" in the Caribbean coastal trade, found his way in a merchant ship back to London, and then, in various voyages, on to Bristol, the African coast, Virginia, Lisbon, Genoa, Leghorn, and Cartagena.[5] Ned Coxere, a late-seventeenth-century merchant seaman and privateersman, summed up his maritime experience this way: "I served the Spaniards against the French, then the Hollanders against the English; then I was taken by the English out of a Dunkirker; and then I served the English against the Hollanders; and last I was taken by the Turks, where I was forced to serve then against the English, French, Dutch, and Spaniards, and all Christendom." Not surprisingly, this able sailor spoke English, Spanish, French, Dutch, and the Mediterranean lingua franca.[6] Coxere was truly an international workingman, finally refusing to participate in the nationalistic

---

[4] The labor process is here defined as the process by which raw materials, other inputs, and labor are transformed into products and services having value. For a sample of the growing literature on the labor process, see footnote 39 of this chapter.

[5] Examination of John Young, HCA 1/54 (1710), ff. 1–2.

[6] *Adventures by Sea of Edward Coxere*, ed. E. H. W. Meyerstein (New York, 1946), 37, 130–4.

violence of "The Era of Trade Wars" and becoming instead a pacifist and a Quaker.

Both Young and Coxere worked among men who, it must have seemed, came from almost everywhere: from every corner of England, America, the Caribbean; from Holland, France, Spain, all of Europe; from Africa and even parts of Asia. Regional, national, and ethnic identities abounded in the ships of the world, even though the Navigation Acts had required that three out of four seamen on English ships be subjects of the crown. Such requirements were rarely enforced, especially in times of war and labor scarcity, when even the British state admitted that half or more of ships' crews could be "foreign."[7]

The global deployment of thousands of seamen in the early eighteenth century was predicated upon the broad and uneven process of proletarianization, through which these men or their forebears were forcibly torn from the land and made to sell their labor power on an open market to keep body and soul together. The major sources for stocking the labor market with "hands" were dispossession – the displacement or eviction of rural producers, most notably by the enclosure of arable farmland – and population growth, which forced the offspring of agrarian laborers or wage workers themselves to sell their mind and muscle for money. England was of course known for its teeming share of these "masterless men and women" in the early modern period. Population growth and dispossession, each with its own oscillating rhythm, combined to swell the number of those who in some way worked for a wage to some 60 percent of Britain's people by the beginning of the eighteenth century. Between 1700 and 1750 the process of proletarianization seems to have stabilized. Population growth reached a certain plateau, showing perhaps a small upturn in the 1740s.[8] The number of colonists in North America grew

---

[7] Davis, *English Shipping*, 327; Ruth Bourne, *Queen Anne's Navy in the West Indies* (New Haven, Conn., 1939), 220.

[8] Wallerstein, *Modern World-System II*, 16, 258; B. A. Holderness, *Pre-Industrial England: Economy and Society* (London, 1976), 11, 24; D. C. Coleman, *The Economy of England, 1450–1750* (London, 1977), 12; Richard S. Dunn, "Servants and Slaves: The Recruitment and Employment of Labor," in Jack P. Greene and J. R. Pole, eds., *British Colonial America: Essays in the New History of the Early Modern Era* (Baltimore, 1984), 158–64; Peter Clark, "Migration

both naturally and by immigration throughout the period, whereas the population of the British West Indies increased only through the massive importation of Africans.[9] There was, with a few exceptions, a general shortage of maritime labor in both areas between 1700 and 1750. But the dominant, over-arching tendency, particularly in Britain and America, was toward ever greater employment of wage labor. Seamen were fitting symbols of the trend.

A labor market is defined as "those institutions which mediate, affect, or determine the purchase and sale of labor power," and here our understanding of maritime labor is deficient, for the actual practices of labor market entrepreneurs in the eighteenth century have not been carefully studied.[10] It is clear that crimps – "agents who traded in recruits when men were in great demand either for the armed forces or to man merchant vessels on the point of sailing" – were crucial to the maritime labor market, certainly in England if not in the New World until the late eighteenth century.[11] An equally important if shadowy figure was the "spirit," described by Edward Barlow as "one of those who used to entice any who they think are country people or strangers and do not know their fashion and custom, or any who they think are out of place and cannot get work, and are walking idly about the streets." Spirits promised great wages and often gave advances in money. Those who

in England during the Late Seventeenth and Early Eighteenth Centuries," *P&P* 83 (1979), 70; Charles Tilly, "Demographic Origins of the European Proletariat," paper presented to the conference on "Proletarianization: Past and Present," Rutgers University, 1983, 40; Robert W. Malcolmson, *Life and Labour in England, 1700–1780* (New York, 1981), chap. 2; John Rule, *The Experience of Labour in Eighteenth-Century English Industry* (New York, 1981), chap. 1.

9 Robert V. Wells, *The Population of the British Colonies in America before 1776* (Princeton, N.J., 1975), 259–96.

10 Richard C. Edwards, Michael Reich, and David M. Gordon, eds., *Labor Market Segmentation* (Lexington, Mass., 1975), xi. Daniel F. Vickers has done fine work on the labor markets in fishing and whaling in "Maritime Labor in Colonial Massachusetts: A Case Study of the Essex County Cod Fishery and the Whaling Industry of Nantucket, 1630–1775," Ph.D. diss., Princeton University, 1981.

11 J. Stevenson, "The London 'Crimp' Riots of 1794," *International Review of Social History* 16 (1971), 41–2. For a good analysis of crimping in the nineteenth century, see Judith Fingard, *Jack in Port: Sailortowns of Eastern Canada* (Toronto, 1982), chaps. 1 and 5.

accepted their offers often found themselves apprenticed as sailors or sold as indentured servants bound to America.[12] Such "recruiters" operated from gin shops, alehouses, inns, and taverns, where they often seized indebted sailors and paid off their bills. In exchange, crimps and spirits gained the right to sell the seaman's services to outward-bound vessels, usually sailing to distant parts of the globe, and to receive the sailor's advance pay. Some crimps did not adhere even to these standards of conduct, preferring instead to raid the pubs, handcuff, drag off, and incarcerate drunk sailors, then to sell them to merchant captains in search of labor.[13] Most of the contracting of maritime labor was probably handled in less formal and exploitive ways, especially in the New World, where labor was scarce and wages higher, through the pubs, inns, or taverns where merchants, ship captains, mates, and seamen gathered and through which information on shipping circulated. Seamen also peddled their own skills in the port cities by going from vessel to vessel, jumping aboard, and asking the ship's route, pay, and fare. Those men who did not possess adequate skills were hired by a master as a ship's boy or as an apprentice to some member of the crew.

Maritime labor in all English Atlantic ports was seasonal and often casual. The rhythms of climate dictated employment opportunities by icing harbors, by fixing the growing seasons of commodities such as sugar and tobacco, or by making parts of the world dangerous with disease or hurricane. Seafaring jobs were most easily found in late spring, summer, and fall, though the demand for labor in each port varied according to the commodities shipped, their destinations, and the length of the shipping season.[14] Many mariners were unable to find year-round employment.[15] Numerous landed occupations, however, were equally seasonal, and for some people, "sailoring was normally a casual employment, into and out of which they drifted as they found employment harder to come by on sea or on

---

[12] *Barlow's Journal,* 27.

[13] Stevenson, "Crimp Riots," 42; Davis, *English Shipping,* 153.

[14] Fingard, *Jack in Port,* is very sensitive to the differences in regional maritime labor markets.

[15] Gary B. Nash, *The Urban Crucible: Social Change, Political Consciousness, and the Origins of the American Revolution* (Cambridge, Mass., 1979), 12; T. S. Ashton, *Economic Fluctuations in England, 1700–1800* (London, 1959), 4.

land."[16] Such opportunities were always greater and more lucrative during war years. Employments connected to shipping "were notorious then, as later, as precarious occupations."[17] Yet throughout the eighteenth century it was increasingly the case for Jack Tar that "once a sailor, the chances were that he would always be a sailor."[18] By 1750 seafaring had become a lifelong occupation for increasing numbers of waged workers.

Seafaring labor consisted mainly of loading, sailing, and unloading the merchant vessel. The essence of the labor process was, quite simply, the movement of cargo. The ship, prefiguring the factory, demanded a cooperative labor process. Waged workers, the preponderant majority of whom did not own the instruments of their production, were confined within an enclosed setting to perform, with sophisticated machinery and under intense supervision, a unified and collective set of tasks. Large parts of this labor were performed at sea in isolation from the rest of the population. The character of seafaring work and its lonely setting contributed to the formation of a strong laboring identity among seamen.[19]

By 1700 seafaring labor had been fully standardized. Sailors circulated from ship to ship, even from merchant vessels to the Royal Navy, into privateering or piracy and back again, and found that the tasks performed and the skills required by each were essentially the same.[20] They anticipated a basic division of labor on each merchant ship, consisting of a master, a mate, a carpenter, a boatswain, a gunner, a quartermaster, perhaps a cook, and four or five able or ordinary seamen. A larger or more heavily manned ship included a second mate, a carpenter's mate, and four or five more common tars.[21] This divi-

---

[16] Davis, *English Shipping*, 116; Malcolmson, *Life and Labour*, 54; Rule, *Experience of Labour*, 49–73.

[17] Charles Henry Wilson, *England's Apprenticeship, 1603–1763* (London, 1965), 344.

[18] Peter Kemp, *The British Sailor: A Social History of the Lower Deck* (London, 1970), 92; Lloyd, *British Seaman*, 86.

[19] Peter Linebaugh, "The Picaresque Proletarian in Eighteenth-Century London," paper presented to the conference on "Proletarianization: Past and Present," Rutgers University, 1983, 27; Vilhelm Aubert, "A Total Institution: The Ship," in his *The Hidden Society* (Totowa, N.J., 1965), 240, 245, 256, 258.

[20] Lloyd, *British Seaman*, 12, 53.

[21] Davis, *English Shipping*, 110–13, 119–20; William Falconer, *An Universal Dictionary of the Marine* (1769; reprint New York, 1970). Colonial vessels were, on the whole, smaller than those owned and operated out of Great Britain.

sion of labor allocated responsibilities and structured working relations among the crew, forming a hierarchy of laboring roles and a corresponding scale of wages.

The organization of labor on each ship began with the master, the representative of merchant capital, who was hired "to manage the navigation and everything relating to [the ship's] cargo, voyage, sailors, &c."[22] Frequently a small part owner himself, the master was the commanding officer. He possessed near-absolute authority. His ship was "virtually a kingdom on its own," his power "well nigh unlimited," and all too frequently, to the muttering of his sailors, he ruled it like a despot.[23] His primary tasks were navigation, tending the compasses, steering the vessel, and transacting the business throughout the voyage. He procured the ship's provisions and usually inflicted the punishments. Except on the largest ships, he ran one of the two watches.[24]

The mate, whose powers were vastly inferior to those of the master, was second in the chain of command. He commanded a watch and oversaw the daily functioning of the ship. He was charged with the internal management of the vessel, setting the men to work, governing the crew, securing the cargo, and directing the ship's course. The mate needed a sure knowledge of navigation, since he was to take charge of the vessel in the event of the master's death, no uncommon occurrence at any time during the age of sail.[25]

The carpenter, an important specialist in a wooden world, was responsible for the soundness of the ship. He repaired masts, yards, boats, machinery; he checked the hull regularly, placing oakum between the seams of planks, and used wooden plugs on leaks to keep the vessel tight. His search for a leak often required that he wade through stagnant bilge water with vapors strong enough "to poison the Devil."[26] His was highly skilled work which he had learned through apprenticeship. Often he had a mate whom he in turn trained.[27]

---

[22] Falconer, *Universal Dictionary*, 191.
[23] Lloyd, *British Seaman*, 230; Davis, *English Shipping*, 127, 131; Barnaby Slush, *The Navy Royal: Or a Sea-Cook Turn'd Projector* (London, 1709), 9.
[24] Davis, *English Shipping*, 123.
[25] Ibid., 126; *Barlow's Journal*, 327; Falconer, *Universal Dictionary*, 192.
[26] Jeremy Roch, "The Fourth Journal," in *Three Sea Journals of Stuart Times*, ed. Bruce C. Ingram (London, 1936), 115; Falconer, *Universal Dictionary*, 78.
[27] Davis, *English Shipping*, 119.

The boatswain, like the mate, functioned as something of a foreman. He summoned the crew to duty, sometimes by piping the call to work that brought the inevitable groans and curses from the off-duty crew. His specific responsibilities centered on the upkeep of the rigging. He had to be sure that all lines and cables were sound and that sails and anchors were in good condition.[28]

The gunner, sometimes with the help of a boy or "powder monkey," tended the artillery and ammunition. He was crucial to an era in which trade itself was regarded by many as a form of warfare, but between 1700 and 1750 his position declined as the convoy system lessened the need for ordnance, and as the removal of cannon and a crewman added to speed while subtracting from the merchant's operating expenses. The gunner needed experience to avert or handle the potential disaster of a cannon bursting, overheating, or recoiling out of control. A knowledgeable gunner was essential to the crew's safety if a ship had any pretense to self-defense.[29]

The quartermaster did not require special training. Rather, he was an experienced or "smart" seaman who was given an additional shilling or two per month to assist the mates. He provided an extra hand in storage, coiling cables, and steering the vessel.[30] The cook, on the other hand, was truly "remarkable for his inability to cook."[31] Often a wounded seaman no longer able to perform heavy labor, his status was rather low. According to the doleful and never-ending complaint of the ship's people, he brought no distinctive talents to his job.

The common seaman, Jack Tar himself, was a "person trained in the exercise of fixing the machinery of a ship, and applying it to the purposes of navigation."[32] He needed to know the rigging and the sails, as well as how to steer the ship, to knot and splice the lines, and to read the winds, weather, skies, and mood of his commander. There were two categories of seamen: the able seaman, who fully knew his trade, and the ordinary seaman, usually a younger and less experienced man. The latter was still learning the mysteries of tying a clove-hitch

---

[28] Ibid., 112; Falconer, *Universal Dictionary,* 41, 100.
[29] Falconer, *Universal Dictionary,* 227.
[30] Ibid., 226; Davis, *English Shipping,* 113.
[31] Kemp, *British Sailor,* 72.
[32] Falconer, *Universal Dictionary,* 259.

or going aloft to reef in a sail in a blustery thunderstorm.[33] In sum, a merchant ship, like a man-of-war, required a wide variety of skills. It was "too big and unmanageable a machine" to be run by novices.[34] Some orbits of trade dictated the need for other crew members. Larger ships, particularly those in the slave trade, carried a surgeon, whose difficult job it was to keep the crew and slaves alive from one side of the Atlantic to the other. Larger ships occasionally procured the services of a caulker in addition to the carpenter. And in the tobacco and sugar trades, a cooper often signed on to assist in packing the product in casks and hogsheads. Coastal pilots were hired when the ship had to be maneuvered through particularly deceptive, uncharted, or unknown waters.[35]

There were, of course, many variations on this standard division of labor, depending upon the related factors of trade route, cargo carried, and ship size. The northern European trade, transporting largely corn, coal, salt, or wine, featured small ships that made quick and predictable voyages. Trade with the Mediterranean, the North American colonies, or the West Indies, carrying food, sugar, and tobacco, used ships of greater size. Some eleven to fourteen men worked a 150- to 200-ton vessel on voyages that lasted for six to nine months. Ships in the African trade were most heavily manned, for security against slave uprisings and as a safeguard against raging mortality, and often bore twenty to twenty-five men on a 200-ton vessel. Slaving voyages took ten to eleven months. Ships of the East India Company were, by eighteenth-century standards, mammoth, often as large as a man-of-war at 300 to 500 tons, and manned to survive a voyage of two years or more. Although ship size varied with the type of trade, the larger the ship's home port, the larger the ship and its crew were likely to be.[36]

It is difficult to determine whether seamen specialized in particular routes, trades, or types of ships. Ned Coxere, for one,

---

[33] Davis, *English Shipping*, 113; Mallis v. Wade, HCA 24/138 (1736).

[34] Slush, *Navy Royal*, 3.

[35] Falconer, *Universal Dictionary*, 60; Davis, *English Shipping*, 112, 120.

[36] Davis, *English Shipping*, 204–93; Jonathan Press, *The Merchant Seaman of Bristol, 1747–1789* (Bristol, 1976), 9; Ian K. Steele, "Harmony and Competition: Aspects of English and Colonial Shipping in the Barbados Trade at the End of the Seventeenth Century," unpublished manuscript, 1980, 23.

seems to have preferred to sail the Mediterranean. Masters and mates, since they had to develop contacts and learn regionally specific business methods, tended to find employment in trade routes where they had already accumulated some experience.[37] As trade orbits matured and the motions of the market chain became more orderly throughout the eighteenth century, such specialization increased. Yet many masters, like their men, had varied careers. Nathaniel Uring, taking to sea in 1698, managed over the next twenty-three years to find his way to Virginia, the Baltic, Africa, Cádiz, the West Indies, New England, Ireland, Cartagena, Campeche, Tunis, Lisbon, and Florence.[38]

The tendency of masters and mates to specialize in certain voyages indicates another crucial part of the maritime division of labor: the distribution of knowledge on board the ship. Masters and mates, as suggested earlier, had to know the principles of navigation, whereas the rest of the crew did not. Yet this separation of mental and manual labor was never complete, indeed never could become as complete as it would in later industrial production.[39] The knowledge of seafaring was still contained largely within a broad system of apprenticeship, but one in which the perils of life at sea placed grave limits upon the advisability of keeping trade secrets. Only later, with the introduction of officers' schools and a growing social distance between the lower deck and the quarter deck, would a consistent separation of conception from execution be effected. Much could be and was learned about navigation through observation of the daily work routine. Consequently older and experienced seamen, whatever their formal position, mini-

---

[37] Davis, *English Shipping*, 129, 159–70.

[38] *The Voyages and Travels of Captain Nathaniel Uring*, ed. Alfred Dewar (1726; reprint London, 1928).

[39] Davis, *English Shipping*, 122–3, 113. My thinking on this subject owes much to the recent works on the labor process, and especially to *The Labour Process and Class Strategies* (London, 1976), a volume produced by the Conference of Socialist Economists. See also Harry Braverman, *Labor and Monopoly Capital: The Degradation of Work in the Twentieth Century* (New York, 1974); Michael Burawoy, "Towards a Marxist Theory of the Labor Process: Braverman and Beyond," *Politics and Society* 8 (1978), 247–312 and *The Politics of Production: Factory Regimes Under Capitalism and Socialism* (London, 1985); Andrew Zimbalest, ed., *Case Studies on the Labor Process* (New York, 1979); and Les Levidow and Bob Young, eds., *Science, Technology and the Labour Process: Marxist Studies* (London, 1981).

mized the differential in knowledge that separated the top of the ship's labor hierarchy from its bottom.

The watch, another decisive element in the social arrangement of each ship, was perhaps the most basic unit for organizing the steady work of sailing the ship. Half of the crew was assigned to the starboard and half to the larboard watch. The captain supervised one, the mate the other. On the largest ships, the first and second mates took responsibility for a watch. Each watch served four hours on duty, then four hours off, alternating in work shifts (also called "watches") around the clock. The dog watch, between 4 and 8 P.M., was subdivided into two-hour shifts. This produced a total of seven shifts, ensuring that a watch would not work the same hours each day. Each sailor alternately worked a ten- and a fourteen-hour day. The starboard and larboard watches were the essential cycle groups on each ship. Their major responsibility was to guarantee the continuity of keeping the vessel running and true. Everyone made a roughly equivalent contribution by helping to keep the ship on course at the highest possible speed.[40]

Even when off duty, Jack Tar was never far from work. Anytime, anywhere, he might hear the mate's fearful cry: "up every soul nimbly, for God's sake, or we all perish."[41] Or in Edward Barlow's dramatic and evocative words: "at night when we went to take our rest, we were not to lie still above four hours; and many times when it blew hard were not sure to lie one hour, yea often were called up before we had slept half an hour and forced to go up into the maintop or foretop to take in our topsails, half awake and half asleep, with one shoe on and the other off, not having time to put it on: always sleeping in our clothes for readiness, and in stormy weather, when the ship rolled and tumbled as though some great millstone were rolling up one hill and down another, we had much ado to hold ourselves fast, by the small ropes from falling by the board; and being gotten up into the tops, there we must haul and pull to make fast the sail, seeing nothing but air above us and water beneath us: and many times in nights so dark that we could not see one another, and blowing so hard that we could not hear

[40] R. J. Cornewall-Jones, *The British Merchant Service* (London, 1898), 296; Falconer, *Universal Dictionary*, 312.

[41] "The Journal of Francis Rogers," in Ingram, ed., *Three Sea Journals*, 144.

one another speak, being close to one another; and thundering and lightning as though heaven and earth would come together."[42] Situations of crisis mobilized both watches in urgent cooperation.

The ship's technical division of labor, while demanding cooperation and interdependence, was also highly graded and specialized relative to the total number employed.[43] A crew of twelve was usually divided into five or six different ranks and an equal or greater number of pay stations. Rarely did more than four or five occupy equal positions in the laboring hierarchy. Rank, knowledge, watch, and pay were objective lines of demarcation and division within the ship's crew. The organization of work in the merchant service assembled a complex and collective unit of labor, only to separate that unit into shifting, overlapping, task-oriented components.

Despite the many specialized positions on each ship, there existed a general set of chores that everyone knew and performed. These duties constituted the core of the labor process in the merchant shipping industry. They logically centered on the industry's essential economic role – the movement of commodities – and the imperative to move them quickly. The labor process contained two fundamental kinds of work: handling the cargo and handling the ship.

The first stage of most voyages consisted of loading the ship. Here seamen, dock workers, and other laborers collectively handled and hoisted the casks, bales, hogsheads, and cases, the ballast, provisions, and stores into the vessel's hold. In addition to the human strength involved in lifting, several mechanical devices were used to load the ship. Seamen used a wide array of tackle, an arrangement of ropes, pulleys, slings, and hooks, to lift and lower cargo into the ship, but also to support the masts, extend the rigging, or expand the sails. The parbuckle, a less elaborate system of leverage, was used when no tackle was available.[44] The heaviest tasks required the use of the capstan or its smaller and, in the merchant service, more popular coun-

---

[42] *Barlow's Journal*, 60.
[43] Vilhelm Aubert, "On the Social Structure of the Ship," in *The Hidden Society*, 260.
[44] Falconer, *Universal Dictionary*, 155–6; David Steel, *The Elements and Practice of Seamanship* (London, 1794), 176–7.

terpart, the windlass. These machines consisted of a "strong massy column of holes" into which seamen inserted bars or levers called "handspikes."[45] This machine worked on the same principle as a horse mill. Seamen turned in a circular movement, and it required "some dexterity and address to manage the handspec [sic] to the greatest advantage; and to perform this the sailors must all rise at once upon the windlass, and, fixing their bars therein, give a sudden jerk at the same instant, in which movement they are regulated by a sort of song or howl pronounced by one of their number."[46] By the use of the capstan or windlass and their systems of ropes and pulleys, heavy items such as masts, artillery, or bulky cargo were elevated and placed aboard, and anchor was weighed. In heaving or hoisting, it was necessary that the men work to the chant of "Together!" acting "all in concert, or at the same instant."[47] Seafaring labor, in its work chants and songs, revealed its profoundly collective nature.

Next, the cargo had to be maneuvered carefully into the hold, the belly of the ship, and stored properly. The arrangement of the cargo was important, and stowage had to take account of the weight, form, and type of commodity, as well as the overall balance of the ship. The heaviest goods had to be placed nearest the keel on the very bottom and at the center of gravity of the ship. Other items were stowed according to their packaging. Bales, boxes, and cases were stacked; hogsheads and casks were wedged into place with chocks. All goods had to be secured to prevent shifting in rolling seas. Ballast was often added, since a proper amount of tonnage had to be on board so that the ship would sit properly, neither too crank (light) nor too stiff (heavy) in the water.[48] The leakiness of any given ship also determined how goods were to be stowed. Some cargo had to be put away "bilge free" to avoid water damage. Each ship was equipped with a pump for the safety of the cargo and the crew. Depending on the size of the ship and the pump, a gang of two to seven men pulled large levers that activated a suction

[45] Steel, *Elements and Practice*, 54; Falconer, *Universal Dictionary*, 61, 210–11, 270, 288.
[46] Falconer, *Universal Dictionary*, 75, 76, 144, 324.
[47] Ibid., 293.
[48] Ibid., 281–2, 262, 81, 28–9; Steel, *Elements and Practice*, 7, 82–151.

cup or a chain and valves, pushing water out of the hold through a channel.[49] A tight ship demanded little pumping, and sailors adored the skillful carpenter who could keep this dreaded, back-breaking work to a minimum. But frequently, a ship decaying with age or damaged by a tempest required its crew to spend long spells at the pump. This "very bad work for the ship's company" usually resulted in deadening fatigue.[50] Lifting, hoisting, heaving, stowing, and pumping were operations in the labor process supervised by the captain and the mate.

Once the cargo had been loaded and secured, the emphasis of work shifted from handling the goods to handling the ship. Three basic chores now confronted the crew: steering the ship, managing the rigging, and working the sails, the skillful performance of which determined the speed and ultimately the profitability of the voyage. Steering the ship, along with the associated duties of keeping lookout and sounding, was a central part of the work effort. The helmsman directed the ship's course with the use of the compass, the sun, the moon, and the stars, according to the officer of the watch. Each sailor took a turn at the helm. The lookout acted as an additional pair of eyes for the helmsman. Soundings were taken in shallow water to determine the surrounding depths and, with the aid of charts, the vessel's location.[51]

The rate of the ship's progress depended directly on the labors performed on the riggings and the sails. There were two kinds of rigging. The standard rigging—shrouds, stays, forestays, and backstays—was the collection of ropes that supported the masts; the running rigging—braces, sheets, halyards, cluelines, and brails—was used "to extend and reduce the sails, or arrange them to the disposition of the wind."[52] A series of lines running through blocks, or pulleys, were used to manage the sails, and although much of this work was done from the deck, frequently a sailor had to climb aloft "hand-over-hand," carefully using the "horses," or rigging made expressly for sailors

[49] Falconer, *Universal Dictionary*, 282, 221–3.
[50] *Ramblin' Jack: The Journal of Captain John Cremer*, ed. R. Reynall Bellamy (London, 1936), 115.
[51] Falconer, *Universal Dictionary*, 277–8, 80, 104, 271–2, 184.
[52] Ibid., 244, 27, 42, 56, 143, 267.

to stand upon or hold, to adjust a sail or a rope.[53] Rigging work also demanded a superior knowledge of tying and connecting ropes, whether by hitches or knots, using lanyards or lashings, or splicing one piece of hemp to another. The tar's strong, nimble fingers deftly arranged a catspaw, a Flemish Eye, a sheep-shank, a timber-hitch, or a diamond-knot.[54]

Most deep-sea ships were either two- or three-masted vessels with a complex arrangement of sails, consisting of the course-sails, topsails, and gallantsails, as well as the smaller staysails, studdingsails, and jibs, among many others. Sailors positioned the sails to accelerate or modify the ship's course by backing, balancing, reefing, shortening, furling, or loosing the enormous pieces of canvas. The tars clambered from the deck to the tops, as high as sixty to seventy-five feet on most merchant-men, expanding this sail or reducing that one, according to the direction and strength of the winds.[55] Like the loading of cargo, work on the helm, the rigging, and the sails required careful coordination.

Once the ship was in port, attention turned back to the cargo. Breaking bulk, or discharging the first part of the cargo, began with the same equipment and labor used in loading. Cargo was lifted, hoisted, or heaved from the hold and transferred with the help of other workers into smaller craft such as hoys, barges, prams, and boats.[56] In the smaller ports, seamen were required to row the cargo ashore. Even here the work remained collective, as Robert Hansell discovered in 1726. He was given a severe beating by his captain, Joseph Wilkinson, because he was "not rowing regularly with the rest of the Boat's Crew as he ought to have done."[57]

The maritime labor process was extraordinarily dangerous. Records do not exist to allow computations of death rates for maritime industries and comparison of these to rates for other occupations. Yet in the judgment of the late Ralph Davis, one of the finest historians of maritime affairs, "the chances of a seaman ending his life in . . . a catastrophe were high, and

[53] Ibid., 143, 37; Steel, *Elements and Practice*, 167, 149–60.
[54] Steel, *Elements and Practice*, 181–5; Falconer, *Universal Dictionary*, 155, 168, 171, 172, 273.
[55] Falconer, *Universal Dictionary*, 27, 28, 135, 157, 184, 186, 239, 252, 286, 293–4, 298; Steel, *Elements and Practice*, 7, 82–151.
[56] Falconer, *Universal Dictionary*, 48, 155, 184, 89.
[57] Hansel v. Wilkinson, HCA 24/136 (1728).

many a man fell from the rigging, was washed overboard, or was fatally struck by falling gear."[58] Indeed, a crucial part of the seaman's socialization consisted of learning to endure physical trial and minimal provisions. As Edward Barlow explained in 1696, those men who "were not used to hardship and had not known the lack of drink" were the first to collapse and die in hard times.[59] Quite apart from the dangers of scurvy, rheumatism, typhus, yellow fever, ulcers, and skin diseases, seamen had to contend with an extensive range of disabilities and afflictions that flowed from their work. Frequently lifting or pulling, seamen were peculiarly susceptible to hernia or the "bursted belly," as they preferred to call it.[60] It was not unusual for a finger to be lost to a rolling cask, for an arm or leg to be broken by shifting cargo, or for a hand to be burned in tarring ropes.[61] Countless men drowned and "took their habitation among the haddocks."[62]

One of the most hazardous aspects of the labor process was the dispensation of discipline, the necessary and bloody complement of the increasing productivity of seafaring labor in the eighteenth century. This "class discipline at its most personal and sadistic," as Peter Linebaugh has put it, resulted in many disabling injuries inflicted by masters and mates upon the common men of the deep. Having been beaten nearly senseless with a pitch mop, John Laws cried to George Burrell, "captain, you have ruined me. I shall never be my own Man again."[63] Such beatings often produced what seamen called the "Falling Sickness": John Marchant, caned in 1735 by mate John Yates, was, as he told the High Court of Admiralty, "troubled with a diziness in his Head . . . in so much that he cannot go aloft without danger of falling down."[64] Others considered themselves "incapable of going to sea," since they were, in their own tragic words, "dam-

---

[58] Davis, *English Shipping*, 156. Knut Weibust, in *Deep Sea Sailors: A Study in Maritime Ethnology* (Stockholm, 1976), 435, notes the solidarity occasioned by the dangerous work environment at sea.

[59] *Barlow's Journal*, 462.

[60] Lloyd, *British Seaman*, 262.

[61] Journal of Surgeon Browne, Sloane Manuscript 1689, BL, f. 23; *Ramblin' Jack*, 73.

[62] Jeremy Roch, "The Third Journal," in Ingram, ed., *Three Sea Journals*, 104.

[63] Laws v. Burrell, HCA 24/138 (1735); Linebaugh, "Picaresque Proletarian," 27.

[64] Marchant v. Yates and Hance v. Jeffrey, HCA 24/139 (1736); Macquam v. Anstell, HCA 15/43 (1744); Clancy v. Bennet, SC ADM (1737), f. 164.

nify'd" like a piece of cargo.[65] Seamen also suffered injury in battle against men-of-war, privateers, pirates, or coastal raiders. Upon discovering in 1713 that their captain had changed the voyage to a more dangerous destination, William Howell penned a protest for his shipmates, saying "that they did not hire themselves to fight" and properly wondering "in case they should lose a Legg or an Arme who would maintaine them and their Familys"?[66] It was a good question, for lucky was the seaman who, after fifteen years of service, could say, "I had my health and was able to seek for more employment."[67]

The deep-sea sailor labored on a frail vessel surrounded by omnipotent forces of nature, and this situation imparted a special urgency to cooperative labor. Upon hitting a rock or being overtaken by a turbulent squall, many crews realized that they had to turn out, all hands high, to "work for our Lives." Ned Coxere and his mates once found themselves surrounded by mountainous waves that soon tossed their vessel on its side, made them think of "their poor wives and children," and made them look "on one another with sorrowful hearts." After the desperate measure of cutting away the mainmast, the seamen took frantically to the pump to save themselves. Eager to know their fate, Coxere took a piece of chalk and marked the dangerously high waterline in the hold. After a strenuous turn at the pump, he returned "to see whether the score of the chalk were above the water." If they had "gained with pumping," their verdict would be "life"; if the mark was underwater, their fate was to be "death." The water had in fact receded by "about an inch," and Coxere and his comrades lived to tell the tale.[68] Their life-and-death example reveals the massive confrontation between the seaman and his work. The labor was physical. It required extraordinary strength, stamina, dexterity, and agility. The labor was dangerous. It required courage and a constant renewal of initiative and daring.

---

[65] Phillips v. Haskins, HCA 24/133 (1722); Macknash v. Wood, HCA 24/134 (1724); Hamilton v. Harris, HCA 24/135 (1728).

[66] Howell v. Rawlins, HCA 24/130 (1714); *Voyages and Travels of Captain Nathaniel Uring*, 66.

[67] *Barlow's Journal*, 262.

[68] William Dampier, "Mr. Dampier's Voyage to the Bay of Campeachy," in his *Collection of Voyages* (London, 1729), 23; *Adventures by Sea of Edward Coxere*, 141, 142, 143.

Many smaller but still crucial chores filled out the shipboard routine of labor. These included shadow work such as over-hauling the rigging, coiling ropes, repairing and oiling gear, changing and mending sail canvas, tarring ropes, cleaning the guns, painting, swabbing and holystoning the deck, and check-ing the cargo.[69] Such maintenance made it possible for seafar-ing work to be almost perpetual. Since the forces of nature dictated many of the tasks to be performed at sea, shadow work was used to fill the hours not directly devoted to sailing the ship. These chores made up one of the most contested domains of the labor process. How much and what kinds of work were seamen willing to perform for their wages? This question had to be answered through a process of negotiation on every change of crew.

One of the central features of seafaring work was its social visibility. Work was a public activity, so public in fact that any seaman, even when off duty, knew what work was being done, and by whom, by the distinctive yell each tar gave during his various exertions. Crews were extremely sophisticated in judg-ing the quality of each man's contribution to the sailing of the ship. Everyone knew how to perform the basic tasks, and most men had been on other ships and had seen every chore, from the captain's duties down, executed by others.[70] Consequently even the lowest ordinary seaman considered himself a judge of his officers. Further, work was closely scrutinized since the col-lective well-being often depended on it. There was considerable pressure to demonstrate one's skills, and when a man could do a job better than his superior, it was rarely a secret. When a captain was unskillful in his station, a crew might follow his incorrect orders with precision just to expose his ignorance.[71] A drunken captain shouting incoherent orders put the ship's company "in great fear and danger of their Lives."[72] Fortu-nately, seamen were usually able to counteract such danger through their own knowledge of the labor process. That such

---

[69] Cornewall-Jones, *British Merchant Service*, 299.
[70] Ibid., 195; Kemp, *British Sailor*, 86; Aubert, "Social Structure," 286; Freder-ick Pease Harlow, "Chanteying Aboard American Ships," *American Neptune* 8 (1948), 88.
[71] Falconer, *Universal Dictionary*, 195.
[72] Brazier v. Kennett, HCA 24/136 (1730).

knowledge was broadly held was central to the negotiations that surrounded the question of work in the merchant shipping industry.

Frequently this extensive knowledge of shipboard affairs translated into severe problems for the captain. He found that some of his men were of an "unruly and Ungovernable Disposition" or a "grumbling unwilling mind."[73] Captains endlessly groused about crew members they described as "self-willed" and "obstinate."[74] Such intransigence usually resulted from one of two situations: Either the seaman was new and unaccustomed to the nature of work and authority on board ship; or, knowing the ways of the merchant service, he objected to the manner in which the ship was being run. This latter attitude was summed up by Ned Ward: "The better sailor he is, he becomes the more lazy, and fancies himself like a sheet-anchor, to be reserved for desperate occasions."[75] Many such seamen had their own ideas about the social relations of work at sea. The organization, the pace, and the process of work became the focus of an often fierce struggle for control.

One way seamen attempted to expand their control over the labor process was by trying to enforce their own notions of what constituted a proper crew. In 1705 John Tunbridge deserted the *Neptune* because "the Ship had not hands enough on board to work her."[76] Seamen commonly complained that their vessels were "too weakly man'd."[77] In 1722 sailors refused to proceed on a voyage from London to northern Europe because the "Master had not eleven hands on board," as he had promised in his "first Agreement."[78] In Charleston, South Carolina, in 1736, a crew of seamen was brought on board the *Fenton,* only to walk out en masse when they discovered how much pumping would be required to stanch a "River"-like leak. A second crew hired by

---

[73] Carr v. Harris, HCA 24/135 (1725); *Barlow's Journal,* 452.

[74] Knight v. Lawson, HCA 24/137 (1732); *Voyages and Travels of Captain Nathaniel Uring,* 235.

[75] Ned Ward, *The Wooden World Dissected: In the Character of a Ship of War* (1708; reprint London, 1756), 67. See also, *The Life and Adventures of Matthew Bishop* (London, 1744), 79: "There is more Prospect of a good Sailor from a Country-man than from a Waterman, that pretends to know more than his Teachers."

[76] Examination of John Tunbridge, HCA 1/53 (1706).

[77] *Ramblin' Jack,* 76; Thompson v. Curling, HCA 24/139 (1735).

[78] Hays v. Russell, HCA 24/139 (1724).

the same master took a similarly quick exit.[79] Captain John Rushton took his crew to court in 1732 for refusing to sail; they too had charged a lack of sufficient men. The judge of the Massachusetts Admiralty sided with the captain, ruling that the seamen were "not proper Judges [of] what hands the Master ought to carry," and ordered that the crew set sail.[80] This form of protest, something of a preemptive strike, was, from the seaman's point of view, frequently too dangerous a tactic. During times of peace, maritime workers were so abundant that they could not exert much pressure without fear of dismissal. Those who made up the reserve navy of the unemployed, those put out of work by the demobilization of the Royal Navy, waited anxiously for any vacant berth. During wartime, as men-of-war and privateers scouted the seas, labor was so scarce that captains often had no alternative but to sail with smaller crews. Seamen usually gained their advantage in the form of higher wages.[81]

Given the limits of this tactic, many mariners resorted to the work stoppage. Some stoppages were primarily defensive, used by seamen to preserve the privileges that previous generations of seafarers had won. They insisted, for example, that their work regimen was to be relaxed while they were in harbor. The sailors of the *Hind* in 1720 complained while lying at anchor that Captain John Hunter "obliged them to work every day & to do more labour & duty than when at Sea."[82] Seamen also insisted that Sundays in port were their own. When Thomas Revit ordered his crew to unload a ship on a Sunday, he was told that "they were Christians and not slaves [and] they would not then work."[83] A significant number of work stoppages resulted from individual acts of defiance. In 1735 Captain Joseph Barnes asked Henry Twine, his carpenter, "what he came to Sea for if he would not do his Business & Duty as Carpenter"; Twine "replyed that he came to Sea for his Pleasure & would do what he pleased & nothing more."[84] Actions of this sort in

[79] Brown v. Graer, HCA 24/139 (1737).
[80] Rushton v. Seamen, MASS ADM (1732), f. 105.
[81] Kemp, *British Sailor*, 105. See Chapter 3 of this book.
[82] Crayton v. Hunter, HCA 24/133 (1721); Sharpless v. Durrell, HCA 24/133 (1720); Wallis v. Wills, HCA 24/133 (1721).
[83] Dunkin v. Revit, HCA 24/133 (1721); Gouldin v. Saunders, HCA 24/133 (1721); Information of Thomas Blood, HCA 1/54 (1715).
[84] Twine v. Barnes, HCA 24/136 (1736).

the workplace were highly visible and carried expansive social meanings, affording examples, perhaps encouragements, to others, and occasionally precipitating collective actions.[85] Everyone on board breathed and worked a bit more easily within the space created by the successful confrontation. When such conflict called the legitimacy of the command into question, seamen dramatically increased their control over the nature and pace of work. As one captain lamented in 1729, those who neglected their duty "did occasion the like neglect in the other Mariners."[86] And as an agricultural-turned-seafaring maxim had it, "One Scaley Sheep spoils a hole Flock."[87]

The most effective work stoppages were collective. In 1729 the seamen of the *Young Prince*, when ordered to heave anchor, "one and all . . . unanimously agreed to stop & swore Goddamn their Bloods if they would heave the Anchor or go any further with the said Ship but would go on Shore."[88] On other occasions, a core of dissatisfied mariners might attempt "to raise a Mutiny . . . and to prevent the other Mariners from proceeding on the said Voyage."[89]

Many of these themes were sharply illustrated in an abundantly documented case heard in the South Carolina Court of Admiralty in 1719. John Clipperton, master of the slave ship *Hanover Succession,* brought charges of mutiny against Jacob Key, John Swain, Samuel Woodbrey, Alexander Spencer, Joseph Coke, Benjamin Waistcoat, and David Allen, seven of his seamen. Clipperton claimed that Key, his mate, had "behaved himself mighty Ill and after a threatning and insolent manner" in their passages from London to Charleston by way of the African coast. Key "absolutely" refused to do his duty and "incensed" other members of the crew "to fall from their Duty and also to declare that they would not goe the Voyage." When the master asked the seamen why they refused, they "all

---

[85] I am indebted here to Martin Glaberman, *Wartime Strikes: The Struggle Against the No Strike Pledge in the UAW during World War II* (Detroit, 1980), 31.

[86] Latouche v. Roure, HCA 24/136 (1729).

[87] *Ramblin' Jack*, 162.

[88] Brazier v. Kennet, HCA 24/136 (1730); Beck v. Seamen, SC ADM (1716), ff. 33–47; Moodie v. Hogg, HCA 24/135 (1726); Mason v. Pomeroy, HCA 24/137 (1701).

[89] Plummer v. Burnaby, HCA 24/135 (1725).

answered [that] the Vessel was incapable," meaning that it leaked badly. Having left Charleston for London, the crew made Clipperton return to the South Carolina port, "reviling him with hard words" all the way. Key "kept severall Caballs" with the other sailors; soon, according to Clipperton, they were "combining together" in an ominous design.[90]

The effects of this combination were visible when Clipperton ordered his men to weigh anchor. Jacob Key bid him defiance. Samuel Woodbrey "threw away his hand spike saying Damn it He would heave no more." Several seamen then announced that unless Captain Clipperton "would be guided and ordered by them they would take from him his Boats and leave him to the wide ocean to perish together with his Ship." The sailors then "drew up a Paper" and Jacob Key told Clipperton, "Wee'll make a Protest against you and nail it on the Main Mast and you are a Young Rascally Dogg and I'le take Charge of the Vessel for you intend to Destroy it." Key then suggested a deep source of tension by adding, "Damn you I'le make you take a Spell at the Pump as well as the rest." Key was soon obeyed by some as captain, and the command had been fully divided. Some seamen apparently continued to support Clipperton because the protest was eventually ripped from the mast. But the ship had to return to Charleston.[91]

Clipperton cursed his "hard usage" by this "bad Crew." The seamen had their own complaints: They were "weary with pumping," having been called up while off duty, and they had but "little Water and Provisions." Key complained that Clipperton had beaten him "without the least Occasion."[92]

Several themes are vividly illustrated here: the coalescence of support around individual resistance, the struggle over the control of work, the negotiation of authority, the efforts of the crew to set standards of safety, and the omnipresence of danger. Allegations of incompetence were crucial, Clipperton calling Key "an Old Rogue and Villain," Key calling Clipperton a "Drunken Fellow" unfit for command.[93] But so too does this case illustrate one of the limits of work stoppage. It was often simply too dangerous. If the ship had not been near Charleston

[90] Clipperton v. Seamen, SC ADM (1719), ff. 493, 494.
[91] Ibid., 494, 495.　[92] Ibid., 507, 505.　[93] Ibid., 589.

when the conflict broke out, little could have been done, and the men would have been obliged to "work for their Lives."[94]

The law also placed sharp limits upon the use of work stoppages at sea. As historian Richard B. Morris has noted, "A strike which might have been treated at common law would, if committed by mariners, be deemed a mutiny."[95] Most seamen, therefore, resorted to another tactic to influence the conditions and character of their work, a tactic summed up in the lyrics of an old sea song:

> O, the times are hard and the wages low
> Leave her, John-ny, leave her
> I'll pack my bag and go below;
> It's time for us to leave her.[96]

If seamen were unable to limit their exploitation by controlling the labor process, they could at least escape it by using their fast feet.

Desertion was one of the most chronic and severe problems faced by the merchant capitalists of the shipping industry.[97] Merchants bought the seaman's labor power in a contractual exchange. Monthly wages were paid for work on a specified voyage. Vast bodies of legislation and legal opinion were produced in an effort to guarantee that exchange. In signing a set of articles, the legal agreement among owner and captain and crew, seamen were usually required to affirm that they would not "go away from, Quit or leave the said Ship . . . in any port abroad, or go on board of any other Ship whatsoever," unless impressed or required to do so by force.[98] But seamen always reserved the right to terminate that contract, to take their chances with the law, and to demonstrate that labor power was a commodity unlike any other. What merchant capitalists and

---

[94] See also Seamen v. Alloyn, SC ADM (1730), ff. 764–802, in which a work stoppage almost produced a disaster.

[95] Richard B. Morris, *Government and Labor in Early America* (New York, 1946), 225.

[96] Quoted in ibid., 248.

[97] Ibid., 247.

[98] Linam v. Chapman, HCA 24/136 (1730); Arthur Pierce Middleton, *Tobacco Coast: A Maritime History of Chesapeake Bay in the Colonial Era* (Newport News, Va., 1953), 273–4. See the many plans proposed to guarantee maritime labor power in J. S. Bromley, ed., *The Manning of the Royal Navy: Selected Public Pamphlets, 1693–1873* (London, 1974).

their lackeys saw as "the natural unsteddiness of seamen" was in fact the use of autonomous mobility to set the conditions of work.[99]

The tactic of desertion was used in complex and ingenious ways. Seamen resorted to desertion to stay out of areas where they were likely to be pressed into the Royal Navy. When William Trewfitt and other mariners in 1735 found themselves sailing toward a port rumored to contain a hot press, they immediately put the ship on another course, "hindring any others of the Mariners on board who attempted . . . to have her keep a proper course." At the first available moment, Trewfitt and several men ran from the ship.[100]

Desertion was also used to avoid sailing to disease-ridden ports. When Captain Robert Ranson altered his voyage to go to Calabar in Africa, some of his men deserted, calling the new destination "a very unhealthy place & for which the said Mar[ine]rs or several of them would not have shipt themselves."[101] Seafarers also ran from their ships to escape inadequate rations of food. Richard Young in 1720 claimed that he and twenty-three others deserted the *Pompey* "by reason that they could not live upon their Allowance of Provisions." A band of seamen left the *William* in 1729 because they "were afraid of being pinched in their Provisions."[102]

Perhaps most crucially, desertion was used to escape the grasp of a brutal master or mate. After one of their fellow tars had jumped overboard, and eventually drowned, in an attempt to escape the "severity" of their captain, William Bedford, John Lake, and John Tunbridge in 1706 collectively deserted. They "being not able to suffer his Tirany any longer took ye Boate and came on Shore."[103] In 1726 William Hamilton, John Slater, Joseph Pattison, Thomas Trummel, and Charles Hicks deserted the *Judith* in Maryland, complaining of the abuses of

---

[99] William Gordon to Thomas Corbett, ADM 1/1827 (Dec. 30, 1742).

[100] Trewfitt v. Storm, HCA 24/138 (1735). It should be noted that desertion from the Royal Navy, into which so many had been impressed, was a very different social phenomenon.

[101] Arnold v. Ranson, HCA 24/129 (1706).

[102] Examination of Richard Young, HCA 1/54 (1720); Macnamera v. Barry, SC ADM (1729), f. 726.

[103] Petition of William Bedford, John Lake, and John Tunbridge, HCA 1/29 (1706?).

Captain Joseph Wilkinson. The captain "had beaten some of them & [they] did not know how soon he might beat ye rest." They swore "they would not go on Board unless they were carried on mens backs" and that for all they cared the captain might be "cut into half crown pieces."[104] In 1737 four seamen of the *Charming Anne* ran from their less than charming captain, Henry Curling. Apparently the seamen had heard that Curling was a rough master, and they signed on for only one part of the voyage to see "if they liked and approved" of the captain's "usage and treatment of them." One of the sailors, Richard Hudschon, claimed that Curling "threatened to Shoot him and to tye him by his private parts and hang him over board." Hudschon and several others deserted, probably with great determination.[105] Mariners endlessly alleged in court that a captain's cruelty was a primary reason for running from one ship to another.[106]

On many occasions, the mere threat of desertion was enough to wrest from a captain an advantage for the crew. Some seamen threatened to desert during harsh weather, and others swore they would leave if a drunken and abusive mate continued in service.[107] One can imagine the fears of Captain Joseph Chapman in 1725 when two seamen "endeavoured to perswade all the Foremastmen on board to leave & desert the sd Ships Service" while the ship was full of slaves. Four men left, and if the Africans "had revolted . . . there could not have been sufficient force to suppress them."[108]

Desertion was encouraged by the extraordinary competition between the Royal Navy and the merchant service for the sailor's labor power. During war years the bidding grew especially intense as privateers joined the rivalry, offering the prospects of greater riches for less work.[109] Merchant captains were notorious for spiriting seamen away from the king's ships by offering high

---

[104] Hamilton v. Wilkinson, HCA 24/136 (1728).
[105] Hudschon v. Curling, HCA 24/139 (1737).
[106] Bennet v. Bride, HCA 24/139 (1740).
[107] Young v. Higgins, HCA 24/128 (1704); Webber v. Prust, HCA 24/138 (1735).
[108] Wistridge v. Chapman, HCA 24/135 (1727).
[109] Lloyd, *British Seaman*, 52–7; Kemp, *British Sailor*, 105; Forest v. Leveron, HCA 24/128 (1704).

wages and generous allotments of rum.[110] The sailor, even during peacetime, could move back and forth between these two enterprises with great profit. As members of the Massachusetts Court of Admiralty heard in 1731: "One great inducement why Sailors so frequently leave the merchants service in these parts is, the Wages given from hence are greater than out of Great Brittain and they don't value loosing two or three months Wages to get clear of a long & tedious Voyage upon smaller Wages and in order the better to do it Enter themselves on board His Majestys Ships that happen to be here and so soon as a profitable Voyage offers, Desert the Kings Service by which practices the Voyage they originally contracted to proceed is very much retarded if not quite overset."[111] At times seamen could desert to the navy without losing any money. According to the Act for the Better Regulation and Government in the Merchants Service, passed in Britain in 1729, those mariners who joined a royal ship were entitled to full pay from the ship they left behind.[112] The enforcement of this statute depended very much upon the court and judge who heard the seaman's case, but in general it seems that sailors successfully used the Admiralty Courts to argue their claims throughout the period. In order to escape contracts, mariners libeled incessantly "for wages and liberation."[113]

The sprawling nature of the international labor market and the empire made desertion extremely attractive. Many seamen, like those who congregated in Massachusetts, migrated to the

---

[110] See, for example, William Gordon to Thomas Corbett, ADM 1/1827 (Nov. 10, 1742), on the "great number of Gallons of Rum" offered to seamen to desert.

[111] Guy v. Skinner, MASS ADM (1731), f. 6.

[112] "An Act for the Better Regulation and Government of the Merchants Service," copy in HCA 30/999; Robinson v. Comyn, SC ADM (1736), f. 51; Lords of Admiralty to William Bull, CO 5/358 (Aug. 14, 1742), ff. 87–9.

[113] Roberts v. Kipping, MASS ADM (1726), f. 6. Although many a sailor deserted to a man-of-war to elude the clutches of a violent merchant captain, some merchant captains in turn used the king's ships as repositories for mutinous and disobedient seamen. Some captains apparently forced seamen from their ships in order to save labor costs. As Edward Barlow lamented in the late seventeenth century, conflicts with a captain led to his being turned out "without a penny of what was my due for the time of my service" (*Barlow's Journal*, 358). See also Pattison v. Beesley, HCA 24/129 (1709); Jones v. Purnell, HCA 24/131 (1715); Vesey v. Yoakley, HCA 24/129 (1707).

edges of the empire where seafaring labor was scarce, taking advantage of high wages and better working conditions. Many a tar was willing "to leave the ship . . . if he could better him-selfe," and such betterment was not hard to find in the West Indies.[114]

By 1700 the plantation mode of production had developed in the Caribbean to the point where free wage labor there had become something of an anomaly. A crippling mortality rate affected practically every ship that sailed into West Indian ports, and this, combined with the scarcity of free labor, created a situation in which sailors quickly seized their advantage. Desertion destabilized the labor market and drove wages up. As one merchant captain explained in 1717, "it was & is usuall for Marriners of Ships who were & are hired at monthly wages to leave & desert their respective services at Jamaica & other parts in ye west Indies & to ship and enter themselves into ye Service of Ships att much greater wages by the Run."[115] Once free of command, seamen were footloose in the port towns, "rambling to and fro about the Country," as one disapproving captain put it.[116] They looked to sell their dear labor for "the run home" to London.[117] "A Rambler in ye West Indies" who made £2 per month on the voyage to Jamaica stood to make £10–20 and ten gallons of rum for the passage back to London.[118] Such bargains drastically reduced the exploitation of maritime labor.

As the examples of William Trewfitt, William Bedford, Richard Hudschon, and their comrades in flight indicate, many seamen ran from their ships "in combination," often leaving behind an incapacitated vessel.[119] Captains thus faced difficult choices. They could look for relatively cheap labor, risking a lengthy delay during which all those sailors who remained in service had to be paid; or they could pay the high wages demanded by the

---

[114] "Account of the Discovery of an Horrid Plot and Conspiracy on Board the Ship *Antelope*," CO 323/3 (1699).

[115] Mathew v. Lawton, HCA 24/131 (1717).

[116] Vincent v. Curtis, HCA 24/139 (1735).

[117] Richard Pares, "The Manning of the Royal Navy in the West Indies, 1702–1763," *Royal Historical Society Transactions* 20 (1937), 31–60.

[118] Thomas Coale to Josiah Burchett, ADM 1/1588 (July 22, 1699). See Lone v. Lewis, HCA 24/131 (1715), and Deverell v. Pierson, HCA 24/129 (1719).

[119] Bruce v. Cathcart, HCA 24/138 (1734).

men attempting to work their way home to London. Often the only option was the latter. Yet it should be noted that not all seamen saw wisdom in desertion. As one man viewed it, anyone who deserted "would be a fool . . . for it was giving his Wages to another Man."[120] And so it was. But in return, many men received wages two, three, four, or more times as high as those they forfeited. Some sailors were even known as chronic deserters, men who, in the words of a vexed captain, "never went out and returned in the same ship a whole voyage." Some were considered "stragling fellows that can't leave their old trade of deserting."[121] Desertion was not so much a trade as a trademark of a footloose maritime proletariat.

Desertion also served as a firm demarcation of the captain's authority and as an affirmation of the sailor's own power. As Henry Fielding perceptively observed during his voyage to Portugal in 1754, the ship captain found that "it was easier to send his men on shore than to recall them. They acknowledged him to be their master while they remained on shipboard, but did not allow his power to extend to the shores, where they no sooner set their feet than every man became *sui juris,* and thought himself at full liberty to return when he pleased."[122]

Desertion was, in all, an essential component of seafaring labor. As the seamen who flew from Fielding's ship demonstrated, it affirmed the "free" in free wage labor. In so doing, it went far beyond and frequently contradicted the free wage labor imagined and endorsed by the merchant capitalist who paid for that labor and the merchant captain who supervised it. Merchants, masters, and government officials made resolute efforts to control the autonomous mobility of maritime workers. They issued acts and proclamations against "straggling" seamen in ports, they ran advertisements in newspapers for deserters, they sued incessantly in court, and they tried to implement a seaman's registry and a certificate system to identify sailors and make their labor readily available.[123] The large measure of power held

[120] French v. Meake, HCA 24/126 (1729).
[121] Wilson v. Parsons, HCA 24/129 (1710). Woodes Rogers, *A Cruising Voyage Round the World* (1712; reprint London, 1928), 299.
[122] Henry Fielding, *The Journal of a Voyage to Lisbon* (1755; reprint London, 1976), 255.
[123] Lloyd, *British Seaman,* 173–91; anonymous officer of an East India Company ship, *Piracy Destroy'd, Or, A short Discourse shewing the Rise, Growth, and*

by these figures gave them some success in controlling Jack's mobility, for the seaman was not only free to find a job but also free to go hungry if he was unable to find one. Yet mobility was an essential component in the seaman's strategy for survival. The mariner had to maintain a continuity of income when often there was no continuity of available work.[124] As Gary Nash has shown, free laborers in the colonial port cities were able to count on little more than 200–250 days of work per year.[125] Jack Tar's rhythm of keeping body and soul together and the merchant's rhythm of capital accumulation did not move in harmony. As a form of struggle and a means of survival, desertion was widespread among maritime workers.[126] The seafarer's mobility was a stellar part of his strategy to control the means of finding employment. The effectiveness of mobility was enhanced by the amorphous collective network through which rumor, reputation, and information circulated among sailors of the English Atlantic.

Let us return for a moment to the tactic of work stoppage, a form of collective disobedience that often shaded into the more ominous crime of mutiny. Many mutinies between 1700 and 1750 were fleeting affairs, ranging from the downing of tools to the violent, almost always temporary, seizure of ships (see Chapter 5). Yet mutiny at times took on a more permanent and material form; it ceased to be a redressive and defensive posture and assumed the aggressive stance of piracy. Sailors then expropriated the workplace and arranged it anew. Since piracy represented a social world constructed apart from the ways of the merchant and the captain – and hence apart in significant ways from capital – robbery at sea can illuminate certain aspects

Footnote 123 (*cont.*):
Causes of Piracy of Late; with a sure Method how to put a speedy stop to that growing Evil (London, 1701), 22; John Dennis, *An Essay on the Navy* (London, 1702), 36–53; "An Act for punishing mutinous and disobedient Seamen and for the more speedy determination of controversies arising between Masters of Ships and their Crews," CO 412/22 (1722).
[124] This paragraph owes much to Michael Sonenscher, "Work and Wages in Paris in the Eighteenth Century," *Manufacture in Town and Country before the Factory*, ed. Maxine Berg, Pat Hudson, and Michael Sonenscher (Cambridge, 1983), 147–72.
[125] Nash, *Urban Crucible*, 55–7.
[126] The complaints and allegations of desertion in the English and colonial admiralty courts were incessant.

of the labor process as seen by those whose lives were shaped by it.[127]

Almost all early-eighteenth-century pirates had worked in the merchant shipping industry, and piracy was deeply imbued with the collectivistic tendencies produced by life and labor at sea. Against the omnipotent authority of the merchant ship master stood the limited authority of the pirate captain and other officers, who were elected by the crew. In contrast to the hierarchical pay system of the merchant service, pirates distributed their plunder in markedly egalitarian fashion. Pirates also exhibited a pervasive consciousness of kind.[128]

The nature of the tasks performed by a seaman did not change for the bold tar who exchanged a life of legal trade for one of illegal plunder. In either employ, the same work had to be performed. Yet once among pirates, the intensity of labor decreased dramatically because pirate ships were hugely overmanned. An average vessel of 200 tons carried eighty or more men, whereas a merchant ship of equivalent size contained only thirteen to seventeen hands. These outlaws maintained the maritime division of labor but strictly limited its tendency to function as a hierarchy of status and privilege. They also altered its relation to income. There were among pirates only three pay stations for some eighty men, rather than five or six slots for fifteen sailors. Even more revealing, pirates abolished the wage. They considered themselves risk-sharing partners rather than a collection of "hands" who sold their muscle on an open market.[129]

Some mariners cast their lot with pirates in order to escape hard labor. As pirate Joseph Mansfield said in 1722, "the love of Drink and a Lazy Life" were "Stronger Motives with him than Gold."[130] Admiral Edward Vernon, taking sixteen suspected pirates aboard his man-of-war, said that since he needed "hands for the pump, it might be of service to carry them out of the way of falling into their old Courses, and that it might be

---

[127] This section draws from material and conclusions that are presented in Marcus Rediker, " 'Under the Banner of King Death': The Social World of Anglo-American pirates, 1716 to 1726," *WMQ* 38 (1981), 203–27. See also Chapter 6 of this book.

[128] Ibid.   [129] Ibid.

[130] "Proceedings of the Court held on the Coast of Africa upon Trying of 100 pirates taken by his Ma[jes]ties Ship *Swallow*," HCA 1/99 (1722), f. 116.

a Means to learn them . . . Working," which, Vernon noted, "they turned Rogues to avoid."[131] And as Woodes Rogers, governor of the Bahama Islands, long experienced in battles against sea robbers, said of pirates: "for work they mortally hate it." Samuel Buck, a long-time resident of the Bahamas, agreed: "working does not agree with them."[132]

Some saw a connection between the seaman's autonomous mobility and piracy. An officer of an East India Company ship observed in 1701 that seamen "run from Ship to Ship, and are encouraged in it by advancing their pay, which makes up what they lost in the other they left, and after they are a little accustomed to this extravagant course of leaving their ships at Pleasure, . . . they seldom care to proceed to their intended Voyage, but getting a custome of Roving, they leave their Commander upon every slight distaste, and at last grow so ungovernable, that nothing will serve them but going where they shall all be equal, or all Masters by turns. This I think is the occasion of such numbers of Pirates." Parliament agreed. In an "Act for the more effectual Suppression of Piracy," it stated that the "deserting of merchant ships abroad in parts beyond the seas" was not only the "chief occasion" of seamen turning pirate but "of great detriment to trade and navigation in general."[133]

The social contours of piracy, although fully congruent with the labor process at sea, were often formed in violent antipathy to that world of work from which many seamen gladly escaped. "Lower class utopias," writes Christopher Hill, for centuries aimed "to abolish wage-labour altogether, or drastically to reduce the working day." The social organization of piracy, even though based upon a relatively new form of collectivism, was part of that tenacious tradition that linked medieval peasants, seventeenth-century radicals such as the Ranters and Levellers, and the free wage laborers of the eighteenth century.[134]

---

[131] Edward Vernon to Josiah Burchett, Aug. 12, 1721, Edward Vernon Letterbook, 1720–1, BL, Add. Ms. 40813, f. 128.

[132] Rogers to Council of Trade and Plantations, CO 23/11 (May 29, 1719); Memorial of Samuel Buck, CO 23/1 (1720), f. 103.

[133] *Piracy Destroy'd*, 15; "An Act for the more effectual Suppression of Piracy" (11 and 12 William III, c. 7, 1700) in Sir Thomas Parker, *The Laws of Shipping and Insurance, with a Digest of Adjudged Cases* (London, 1775), reprinted in *British Maritime Cases* (Abingdon, Oxfordshire, 1978), vol. 24, p. 45.

[134] Christopher Hill, "Pottage for Freeborn Englishmen: Attitudes to Wage

Piracy illustrates only one of the ways in which the cooperation and interdependence of the labor process produced solidarity among seafaring workers. Many types of collective disobedience were common in the merchant service between 1700
and 1750. According to merchant captains, sailors often
formed "cabals" among themselves, and support usually co-
alesced around a particularly defiant member of the crew. For
example, Captain Thomas King in 1723 called Peter Lester a
"mutineer," a man with whom "most part of the Sailors seemed
to be in a cabal." King tried to maneuver Lester out of the ship
but had "much difficulty . . . for noe Violence cou'd be us'd
where the Major part of the Ships Company were inclin'd to
favour him."[135] Off the African coast in 1736, another crew
attempted "to raise a mutiny" in response to the harsh punishments administered by their captain for work-related offenses.
One of the sailors was placed in irons for his role in the rising.
When asked by the captain of another merchant vessel why
they were so angry, the seamen said, "by God, they would not
be serv'd so, no Man shou'd confine any of them, for they were
one & all resolved to stand by one another."[136] In 1721 John
Sedgewick and several other mariners plotted to desert their
ship. On arrival in St. Kitts and when ordered by their captain
to load some casks of sugar, Sedgewick replied, "God damn
you take them on board yourselfe. [H]ere is one Boat on Shore
& another at anchor, look after them & be damned." The captain persisted in his order and was told by several men, "God
damn y[ou]r Blood carry them on Board your selfe for wee will
not sett our feet on Board y[ou]r Ship any more." A band of
men deserted, but they were soon captured and taken before a
magistrate who threatened them with jail. Sedgewick then reportedly "damned his Blood & sayd they were one & all." One
and all they were, and this was precisely how they went to jail:
one and all.[137]

In 1714 the crew of the *St. Joseph* "all as one" refused to go
any further once their captain had changed the destination

Labour," in his *Change and Continuity in Seventeenth-Century England* (Cambridge, Mass., 1975), 235. See Linebaugh, "All the Atlantic Mountains
Shook," for a pathbreaking analysis of many of these continuities.
[135] Lester v. King, HCA 24/134 (1723).
[136] Powell v. Hardwicke, HCA 24/139 (1738).
[137] Sedgewick v. Burroughs, HCA 24/134 (1723).

stipulated in their original agreement.[138] In other disputes, seamen swore that "they would stand by one another and stand Knock for Knock . . . meaning they would Resist" their master "by Force."[139] To avert the captain's wrath over some anonymous misdeed, sailors often must have "turned freemasons and kept a secret."[140] Not for nothing did seamen call each other "Brother Tar."[141]

Perhaps the most telling evidence, much of it dating from the later eighteenth century, of the increasingly collective consciousness and activity among seamen lay in their resort to the strike. Given, in fact, the logic of collectivism that informed seafaring work, it comes as no surprise that the very term "strike" evolved from the decision of British seamen in 1768 to "strike" the sails of their vessels and thereby to cripple the commerce of the empire's capital city. The strike may have been born of shipboard cooperation, but as a concept in language and in practical political and economic activity, it began to circulate with increasing velocity among all men and women involved in collective industrial labor.[142]

These are some of the many ways in which the relationships initiated by the concentration of labor on the ship were soon transformed by seamen into a new basis for the organization of community. Sharing a total life situation as a "community apart," separated from family and church, seafarers forged new social relations. The dangers of their work and their collective need for safety intensified their solidarity. Their new ties were sometimes undercut by the diversity of the men who made their living by the sea, as well as by the mobility and dispersion that were essential features of their work.[143] Yet for all of these men, self-protection – from harsh conditions, excessive work, and oppressive authority – was necessary to survival. Too often,

---

[138] Longust v. Youron, HCA 24/130 (1714).

[139] Parker v. Boucher, HCA 24/132 (1719).

[140] *Ramblin' Jack*, 86.   [141] Ibid., 117.

[142] *Oxford English Dictionary*, s.v., "strike"; Dobson, *Masters and Journeymen*, 154–70, for a partial listing of seamen's strike activity.

[143] Aubert, "Total Institution," 257. Jesse Lemisch, in "Listening to the 'Inarticulate': William Widger's Dream and the Loyalties of American Revolutionary Seamen in British Prisons," *Journal of Social History* 3 (1969–70), 1–29, discusses this same collectivistic ethos as it appeared in the revolutionary era.

claimed Edward Barlow, when under command, "all the men in the ship except the master" were "little better than slaves."[144] Social bonds among sailors arose from the very conditions and relations of their work. These men possessed a concrete and situational outlook forged within the power relations that guided their lives. Theirs was a collectivism of necessity.

The coexistence and integration of diverse types of labor, the coordination of efforts to combat a menacing laboring environment, the steady shifts of work as organized by the watch system, and the interdependence of the stages of production combined to produce a laboring experience uncommon to the first half of the eighteenth century. The seaman, in sum, was one of the first collective workers. There were, to be sure, several broad continuities in the nature of work between the early days of sail and the eighteenth century. Certain aspects of the division and organization of labor, and some of the chores, tasks, and dangers remained essentially the same. Yet there were also decisive changes in the nature, pace, and context of work at sea, both in the labor process and, perhaps even more importantly, in the maritime labor market.

Several technological changes affected the labor process between 1700 and 1750. Major alterations were made in rigging, steering, and the complexity of sails.[145] By 1700 vessels were being designed and built for smaller crews, and the production of more manageable two-masted ships, brigs and snows, increased significantly. Merchants deployed wide-bottom Dutch hull forms in order to ship larger amounts of cargo with fewer workers.[146] Throughout the eighteenth century, crew sizes decreased in relation to tonnage. A typical 200-ton Virginia trader carried twenty or twenty-one crew members in 1700, about sixteen in 1750, and as few as thirteen by 1770.[147] The number of tons of cargo handled per seaman increased from

---

[144] *Barlow's Journal*, 339. See also Rule, *Experience of Labour*, 207, 194; Weibust, *Deep Sea Sailors*, 443.

[145] Parry, *Trade and Dominion*, 207–9.

[146] Davis, *English Shipping*, 72, 65–6; Abbott Payson Usher, "The Growth of English Shipping, 1572–1922," *Quarterly Journal of Economics* 42 (1928), 476.

[147] James F. Shepherd and Gary M. Walton, *Shipping, Maritime Trade, and the Economic Development of Colonial North America* (Cambridge, 1972), 73–81; Davis, *English Shipping*, 71–8; Parry, *Trade and Dominion*, 214.

the 1720s to 1770.[148] Some of these declining crew sizes, however, were offset by an increase in the size of the average transatlantic vessel.

Yet what appeared to the merchant capitalist or captain as an increase in productivity often appeared to the seaman as an increase in exploitation. As crew sizes were reduced through the removal of ordnance, the specialization of function, and technological change, more work was required of the seamen who remained on each ship. As Robert K. Schaeffer has written of the seventeenth and eighteenth centuries, "The multiplication of sails and rigging and the use of block and tackle made the work of running the ship much more complex." Mastery of shipboard labor required crews both to learn more and to "work harder."[149] The smaller crews, subjected over time to ever harsher discipline, were forced to take part in a more intensively cooperative labor process. Paradoxically, as merchants hired fewer men to do seafaring work, they simultaneously required greater concert from those hired. A quantitative reduction of the collectivity of the crew led to a qualitative expansion of collectivized work.[150]

The maritime labor market also witnessed crucial changes. As the luxury trades of the period 1450–1650 gave way to the bulk trades of the late seventeenth and eighteenth centuries, the merchant shipping industry created increasingly stable, lifelong employment for an ever-larger mass of waged workers. Thus the seaman's work was collective not only within the technical process and division of labor that existed on each ship but also, more broadly, within the social division of labor. Occupying a central position in the international economy, the seaman came into contact with an extraordinary assortment of other laborers, working alongside lightermen, porters, coastal traders, dock workers, and others in Europe's port cities, and with slaves, indentured servants, and day laborers in the colonies. He regularly crossed paths with customs officials, provisioners, merchants, supercargoes, coopers, shipbuilders, and ship

[148] Parry, *Trade and Dominion*, 215.
[149] Robert K. Schaeffer, "The Chains of Bondage Broke: The Proletarianization of Seafaring Labor, 1600–1800," Ph.D. diss., State University of New York at Binghampton, 1984, chap. 3.
[150] Davis, *English Shipping*, 154.

chandlers, to name but a few of those who did dockside labor.[151] The turnover of personnel from ship to ship brought the sailor into association with an exceptionally large number of his fellow tars. The cooperative character of his position owed much to his mobile circulation within an expansive labor market, and extended from the technicalities of the workplace to the production and exchange of goods within the empire and beyond, to the international market chain, the global economy increasingly dominated by Europe. The international capitalist economy was emerging as an increasingly cooperative totality, and the strategically situated merchant seaman provided many of the links in the system.

In this age of growing manufacture and trade, merchant capitalists such as those in international shipping gradually took over existing labor processes that in many cases had "developed by different and more archaic modes of production." They introduced gradual changes, such as the regularization and intensification of work, but their control remained merely formal. There existed "no fixed political and social relationship of supremacy and subordination" between capital and labor. Revolutionary changes wrought by the large-scale introduction of machinery came later, arriving, in shipping, with steam power.[152] Eighteenth-century seafaring work, therefore, even though highly synchronized and continuous, remained distinct in one crucial respect from the machine-dominated factory of the nineteenth century. It depended in the final instance upon nature, upon the movements of wind and water. As Edward Barlow insisted, "a fair wind . . . is a seaman's best friend."[153] Or in the verse of sailor John Baltharpe:

> The Merchants Ships did with us Sail
> Bound towards *Legorne*, with merry Gale;
> But four days after we did want
> No wind but fair, one which was scant,
> And ne're unwelcome is to Seamen,

[151] Peter Linebaugh, "Socking: Tobacco Porters, the Hogshead, and Excise," in *The London Hanged: Crime and Civil Society in the 18th Century* (forthcoming).
[152] Karl Marx, *Capital: A Critique of Political Economy*, trans. Ben Fowkes (New York, 1977), 1021, 1026, 1019–38. Marx would have called the transition from sail to steam in shipping an example of the movement from the "formal subsumption of labor under capital" to the "real subsumption."
[153] *Barlow's Journal*, 243.

> For by that means he is a Freeman
> From toylsom Labour, and sad Care,
> Which winds contrary bring for fare.[154]

The sailing ship did not rely upon the continuous application of mechanical power for its progress, and consequently the labor process could not be infused with as much continuity, uniformity, regularity, order, or intensity as would characterize later industrial production.[155] The seaman's workday remained "porous," marked by periods of intensity and inactivity that could not easily be filled with steady toil.[156] Labor's subordination to capital remained formal so long as a "merry Gale" made a seaman into a "Freeman."

Yet the experience of the early-eighteenth-century seaman illuminates a vital moment in the transition to a free wage labor system.[157] Seamen occupied a pivotal position in the movement from paternalistic forms of labor control to the contested negotiation of waged work. The completely contractual and waged nature of maritime work represented a capital–labor relation quite distinct from landlord–tenant, master–servant, or master–apprentice relationships. The sailor was both a free wage laborer located in a critical sector of the economy and a collective laborer located among an unprecedented number of men much like himself. Like others, including those wage laborers in agriculture and manufacture who had no alternative incomes from the land, the seaman found that he had only "a pair of good Hands, and a stout Heart to recommend him."[158] Such was the central reality of proletarian life.

The seaman's world of labor was a complex blend of cooperation and confrontation. Within this world he devised many tactics to break the "formal" control of capital and to assert his own ends against those mandated from above. He resorted to preemptive strikes, work stoppages, piracies, and mutinies.

---

[154] John Baltharpe, *The Straights Voyage, or, St. Davids Poem*, ed. J. S. Bromley (1671; reprint Oxford, 1959), 38.

[155] Marx, *Capital*, 465.

[156] Christian Palloix, "The Labour Process: From Fordism to Neo-Fordism," in *The Labour Process and Class Strategies* (London, 1976), 149.

[157] E. P. Thompson, "Patrician Society, Plebeian Culture," *Journal of Social History* 7 (1974), 384, 383.

[158] Slush, *Navy Royal*, 11. See Malcolmson, *Life and Labour*, 136–59, and Rule, *Experience of Labour*, 194–216.

But his greatest source of power, at least in the early eighteenth century, was his mobility, and desertion was a crucial part of the self-activity of maritime working people. As Barnaby Slush said, early-eighteenth-century seamen "will not bellow forth their complaints, like a Mob of Spittle-Fields Weavers, they e'en shrug up their loaded shoulders, and suppress their groans, but yet with an unchangeable Resolution of deserting at the first opportunity."[159] Just as the merchant financed the aggregation of labor for the sake of productivity and the accumulation of capital, seamen, through desertion, asserted their power to disaggregate that labor, to disrupt that productivity and accumulation, and to contest the course of capitalist development.[160]

In the end, we see that the abstract themes with which we began – the growth of international capitalism, the labor process, and the creation of the free and collective worker – were for the seaman concretely and densely interrelated. As seamen confronted their lot as collective laborers within the sprawling and thriving capitalist economy of the North Atlantic, they began to understand their responsibilities to each other and to see the wisdom of the advice given Jack Cremer by some "Brother Tars": "It is not going voages abroad that makes a Man, but makes Slaves, if we have no Socciaty."[161]

[159] Slush, *The Navy Royal*, 63.
[160] See the excellent article by James O'Connor, "Productive and Unproductive Labor," *Politics and Society* 5 (1975), 297–336.
[161] *Ramblin' Jack*, 211.

3

THE SEAMAN AS WAGE LABORER

The Search for Ready Money

Barnaby Slush, an early-eighteenth-century "Sea-Cook," observed in 1709 that the vocation of seaman was "a universal Pasport, that renders him welcom, and finds him ready Money, in almost every Corner of the Globe."[1] The seaman, as we have seen, was a free and mobile worker in an expansive international economy. His life concretely embodied the abstract phrase "free wage labor." This chapter explores another aspect of that experience: the seaman's quest for wages, or, in Slush's more all-embracing words, his search for "ready Money."

The investigation contains three parts. The first surveys the monetary wage: the types of contracts and agreements, their regulation by law, and the changes in wage rates over time for maritime occupations. The second section considers the "social wage": the money, food, drink, perquisites, and customs that constituted the seaman's total resources for subsistence. The third part sets the first two in motion, examining the many complex struggles and negotiations that determined the sailor's wages. The conclusion discusses some of the social effects of early-eighteenth-century wage relations.

Most seamen engaged in wage relations by selling their labor power along the waterfront. William Gittus, for example, went down to Shadwell Dock on the River Thames in 1717, eyed a likely vessel, went aboard, and asked the mate "whither she was bound and whether she wanted any hands and what

---

[1] Barnaby Slush, *The Navy Royal: Or a Sea-Cook Turn'd Projector* (London, 1709), 92.

Wages her master gave." He discovered that the *Unity* was bound for Norway and that it did indeed want workers to take it there. Even though the wages were low, just as they had been since the end of the War of the Spanish Succession in 1713, Gittus signed on.[2]

Gittus, like his many brother tars, probably signed a wage contract, a complex agreement that formalized and mediated the relations among owners, captain, officers, and crew. The essential features of the contract, as Gittus's questions made clear, were the nature, and hence length, of the voyage and the money offered. In addition, the contract usually contained a formal vow of obedience to the captain's command and specified the particular labors expected of seamen while in port. A significant part of the wage agreement, relating to food, drink, and perquisites, was left to custom and was not normally outlined in the agreement.

The stipulation of the voyage was fundamental to the contract, and controversy surrounded the captain's prerogative to alter it. Some contracts, for example, specified voyages from London to New York to the West Indies "or where else her sd Master should think fitt to Proceed with her," or from London to Falmouth to Venice and "such other Ports & Places in the Meditaranian as her sd Ma[ste]r should think most advantageous."[3] Others detailed the voyage precisely, outlining a specific set of passages in a round-trip pattern or designating a time by which the vessel had to return to its port of origin. Alexander Roberts of the *Dorset* understood his voyage to run from Amsterdam to Portsmouth to Jamaica to Honduras to Amsterdam "and no other voyage whatsoever." Ramblin' Jack Cremer and his shipmates signed a contract at Gravesend for a voyage that was "all to be voide if [they were to] proceed in any other ways." Ramblin' Jack later described a distinctly different wage contract of the 1720s, one that granted the captain vast powers. Cremer signed to go from London to Geneva to Lisbon "and Elsewheair as the Master shall proceed for the Good of the Owners. Noe time limited, or wheair to demand my

---

[2] Gittus v. Bowles, HCA 24/132 (1718).
[3] Whitman v. Eyres, HCA 24/131 (1716); Blaker v. Blackbourne, HCA 24/132 (1720).

Discharge, but as the Master thought fitt." Jack somberly concluded: "Soe unhappy was I in my agreement."[4]

The captain's ability to fix the voyage was determined by a complicated array of factors, the most crucial of which was the overall availability of labor. When maritime labor was abundant and scores of seamen searched North Atlantic harbors for berths, the powers of the owner, the merchant, the captain – of capital generally – expanded; in times of scarcity, seamen had greater power to specify or limit the procession of their voyage. At the very least, they were able to choose the vessels that offered more definite sailing schedules.

The wage contract usually specified the seaman's responsibilities once in port. The men were generally required "to continue on board and serve in such ships til they are wholly unladen and such Voyage is not ended til that time." Some contracts, again depending on the fluctuations of the economy and on numerous negotiations between captain and crew, stipulated that, for instance, sailors were "to be discharged in eight & forty hours after said Ship is Safe at her Moorings." The custom in Bristol was for each seaman to guarantee nine days' labor for unlading.[5]

A second main concern was money, which was paid in three basic types of wage agreements. First and least used was the share system, which originated among ancient mariners and remained a dominant form of pay in medieval shipping. The shift from shares to wages began in the sixteenth century, part of a broader movement in property law. By the early eighteenth century, the share system was used only by fishermen, whalemen, privateersmen, and pirates, though with different methods and emphases by each. Among all of these groups, however, the men were paid with a proportional share of the take. Fishing, whaling, and privateering expeditions allocated a substantial percentage of the produce – whether fish, whales, or loot – to the owners of their vessels and corresponding, dimin-

---

[4] Robertson v. Winterbourn, SC ADM (1738), f. 202; *Ramblin' Jack: The Journal of Captain John Cremer*, ed. R. Reynall Bellamy (London, 1936), 226, 205, 103. See also Edmondson v. Palmer, HCA 24/129 (1708); Arthur v. Willey, HCA 24/138 (1736).
[5] Gittus v. Bowles, HCA 24/132 (1718); Accountbook of Benjamin Mollish, HCA 24/133 (1720); Twine v. Barnes, HCA 24/139 (1736).

ishing shares from the captain down to the common tar. Pirates, of course, had no owners to pay and distributed their plunder in a remarkably egalitarian way.[6]

A second wage agreement exchanged a fixed amount of money for labor on a particular voyage. Lump sum payments were most prominent in the Northern European trades, where voyages were quick and predictable. Seamen earned their money "by the run," accepting a voyage unlikely to be changed, but also agreeing implicitly to absorb losses if anything extraordinary happened while at sea.

The final and most common form of money payment for deep-sea sailors was the monthly wage. Seamen agreed to monetary wages of 22 to 35s. per month in peacetime or 35 to 55s. per month during wars. The money was to be paid in two or more parts: first, at the second port of delivery and at every second port thereafter; and finally, upon the completion of the voyage in the home port.

The proliferation of vice-admiralty courts throughout the British Empire in the seventeenth century was part of the overall expansion and rationalization of commerce. (See Appendix F.) One of the main functions of these courts was to handle seafaring wage disputes. By 1700 admiralty law had clearly established criteria to guarantee the seaman's pay. As Richard B. Morris pointed out, "In admiralty law the ship was pledged for the payment of wages to the last plank and the last nail." Vice-admiralty judges recognized the indispensability of maritime labor to the orderly movement of commodities and the accumulation of capital, and they did not hesitate to condemn and sell merchantmen at public auction. Since the colony, the court, and the judge benefited by such sales, numerous ships and cargoes were sold to satisfy wage contracts. Speaking of the security given seamen by the lien on the ship, a Pennsylvania

---

[6] William McFee, *The Law of the Sea* (Philadelphia, 1951), 54, 72; F. R. Sanborn, *Origins of the Early English Maritime and Commercial Law* (New York, 1930), 66, 96; Ralph Davis, *The Rise of the English Shipping Industry in the Seventeenth and Eighteenth Centuries* (London, 1962), 133; Richard B. Morris, *Government and Labor in Early America* (New York, 1946), 226; Olof Hasslof, "Maritime Commerce as a Socio-Historical Phenomenon," *Ships and Shipyards, Sailors and Fishermen: Introduction to Maritime Ethnology*, ed. Hasslof, Henning Henningsen, and Arne Emil Christensen (Copenhagen, 1972), 83–4. See Chapter 6 of this book.

vice-admiralty judge observed, perhaps overgenerously, in 1735: "the Law seems to be very favourable and tender of Mariners by providing them so safe, so many, & so easy methods as it has for coming at their Right."[7]

One way of coming at this right was salvage. Sailors whose vessels sank or were severely damaged by the elements frequently claimed salvage rights as defined by the vice-admiralty courts. Salvage law tried to mediate the interests of owner and seaman by requiring the sailor to save all possible cargo and equipment in order to be eligible for his wages after the sale of such goods. Seafarers often "w[i]th Great diligence & pains saved all of the greatest part of the Cargo" of their damaged ship, and they always seemed to know when salvage was "much more than sufficient to pay all the Wages due to all the Marriners."[8] They also often knew when a ship was "insured by the Owners," another situation that guaranteed their wages.[9] Seamen sometimes exploited the calamity of emergency salvage to benefit themselves at the owner's expense. Drewry Ottley wrote to owner William Coleman in 1717 that the "Scoundrell Kidgell" somehow "saved Tenn Ounces of Gold" from a wrecked vessel, although, of course, "he Deny'd that he had any."[10]

Admiralty law was not, however, designed simply to protect seamen and their access to wages. It had another side, the cardinal responsibility of which was to uphold and protect the interests of the owner, merchant, and captain of the shipping industry. Numerous legal provisions required the forfeiture of wages by seamen. If a sailor "be mutinous, disobedient, or desert the ship, he makes a total forfeiture of all his wages." Further, if he "purloin, or embezzle any of the goods, or be faulty in the due stowage thereof, or damage happens for want

---

[7] Seamen v. John, Records of the Pennsylvania Vice-Admiralty Court (1735), Manuscripts Division, LC, f. 19; Morris, *Government and Labor*, 243, 229, 232, 233.

[8] Brown v. Hopkins, MASS ADM (1721), f. 86; Weeds v. Nicholls, HCA 24/139 (1739). For an inversion of the old saying about the captain going down with his ship, see Stanley v. Turner, HCA 24/129 (1707), in which the captain ordered the crew to abandon ship, and was refused because his seamen wanted to claim their salvage rights.

[9] Bushby v. Studley, HCA 24/135 (1728).

[10] Drewry Ottley to William Coleman, HCA 24/132 (Oct. 9, 1717).

of pumping, or through his default, his wages will be liable to a proportionable satisfaction."[11] The passage of "An Act for the Better Regulation and Government of the Merchants Service" in 1729 reaffirmed and extended these rulings. All contracts were formalized in writing. Deserters, in addition to losing their wages, were to pay a £5 fine for running and were to be committed to the nearest "House of Correction, there to be kept to hard Labour not exceeding Thirty days, nor less than Fourteen days." Time away from the ship without consent was punished by docking two days' pay for each day away. One month of pay was forfeited for leaving the ship before completing the unloading of cargo and gaining formal discharge.[12] This side of admiralty law had three primary functions: to protect the merchant's and owner's investments against the encroachments of the seamen, to attach the interests of sailors to the interests of their employers, and to discipline and make available enough maritime labor to suit the needs of commerce and capital.

Wages for masters of transatlantic voyages were remarkably stable and consistent between 1700 and 1750, ranging from £5 to £6 per month. Wartime wages were only 10 percent higher than the peacetime average, and captains were thus less affected by the oscillations of war and peace than any other category of maritime worker. Their rates of pay, like those of all other officers, did, however, vary significantly with vessel size. The man who took charge of a large East India Company ship occasionally received £10 per month plus lucrative perquisites, whereas the master of a small vessel in the Northern European trade got only a standard £5 per month and perhaps a bit of "privilege."

The mate, or first mate, of a merchantman usually made

---

[11] *Reasons for Settling Admiralty Jurisdiction and Giving Encouragement to Merchants, Owners, Commanders, Masters of Ships, Material Men, and Mariners* (London, 1690), in *Harleian Miscellany* (London, 1810), vol. IX, 472. It would seem that when admiralty jurisdiction was finally established in 1696, benefits accrued, largest to smallest, in precisely the order in which the occupations were listed in this pamphlet.

[12] A copy of the act is in HCA 30/999. For examples of its enforcement, see Linam v. Chapman, HCA 24/136 (1729), and Fox v. Walker, HCA 24/137 (1731).

between £3 and £4, an average wage of £3.63 per month in the first half of the eighteenth century. His peacetime pay was £3.26; his wages during war years were more than a third higher at £4.38 per month. The second mate, present only on the larger vessels, made between £2.50 and £3 monthly, averaging £2.55 during peacetime and £3.47 when his nation was at war.

The carpenter was one of the highest paid members of the crew at £3 to £4 a month. He received an average wage of £4.09 in years of war, £3.08 in peace. Frequently the carpenter trained a mate as an apprentice and got an extra £2 to £3 for his services. The boatswain was a ubiquitous member of seafaring crews. He was given an average of £2.52 per month between 1700 and 1750, £2.06 during peacetime and £3.20 in war. The boatswain, situated in the lower middle of the laboring hierarchy, strongly felt the effects of the transition between war and peace. His wartime wages were more than 50 percent higher than those he received in times of peace. He too occasionally had a mate, a helper who got around £2 per month for his labors.

The gunner appeared with decreasing frequency on eighteenth-century merchant craft, especially after the repression of piracy in 1726. He made £2 to £3 monthly, and his skills and experience were understandably in greatest demand during wartime, when he made an average of £3.20, as compared to £2.10 when Britain was at peace. On large vessels the gunner often oversaw the work of a mate, who made £2 to £2.50 each month.

Certain ships, most notably those involved in the African slave trade, required the services of a surgeon, who made £3 to £4 per month. He was one of the few shipboard workers whose wages showed a long-term increase in the first half of the eighteenth century. His wages averaged £3.06 during peacetime and increased by a third to £4.09 when international hostilities broke out.

Other skilled workers or maritime officers who signed on some merchant vessels were the cooper, caulker, sailmaker, and armorer. The cooper, instrumental to the tobacco and sugar trades, where commodities were shipped in casks and hogsheads, made £2 to £3 per month, £2.80 during war and £2.07

in peace. The very largest merchant ships, particularly those in the East India trade, carried sailmakers and armorers at £2 to £3, and sometimes a trumpeter.

In sum, maritime officers and skilled workers in the first half of the eighteenth century made an average of £3.43 per month, ranging from £2 to £6 according to position, skill, and responsibility. Peacetime wages were £3.10, those of war, £3.96. The transition from peace to war brought an average increase of 27.7 percent, whereas the reverse resulted in a decrease of 21.7 percent. This, as we shall see by comparison with the lesser skilled occupations, was a remarkably stable rate for maritime monetary wages. (See Appendix C.)

First among the less skilled, or "ship's people," as they were called, was the cook, whose extraordinary lack of skill was the bane of almost everyone on the ship. The cook made around £2 for his monthly labors, dipping down to £1.62 in peace and reaching £2.40 during war. The quartermaster, essentially an experienced or "smart" seaman, was given a couple of shillings over the wages of the common tars. He averaged about £2 monthly: £1.65 in peace and £2.58 in war.

Finally, we come to the largest category of maritime worker: the foremastman, able seaman, or common tar. He received average wages of £1.66 in the first half of the eighteenth century. The differential between peace and war was enormous: £1.46 in the former, increasing by fully 50 percent to £2.20 in the latter. The peacetime wages of foremastmen were remarkably low but stable, whereas war produced increases along with violent fluctuations. The scarcity of maritime labor, plus the added danger of impressment, resulted in the greater range and amount of wartime wages.[13] Owners and masters of merchant ships, eager to reduce the wages that constituted shipping's greatest expense, often, when the end of a war seemed near, made their seamen agree that "in case the Warr should cease or a peace be made between England and France before the sd Voyage was ended then the sd Mariners were to have no

[13] For a year-to-year breakdown of wage rates by occupation in the merchant shipping industry, see Marcus Rediker, "Society and Culture among Anglo-American Deep Sea Sailors, 1700–1750," Ph.D. diss., University of Pennsylvania, 1982, 318–28. On war and wages, see Robert Crosfeild, *England's Glory Revived* (London, 1693).

more Wages or Salary per month than should at that time be given for the remainder of the Term."[14]

The "people" of the merchant service – cooks, quartermasters, common tars – earned a mean wage of £1.47 in times of peace, £2.23 in war. The outbreak of war portended a 50 percent increase; the signing of a peace treaty sent wages plunging by more than a third. Officers made 77.6 percent more than the people in war and 101.9 percent more in peace. The conditions of war modified the maritime wage structure, producing significantly greater equality among officers and men. Yet there were limits. Throughout the 1700–50 period, the men made only half as much as their officers, and their wage rates were much less stable. Thus did the lower end of the seafaring laboring hierarchy bear the greatest portion of the risks, uncertainties, and insecurities of the early eighteenth-century Atlantic wage economy. The material standards of the common seaman's life vacillated sharply between periods of war and peace. The sailor, through his wages, absorbed many of the shocks of an unstable, expansive capitalist economy.

Further, it is important to note that there was no long-term secular increase in seamen's wages in the first half of the eighteenth century, either for officers or for men. In fact, given the moderate inflation of the period, it would seem that the real wages of seamen were falling. The decline was part of a longer trend, spanning the period 1450–1750, that affected most English working people. In the American colonies, urban workers seem to have experienced a measure of stability and perhaps a slight increase in real wages between 1700 and 1750. The same was true for London workingmen, who witnessed a small rise in real wages during the same period. Yet the overall picture of the merchant shipping industry in this era is one in which wages were stagnant or slightly falling in real terms. This overarching reality set the stage for intense and various struggles over the amount and form of the wage of the maritime worker.[15]

---

[14] Jones v. Cleare, HCA 24/130 (1713).

[15] Gary B. Nash, *The Urban Crucible: Social Change, Political Consciousness, and the Origins of the American Revolution* (Cambridge, Mass., 1979), 115, 392–4; B. A. Holderness, *Pre-Industrial England: Economy and Society, 1500–1750* (London, 1976), 21; D. C. Coleman, *The Economy of England, 1450–1750* (London, 1977), 102.

A crucial part of the "social wage," the full set of life-maintaining resources available to seamen, was the advance that many deep-sea sailors got on their pay. The longer the voyage they signed on for, the larger the advance was likely to be. The East India Company, whose voyages frequently lasted for two years, usually gave two months' pay in advance. Other long-distance sailings, to the West Indies, North America, or the Mediterranean, offered a front of one month's wages. Seamen used advance pay in numerous ways: to pay off debts accumulated while ashore, to fund a rakish binge before taking to sea for a year, or to help sustain a family during the impending absence of a wage earner.[16]

The advance system was designed primarily to guarantee the labor supply in an industry so harsh that it occasionally had trouble attracting workers. Yet the system, from the point of view of capital, did not work well in periods of extensive labor scarcity, and sometimes it did not work at all. Jack Cremer reported that as soon as his crew bound to Leghorn had received one month's wages at Gravesend, six men immediately deserted. Captain Samuel Bromley, who gave advances to seamen in both money and bills of credit in order to secure enough workers to get home to London, reported to his owners in 1701: "Now since giving them money & bills two are deserted." Advances plus desertion equaled a means of getting ready money for no work.[17]

A variation on the advance system paid seamen from the moment they signed on with a ship lying at harbor. But this arrangement also changed according to the general availability of labor. William Bevill testified before the High Court of Admiralty in 1704 that "it was and is the constant usage and custom within the port of London in time of War for Mariners to be allowed full pay from the time of their first comeing on board or entering the ships service."[18] Edward Barlow explained the peacetime procedure: "from the time that [seamen] are shipped on board and all the time they lie in the river till they depart from Gravesend, they have but half of their pay

---

[16] Child v. Clark, HCA 24/127 (1702).
[17] *Ramblin' Jack,* 129; Samuel Bromley to Thomas Ekines and Samuel Mitchell, HCA 24/127 (Apr. 14, 1701).
[18] Bevill v. James, HCA 24/128 (1704).

that they are shipped for a month . . . and that day you go from Gravesend you enter into your whole pay always, your half-pay being paid to you the day before you go from Gravesend."[19] This arrangement, too, was apparently negotiable. Several sailors from the *Anne,* for example, claimed that they were told by their shipowners in 1717, a year of peace, "that they should receive whole pay all the time that the said Ship should lye in the River Thames."[20]

Similarly, seamen received half-pay when they were quarantined in a foreign port. And when seamen were stranded in a frozen harbor, which was not uncommon in the North Sea and Baltic trades, they were to receive "winter money," usually 30–50s., "for the loss of the time they continue[d] frozen up." These were among the many supplements to formal wages.[21]

A second major part of the seaman's living wage was his "customary usage" in the "necessaries of life": his share of the food and drink dispensed on board the ship. This "usage" was subject to numerous interpretations and sometimes became the focus of fierce argument and contest, not least because there was a direct relationship between the amount and quality of victuals given to the crew and the overall profitability of the voyage. This part of the wage relation sometimes pitted profits against human life. As an English tar said of the Royal Navy, but could as easily have observed of the merchant shipping industry, "A hot country, stinking Meat, and maggoty Bread, with the noisom and poisonous Scent of the Bilge Water, have made many a brave English sailor food for Crabs and sharks."[22] Edward Barlow thought that naval vessels were "better victualled than most merchant ships," but in any case, captains, mates, stewards, pursers – in short, anyone responsible for giving out food and drink – were almost universally detested for their conniving and exploitive ways.[23] Some gave

[19] *Barlow's Journal,* 140.

[20] Clark v. Westerdale, HCA 24/132 (1718). See also Ebrard v. Joyeaux, HCA 24/131 (1716); Lowry v. Toben, HCA 24/132 (1719).

[21] Crayton v. Hunter, HCA 24/133 (1720); Cunningham v. Donaldson, HCA 24/132 (1719).

[22] An English Sailor, *The State of the Navy Consider'd in Relation to Victualling* (London, 1699).

[23] *Barlow's Journal,* 426.

only fourteen ounces of food for the allotted pound; others served beer "as bad as water bewitched" or food so bad, some seamen sneered, that the rats would not eat it. John Baltharpe put the matter simply in verse:

> Purser, Steward, Mate, all three
> I wish them hang'd upon a Tree.[24]

In 1722 pirate John Philps called John Wingfield "a Super Cargo Son of a B – – – h" and claimed that "he starved the Men, and that it was such Dogs as he as put men on Pyrating."[25] Seamen regularly voiced complaints similar to those made by the crew of the *Mansell* in 1728. Their captain had "no reason to put his Marriners to short allowance w[hi]ch he began three days after he left Lisbon & continued it all the Voyage to the grievous hurt of his Men & his Government on board his ship."[26]

Occasionally merchant captains had to put seamen to "short allowance" in order to make the food supply last through a voyage that had been lengthened by contrary winds, storms, or currents. Many captains, of course, seized upon this excuse to save on expenditures of food and drink. When deliberately kept short of victuals, seamen seem to have been technically entitled to receive "pinch-gut money," a designated monthly sum to supplement wages. Seamen also claimed their traditional right to fresh, as opposed to salt-preserved, victuals while in port. Although the custom varied according to time and place, standard fare included one pound of meat – salt beef (called "Irish horse"), pork, bacon, or at times fish – four times a week, with additional portions of cheese, peas, butter, and biscuit, and rations of wine, brandy, small beer, or rum, all of which had to be of reasonable quality. Fresh provisions were to be given whenever possible. This shifting set of standards ad-

---

[24] Ibid., 51, 127, 339; John Baltharpe, *The Straights Voyage, or, St. Davids Poem*, ed. J. S. Bromley (1671; reprint Oxford, 1959), 38.

[25] "Proceedings of the Court held on the Coast of Africa upon Trying of 100 Pirates taken by his Ma[jes]ties Ship *Swallow*," HCA 1/99 (1722), f. 102. A supercargo was the merchant's official representative on board the ship. As the international market chain became more orderly, the need for a supercargo to police the merchant's goods declined.

[26] Gray v. Travis, MASS ADM (1728), f. 56.

ded up to "the usual Custom of Entertaining Mariners on board of Merchant Ships."[27]

Seamen actively sought to supplement this part of the living wage with extra food procured by fishing and hunting. Sailors in general and Scottish tar Alexander Selkirk in particular were, after all, the models for Daniel Defoe's *Robinson Crusoe*. Perhaps the era's most sophisticated seafarers in this respect were the buccaneers and privateers, many of whom were extremely literate and left journals and diaries that were, in one crucial respect, detailed manuals of survival. Drawing upon the knowledge gained from the native populations of Latin America, Africa, or the East Indies, these seamen endlessly catalogued what could and could not be eaten and how various catches could be prepared.[28] Turtle, for instance, could be boiled, roasted, fried, baked, or stewed. Booby birds, privateersman William Funnel noted, "taste very Fishy; and if you do not salt them well before you eat them, they will make you sick."[29] Seamen also caught and ate fish of all varieties – albacore, catfish, mullet, smelt, rockfish, grouper, dolphin, snapper – as well as shellfish and even sharks. Nathaniel Uring, on an early-eighteenth-century voyage, lamented the "Loss of our Fish-gigg," which "was a very great Misfortune to us, having no more on Board, and therefore could strike no more Fish, by which means we lost many a good meal during the Voyage."[30] Other meals, perhaps in more of an emergency, could be culled from seals, sea cows, penguins, and wild vegetation of all types. Probably no one in the eighteenth

[27] F. N. L. Poynter, ed., *The Journal of James Yonge* (Hamden, Conn., 1963), 48; Baltharpe, *Straights Voyage*, 23; Seamen v. Powell, MASS ADM (1732), f. 129; Seamen v. Barry, SC ADM (1729), ff. 713–14; Charlton v. Dover, HCA 24/139 (1738). Struggles over the distribution of food and drink helped to create a distinctly egalitarian tendency among seamen when it came to dividing up shares. See Chapter 5 of this book.

[28] See, for examples, the works by John Wood, Bartholomew Sharp, and Captain Crowley in William Hacke, ed., *A Collection of Original Voyages* (London, 1699), and especially William Dampier, "A New Voyage round the World," in Dampier, ed., *A Collection of Voyages* (London, 1729); Edward Cooke, *A Voyage to the South Sea* (London, 1712); and Woodes Rogers, *A Cruising Voyage Round the World*, ed. G. E. Manwaring (1712; reprint London, 1928).

[29] William Funnell, *A Voyage Round the World* (London, 1707), 10. See also *Journal of James Yonge*, 54, and G. E. Manwaring, ed., *The Diary of Henry Teonge* (1825; reprint London, 1927), 146.

[30] *The Voyages and Travels of Captain Nathaniel Uring*, ed. Alfred Dewar (1726; reprint London, 1928), 23.

century was better steeled in the crafty art of self-preservation than the seaman. Many of his skills and much of his knowledge developed as ways to escape the exploitive nature of the wage system, especially as it related to the near-dictatorial control of food and drink on board the ship.

Many seamen added to their wages through embezzlement, taking a cut of the product that their labors carried to market.[31] Probably the most popular item pilfered was alcohol. Seamen were frequently sued in admiralty courts by their masters and shipowners for the "embezelm[en]t of Liquors," for drinking wine or rum from often deliberately damaged casks. But seamen also took other commodities, in particular East India goods (which provoked strict regulation and punishment from the company), sugar, and tobacco. The quantities of such pilferings seem to have been relatively small: a few handkerchiefs, a few pounds of produce. But given the opportunity occasionally presented, for example, by shipwreck, seamen might "committt very great Ravage and Plunder." In 1713 they "imbezeled or carried away part of [the] provisions and several goods" of the *Lady Mary*. They also took "gold, silver, diamonds, jewels, precious stones" and "other goods and merchandizes," as new legislation announced in 1734.[32]

Embezzlement, it must be stressed, was nearly universal aboard ship. The captain, officers, seamen, boys – almost every-

---

[31] The seminal study of embezzlement, to which I am much indebted, is Peter Linebaugh's "Socking: Tobacco Porters, The Hogshead, and Excise," which will appear in *The London Hanged: Crime and Civil Society in the Eighteenth Century* (forthcoming). Some of Linebaugh's comments on embezzlement can be found in E. P. Thompson, Peter Linebaugh, and Douglas Hay, "Eighteenth Century Crime, Popular Movements, and Social Control," *Bulletin for the Society of the Study of Labour History* 25 (1972), 9–17. Some of these ideas have been discussed in John Rule, *The Experience of-Labour in Eighteenth-Century English Industry* (New York, 1981), chap. 5.

[32] Adams v. Barlow, MASS ADM (1723), f. 163; Pattison v. Beesley, HCA 24/129 (1709); Wood v. Germain, HCA 24/136 (1729); Hunter v. Hill, HCA 24/131 (1717); Pim v. Goodloe, HCA 24/131 (1717); King v. Jesson, HCA 24/133 (1721); Chapman v. Hudson, HCA 24/138 (1734); Greengrass v. Brown, HCA 24/138 (1735); Hillier v. Burnett, HCA 24/134 (1724); Warner v. Stephens, HCA 24/130 (1713); Information of Phillip Peers, HCA 1/54 (1717), f. 48; "An Act to settle how far Owners of Ships shall be answerable for the Acts of Masters or Mariners" (7 George II, c. 15, 1734), in Sir Thomas Parker, *The Laws of Shipping and Insurance, with a Digest of Adjudged Cases* (London, 1775), reprinted in *British Maritime Cases* (Abingdon, Oxfordshire, 1978), vol. 24, 127.

one took a cut. The area of control defined by one's labor produced the prospects for embezzlement. Boatswains dealt in hemp and cordage, carpenters in wood, gunners in metals and weapons, captains and mates in almost anything and everything. Indeed, the frauds perpetuated by captains, pursers, and supercargoes, denying seamen their proper usage in food and drink, can be seen as a kind of embezzlement from above. Although it is impossible to establish the extent to which embezzlement served to supplement monetary wages, it is clear that it was widely practiced and that the goods procured were considered a fundamental part of the social wage.[33]

Closely related to the contest over access to the product was a struggle over the use of space on the ship. The matter was summed up well by historian Ralph Davis: "widespread was the crew's customary right – its legal standing is very doubtful – to carry some cargo on their own account, possibly in their own quarters, but sometimes occupying part of the hold, freight free."[34] Richard B. Morris made the same point: "In addition to stipulated wages and food, the sailor customarily had the right to ship on board a small amount of cargo for himself, both outgoing and returning, or in lieu thereof the freight payable to the ship in the amount of cargo which they might have embarked."[35] This custom apparently dated back to the greatest maritime code of the medieval period, the Laws of Oleron (1194), which, in the words of historian Timothy J. Runyan, guaranteed that the seamen "could use part of the storage space to freight a cargo of his choice (*mareage*), or he could take a portion of the general freightage as his share of the profits from the sailing venture."[36] The carrying of cargo as part of the wage took two major forms: "privilege" and "venture."

---

[33] Ned Ward, *The Wooden World Dissected: In the Character of a Ship of War* (1708; reprint London, 1756), 49, 58.

[34] Davis, *English Shipping*, 147.

[35] Morris, *Government and Labor*, 238. See also C. Ernest Fayle, *A Short History of the World's Shipping Industry* (London, 1933), 71, 96, 97.

[36] Timothy J. Runyan, "Ships and Mariners in Later Medieval England," *Journal of British Studies* 16 (1977), 15. Article XVIII in the *Black Book of English Admiralty*, the summary of English medieval law and custom, stipulated that "mariners may embark a small quantity of freight on their own responsibility": see Sanborn, *Origins of Early English Maritime and Commercial Law*, 66.

Privilege was a multiform arrangement that, by the eighteenth century, seems most often to have benefited the officers of merchant vessels. The extent and nature of privilege depended upon the specific voyage, the commodity carried, and negotiations among the owner, master, and crew. Masters of merchantmen were entitled to the greatest privilege, or "clapleighton," as they sometimes called it. It was customary "for Mates of Ships or Vessels who use the Holland Trade to have the profitt and advantage of their Cabbins allow'd to them for a passenger who shall make use thereof." Masters, mates, carpenters, and surgeons involved in the slave trade usually got to carry one or more Africans as privilege, taking the slave's fare and provisions from the ship's stores. Carpenter John Scroge in 1731 arranged his wages so that he was able to carry one slave and two parrots to the West Indies "freight free."[37] Other mates, like Nicholas Worsdale, who was experienced "on the Coast of Angola, where he had been already two voyages," articled to receive £4 for every £100 worth of slaves delivered by his vessel in the Caribbean.[38] Similarly, surgeons in the "Guinea Trade" often received monetary wages plus a reward of "5s. for every Negro delivered alive att Jamaica."[39]

Other arrangements permitted mates "two Barrels in the Hold Customary Privilege" or "ye priviledge of three Barrels out & home, & a Doz[en] of Geese, a Shoat or Sheep." Some agreements gave "half a Ton of Logwood Privilege."[40] The East India Company, according to J. H. Parry, allowed about 5 percent of its cargo space in each ship for "private trade": "The captain naturally got the lion's share; but every man in a company ship, from captain to cabinboy, had his 'privilege,' his allotted space, according to his rank, for goods which he might purchase at one end and sell at the other on his private account." This produced a chronic conflict between the com-

---

[37] Forster v. Van Leer, MASS ADM (1720), f. 62; Dawson v. Latham, HCA 24/135 (1726); Patrick v. Smith, HCA 24/137 (1732); Wiseman v. Cater, HCA 24/127 (1702); Scroge v. Stewart, HCA 24/136 (1731).

[38] Worsdale v. Barry, SC ADM (1729), f. 657.

[39] Thornburgh v. Berry, HCA 24/127 (1703).

[40] Serjant v. Coffin, MASS ADM (1727), f. 21; Gardiner v. Tompkin, MASS ADM (1727), f. 27; Bennett v. Benny, MASS ADM (1727), f. 19; Arno v. Robbins, MASS ADM (1742), f. 102; Littleton v. James, MASS ADM (1718), ff. 9–10; Seamen v. Neal, CO 5/1311 (1698).

pany and the crew over space, and seamen logically preferred to trade on their own account.[41] It is unclear how widespread customary privilege was in the early eighteenth century, though it probably was not as common as it had been in the medieval period. All that can be said with certainty is that officers had enforceable legal claims to privilege. The ship's people, no matter what the law said, almost certainly interpreted this custom in ways that gave an additional dimension to their wages.

The venture or "adventure" system was available to all crew members who were willing and able to pay freight charges on small shipments of their own. Edward Barlow's venture was "to help bear out my wage": "if I carried a small venture in some sort of Goods I might gain a little money by it, intending if it were possible to get myself a little money beforehand that I might drive some trade or way to live ashore and leave the sea before I came to be old . . . and if I could but accomplish so much it would be for my good."[42] Seamen padded their wages by selling "on their own account" commodities from one part of the world that were scarce and exotic in another. It was, after all, their labors that had created the additional value. Captain Theodore Boucher argued in 1719 that sailors stood to make 50–70 percent on items bought in Virginia and carried to market in London.[43]

Ramblin' Jack Cremer, with customs officers in hot pursuit, "youst to goe of an evening with a half dozzen of Florence Wine & Small things, and land at Wappin' old Stayers [stairs] and go the way from White Chappell Mount to Shoardidge Church all through fields and brick-feilds" to sell his venture.[44] The East India and other trading companies sought to limit such private commerce. Captain Thomas Barry in 1729 made seaman Christopher Harvey "open his Breeches from which he took two

[41] J. H. Parry, *Trade and Dominion: The European Overseas Empires in the Eighteenth Century* (New York, 1971), 64.

[42] *Barlow's Journal*, 204, 194.

[43] Parker v. Boucher, HCA 24/132 (1719). It should also be mentioned that the space question had another dimension. The greater the cargo carried, the smaller the living area for the crew. See Slush, *Navy Royal*, 27.

[44] *Ramblin' Jack*, 126, 175–6.

strip'd India Handkerchiefs."[45] Such "small things" made a big difference in the wages of eighteenth-century seamen.

Now let us turn from the various elements of the wage to the contests over the wage, to the complex range and processes of negotiations whose results determined the actual content – monetary or otherwise – of the seaman's well-being. Such negotiations began the moment the seaman hopped aboard a ship at anchor and asked "whither she was bound and whether she wanted any hands and what wages her Master gave."[46]

An important, even if amorphous and, to our eyes, somewhat inaccessible, reality lay behind this set of questions. This was the broad, diffuse, informal network of experience, knowledge, and reputation that was central to life and work at sea in the eighteenth century. There were, in fact, two networks that carried very different kinds of information. One purveyed information about ship masters and their "customary usage" of sailors; the other carried reports of the discipline, skills, and behavior of maritime workers. The former was constructed by and for seamen, the latter by and for ship owners, merchants, and captains.

The seaman's network took shape within and around the port city institutions most basic to the seafaring life: the ship, the docks, the brothel, the jail, and the pub or tavern. There were, in Port Royal, Jamaica, and every other port "Publick Houses" that entertained "Lewd dissolute fellows," frequently seamen searching for a voyage, passing through, or just deserted from a merchant or naval vessel. Such places, at least in Jamaica, served as free and open spaces for seamen, places where the "whole Mobb of the Towne" was "ready on all Occasions, to knock any of the Officers of ye Kings Ships on the Head, who shall attempt doeing their Duty [of impressment] there." Civil magistrates, Admiral Edward Vernon claimed, were of no help, since they had no control over the "dissolute rabble." So "dissolute" was this particular "Mobb" that it rescued a soon-to-be-hanged pirate "from under the Gibbet" in 1716 and then turned its collec-

[45] Worsdale v. Barry, SC ADM (1729), f. 703; King v. Norton, MASS ADM, (1721), ff. 78–80.
[46] Gittus v. Bowles, HCA 24/132 (1718).

tive attention to successfully retaking the pirate's ship from the clutches of the Royal Navy.[47]

The very success of pirates between 1716 and 1726 depended upon their access to the information that flowed through this informal network. Edward Vernon pointed out in 1720 that piratical excursions in the West Indies were difficult to stop, "for the daily intelligence they have from [Jamaica] will caution them, to keep them out of the way of our Ships."[48] Alexander Spotswood, looking for a safe passage to England but fearing revenge for his bloody part in clearing the Virginia shores of pirates, told the Board of Trade in 1724 that he would have to go to some port far to the north, "where neither Master nor Sailors know me, & so [that I] may possibly escape the knowledge of ye pirates."[49]

Seamen used this same network to search for safe vessels, good voyages, plentiful wages and provisions, and, perhaps most importantly of all, decent and fair masters of vessels. As Edward Barlow commented, seamen searched for that captain who had "the clearest report for his civil and honest carriage towards his men and servants." But such masters were often difficult to find, as Barlow himself explained when he took an East India voyage under a commander who "had none of the best commendation for kindness or civility to his men." The warning about the captain turned out to be essentially correct, and Barlow later wished he had "gone in another ship for forty shillings the month less" rather than proceed with this "very unfortunate" voyage.[50]

The ability to make use of the network was at times effectively limited by labor gluts, the sluggishness, or stagnation of the Atlantic economy. Sometimes berths were so scarce that sailors had no choice but to sail with a master reputed to be something less than "civil and honest." Such would appear to

---

[47] Edward Vernon to Josiah Burchett, Oct. 28, 1719, Edward Vernon Letterbook, 1719–20, BL, Add. Ms. 40811; "A Proclamation prohibiting the Entertainment of Sailors belonging to his Majesty's Ships and Preventing the Desertion of Such Sailors," CO 5/1321 (1728).

[48] Edward Vernon to Josiah Burchett, Nov. 7, 1720, Edward Vernon Letterbook, 1720, BL, Add. Ms. 40812.

[49] Alexander Spotswood to the Board of Trade, CO 5/1319 (June 16, 1724), ff. 190–2.

[50] *Barlow's Journal*, 352, 386.

have been the case when Gouche Certiss boarded the *Mermaid* in 1734 and quickly informed captain Hugh Crawford, apparently within full earshot of the whole crew, that he knew that the commander "had killed a man on board the said Ship a former voyage, but that he should not kill him."[51] Brutal captains were clearly, even if not always effectively, targeted within the seaman's network of information and reputation.

Ship owners, merchants, and masters used a similar network of preferment and patronage. Part of its operation was revealed in the frustrated words of Jack Cremer, searching in 1714 for work after the War of the Spanish Succession had ended and the navy demobilized: "the best Sailors ever known, had but 22s./6d. per Month, with strong recomindations for theair good behaviour and honesty."[52] Ship captains tried to establish a means to recommend the most industrious, trustworthy, and disciplined seamen and to exclude troublemakers who obstructed voyages, were likely to desert, had mutinous or piratical tendencies, or took cuts of the product as a supplement to wages. The use of certificates of recommendation, which represented an early form of blacklisting, was probably not very successful except in times of extreme labor abundance. The extent of their use is unknown. They were, however, part of a larger network serving capital, which itself was the logical and functional antithesis of the network built and used by the common tar.

Both networks were literally shaped by the transatlantic economy, more particularly by the disparate and diverse labor markets linked, used, and exploited by the merchant shipping industry. As capital and labor moved in increasingly international orbits in the early modern period, Anglo-American seamen sailed in "the Russian Fleet, ships of Europe, even Spanish Privateers." William Dampier noted in the late seventeenth century that "Our seamen are apt to have great Notions of I know not what profit and Advantage to be had in serving the Mogul

---

[51] Certiss v. Crawford, HCA 24/138 (1734); N. Bostorh to Lords of Admiralty, ADM 1/1462 (1699); Powell v. Hardwicke, HCA 24/138 (1738). Francis Rogers in 1704 noted the reputation of a Captain Carleton, who had "killed one, 2 or more men very barbarously" and who had thereafter suffered from "a wounded conscience." See "The Journal of Francis Rogers," in *Three Sea Journals in Stuart Times*, ed. Bruce Ingram (London, 1936), 275.

[52] *Ramblin' Jack*, 66, 116.

[of India]; nor do they want for fine stories to encourage one another to it." A tar's skills, as Barnaby Slush indicated, brought "ready Money, in almost every Corner of the Globe."[53]

Britain's overseas colonies, as suggested in Chapter 2, made up the most significant – and to sailors, the most advantageous – of these regional labor markets. Charleston, the Chesapeake, Philadelphia, New York, Boston, Port Royal, Bridgetown, and many lesser ports were the sites for numerous wage struggles, primarily because of the scarcity of free wage labor in general and maritime labor in particular in these colonial ports. Jack Cremer, like so many others who arrived in Boston, "wanted to run away, [there] being great wages given for Sailors, and they were very skarce."[54] Desertion abounded throughout the colonies, not least because of the discerning choices of seamen and the pressing practices of the Royal Navy. Captain Nathaniel Uring noted in 1712 that Jamaican seamen refused to sail to Europe "for fear of being imprest." It was often "difficult to provide such a number of Men as was proper" for certain voyages.[55]

When the seamen of labor-scarce markets decided to sail to Europe, they frequently made their employers pay a hefty price for their services. Sailors negotiated a lump-sum payment for the "run home to London" or some other European port. Such wages were available at various times in almost every port, depending on the local labor supply and the patterns and rhythms of commodity shipment. Wages by the run ranged from £6 all the way up to £30 for voyages completed in an average of six weeks. The most common payment was £10 or £12, and frequently seamen negotiated wages of £10 and ten gallons of rum.[56] As Daniel Lawlore testified before the High

---

[53] James Edward Oglethorpe, "The Sailor's Advocate" (1728) in J. S. Bromley, ed., *The Manning of the Royal Navy: Selected Public Pamphlets, 1693–1873* (London, 1974), 73; Dampier, "New Voyage," 507; Slush, *Navy Royal*, 92.

[54] *Ramblin' Jack*, 87; Arthur Pierce Middleton, *Tobacco Coast: A Maritime History of Chesapeake Bay in the Colonial Period* (Newport News, Va., 1953), 266.

[55] *Voyages and Travels of Captain Nathaniel Uring*, 165.

[56] Smith v. Gillebrand, HCA 24/128 (1706); Clark v. Gilhamas, HCA 24/129 (1707); Jenkinson v. *Barclay Castle*, HCA 24/130 (1713); Vaughn v. Rattray, HCA 24/131 (1715); Lone v. *Great Cyrus*, HCA 24/131 (1715); Danedge v. Cuthbert, HCA 24/131 (1716); Corbett v. *Craven*, HCA 24/131 (1715); Boson v. Hanover, HCA 24/132 (1718); West v. King, HCA 24/132 (1719); Crafts v. Darby, HCA 24/132 (1719); Deverall v. Pierson, HCA 24/132 (1719); Lewis v. Beck, HCA 24/132 (1719); Clipperton v. Hanover, HCA

Court of Admiralty in 1706, "in time of Warr English Seamen, her Maj[est]ies subjects are difficult to be met with in parts beyond the Seas, and as Wages now go, 'tis usuall, and common to allow Men serving in such Capacities, by the Voyage, or for the Runn from Virginia to any port in England" £12 or more.[57] Around 1717 Jack Cremer got £12 and six gallons of rum for the run from Boston to London.[58] And as Captain Richard Chapman wrote to a merchant, a Mr. Hudson, in 1729: I "cant hier a man by the Mounth but all by the Run home. [T]his gives for the run 10 or 12 pound."[59] Seamen creatively employed a wage form normally used in shorter, more predictable voyages and gained immensely by their resourcefulness.

The Act for the Better Regulation and Government of the Merchants Service, passed in 1729, seems to have been an attack on this particular form of the maritime wage. According to the wages by the run recorded in the High Court of Admiralty, this sort of payment for labor was most common in the late 1720s, particularly in 1728 and 1729, just before the act was passed. As the act stated, when merchant vessels were brimming with cargo and ready to leave port, seamen would "refuse to proceed with them, without coming to new Agreements for

---

24/132 (1719); Hepburn v. ?, HCA 24/132 (1718); Finch v. Charles, HCA 24/133 (1720); Shaw v. Boyd, HCA 24/133 (1723); Rowles v. Kerfoot, HCA 24/133 (1724); Judge v. Wilson, HCA 24/135 (1727); Cook v. *Henry & Jane*, HCA 24/135 (1727); Leavell v. Whitaker, HCA 24/136 (1728); Higgon v. Mathews, HCA 24/136 (1729); Harding v. Malthus, HCA 24/136 (1729); Clymer v. *Lively*, HCA 24/136 (1729); Hansell v. Wilkinson, HCA 24/136 (1728); Cruse v. McArthur, HCA 24/136 (1730); Fentiman v. Kittle, HCA 24/136 (1730); Linam v. Chapman, HCA 24/136 (1730); Calhoun v. Stewart, HCA 24/136 (1730); Butterworth v. Smith, HCA 24/136 (1730); Ward v. Corne, HCA 24/136 (1730); Lewis v. Showers, HCA 24/136 (1730); Mahoney v. Payne, HCA 24/136 (1731); Ellis v. Randall, HCA 24/136 (1731); Wensley v. Papps, HCA 24/136 (1731); Cecill v. Ralls, HCA 24/136 (1731); Rook v. Hodgson, HCA 24/138 (1735); Vincent v. Curtis, HCA 24/139 (1736); Wilkinson v. Haskins, HCA 24/139 (1736); Webber v. Baggatt, HCA 24/139 (1734); Thompson v. Hanton, HCA 24/139 (1736); Charlton v. Dover, HCA 24/139 (1738); Bevan v. *George*, HCA 15/42 (1741); Mountier v. *Charming Jenny*, HCA 15/42 (1741); Macquam v. Anstell, HCA 15/43 (1744); Deposition of Bartholomew Gould, HCA 1/19 (1735). It should be noted that the dates just listed indicate when the cases were heard in court, not when the wage agreements were made.

57 Lawlore v. Bassett, HCA 24/128 (1706).
58 *Ramblin' Jack*, 116.
59 Richard Chapman to Mr. Hudson, HCA 24/136 (May 19, 1729).

increasing their Wages, and many of them will leave their Ships and Vessels, and not proceed on their Voiage." Such strategies on the part of seamen not only held up the flow of commodities but also – since wages were the major expense of shipping – cut deeply into merchants' profits.[60] The act of 1729 was part of a continuing initiative on the part of employers to control the autonomous mobility of maritime workers, and thereby to enhance the accumulation of capital.

The nature of the voyage, as mentioned earlier, was another chief and persistent focus of wage conflict. Once again the interests of the ship owner, merchant, and master diverged dramatically from those of the crew. Early-eighteenth-century shipping, responding to irregular, weather-dependent production schedules and enormous distances between international buying and selling markets, confronted numerous risks and uncertainties that, in turn, created among merchants and ship captains a need for flexibility in transport activities. These capitalist traders sought to maintain the prerogative to fix a ship's voyage in any way that the master and merchant "should think most advantageous." Captain William Wrougham told his people in 1718 that "he must go to Norway & that if he had a mind to go to the East or West Indies or any other p[ar]ts of the Universe he wou'd or cou'd make them go with him."[61] Many seamen begged to differ with such a claim and often asserted contrary concerns. Seaman Lemon Bacon complained in 1723 that his voyage had been changed so many times that he "despairs of ever seeing his Country & Relations again."[62]

Jack Cremer frequently noted seamen's efforts to "begin a new Contract" with each alteration of the ship's course. On one voyage his "first Mate, an old Surly Jack Tar, put all the men in mind to raise their wages theair to 30s./pr Month" if they "went further abroad" after reaching Leghorn, and "to be paid every Second delivering port soe much Starling for a Twelve month certain." The alteration of a later voyage, to pass through Charleston, South Carolina, "made our Contract Voide; but wee young fellows made noe Objections. But our old brute of a

[60] "Act for the Better Regulation . . . ," HCA 30/999. See also Rane v. Clarke, HCA 24/136 (1730).
[61] Ellis v. Wrougham, HCA 24/132 (1718).
[62] Bacon v. Boyce, MASS ADM (1723), f. 164.

matte directly told us we wear [were] all free men to Leave the Ship, & we might get good Voages and Wages." Soon, Cremer commented, "We was all Separated, and every one took his Voage [as] he liked."[63]

As a general rule, seamen, like Ramblin' Jack's mates, pressed to renegotiate the wage with almost every violation or alteration of the originally stipulated voyage. Some sailors got an extra "months pay" to "confirm this agreement" after a change. Other seamen got 5s. "added to each Person's Wages." Others got even more money, especially if the deviation produced new risks to the crew. As a sailor said before the High Court of Admiralty in 1702:

the Voiage from Jamaica to the Bay of Campeachy was and is looked upon and esteemed to be very dangerous and such Mariners as proceed or go the said voyage run great hazard and risque of their lives or of being taken and made Slaves by the Spaniards, in consideration of which danger and risque it was and is usuall and customary to give and directly allow such Mariners greater wages, than in other voyages, when they return directly from Jamaica to England.[64]

Such trips to Campeche were usually arranged when a sufficient cargo was not available in Jamaica, and many an agreement was negotiated to pick up logwood on the western shore of the Caribbean. A master was often forced by the courts to give "Consideration" to seamen after a deviation, "so much more as any others get in the like alteration and voyage." The captain could be sure that his seamen would know how much more they were entitled to receive.[65]

The reasons that lay behind these alterations were not lost on maritime workers. Seamen complained that they were due higher wages after a modified voyage because "the Owners of the said Ship have thereby gaind and acquird very great profitt & Advantage" or because the changes "were very profitable and advantageous to the owners of the said Ship and they were very considerable gainers thereby."[66] Seamen thus demon-

---

[63] *Ramblin' Jack*, 76, 74–5, 110, 111.
[64] Duce v. Smith, MASS ADM (1729), f. 67; Seamen v. Furrs, MASS ADM (1733), f. 142; Warden v. Searle, HCA 24/127 (1702).
[65] Seamen v. Spatman, MASS ADM (1722), f. 103; Miller v. Howard, MASS ADM (1723), f. 147; Hutton v. Seamen, MASS ADM (1719), f. 27.
[66] Peterson v. Mackley, HCA 24/128 (1706); Warden v. Searle, HCA 24/127 (1702).

strated their understanding of the ways in which their labors enriched their employers.

Seamen not only resorted to the courts to press their advantage upon a change; they stopped work, deserted or threatened to desert, or even "threttend blows" with the captain or officers. When Captain William Cannum refashioned his route, his seamen refused to proceed until he made "a new agreement with them . . . [which the captain] rather than to overthrow or delay the Ship's voyage was compelled and forced to submit to." Such forced submission was, of course, much less likely when a captain was "in a Country where he could have had men enough if his whole Ships Company had left him."[67]

Many sailors, like Jack Cremer's fellow tars, aspired to be "free men" when, after an alteration, they landed in a place where maritime workers were scarce. They incessantly sued in court for "liberation" from ships that had veered from their original voyages. But seamen found the vice-admiralty courts much less sympathetic on this score than regarding the payment of monetary wages. Judges in the colonies were extremely unlikely to "liberate" sailors from their ships, even when the tars' charges were just and accurate. As Richard B. Morris wrote: "Where there was a serious deviation without their consent the seamen were entitled to their discharge, but in practice the vice-admiralty courts were reluctant to enforce the letter of the law and did not construe shipping articles too strictly."[68] Thus the courts upheld the prerogatives of capital – despite the legality of the matter – enabling merchants and masters to respond as profitably as possible to international market opportunities.[69]

The Act for the Better Regulation and Government of the

---

[67] *Ramblin' Jack,* 157; Taylor v. Cannum, HCA 24/136 (1730); Wayte v. Davy, HCA 24/128 (1704).

[68] Morris, *Government and Labor,* 260.

[69] The following are examples of vice-admiralty judges granting seamen wages, usually because of a broken contract or an alteration, but refusing them liberation: Partridge v. Bennet, MASS ADM (1720), f. 59; Seamen v. Clarke, MASS ADM (1723), f. 134; Wallace v. Abbott, MASS ADM (1723), f. 152; Seamen v. Hirst, MASS ADM (1724), f. 209; Fielding v. Cleeland, MASS ADM (1729), ff. 70–1; Seamen v. Cornish, MASS ADM (1731), f. 97; Seamen v. Sanders, MASS ADM (1733), f. 133.

Merchants Service of 1729 limited such prerogatives in one crucial way. In an effort to stabilize the maritime labor supply, the act tried to eliminate problems, especially desertion, that flowed from the ambiguities in seafaring wage agreements. In so doing it formalized the wage contract and thereby reduced the captain's ability to take the vessel where he pleased. Once the voyage had been clearly specified, seamen had a greater chance to press in court for liberation if such contracts had been broken. Even though judges continued to deny many sailors their liberation, it is clear that the number of men set free after altered voyages increased after 1729.[70]

Sometimes, however, the courts did the very opposite of liberating the seaman, taking bold steps to guarantee the continued availability of his labor, even to the captain who had knowingly violated a contract. Seamen who had left the ship had their "Chest & Goods" taken back aboard the ship "for Security." Others were ordered to leave with the court a £5 bond as assurance that they would continue their voyages. Still others were "ordered by the Marshall of the Court" to be carried "to Gaol for Security of their fulfilling" the court's decree of persisting in a voyage. Some seamen were placed back aboard a vessel even when their captain, they insisted, had threatened to shoot them, much "to the terrour of their Lives."[71]

Another conflict, closely related to voyage alteration, centered on the captain's practice of lingering in port in order to get a full or proper cargo. Seamen often tried both to specify in their contracts the duration of a voyage and to minimize the amount of time to be spent in port, in large part because they frequently received no wages or necessaries while at anchor. To add to their wages during "dead time," sailors went ashore as casual laborers, usually as stevedores or rope walkers on the docks, or took short voyages, lasting two or three weeks, in the West Indian or North American shuttle trades. The interests of

[70] "Act for the Better Regulation . . . ," HCA 30/999; Perry v. Tyng, MASS ADM (1731), f. 101.
[71] Cooke v. Purvis, MASS ADM (1720), f. 53; Seamen v. Sanders, MASS ADM (1733), f. 133; Fonds v. Seamen, MASS ADM (1730), f. 83; Newby v. Odar, MASS ADM (1727), f. 20; Seamen v. Odar, MASS ADM (1728), f. 37; Foy v. Seamen, MASS ADM (1727), f. 33; Seamen v. Templeton, MASS ADM (1728), f. 48; Roberts v. Kipping, MASS ADM (1726), f. 6.

capital and labor once again came into conflict over the management of the voyage.[72]

Seamen needed money once they were in port, and many conflicts followed from the seaman's legal right to be paid in every second port of delivery. Jack Cremer observed that his crew once decided to "have all theair wages – it being a Second delivering port – and would not doe a Stroak of work, nor wash or Clean the Ship."[73] Edward Poundey brought his voyage to a quick halt in port by saying that he would "be the Death of yt man yt offers to unmore ye Vessall till he has his Wages."[74] Second-port payment vexed the captain because his ship was frequently docked in the colonies, where his men were eager to desert. Ship owners Thomas Ekines and Samuel Mitchell outlined the dilemma and proposed a technically illegal solution in their letter to Captain Owen Searle: "Y[ou]r wages must be paid off at Jamaica but if you want men and feare theire leaving you its best [to] stop 2 or 3 months pay . . . of those you Distrust."[75]

Just as seamen deserted to advance their own causes, masters of ships got rid of seamen to enhance profits by eliminating wages as costs. James Stadden in 1719 threatened to kill Samuel March or "to confine him in prison or put him on board a man of war and oftentimes declared that he used him in that manner to force him to leave the said Ship for he would not carry him back to England."[76] Other captains "marooned" their seamen, leaving them "on a desolate Island" or in a foreign port, refusing to carry them the full stipulated voyage and hoping, obviously, never to see them again.[77] Chronic differences of these sorts were summed up in Edward Barlow's description of "most commanders" he had sailed with in his long career at sea: "they care not how much or in what way they can

[72] Morris, *Government and Labor*, 242; Seamen v. Tudar, MASS ADM (1719), f. 35; Mattear v. Turner, HCA 24/132 (1718); Arnold v. Ranson, HCA 24/129 (1706); Shaw v. Boyd, HCA 24/134 (1723); Ward v. Corne, HCA 24/136 (1730); Brown v. Graer, HCA 15/40 (1738).

[73] *Ramblin' Jack*, 157.

[74] Poundey v. Shortridge, HCA 24/130 (1712).

[75] Thomas Ekines and Samuel Mitchell to Owen Searle, HCA 24/127 (June 8, 1700).

[76] March v. Stadden, HCA 24/133 (1721).

[77] Rex v. Winkley, MASS ADM (1728), f. 39; Hakes v. Emms, MASS ADM (1723), f. 148; Holley v. Vitt, HCA 24/131 (1715).

get all to themselves, and care not what little other people get that are under them"; they were all out "to gain what they can, either by hook or crook."[78]

Captains also denied seamen their proper wages by withholding their rightful necessaries. The difference padded profits. Again, Edward Barlow:

Merchants and owners of ships in England . . . will put no more victuals or drink in the ship than will just serve so many days, and if they have to be a little longer in their passage and meet with cross winds, then the poor men's bellies must be pinched for it, and be put to shorter allowance, so that many times in long voyages men are forced to spend half their wages in buying themselves victuals, but they never have any recompense for it.[79]

The various ways in which the seaman's body was made to absorb the uncertainties of sea passage ultimately served as insurance to guarantee the merchant's accumulation of wealth.

Captains cut further into mariners' wages by selling basic necessities to seamen, often at enormous profits. They sold brandy, rum, wine, additional food, sugar, tobacco, caps, coats, shirts, trousers, breeches, stockings, shoes, and thread. They made further deductions for the Greenwich Hospital fund and the surgeon's fees. Master John Murrin asserted that "its usual for Masters of Ships to make profit of[f] what goods they sell to their Marriners."[80] The costs of such goods were always deducted from the tar's wages, and not infrequently did a man "make a Bristol voyage of it," using up more value in these necessities than was due him in wages at the voyage's end. Such arrangements gave the master a claim on that seaman's labor for the future.[81] This formal structure of debt must be counterposed to the less visible but no less important practice of em-

---

[78] *Barlow's Journal*, 529, 540.   [79] Ibid., 83.

[80] Ibid., 152; George St. Lo, *England's Safety: Or, a Bridle to the French King* (London 1693), 17; McNamera v. Barry, SC ADM (1729), ff. 634–50; *Ramblin' Jack*, 86; Lamb v. Murrin, HCA 24/129 (1707); Davis, *English Shipping*, 144; Morris, *Government and Labor*, 252. See also Collins v. Lillie, MASS ADM (1722), f. 110. For a reverse situation in which seamen got "double provisions" to sustain them through exceptionally arduous toil, see Foot v. *George & Martha*, HCA 24/130 (1711).

[81] Daniel F. Vickers, "Maritime Labor in Colonial Massachusetts: A Case Study of the Essex County Cod Fishery and the Whaling Industry of Nantucket, 1630–1775," Ph.D. diss., Princeton University, 1981, chap. 4.

bezzlement. These were two differently sanctioned systems of access and legitimacy to handle the social distribution of the same commodities on board the ship.

A cluster of struggles surrounded the last stage of the wage arrangement, that is, the final payoff. Seamen sought nothing more than an honest accounting of wages due at the end of a voyage. Upon returning from the Levant, Jack Cremer observed that his had been a particularly "happy voyage," not least because the sailors received their wages "honestly."[82] Many seamen felt they could not expect such fair and just treatment, and the volume of admiralty business on wage disputes underscores the legitimacy of their fears.

Seamen voiced one of their most bitter complaints against the legal right granted to merchants and masters to dock mariners' wages for "such damages as do arise and acrue by ill stowage, imbezelments and want of goods." Captains also sued for damages caused by their crews' alleged refusal to pump water from the hold.[83] The unrelenting abuse of this law by masters and merchants produced eloquent denunciations penned by Edward Barlow, and no doubt many others no less eloquent, even if a good bit saltier. Too often, wrote Barlow, "when pay-day came" after a long, exhausting voyage, "our commander and the owners of the ship would stop £3 from every man out of his wages for goods that had been damnified and spoilt in the ship, which they said the men in the ship were the fault of, for not stowing them better and not taking enough care of them." But in fact, Barlow claimed, the damage had been caused by storms, the "extremity of the weather," an "old and leaky" vessel, overfilling the ship with cargo, and imperfections in the goods that existed before loading. This "custom" of docking wages had been "too long used in England to the oppression of poor seamen": so long, in truth, that "a great many

[82] *Ramblin' Jack*, 101.
[83] Holland v. Waters, HCA 24/128 (1705); Sherman v. Philips, HCA 24/129 (1707); Hunter v. Hall, HCA 24/131 (1717); Evans v. Ricketts, HCA 24/132 (1718); Topliffe v. Groom, HCA 24/130 (1711); Davis, *English Shipping*, 145; Sanborn, *Origins of Early English Maritime and Commercial Law*, 264, notes that 32 Henry VIII, c. 14 (1540), gave the admiral "further jurisdiction to try summarily matters of freight and damage to cargo caused by the negligence of mariners, a statute apparently passed with a view to attracting business to his court."

seamen" deserted "their own native country and go serve other nations, for they have more freedom and better pay. So that a seaman sailing in an English ship is never sure of what he works for till he hath it in his pocket." England, Barlow continued, had become "the worst kingdom in Christendom for poor seamen, . . . paying for damnified merchants' goods, they being no fault of it . . . , no other Christian nation doing the like to their poor seamen, but letting them have what they work for, for they earn it with hardship enough." The practice of deduction for loss, Barlow concluded, was "both unjust and unreasonable, depriving the poor man of his lawful hire."[84] Barlow's anger, which recalls the language of the radical sects such as the Levellers in the English Revolution, was righteous and justified, for the act of docking wages for damage served as a flexible, effective insurance system for merchants, deflecting many of capital's risks in transoceanic commerce onto the collective back of the maritime working class.[85]

Another problem with payoff came during wartime when men were pressed from merchant vessels into the Royal Navy. Again, Barlow: "Many times the master of a ship payeth what he pleaseth when a man is pressed and not there to answer for himself; and some men having no friends or acquaintances to take that care for them, then that poor man loseth all, which is a great loss and hindrance to a poor man who hath nothing but what he must get by hard fare and sore labour." Seamen endured much to collect their proper due. Losses were frequent and devastating. Sailors suffered losses when captured by the enemy or by hostile privateers in wartime. They also had to withstand shipwrecks, "many times losing more in a moment than they can get again, maybe in all their lifetime": That seaman who "suffereth neither shipwreck, nor falleth into the hands of one enemy or another, that maketh prize of him, may count himself among the happy and fortunate of seamen."[86]

Yet another conflict over the payoff was the crew's resistance to being paid their wages in deflated colonial currencies. Money amounts in contracts were almost always specified in

[84] *Barlow's Journal*, 89, 90, 165, 166, 326, 341, 350, 385.
[85] See Christopher Hill, *The World Turned Upside Down: Radical Ideas during the English Revolution* (New York, 1972).
[86] *Barlow's Journal*, 146, 226.

pounds sterling, and wages, seamen argued, "ought to be paid full and in Sterling Money without discompt or abatement by reason of the difference of Exchange or any other pretence whatsoever."[87] Captains tried to defraud their crews and add to the voyage's profits by paying men off on "cross dollars," Jamaica, Carolina, or Massachusetts currencies, all of which were valued 25–50 percent less than "Sterling Money."[88]

In a final clash, a great many seamen responded to the iniquities of the wage system by withdrawing from the wage economy altogether. They had essentially three options. First, they turned pirates, an alternative discussed at length in a later chapter. Second, they moved to landed labor, some to farming. Third, many chose a "marooning life," a conscious withdrawal from the imperial economy and culture to a non-accumulative life on the world's periphery. Perhaps the most important group of marooners were the "Baymen," or logwood cutters, who labored at the Bay of Campeche, in Honduras, or in Belize. Described by outsiders as a "rude drunken crew," the logwood men were "Privateers [actually buccaneers] who had hitherto lived upon plundering the *Spaniards*"; they created independent communal settlements around the Caribbean. The abuses inherent in the wage system undoubtedly drove many men away from official society as they had known it and toward fundamentally different ways of life on the margins of the world.[89]

Seventeenth- and eighteenth-century observers of life at sea never tired of pointing out how seamen were "careless" and "irresponsible" with their money: not inclined to save but rather to engage in unruly debauches and sprees of spending

---

[87] Martin v. Dinwiddie, HCA 24/132 (1717).

[88] Parker v. Boucher, HCA 24/132 (1719); Jenkinson v. Cleeland, HCA 24/136 (1729); Seamen v. Loan, SC ADM (1717), ff. 70–83; Seamen v. Norman, MASS ADM (1720), f. 65; *Barlow's Journal*, 540. See also Morris, *Government and Labor*, 237.

[89] Examination of Thomas Jones, HCA 1/55 (1724), f. 52; *Voyages and Travels of Captain Nathaniel Uring*, 241, 124–5; William Dampier, "Mr. Dampier's Voyage to the Bay of Campeachy," in his *A Collection of Voyages*, 53; Dampier, "New Voyage," ii; "Voyage to Guinea, Antego, Bay of Campeachy, Cuba, Barbadoes, &c., 1714–1723," BL, Add. Ms. 39946, ff. 10–14; Robert C. Ritchie, "Marginal People on the Periphery of Empire," paper presented to the annual convention of the Organization of American Historians, Cincinnati, April 1983.

that squandered many months of wages in a matter of days; not inclined to look to the future, but immersed in the rich pleasures and profuse living of the present. Statistical work by Gary B. Nash confirms one part of this picture: "Merchant seamen were by far the largest occupational group represented in the bottom 30 per cent" of Boston's decedents who left inventories of their possessions.[90] Most seamen, it seems, left no inventories at all. Nash's finding is strongly conditioned by several factors: the relatively low pay and status of seafaring jobs; the very nature of sailoring, which encouraged rollicking rampages after months of incarceration on the ship; and mobility, which made transportability a central criterion in the physical accumulation of property. As Jack Cremer said, "a Rowling Stone never gathers Moss."[91]

A nonaccumulative ethic among seamen ran very deep. Certainly it was enshrined in many of their favorite sayings. "Never mind the main chance," they bellowed, meaning not to worry about old age, the likeliest course to success, or "the opportunity of enriching oneself."[92] Or "Never let us want when we have it and when we have it not too." One seaman in *Roderick Random* announced to the purser, whose stock he was plundering, "let us live while we can." Such sentiment caused some seamen to think it a shame to go to war against France, a nation that "produces so much good Wine and Brandy."[93] Merchants had to be sure that men possessed of such attitudes did not come to control their vessels. On the slave trader *Swift,* for example, in 1739, captain William Cole died, and was quickly followed into the watery blue by his first and second mates. The only man who knew navigation, Hugh Everard, took the helm of the ship, promptly put it on a new course, went straight to port, sold the cargo, and "spent all of the said Mony in drinking and Extravagant Living."[94]

Perhaps the most common as well as the most revealing of these aphorisms was spoken by Jack Cremer: "Sailor-like, [I]

[90] Nash, *Urban Crucible,* 64, 398.
[91] *Ramblin' Jack,* 39.
[92] Ibid., 194; Tobias Smollett, *Roderick Random* (1748; reprint London, 1927), 210; *Oxford English Dictionary,* vol. VI, 49.
[93] *Barlow's Journal,* 160; Ward, *Wooden World,* 38.
[94] Information of Ephraim Tiffany, HCA 1/57 (1740), f. 39.

was always for a Short life & a merry one."[95] Edward Barlow spoke of his fellow tars as "running out so most part of their wages, crying, 'A merry life and a short one,' and 'Longest liver take all.' "[96] The outlook was probably summed up best in the words attributed to pirate Batholomew Roberts by Daniel Defoe: "In an honest service," said the famous freebooter, "there is thin Commons, low Wages, and hard Labour; in this [as a pirate], Plenty and Satiety, Pleasure and Ease, Liberty and Power; and who would not ballance Creditor on this Side, when all the Hazard that is run for it, at worst, is only a sower Look or two at choaking. No, *a merry Life and a short one,* shall be my Motto."[97] By the late seventeenth century this motto, glorifying the delights of the present, was already counterposed to the desire to accumulate riches. Similarly, a "rolling stone" was already regarded as a rambler, a wanderer, who put immediate enjoyments before long-term security.[98]

These phrases echo some of the radical ideas of the English Revolution. Christopher Hill's *The World Turned Upside Down* discusses the plebeian opposition to the Protestant ethic in the mid-seventeenth century, the men and women who rejected "asceticism for unashamed enjoyment of the good things of the flesh."[99] Such affirmations stood in stunning contrast to the words written by John Flavel in his pamphlet, *A Pathetical and Serious Disswasive From the Horrid and Detestable Sins of Drunkenness, Swearing, Uncleanness, Forgetfulness of Mercies, Violation of Promises, and Atheistical Contempt of Death.* Dedicating his work to merchant John Lovering, Flavel insisted of seamen: "The *Death* of their Lusts, is the most *Probable* means to give *Life* to your Trade."[100]

Seamen, like their wage-earning brothers and sisters in the

---

[95] *Ramblin' Jack,* 194, 39, 38.

[96] *Barlow's Journal,* 160.

[97] Captain Charles Johnson [Daniel Defoe], *A General History of the Pyrates,* ed. Manuel Schonhorn (1724, 1728; reprint Columbia, S.C., 1972), 244.

[98] *Oxford English Dictionary,* vol. VIII, 703. See also Bartlett Jere Whiting, *Early American Proverbs and Proverbial Phrases* (Cambridge, Mass., 1977), 260. See also Captain J. Evans to the Admiralty, 1707 (quoted in Christopher Lloyd, *The British Seaman, 1200–1860: A Social Survey* [Rutherford, N.J., 1970], 61), where he noted that when seamen were confronted with the prospect of hanging, they responded by saying, "it is not a minute's pain."

[99] Hill, *World Turned Upside Down,* 275 and chap. 18, appropriately entitled "Life Against Death."

[100] Flavel, *A Pathetic and Serious Disswasive . . .* (Boston, 1725), 134.

radical sects, sought money but not capital; acquisition but not accumulation; the present, often at the expense of the future; gratification and consumption over deferral and savings. Seamen quite literally wanted "ready Money": the generalized value that permitted sustenance and pleasure in this world. Pirates, no matter what nineteenth-century writers would have us believe, did not bury their treasure. Their "first care," as the *American Weekly Mercury* reported in 1720, was always "to find out a Tavern, where they might ease themselves of their Golden Luggage."[101] The trials and tribulations of life at sea made sailors, notorious for their irreligion, a bit contemptuous of the next world. No pie up in the sky waiting for you when you die. Many seamen decided to have their share in their here-and-now.

These seamen lived in an era when the ways of getting a share were changing. The eighteenth century was crucial for its "erosion of half-free forms of labor, the decline of living in, the final extinction of labor services and the advance of free, mobile wage labor."[102] The classical relationships between masters and journeymen, masters and servants, and lords and peasants in the early modern world were not only or even primarily economic, but rather social. They were characterized by the exchange of goods and services and by the paternalistic authority, mutual responsibilities, and deference of the workshop, the household, and the estate.[103] These wage relations "appeared simultaneously as economic and social relations, as relations between men, not as payment for services and things."[104]

---

[101] *American Weekly Mercury*, Mar. 17, 1720. Pirates apparently followed the customs of buccaneers, who, according to Pere Labat, did not "take money to sea with them, so if they have any money in their pockets they spend it in a cabaret before they sail." See Jean Baptiste Labat, *The Memoirs of Père Labat, 1693–1705* (London, 1931), 232.

[102] E. P. Thompson, "Patrician Society, Plebeian Culture," *Journal of Social History* 7 (1974), 382.

[103] See Karl Marx, "The German Ideology," in Marx and Frederick Engels, *Selected Works* (Moscow, 1969), 53, where he writes: "The patriarchal relationship existing between [journeymen] and their masters gave the latter a double power – on the one hand because of their influence on the whole life of the journeyman, and on the other because, for the journeymen who worked with the same master, it was a real bond which held them together against the journeymen of other masters and separated them from these."

[104] Thompson, "Patrician Society, Plebeian Culture," 384–5.

This arrangement was altered by the rise of manufacturing, by the ascent of primarily economic relations, mediated by the wage, between capitalist and worker. The wage economy expanded at an extraordinary rate in the eighteenth century, paternalistic controls over laboring people consequently weakened, and a new world of struggle and negotiation began to unfold.[105] The Act for the Better Regulation and Government of the Merchants Service in 1729 accelerated the development of a system of free wage labor at sea as it signaled a momentous breakdown in a long-standing customary agreement between seafaring masters and men. The insistence upon a formal contractual agreement acknowledged the pervasive conflict over the wage and attempted to contain it within punitive and institutional boundaries. The conflict was, as we have seen, both diverse and intense, primarily because seamen, as landless proletarians, depended upon the monetary wage. They often had no choice but to fight. But seafaring still bore the marks of the transition to capitalist labor relations.

Merchants and captains appealed to contract and law when their interests suffered by desertion or embezzlement. They appealed to custom, invoking the memory of the long lapsed share system, when they sought to make their crews responsible for the safety of the ship's cargo. Seamen, on the other hand, used custom to guarantee their privilege and their right to "the necessaries of life" while appealing to contract to fight the alteration of voyages or unfair payments of wages. By the middle of the eighteenth century, the language of contract had in many ways supplanted the language of custom at sea.

But seamen were not willing to accept complete dependence on the monetary wage. Their practices indicate that they conceived the wage in broad terms that stressed their right to a life of decent quality. This was made easier since their wages were monthly and bore no direct relationship to the intensity or even the precise amount of time spent working.[106] They pursued their right to a decent competency in a variety of ingenious ways.

[105] Ibid., 382.
[106] Michael Sonenscher, "Work and Wages in Paris in the Eighteenth Century," in *Manufacture in Town and Country Before the Factory*, ed. Maxine Berg, Pat Hudson, and Sonenscher (Cambridge, 1983), 159, 166, 172.

The world of negotiation in the merchant shipping industry revolved around two inherently antagonistic sets of interests. Ship owners, merchants, and ship captains aspired to enhance the accumulation of capital by controlling wages, food and drink or "customary usage," social access to the product, spatial prerogatives, and the nature of the voyage. Indeed, the very process of accumulation was built not merely upon the formal exploitation of seafaring labor but upon the bilked wages, the pinched guts, and often the very lives, prematurely ended, of men of the sea. A central part of capital's plan during the early and uncertain stages of expansion was to shift as many of the burdens and risks associated with the growing but unstable Atlantic economy as possible to the seaman's shoulders.

Fortunately the seaman wore his "fearnought" jacket across those shoulders, and he fought back. He tried to maximize his wages, but simultaneously he fought to protect his nonmonetary supports: his access to proper provisions, his access to the product, his use of shipboard space, and his control of the voyage. The seaman's major interest, distinct from and continually at odds with accumulation, was the quality of life as defined by the social wage. The seaman's concern was to look after his "own account" and to help look after the accounts of those situated much like himself.

The social wage was, more than anything, a contest between these two sets of interests. Complex and subtle tactics were used on both sides: desertion and marooning, embezzlement and pinching provisions, reputation spreading and blacklisting, legal maneuvering, intimidation, and many others. Formal and informal organization took shape around issues such as labor mobility and scarcity in the peripheral parts of the world. Merchants and masters used the wage relation to create stability and continuity in an often anarchic labor market, to control the mobility that seamen used so effectively. Seamen employed their access to ready money to expand their autonomy and to live as well as they could in the world they inhabited. All of these matters were, to be sure, profoundly conditioned by larger patterns of economy and demography, by the process of capitalist development, and by the oscillations of war and peace. But all of these impersonal forces found coordinates in particular human lives, in the experiences that made up these lives.

Seamen led the exploration of a new world of wage conflict and negotiation; they were self-consciously creative, developing new tactics and organizing themselves around key issues. Their diverse activities and negotiations lay ever so materially and ever so crucially behind the quantitative character of the wage. Such matters were obscured in the past by the inert figures that lay in portledge bills and the merchant's ledgerbooks, and in the present by the detached, abstract analysis of labor supply and demand offered by neoclassical economics. The wage struggles of seamen reveal a robust world of working-class self-activity belied by the "reassuringly neutral figurative appearance" of the wage relation.[107] Such was the seaman's search for "ready Money."

[107] Sonenscher, "Work and Wages," 172 (quotation), 160, 167.

4

THE SEAMAN AS PLAIN DEALER

Language and Culture at Sea

To his contemporaries the early-eighteenth-century seaman appeared to be foul-mouthed but plain-spoken, superstitious but irreligious, courageous and dependable but rowdy and difficult to discipline. The Reverend George Whitefield, who crisscrossed the Atlantic in religious mission, doubted whether working sailors could "pull their ropes without swearing." Dramatists and writers from Wycherly to Defoe and Smollett depicted Jack Tar as a blunt, straight-talking "plain dealer." Seamen believed in omens and apparitions, but they did not believe many of the teachings of the Church of England, or any other church for that matter. Amid rolling seas and high winds, "able Sailors, like true Sons of Neptune, [were] most Vigourous and Brave," but in other situations the same able seamen were wild, refractory, even mutinous.[1] These traits were distinctive features of maritime culture.

In this chapter we shall explore the material sources of these features of maritime culture, as well as some of the crucial relationships among maritime work, language, and belief. We will discuss the seaman's speech, religion, rituals, and general worldview. In order to understand culture at sea, we shall enter into conversation with those common Anglo-American seamen

---

[1] *George Whitefield's Journal* (Guildford and London, 1960), 150; William Wycherly, *The Plain Dealer* (1677; reprint London, 1971); Daniel Defoe, *Robinson Crusoe* (1719; reprint New York, 1980); Tobias Smollett, *Roderick Random* (1748; reprint London, 1927); John Dennis, *An Essay on the Navy* (London, 1702), 38 (quotation on "able Sailors").

judged by a condescending sea captain to be the "most uncon-versable Part of Mankind."[2]

Maritime culture was forged from two related confron-tations, each of which was central to seafaring work. The first was the confrontation between man and nature, the seaman's perpetual, ever-vigilant struggle to survive in the face of the nearly omnipotent forces of the deep. Tobias Smollett, whose many months at sea informed his picaresque novel *Roderick Random,* described a storm in which the "sea was swelled into billows mountain high, on the top of which our ship sometimes hung as if it was about to be precipitated into the abyss below!"[3] Surrounded by deafening crashes of thunder, lightning of siz-zling intensity, and violent, churning seas, the seamen often dangled at the edge of eternity, suspended between life and death. The sea's natural terror, its inescapable threat of apoca-lypse, imparted a special urgency to maritime social and cul-tural life. The chances for survival improved markedly as the ship's company became an effective, efficient collectivity, bound together in skill, purpose, courage, and community. Maritime culture could not fail to reflect this imperative, which found expression in the popular adage, "we're all in this boat together."

A second confrontation, detailed in Chapter 5, also exercised a decisive influence upon the development of maritime culture: the showdown between man and man, the class confrontation over the issues of power, authority, work, and discipline. This encounter produced within the larger culture a sharply antago-

---

[2] *The Voyages and Travels of Captain Nathaniel Uring,* ed. Alfred Dewar (1726; reprint London, 1928), xxxiii. It should be noted that it is impossible to separate the work experiences and the cultural life of the merchant service and the Royal Navy in the seventeenth and eighteenth centuries. Although I have not generalized about the navy, I would argue that many of the pro-cesses and developments described in this chapter were present there, al-though usually in modified form, given the navy's vastly larger scale of operation. On the overlap between the two enterprises, see Christopher Lloyd, *The British Seaman, 1200–1860: A Social Survey* (Rutherford, N.J., 1970), 12, and Peter Kemp, *The British Sailor: A Social History of the Lower Deck* (London, 1970), lx. For a brief survey of maritime culture in the seven-teenth century, see Charles A. Le Guin, "Sea Life in Seventeenth-Century England," *American Neptune* 27 (1967), 111–34.

[3] Smollett, *Roderick Random,* 165. For the example of the *Dove* in a severe storm, see the Introduction to this book, pp. 1–2.

nistic tendency, a subculture or "oppositional culture" shared by common seamen, with a distinctive set of attitudes, values, and practices. Maritime culture, then, was fractured. The corporate culture, which grew out of the struggle with nature, was cleft by a subculture of class that emerged from the basic relations of production in shipping.

The wellsprings of maritime culture lay in the realities of work and authority aboard ship. The division of labor linked all members of the ship's crew in a hierarchical and functional way, but at the same time it facilitated the emergence of discrete communities at the top of the hierarchy, among the officers, and at the bottom, among the men. Relations of authority marked the division, frequently producing the phenomenon of "command isolation." Ned Ward, writing of the captain of a man-of-war, also described many a master in the merchant service by characterizing him as "an everlasting Admirer of that old Saying, *Familiarity Breeds Contempt*." Yet isolation was often not only a technique of rule but also part of an active exclusion – an ostracism – practiced against the captain by his crew. The social isolation of the captain, like so much of maritime culture as a whole, thus resulted from two very different social dynamics: the search from above for corporate authority and the search from below for autonomy.[4]

Maritime workers were a diverse lot, and diverse were the sources of maritime culture. A late-seventeenth-century seafarer observed that "a ship is not improperly called a wooden world, [and] various occasions show the various tempers of the men there; we had some of several Nations, humours, and abilitys."[5] First of all, seafaring was an occupation sharply segregated by sex and class, restricted to men and populated chiefly by the poor. Neither women nor the well-to-do ordinarily went to sea. Further, these sailor men were overwhelmingly of humble birth, often driven to the seas by economic neces-

[4] Ned Ward, *The Wooden World Dissected: In the Character of a Ship of War* (1708; reprint London, 1756), 5, 6. See also B. R. Burg, *Sodomy and the Perception of Evil: English Sea Rovers in the Seventeenth Century Caribbean* (New York, 1983), 125. See also Knut Weibust, *Deep Sea Sailors: A Study in Maritime Ethnology* (Stockholm, 1976), 252.
[5] "Richard Simsons Voyage to the Straits of Magellan & S. Seas in the Year 1689," BL Sloane Ms. 86, f. 43; *Ramblin' Jack: The Journal of Captain John Cremer*, ed. R. Reynall Bellamy (London, 1936), 137.

sity.[6] The huge majority of seamen were of European birth and background. French, Dutch, Portuguese, Spanish, or Scandinavian sailors turned up on British-owned vessels, as did subjects of the British crown, from both the Old World and the New – England, Scotland, Ireland, Wales, North America, and the West Indies. African, Asian, and native American seamen also served on Anglo-American craft. Even more notoriously international were the crews of pirate ships, as suggested by the instance when several sea robbers "fell to drinking very hard" and "prophanely singing at Suppertime Spanish and Ffrench Songs out of a Dutch Prayer Book."[7]

High mortality rates and the rigors of maritime work made seafaring a young man's occupation and culture. Most seamen were in their twenties or thirties. Captains, chief mates, surgeons, and lesser officers tended to be in their early to middle thirties, and the average common tar was twenty-seven.[8] The seventeen-man crew of a large vessel had ten common seamen who on average consisted of one man in his late teens, three men in their early twenties, three in their late twenties, two in their thirties, and one in his forties or even early fifties. Despite their relatively small numbers, older seamen, both officers and men, performed principal roles in the transmission of maritime culture because seafaring was characterized by high mortality, rapid turnover of personnel, and geographic mobility and dispersion. This "core population," made up of the "old salt" or perhaps the "old Surly Jack Tar," collectively bore many of the

[6] Ralph Davis, *The Rise of the English Shipping Industry in the Seventeenth and Eighteenth Centuries* (London, 1962), 153.

[7] "Proceedings of the Court Held on the Coast of Africa upon Trying of 100 Pirates Taken by his Ma[jes]ties Ship *Swallow*," HCA 1/99 (1722), f. 139. See also Governor Nicholas Laws to Council of Trade and Plantations (hereafter CTP), Jan. 31, 1719, *Calendar of State Papers, Colonial Series, America and the West Indies* 31 (1719–20), 19, and James Vernon to CTP, Dec. 21, 1697, *Calendar of State Papers*, 16 (1697–8), 70, who said that pirates "acknowledged no countrymen, [and said] that they had sold their country." See also "An Act for the Better Supply of Mariners and Seamen to serve in his Majesty's Ships of War, and on board Merchants Ships, and other trading Vessels and Privateers" (13 George II, c. 3, 1740), in Sir Thomas Parker, *The Laws of Shipping and Insurance, with a Digest of Adjudged Cases* (London, 1775), republished in *British Maritime Cases* (Abingdon, Oxfordshire, 1978), 137, where it is indicated that during times of war three of every four seamen could be foreign born.

[8] On ages, see Appendix A of this book.

cultural traditions of the sea.[9] The older seaman's experience frequently provided the measure and understanding of events and activities. The intensity of storms, for example, was always gauged against the memory of the old salts. Any storm so powerful "as was never felt by the oldest man on board" probably passed into tale and folklore.[10] The younger men respected the older ones for their knowledge of the sea, the ship, the signs of nature, the methods of maritime labor. Daily wrangles with masters and mates made many sailors esteem the savvy old tars who knew the ins and outs of desertion, mutiny, or even piracy.

However rich his stock of lore and knowledge, the older seaman was often a tragic and pitiable figure. Edward Barlow declared sadly that "there are fewer old seamen in want far than landmen, for they seldom live until they be old, for they either die with want or with grief to see themselves so little regarded" when they are "old and in need."[11] It was not unusual to encounter, as Jack Cremer did, a poor old mate, approaching sixty, "unhappily drowning himself in Liquor." Barlow himself spoke fearfully but eloquently of his own future: "I saw by daily experience that . . . if I went to sea when I should be grown in years, that then I should be little better than a slave, being always in need, and enduring all manner of misery and hardship, going with many a hungry belly and wet back"; this, he saw, "would be a great grief for an aged man."[12] And so it was. Younger seamen often tried to protect the older ones by giving them more or better provisions or by shielding them from an abusive captain. In 1749 a drunken captain named Thomas Sanderson struck his boatswain, "whereupon the Crew rose and said that he (meaning the Captain) should not beat the old Man (meaning ye Boatswain who was a very old Man)."[13]

---

[9] *Ramblin' Jack*, 58, 75, 78, 110; Ira Dye, "Early American Merchant Seafarers," *Proceedings of the American Philosophical Society* 20 (1976), 337.

[10] "The Journal of Francis Rogers," in Bruce Ingram, ed., *Three Sea Journals of Stuart Times* (London, 1936), 145. See also William Dampier, "A New Voyage Round the World," in Dampier, *A Collection of Voyages* (London, 1729), 70, 416; E. B. O'Callaghan, ed., *The Voyage of George Clarke, Esq. to America* (Albany, 1867), 23–4; *Whitefield's Journals*, 168; William Funnell, *A Voyage Round the World* (London, 1707), 76; "Simsons Voyage," f. 43.

[11] *Barlow's Journal*, 165.

[12] *Ramblin' Jack*, 202; *Barlow's Journal*, 162.

[13] Information of William Steele, HCA 1/58 (1750), f. 8; "Simsons Voyage," f. 21.

Such "old men" were valued for their intimate grasp of maritime lore, which they communicated through an oral tradition crucial to an occupation marked by many degrees of literacy. Some seamen were entirely illiterate, whereas others not only possessed all the skills of literacy but used them in remarkably talented ways. As many as three-quarters of the sailors employed in the merchant shipping industry between 1700 and 1750 were literate if judged by the standard of the ability to sign one's own name. But there is reason to suspect that the actual proportion of the literate may have been considerably smaller, because not all who could sign their names could read and write. Seaman Jacob Mason, for example, signed his deposition before the High Court of Admiralty, claiming that he "cannot read written hand."[14] Since the contract, so essential to free wage labor, loomed large in the sailor's life, some seamen no doubt learned to sign their names, but little more. Further, to say that one in four was illiterate is to obscure the uneven distribution of illiteracy among seafarers. All captains, mates, and surgeons were literate, but, at best, only two of three common seamen could even sign their name. More than nine of ten officers and skilled workers were literate, whereas fewer than seven of ten among the "ship's company"–those at the bottom of the hierarchy such as cooks, quartermasters, foremastmen, and apprentices–were literate.[15] Maritime life contained cultural forms for the literate and illiterate. Books, tales, and ballads all functioned as important means of communication, education, and entertainment.

The deep-sea vessel, so far-flung about the oceans of the globe as to be isolated from any landed society and its dominant patterns of social life, also shaped maritime culture. Work in the wooden world required mobile laborers to move the world's commodities, and movement had a strong bearing on maritime culture. Tars spoke of themselves as leading a "Roving Course of Life," as possessed of an "unhappy mind of

---

[14] Examination of Jacob Mason, HCA 1/55 (1723), f. 32. For the unusual case of a seaman who learned to read and write after he went to sea, see *Barlow's Journal*, 29.

[15] For a statistical breakdown of literacy among seafarers, see Appendix D of this book.

Rambling," as never "properly Setteled."[16] When Jack Cremer got around to writing of his life at sea, he began by saying, "As I have been a Rambling Sort of Chap, and have had no order or regularity, nor proper learning or conduct in my life, it will not be at all Suprising that I do not observe much in the relating of it."[17] Mobility, fluidity, and dispersion were intrinsic to the seaman's life. Seafaring culture necessarily took shape without firm geographic boundaries or stable residence. Seamen were in many ways nomads, and their mobility ensured a rapid diffusion of their culture.

Working on a merchant ship also meant prolonged, painful separation from family and friends. The vessel lay loaded and ready to sail: "Here," said Edward Barlow, "hath the husband parted with the wife, the children from the loving parent, and one friend from another, which have never enjoyed the sight of one another again, and some by war and some by peace, and some by one sudden means and some by another."[18] The "sudden means" that transformed temporary separation into permanent loss included accident, disease, even murder. Disasters both natural and man-made befell the seaman so often that his return was chronically uncertain. One of the most popular songs of the period was "Loath to Depart."[19]

Work at sea also meant virtual incarceration, as the seaman was forcibly assimilated into a severe shipboard regimen of despotic authority, discipline, and control. Shipboard life constituted a binding chain of linked limits: limited space, limited freedom, limited movement, limited sensory stimulation, and limited choices of leisure activities, social interaction, food, and play. There was too little space aboard the ship and too much space outside.[20]

---

[16] Dampier, "New Voyage," 497; *Ramblin' Jack*, 193; George Phinney to Lord Carteret, CO 23/13 (Jan. 2, 1724), f. 157; *The Life and Adventures of Matthew Bishop* (London, 1744), 46.

[17] *Ramblin' Jack*, 32.

[18] *Barlow's Journal*, 31; Woodes Rogers, *A Cruising Voyage Round the World*, ed. G. E. Manwaring (1712; reprint London, 1928), 5.

[19] Charles Napier Robinson, *The British Tar in Fact and Fiction: The Poetry, Pathos, and Humour of a Sailor's Life* (London and New York, 1911), 425. For an overview of maritime song, see C. H. Firth, *Naval Songs and Ballads* (London, 1908), vol. 33.

[20] *Nipper v. Bruce*, HCA 24/128 (1704); Deposition of Samuel Miller, CO 5/1315 (1706), f. 36; *Wise v. Beekman*, HCA 24/131 (1716). For studies of present-day seamen, see Peter H. Fricke, ed., *Seafarer and Community: To-*

Most of the too little space on the vessel was filled with cargo or ballast. The seamen's cramped living quarters in the steerage of the ship (in the forward part of the hold) made for a densely communal social life. Here each seaman – except the highest officers, who often had their own cabins – stored his sturdy sea chest, his few and simple clothes, and his bedding. The sailor's hammock, adopted from that of the Arawak Indians of the Caribbean in the late sixteenth century, was a piece of canvas, usually 3 by 6 feet, "hung horizontally under the deck, lengthways, for the sailors to sleep therein."[21] Strung up side by side, often only a few inches apart, the hammocks rocked and rolled with the motions of the vessel upon the sea. Jack Tar always sought a good hammock, perhaps because sleep offered at least some escape from his confinement. Sir Thomas Overbury noted of the seventeenth-century tar that "His sleepes are but reprevals of his dangers." In any case, a hammock was certainly better than sleeping on the "softest Plank" he could find. The distance between the decks was minimal, ranging from 4 feet 6 inches on the smaller ships to 6 feet 6 inches on the very largest. Most ships had decks that ranged between 5 feet and 5 feet 6 inches.[22] Seamen lay in their hammocks, singing or telling tales; they played cards by candlelight on a worn, crusty sea chest. Their isolation was communal. They could escape neither their loneliness nor each other.

Human beings were not the only incarcerated creatures on the early-eighteenth-century merchant vessel. Animals, some of them welcome, others cursedly unwelcome, swarmed the ship. Rats, cockroaches, and maggots infested every deep-sea vessel. Another fellow traveler was *teredo navalis,* the insidious sea worm that ate its way through many a hull. But there were also

Footnote 20 (*cont.*):
wards a Social Understanding of Seafaring (London, 1973), especially the essays by Jan Horbulewicz and Bryan Nolan.

[21] William A. Baker, "The Arrangement and Construction of Early Seventeenth-Century Ships," *American Neptune* 15 (1955), 266. Quotation: William Falconer, *An Universal Dictionary of the Marine* (London, 1769; reprint New York, 1970), 143.

[22] John Leyland, "Another Seventeenth Century Mariner," *Mariner's Mirror* 2 (1912), 154; "Mr. Roberts and His Voyage to the Levant," in William Hacke, *A Collection of Original Voyages* (London, 1699), 5; Baker, "Arrangement and Construction," 267; William A. Baker, "Deck Heights in the Early Seventeenth Century," *American Neptune,* 22 (1962), 99–105.

pets – dogs, cats, parrots, even an occasional "pet penguin." And there were animals brought on as stock, kept on board until slaughtered for food. These included cattle, sheep, goats, and pigs, and they sometimes provided more than meals. As a man related of one voyage, "the roughness of the weather" made three hogs so seasick that "no man could forebear laughing to see them go reeling and spewing about the decks." The scene was all the funnier because the men on board had surely done their own share of "reeling and spewing" at one time or another.[23]

The ship was not only a self-contained world but very much a world apart. The dominant institutions of eighteenth-century English and American societies played relatively small parts on the deep-sea craft. The absence of family, church, and state – the primary institutions that organized social life – created a power vacuum within the wooden world. Into the vacuum, as we shall see in Chapter 5, stepped the merchant captain, armed with extraordinary powers. Such concentration of authority tended to nullify at the outset many of the social, political, and cultural compromises that had been worked out between working people and the various authorities of church, state, and labor. But into the same vacuum stepped the seaman, determined to reestablish protections and some degree of autonomy. The isolation of life at sea produced within the tar intensified awareness of the actual and symbolic uses of power and a powerful need for self-defense. The common seaman developed numerous tactics that he used in negotiation with his mighty master. Survival often depended as much on checking the forces of authority as those of nature.

Maritime culture was thus necessarily constituted by material relationships with nature and among men, by the basic relations of production in shipping. Emerging primarily from the complex and contested realities of work and authority, that culture was shaped by the social characteristics of the sailors

[23] Tom Glasgow, Jr., "Sixteenth-Century English Seamen Meet A New Enemy – The Shipworm," *American Neptune* 27 (1967), 177–84; "Simsons Voyage," ff. 3, 4; Captain John Strong, "Journal of the Voyage to the Straits of Magellan and the South Sea," 1689, Sloane 3295, ff. 37, 53. Quotation: Henry Teonge, *The Diary of Henry Teonge*, ed. G. E. Manwaring (New York, 1927), 233.

themselves—sex and class, race, nationality, and literacy—and by the concrete environment of the ship.

Language, a pivotal part of any culture, held a special significance in the wooden world, the solitary vessel of seafaring life. To learn and finally to master the peculiar argot of the sea was to become a seaman. Such learning left its mark. One writer noted in 1757 that seamen displayed "a dialect and manner peculiar to themselves": "they are a species of man abstracted from every other race of mortals."[24] Abstracted—that is, separated and removed—from landed society by their work, seamen expressed their alienation in their speech. Their removal from land to sea, from farm or workshop to the ship, was simultaneously a movement from one work language to another. To be socialized anew into the ways of the deep-sea craft was necessarily to be weakened or stripped of previous attachments to local and regional cultures and ways of speaking. The ship thus served as a mechanism of cultural dispossession, but it simultaneously created new bonds among those who went to sea, one of which was a common language.

Jack Cremer, who was apprenticed as a youth to an officer aboard a man-of-war, vividly described his startled entry into the world of maritime language, objects, and work: "I was not taken notice of for a day or two, nor could I think what world I was in, weather [whether] among Spirits or Devills. All seemed strange; different languidge and strange expreshions of tonge, that I always thought myself a sleep or in a dream, and never properly awake." In this nightmarish state, young Jack was "always dreading what was the matter." But soon the grotesque began to fade into the familiar; objects acquired terms and meanings. Other seamen, Cremer explained, "began to learn me to call names, which was the first Rhudiment of that University," the first big step into the world of the deep-sea sailor.[25]

Cremer's first step, like that of every new seaman, consisted of learning the tasks of the maritime labor process. The novice

---

[24] Cited in Nathan Comfort Starr, "Smollett's Sailors," *American Neptune*, 32 (1972), 86.
[25] *Ramblin' Jack*, 43. See also *Adventures by Sea of Edward Coxere*, ed. E. H. W. Meyerstein (New York, 1946), 30–1.

entered what was essentially a language apprenticeship. As the old saying had it, he had "to learn the ropes," and he had to find out what to call them as well as what they did. The deep-sea ship was one of the early modern world's most sophisticated pieces of technology; its labor process was complex, and its linguistic complement could be no less so. The young tar studied the differences between stem and stern, port and starboard; how to distinguish among backing, reefing, balancing, furling, and loosing the sails; how to tell a splice from a hitch from a knot. He had to learn the difference between cat-harpins and nippers, belaying pins and can-hooks. He had to learn the division of labor, from captain to cabin boy. He had to learn to recognize the various types of vessels – brigs, snows, schooners, shallops, and many others. He had to master the terms for the rigging, masts, and sails. And he had to understand the ship's basic maneuvers, such as beating against the wind, tacking, or box-hauling.[26]

The green hand also had to acquire a new vocabulary for the elements. There were trade winds and their patterns, variable breezes, slatches, "cats' paws," gales, and fresh gales. He encountered "fair winds" that favored the ship's movement on course and "foul winds" that hindered it. He had to master the terms associated with the oceans and seas, their currents, calms, swells, and breakers. The seaman studied the types of storms, squalls, and tempests, and even the "scuds," clouds, and their formations. He had to be able to identify the constellations of heavenly bodies by which he steered the vessel.

The seaman thus learned a language of "technical necessity," a language "remarkable for its terseness and accuracy," a language that, to novelist Joseph Conrad, was "a flawless thing for its purpose."[27] Maritime language was marked by lack of ambiguity. Each object and action had a word or phrase – short, clear, and unmistakable – to designate it. Acknowledging the struggle against nature for survival, maritime language was constructed to serve as a precise set of relays for authority, to link captain and crew with a machinelike efficiency.[28]

[26] For a description of the maritime labor process, see Chapter 2 of this book.
[27] See the excellent article by J. H. Parry, "Sailor's English," *The Cambridge Journal* 2 (1948–9), 660–70; quotations: 662, 670.
[28] Burg, *Sodomy and the Perception of Evil*, 151; Dell Hymes, *Foundations in Sociolinguistics: An Ethnographic Approach* (Philadelphia, 1974); Basil Bern-

But this terse, accurate, and technical language also expressed a set of social relations. As the seaman learned maritime language, he also learned the requirements of the ship's social structure, for maritime speech ordered social relations within the wooden world. He quickly understood that the always primary form of communication aboard the ship was the command. Thus the seaman at once learned maritime language and social life, relations of community and relations of class.

The efficiency of seafaring language and social relations might guarantee obedience even when survival was not at stake, or at least the captain hoped so. In those moments when obedience was not forthcoming (and often it was not), another part of the maritime vocabulary might be called upon: the language of punishment. The cat wailed on "market day," and mutinous seamen were "dried out in the shrouds" or "marooned" on a deserted island. Such activities reinforced the relay of authority through the language of command, but simultaneously indicated that there was more at issue than "technical necessity."[29]

The language of work was thus central both to the socialization process and to the nature of social life at sea. A newcomer had to learn the language before he could move from ordinary to able seaman and beyond, and thereby gain a substantial increase in pay. And maritime speech had to be mastered before a man could become a fully accepted member of the fraternity of deep-sea sailors. The language of the sea provided a broad basis for community, linking the top and the bottom of the ship's hierarchy. Masters and chief mates, who were frequently the most knowledgeable about the technicalities of language and labor, were often the dominant figures in this community, though seamen learned much of the language of the sea from their peers. The "speech community" contained within it a set of bonds, the basis for a consciousness of kind and a collectivism among all those who lived by the sea.[30]

Footnote 28 (*cont.*):
stein, "The Limits of My Language Are Social," in Mary Douglas, ed., *Rules and Meanings: The Anthropology of Everyday Knowledge* (New York, 1973), 203–6 and especially 205 on language and social structure.
[29] *Ramblin' Jack*, 45; *Adventures by Sea of Edward Coxere*, 30; *Barlow's Journal*, 29. See Chapter 5 of this book on authority and discipline.
[30] *Adventures by Sea of Edward Coxere*, 30–1.

Seafaring speech did not, however, constitute a total language. It was primarily a language of work and could not encompass and express all aspects of existence. Maritime language was thus grafted onto a wide array of plebeian forms and patterns of speech, some aspects of which intensified in the peculiar setting of the wooden world. It was, for example, a commonplace that seamen were the greatest of cursers and swearers, hence the superlative phrase "with seamanlike profanity." Jack Tar was, according to Jesse Lemisch, bred in the "very shambles of language": "he is foul-mouthed, his talk alien and suspect."[31] An eighteenth-century royal official considered such language to be part of "the Nature of a Comon Sailer whose prejudiced education may plead for their rudeness Tho in no way Justify it."[32] Ned Ward insisted that the man-of-war, and indeed almost any deep-sea vessel, was "Old Nick's Academy," where the "seven liberal Sciences" were "taught to full perfection." "Swearing" ranked first among the "sciences," just ahead of "Drinking, Thieving, Whoring, Killing, Cozening, and Backbiting."[33]

Seamen had tongues as nimble as they were razor sharp. Tars performed their work "with Volleys of Oaths"; sometimes addressed their officers with "abusive and reviling Language accompanied with the most bitter and prophane Oaths and execrable Curses"; and swore like "madmen" or "demons."[34] Now playfully, now seriously, they damned each other's blood, cursed each other's bodies, and wished misery and destruction on their foes. Seamen hurled insults at each other and at their officers: You fat-gutted chucklehead! You lazy skulking son of a bitch! Blood and thunder, you damned knave! Richard Peard, "just before he dyed" of a captain's beating, "prayed that the ship might never prosper and the Capt[ain] never thrive." Such curses could as easily be used against victims as by them. Another mortally injured victim of a beating was made to repeat by his captain: "I wish the Devil may eat my fflesh off

[31] Jesse Lemisch, "Jack Tar in the Streets: Merchant Seamen in the Politics of Revolutionary America," *WMQ* 25 (1968), 371–2.
[32] Deposition of Governor Robert Daniel, CO 5/387 (July 14, 1716), f. 27.
[33] Ward, *Wooden World*, 12.
[34] *Ramblin' Jack*, 192; Hopkins v. Tennel, SC ADM (1737), f. 103. See also Murray v. Hyde, HCA 24/135 (1726); *Voyages and Travels of Captain Nathaniel Uring*, 131; Hamilton v. Wilkinson, HCA 24/136 (1727).

of my bones if ever I discover this [bad usage] to ffather or mother or any body else."[35] Seamen also taunted each other. One told his captain that he hoped "to piss on his Grave." Nicholas Worsdale, mate of the *William,* informed his captain, supposedly the most knowledgeable man on the ship, that "he valued him no more than a ballad singer."[36] Ballad singers, however important between watches, did not, in Worsdale's estimation, contribute much to the actual running of the ship. Such insults always took on special meaning when addressed by a crewman to a master or mate, because they represented a kind of verbal mutiny, a small but important – and easily understood – attack on the social order of the ship.

In situations of gravity and danger, seamen pledged oaths. Mutineers swore among themselves to be true to each other, even to "the last drop of blood," and to guard their common secrets.[37] Likewise, those seamen who became pirates were often required to take "a very severe Oath" not "to betray" each other. They pledged to be "true to the crew."[38] Such pledges were often accompanied by ritual, drink, and cheer.

"Rough talk" at sea had distinct social implications. Such language expressed clear opposition to the "polite," mainly bourgeois elements of society. Since the English Revolution, if not before, blasphemy, cursing, and swearing had implied defiance of middle-class society and its ideals of gentility, moderation, refinement, and industry. Rough speech was thus essentially transgressive. It owed much to an all-male environment, to shipboard isolation and incarceration, and to the many frustrations and resentments engendered by a rough line of work.[39]

---

[35] Information of John Daftor, HCA 1/56 (1733), f. 75; see also Information of Edward Bingley, HCA 1/56 (1733), f. 79; (second quotation): Information of Henry Hull, HCA 1/56 (1729), f. 31.

[36] Nairn v. Rogers, HCA 24/130 (1712); Worsdale v. Barry, SC ADM (1729), ff. 693 695, 697, 700.

[37] Morgan v. Man, HCA 24/127 (1700); Examination of Anthony Hart, in "Account of the Discovery of an Horrid Plot and Conspiracy on Board the Ship *Antelope,*" CO 323/3 (1699).

[38] Examination of Richard Capper, HCA 1/54 (1718), f. 70; Examination of William Ingram, HCA 1/54 (1724), f. 141. See also Information of John Stephenson, HCA 1/55 (1721), f. 5; Sedgewick v. Burroughs, HCA 24/134 (1723).

[39] Christopher Hill, *The World Turned Upside Down: Radical Ideas in the English Revolution* (New York, 1972), 162; Leonard W. Levy, *Treason Against God: A History of the Offense of Blasphemy* (New York, 1981), xv, 245. In the relatively

Rough talk obviously had strong antichurch overtones. The scoffer and blasphemer had long been a key figure in the history of popular irreligion, and seamen kept the tradition alive. Ministers who wrote manuals for the seaman's "spiritual navigation" waged holy war against his profane manner of speech, especially since, as *The Mariner's Divine Mate* put it, "A tongue that swears does not easily pray." George Whitefield bristled as seamen damned his prayers and filled their normal rounds of work with bawdy talk. A seaman's tongue expressed, in a sharp and salty way, his alienation from the polite and religious elements of landed society.[40]

Suppression of rough talk was actively, though only occasionally, undertaken by authorities in the major maritime industries – the Royal Navy, privateering, and the merchant shipping industry. Navy officers clamped the "speculum oris" into the mouth of swearers and blasphemers "till their mouths [were] very, very bloody." Privateering captains like Woodes Rogers "had Ferula's made to punish Swearing, by which," he claimed, "we found the Men much broke of that Vice." Merchant captains also joined the struggle for proper language. In 1727 the Massachusetts Court of Vice Admiralty congratulated Captain Henry Atkins because he had "endeavoured to Discountenance profaneness & acted during the Voyage the part of a good Christian as well as a Judicious Commander."[41]

Yet the content of the sailor's speech was not merely negative. It embodied a distinctive kind of working-class speech –

more religious society of America, "rough talk" may have taken on an even stronger social meaning. Carl Bridenbaugh has pointed out that swearing, cursing, and blaspheming were increasing among urban plebeians in the eighteenth century. See his *Cities in the Wilderness: The First Century of Urban Life in America, 1625–1742* (London, 1938), 228, 390.

[40] *Mariner's Divine Mate* (Boston, 1715), 50; *Whitefield's Journals*, 513, 107. See also John Flavel, *A Pathetical and Serious Disswasive From the Horrid and Detestable Sins of Drunkenness, Swearing, Uncleanness, Forgetfulness of Mercies, Violation of Promises, and Atheistical Contempt of Death* (Boston, 1725), 155; Bridenbaugh, *Cities in the Wilderness*, 423.

[41] Teonge, *Diary*, 219; Edward Cooke, *A Voyage to the South Sea* (London, 1712), 122; Broughton v. Atkins, MASS ADM (1727), f. 25. See "Instructions to be Observed by Captain Daniel Plowman, Commander of the Briganteen Charles of Boston in Pursuance of the Commission Therewith Given Him," HCA 49/106 (1703): "You are to keep such good order among your sd Brigantines Company that Swearing, Drunkenness, Prophaneness be Avoided or duely Punished [and] that [God Be] Duely Worshipped." See also Pitchel v. Lawrence, MASS ADM (1737), f. 101; *Ramblin' Jack*, 214–15.

"plain speaking." In the late seventeenth century, precisely when the numbers of maritime wage workers swelled swiftly to accommodate the new imperatives of trade and empire, dramatists began to depict the seaman as an uncommonly honest, straightforward, and unconventional speaker, someone not much given to politeness but usually committed to telling the unvarnished truth. The seaman was a plain dealer.[42] He spoke in immediate, direct, clear, expressive, and forceful ways, even if it got him in trouble, as sometimes it did. Edward Barlow's relations with one of his captains were vexed, he believed, not because he went behind the captain's back, but rather "for speaking too much to his face and plainly telling him of his actions and behaviour and what I thought of him."[43]

The seaman's language, as many heard it, was not merely foul-mouthed but lacking in deference, at least when the seaman found himself beyond the social world of the ship. Tars were "not very much given to complimenting"; they did not always bother to give way to "every Pouder'd Bob" they met in the streets. Tom Bowling, the quintessential honest tar depicted in Smollett's *Roderick Random,* illustrated this absence of deference after he was attacked by the hounds of a young fox-hunting squire. Bowling quickly killed both dogs and addressed the squire thusly, "Lookee, you lubberly son of a w—e, if you come athwart me, 'ware your gingerbread work, I'll be foul of your quarter, damn me." The young gentleman, taken aback, threatened to have Bowling hanged. "None of your jaw, you swab – none of your jaw," replied Tom, "else I shall trim your laced jacket for you – I shall rub you down with an oaken towel, my boy – I shall."[44]

An important reason for the seaman's plain dealing lay in the monetized character of his wage, a subject explored at length in the previous chapter. Money nibbled away at paternalistic authority and conferred a degree of independence and autonomy, both psychological and social, upon the wage laborer. Language could not fail to be affected by the waged as-

---

[42] See "Editorial: Language and History," *History Workshop Journal,* 10 (1980), 1–5. See also Weibust, *Deep Sea Sailors,* 171; Robinson, *British Tar,* 196.

[43] *Barlow's Journal,* 544.

[44] *Adventures by Sea of Edward Coxere,* 139; Barnaby Slush, *The Navy Royal: Or a Sea Cook Turn'd Projector* (London, 1709), 83; Smollett, *Roderick Random,* 17.

pect of social relations, whatever the formal authority of communications at sea. Nondeferential, sometimes defiant speech expressed one of the ways in which maritime culture was linked to the process of class formation.[45]

The story was told of a priest, a passenger of small sailing experience, who made his way amid a squalling tempest and groaning timbers to the captain's cabin in order to ask about the perils of the surrounding storm. The captain puzzled the priest when he told him to go on deck and listen to the sailors as they worked the masts and sails. The priest complied, only to find that the fury of the seamen's language matched that of the elements. Bursting back into the captain's quarters, he reported that the sailors were cursing and swearing like madmen, to which the captain nonchalantly responded that there was no great danger. Still later, the priest returned with news that the seamen cursed no longer, but now occupied themselves with prayer. The captain gravely replied, "Oh, I am afraid that if they have stopped swearing and started praying there is no hope for us."[46]

This incident, although taken from a later period, throws a sharp shaft of light upon the nature of religion at sea in the eighteenth century. The ship was an environment where work, activity, and self-help necessarily took precedence over religious meditation or supplication. Religious belief and practice had to be broadly congruent with the imperatives of work and survival. This necessity, reinforced by the ship's isolation and distance from religious institutions, joined with long-standing plebeian traditions of skepticism and anticlericalism to make sailors one of the most notoriously irreligious groups of the early modern period.[47]

Commonplace were the moans and complaints about the sailor's ungodly ways. Edward Braithwaite, writing in the seventeenth century, said of Jack Tar: "He converseth with the

---

[45] On this point, see the Conclusion of this book.

[46] Walter Runciman, *Windjammers and Sea Tramps,* quoted in Weibust, *Deep Sea Sailors,* 204.

[47] Why irreligion took root in the maritime milieu has not, to my knowledge, been investigated. The key period would seem to be the seventeenth century.

starres, observes their motions, and by them directs his compasse. Singular notions derives hee from them; meane time he is blind to Him that made them. He sliceth the depths, and is ignorant of Him that confines them; he cutteth the surging swelling waves, and thinks not of Him that restraines them; he coasteth by the shelfes, and forgets Him that secures him." Blind, ignorant, thoughtless, and forgetful: common words in the description of the seaman's relation to religion. "Defiant" might have been equally appropriate, as a Mr. Young of the Society for the Promotion of Christian Knowledge discovered during his efforts to convert the seamen at Plymouth Hospital. The tars found that they could best use Young's moralistic tracts to light their pipes.[48]

Ned Ward wrote that the seaman "loves short Voyages, as he does short Prayers, and it is hard to say which of the two he makes oftenest."[49] This man of short prayers (or no prayers at all) prompted numerous authorities to prepare pamphlets designed to overcome his "Worldly Lusts" and "disordered affections" and to turn his attention to hymn, meditation, and the state of his soul.[50] In 1725 Bernard Mandeville observed that "Amongst our Seafaring Men, the Practice of Piety is very scarce: Abundance of them lead very bad lives"; "There are not many that are well grounded in the Principles of their Religion."[51] John Woolman, the Quaker who championed the causes of many oppressed people in the eighteenth century, found but little "Fear of the Lord" at sea. "Great is the present defect among seafaring men in regard to virtue and piety," he cried, bemoaning the "lamentable degeneracy" that made life at sea "so full of corruption and extreme alienation from God," so "manifestly corrupt and profane."[52]

---

[48]   Edward Braithwaite, quoted in Robinson, *British Tar,* 98; Archive of the Society for the Propagation of Christian Knowledge, "Minutes of the S.P.C.K., 1706–1709," p. 20. I would like to thank Tim Hitchcock for this reference.

[49]   Ward, *Wooden World,* 68.

[50]   *Mariner's Divine Mate,* 1, 4, 48, 49, 50.

[51]   Bernard Mandeville, *An Inquiry into the Causes of the Frequent Executions at Tyburn* (1725; reprint Los Angeles, 1964), 48–9. See also *The Journal of John Fontaine: An Irish Huguenot Son in Spain and Virginia, 1710–1719,* ed. Edward Porter Alexander (Charlottesville, Va., 1972), 58.

[52]   *The Journal of John Woolman and a Plea for the Poor* (Secaucus, N.J., 1972), 192, 195, 206, 206, 195.

Men of the sea often made the same general judgment on the irreverence rampant among their kind. "We were all of us too wild and little considered the mercies we received," noted Ned Coxere; there was "little of the fear of God amongst us." The captain of an East India Company ship said that there was "no hearing the name of God or Christ among [seamen], unless in profane Swearing."[53] Tom Bowling, who hoped "to be saved as well as another," declared that he trusted "no creed but the compass."[54]

These comments do not mean that religion was entirely absent among seamen. The actual religious practices on board the merchant ships of the North Atlantic varied widely. As a general rule, the larger the ship, the greater the likelihood of formal religious services. The law required the Royal Navy to use chaplains to lead the solemn, orderly, reverential, and "public worship of Almighty God." But such leaders, Ned Ward only half satirically explained, were "much better at composing a Bowl of Punch than a Sermon."[55] Some privateering captains, such as Woodes Rogers, arranged for formal religious services by the book of the Church of England. And on merchant vessels, religious services were usually held at the insistence of the captain and conducted by him or by a more pious officer or crew member. Some ships had occasional services, some none at all. On one of Jack Cremer's craft, "Prayers we had once a week if [the wind] blowed hard, if little winds, knone."[56]

---

[53] *Adventures by Sea of Edward Coxere*, 40, 64; Anonymous officer of an East India Company ship, *Piracy Destroy'd, Or, a Short Discourse Shewing the Rise, Growth, and Causes of Piracy of Late, with a Sure Method How to Put a Speedy Stop to that Growing Evil* (London, 1701), 6; Smollett, *Roderick Random*, 237. John Bromley has observed of John Baltharpe's poetic account of life at sea that "[t]here is scarcely a word of religion in the whole narrative." See Baltharpe, *The Straights Voyage, Or, St. Davids Poem*, ed. J. S. Bromley (1671; reprint Oxford, 1959), xlv.

[54] Smollett, *Roderick Random*, 237.

[55] "An Act for amending, explaining and reducing into One Act of Parliament, the Laws relating to the Government of his Majesty's Ships, Vessels and Forces by Sea" (22 George II, c. 33, 1749), in Parker, *Laws of Shipping*, 179; Ward, *Wooden World*, 29, 30.

[56] Rogers, *Cruising Voyage*, 26, 165; *Ramblin' Jack*, 84. Sometimes the presence of an especially religious passenger made a difference in the ship's spiritual atmosphere. George Whitefield and John Woolman are cases in point. Whitefield held public prayers on the open deck and even used dramatic techniques such as preaching in a rising storm to impress the seamen: "while the winds and storms were blowing over me, I made earnest supplications to

But frequently religious meetings bore the imprint of the seaman's peculiar faith. Ned Coxere disclosed that sea devotions consisted of a prayer and a psalm, followed by "swearing, cursing, and lying," and then a "laugh, scoff, and jeer." Soon, "instead of singing with melody in the heart unto the Lord," the seamen lustily sang "vain, idle songs with ungodly words and action."[57] Irreverence and unruliness thus marked religious observances themselves. From the 1690s came the story of two seamen, George and Robin, and their discussion about religion: "Poor George, thus disturbed at his devotion, would look over his shoulder, and, at the end of every petition, would make an answer to old Robin with a 'God d—n you, you old dog! can't you let a body pray at quiet for you, ha? A plague rot you! Let me alone, can't ye?' Thus the one kept praying and cursing, and t'other railing for half an hour, when a great log of wood, by the rowling of the ship, tumbled upon George's legs, and bruised him a little; which George, taking up into his hands, and thinking it had been thrown at him by old Robin, let fly at the old fellow, together with an whole broadside of oaths and curses, and so they fell to boxing."[58]

It is impossible to know how many seamen would have emulated George, who prayed for half an hour despite disruptions, or how many would have taken old Robin's part as spoiler. There would seem to have been more Robins than Georges. But it is clear, the preceding boxing match notwithstanding, that the private practice of religion was both diverse and widely tolerated.

Little is known about the specific religious beliefs of seamen. Their thoughts about the body and the soul, salvation, sin, and the nature of heaven and hell have not been preserved. Yet formal religious affiliations among seamen were many, ranging from Catholic to Protestant, from the Church of England to

Footnote 56 (*cont.*):
God for them." Woolman also held religious meetings to which, after a while, "[t]he sailors usually came." See *Whitefield's Journals*, 99, 100, 102; *Journal of John Woolman*, 198, 204.

[57] *Adventures By Sea of Edward Coxere*, 131–2. Daniel F. Vickers notes the peculiar religiosity of fishermen in seventeenth- and eighteenth-century New England in "Maritime Labor in Colonial Massachusetts: A Case Study of the Essex County Cod Fishery and the Whaling Industry of Nantucket," Ph.D. diss., Princeton University, 1981, 127–8.

[58] Quoted in Robinson, *British Tar*, 110.

Presbyterianism and Quakerism. Almost every denomination was represented. African, Asian, and native American seamen extended the range of religious belief. Catholics and Protestants had their differences, as reflected on one side by the popularity of seafaring ballads on "popery."[59] But even this antagonism seems to have abated as the eighteenth century progressed. Since maritime culture did not on the whole take religious forms, coexistence was relatively easy. Indeed, seamen demonstrated remarkable tolerance of the diverse and heterodox beliefs they encountered on nearly every sizable merchant ship, so long as such beliefs did not interfere with work and survival. Speaking of religion, Tom Bowling announced, "I meddle with nobody's affairs but my own."[60] Tolerance, however, did not preclude strong belief. Fervent religiosity and extensive knowledge of the Bible, for example, sustained Joshua Gee, a late-seventeenth-century mariner from Massachusetts, through the trials of slavery in Algeria, off the Barbary Coast.[61] But it is noteworthy that most seamen apparently had scant knowledge of the Bible and few religious beliefs central to their identities. For the majority of seamen, religion was in almost all respects a distinctly secondary matter.

Why should this have been so? A definitive answer is impossible, owing to the limited and fragmentary nature of the evidence on religious belief among seamen. But it is clear that several factors would have weakened the force of religious ideas in the seaman's consciousness. First and foremost was the simple but profound fact of the ship's isolation, its social and geographical distance from landed society and the church. The deinstitutionalized setting of seafaring life allowed maritime culture to develop in a relatively autonomous way, since seamen lived apart from the conventions, symbols, and rituals of

---

[59] For evidence of prejudice against Catholics, see *Ramblin' Jack*, 139; *Barlow's Journal*, 405–6. For the comical case in which English seamen converted to Catholicism, got drunk, and then demolished an image of a saint, see William Betagh, *A Voyage Round the World* (London, 1728), 255.

[60] Smollett, *Roderick Random*, 237. Christopher Hill has written: "As *Robinson Crusoe* shows, the world of the Caribbean, with its frequent shipwrecks and sea rescues, led to a mix-up of nationalities and creeds in which religious intolerance would have been extremely inconvenient, to say the least." The same principle often applied to shipboard life. See Hill's "Robinson Crusoe," *History Workshop Journal*, 10 (1980), 11.

[61] *The Narrative of Joshua Gee, 1680–1687* (Hartford, Conn., 1943), 17.

mainstream religious society for extended periods. As Edward Barlow pointed out, something as elementary as the religious calendar had hardly a place at sea: "Yea, I always knew that the worst of prentices did live a far better life than I did, for they had Sundays and other holy days to rest upon and take their pleasures; but all days were alike to us, and many times it fell out that we had more work on a Sabbath day than we did on other days."[62] Work at sea obliterated the plebeian calendar of holy days: "all the days were alike to us." Work itself – the central reality – dictated much of the rhythm and nature of cultural life. No matter how often Cotton Mather instructed seamen to admit to God that "thine Eye is always upon me," the seaman knew that life at sea was exceptional. God's eyes may have been upon him, but those of minister and magistrate most emphatically were not.[63]

The seaman's work experience also tended to generate irreligion through a process of dechristianization. Certain forms of religious belief were actively discouraged, even eradicated, by seamen. The process was succinctly described by Daniel Defoe, a writer uncommonly knowledgeable about things maritime, when he had Robinson Crusoe utter these words: "But alas! falling early into the seafaring life, which of all the lives is the most destitute of the fear of God, though His terrors are always before them; I say, falling early into the seafaring life, and into seafaring company, all that little sense of religion which I had entertained was laughed out of me by my messmates, by a hardened despising of dangers, and the views of death, which grew habitual to me by my long absence from all manner of opportunities to converse with any thing but what was like my self, or to hear any thing that was good or tended toward it."[64] Defoe's insight was precise. Learning to live as a seaman meant subordinating religious preferences to practical activity, for in

---

[62] *Barlow's Journal*, 61.
[63] Cotton Mather, *The Lord High Admiral of All the Seas, Adored* (Boston, 1723), 22.
[64] Defoe, *Robinson Crusoe*, 142. The seminal study of dechristianization is Michelle Vovelle, *Piété Baroque et Déchristianisation en Provence au XVIIIe Siècle* (Paris, 1973). See also Marc Venard, "Popular Religion in the Eighteenth Century," in William J. Callahan and David Higgs, eds., *Church and Society in Catholic Europe of the Eighteenth Century* (Cambridge, 1979), 138–54.

the context of ever-doubtful survival, self-help was valued above religious sentiment.

During times of crisis, religion could be worse than irrelevant; it could be dangerous if allowed in any way to stand between a seaman and the task at hand. Seaman John Baltharpe made the same point in verse: " 'Tis ne're the near to cry, God help/And nothing to do to save our self."[65] Appeals to God served no purpose unless everything humanly possible had already been done. Religious belief thus had to be generally compatible with the imperatives of life at sea. Sir Thomas Overbury said that Jack Tar "can pray, but 'tis by rote, not faith, and when he would he dares not, for his brackish belief hath made that ominous."[66] No prayers until all was lost, because praying was, in a sense, an admission that human effort had failed. Praying was "ominous," as the priest in the storm discovered. Once certain religious beliefs and practices had been "laughed out" of a seaman, the irreligious tendency, as Defoe suggested, was reinforced by the powerful isolation, social and spatial, of life at sea, and by the class composition of the maritime labor force.

Irreligion at sea drew upon and was further sustained by ancient traditions of skepticism and disbelief within plebeian culture. The work of Christopher Hill, Keith Thomas, and Jon Butler has demonstrated that heterodox belief was rife among English and American populations in the seventeenth and eighteenth centuries, and that the Toleration Act of 1689 and the declining power and discipline of English ecclesiastical courts facilitated a broad undergrowth of plebeian irreligion. "Popular scoffers and blasphemers," skeptics, and anticlericals abounded.[67] Practically no one scoffed and blasphemed as vig-

---

[65] Baltharpe, *The Straights Voyage*, 60.
[66] Quoted in Robinson, *British Tar*, 256.
[67] Hill, *The World Turned Upside Down*, 21, 29; Keith Thomas, *Religion and the Decline of Magic* (New York, 1971), 159–73; Jon Butler, "The Future of American Religious History: Prospectus, Agenda, Transatlantic *Problematique*," *WMQ* 42 (1985), 167–83; idem, "Magic, Astrology, and the Early American Religious Heritage, 1600–1760," *AHR* 84 (1979), 317–46; G. E. Aylmer, "Unbelief in Seventeenth-Century England," in Donald Pennington and Keith Thomas, eds., *Puritans and Revolutionaries: Essays in Seventeenth-Century History Presented to Christopher Hill* (Oxford, 1978), 25, 31, 41; Robert W. Malcolmson, *Life and Labour in England, 1700–1780* (London, 1981), 84–

orously as Jack Tar, and he could be as skeptical and anticleri-
cal as anyone.

A Reverend Ogilvie bound to New York aboard the *Tartar* in
1725 apparently made the mistake of trying to distribute Bibles
among the less than receptive members of the ship's crew. During the voyage the poor reverend was "abus'd in a most barbarous manner." The seamen sneaked into his quarters and "cut
him down" as he lay "in his Hammock . . . so that he fell upon
one of the Guns," which did him "a bodily prejudice." Further,
they "several times attempted to commit Sodomy with him." Of
course, they had nothing "to accuse him of, only that he wou'd
not swear and drink as fast as they, and seemingly show'd his
dislike of those vices[,] w[hi]ch they so much resented." Probably the greatest indignity came when they beat him violently on
the head with his Bible.[68]

Pirates gave the clearest form to ruling-class fears about the
casting aside of religion, strenuously denying religious teachings and wisdom. Philip Ashton, taken captive by pirates in
1725, put the matter plainly. Among these outlaws "every thing
that had the least face of Religion and Virtue was entirely
banished."[69] One merchant captain believed that pirates not
only expressed irreligion, but that irreligion caused piracy in
the first place. The "real cause" of piracy, he asserted, "is un-

---

Footnote 67 (*cont.*):

5. See also Bridenbaugh, *Cities in the Wilderness*, 422, 423, where he argues
for increasing heterodoxy and secularization in the eighteenth century. Robert Currie, Alan Gilbert, and Lee Horsley suggest that church attendance in
the mid-eighteenth century was low, dipping to 10 percent in some areas of
England. See their *Churches and Churchgoers: Patterns of Church Growth in the
British Isles Since 1700* (Oxford, 1977), 2, 21, 22. See also Alan D. Gilbert,
Religion and Society in Industrial England: Church, Chapel, and Social Change
(London, 1976), 7, where it is argued that the "dark corners of the land,"
where religious indifference reigned, were growing darker in the early eigh-
teenth century.

[68] Richard Hewitt to the Bishop of London, Warwick County, July 29, 1725,
Fulham Palace Papers 14, Lambeth Palace, London, No. 65. This reference
to sodomy is one of the extremely few references to sexuality among early-
eighteenth-century seamen. Although it is certain that alternative sexual
practices were common, even sanctioned, at sea, it is impossible to know how
widespread they were or what seamen thought of them. See Burg, *Sodomy
and the Perception of Evil*, and more importantly, A. N. Gilbert, "Buggery and
the British Navy, 1700–1861," *Journal of Social History*, 10 (1976), 72–98.

[69] John Barnard, *Ashton's Memorial: An History of the Strange Adventures, and
Signal Deliverances of Mr. Philip Ashton . . .* (Boston, 1725), 18, 7.

doubtedly the depravation of the Seaman's manners, and their little or no sense of Religion."[70]

Cotton Mather and Benjamin Colman, two Boston ministers who preached at pirate executions, could not have agreed more fervidly. Mather said that the pirate *"Mocks at Fear,* and like an Horse rushing into the Battel, he rushes upon the Grossest Abominations. *Riots, Revels,* Debauches grow familiar with him. Horrid *Oaths,* & the Language of Fiends, proclame his *Tongue set on fire of Hell.* Bawdy and Filthy *Songs,* enough to infect the very Air they are uttered in, are the finest of his Vocal Music. *Dishonest Gaming* becomes no little part of his *Business.* It is not long before his Impiety improves into *Malignity.* He forsakes, he abhors the *Churches* of God." Worse still, the pirates "bid intolerable *Defiances to Heaven* in their Blasphemies." And worst of all, *"Monstrous Undutifulness* to their Superiors is expressed by them. They *Mock* the Ministers and Messengers of God, with outrageous Insolencies." Colman could only add "amen." These pirates, audaciously "laughing at the very thunders of God," might easily have beheld His "wonders . . . in the deep," yet never were they "thinking of Him," but rather "always defying and blaspheming Him."[71]

Militant irreligion suffused the pirates' social world. Pirate captain Charles Bellamy felt himself a "free Prince" entitled to make war against the whole world; this, he added in antinomian fashion, "my conscience tells me." But he went further to criticize those seamen "who allow Superiors to kick them about Deck at Pleasure; and [who] pin their Faith upon a Pimp of a Parson; a Squab, who neither practices nor believes what he puts upon the chuckle-headed fools he preaches to."[72] Here

---

[70] *Piracy Destroy'd,* 3.

[71] Cotton Mather, *Useful Remarks: An Essay Upon Remarkables in the Way of Wicked Men: A Sermon on the Tragical End unto which the Way of Twenty-Six Pirates Brought Them . . .* (New London, Conn., 1723), 13, 15; Benjamin Colman, *It is a Fearful Thing to Fall into the Hands of the Living God . . .* (Boston, 1726), 22, 27. See also Mather, *Fearful Warnings to Prevent Fearful Judgments* (Boston, 1704), 41.

[72] Captain Charles Johnson [Daniel Defoe], *A General History of the Pyrates,* ed. Manuel Schonhorn (1724, 1728; reprint Colombia, S.C., 1972), 587. Other pirates apparently shared Bellamy's feelings. A novel of the early eighteenth century, probably written by Defoe and perhaps based on real incidents, chronicled the adventures of merchant captain George Roberts, who was taken by pirates and proposed by some for a chaplain. But apparently the

skepticism and anticlericalism rushed together in one swift, sure condemnation.

Although some seamen – and pirates here would appear to be the extreme example – took irreligion as a way of expressing their numerous disaffections, there were of course other alternatives. Some men made a specifically Christian critique of their treatment by the merchants and captains for whom they hauled the treasures of the world. Edward Barlow denounced the un-Christian practices of his commanders with equal passion and regularity.[73] Jack Cremer complained of his "Proud" and "arberterry" captain, who should have "yoused *us* moore Christian like."[74] Other seamen claimed their right to "Christian burial," especially when the alternative was being dumped, without ceremony or care, into the deep. As stated in verse: "In seas the greater Fish the less devour/So some Men crush all those within their power."[75] It was a metaphor readily accessible to seamen, and no less a reality to which they had to respond. Some men expressed disaffection through irreligion, whereas others did so within a religious idiom.

The seaman's religion was thus a complex array of belief, doubt, and disbelief. Some sailors held religious beliefs that sustained them through trial and hardship; many used a sense of Christian ethics to fault their situation and treatment. Probably a greater number took a distant and skeptical attitude toward religion, doubting and ignoring the official teachings of the various churches and their representatives. For reasons both social and work-related, religion took a secondary place in the worldview of most seamen.

William Byrd II, the patriarchal Virginia planter, once argued, " 'Tis Natural for helpless man to adore his Maker in

Footnote 72 (*cont.*):
majority of sea robbers sided with the pirate who replied, "No, they wanted no Godliness to be preached there: That pirates had no God but their *Money*, nor *Saviour* but their *Arms*." See Roberts, *The Four Years Voyages of Capt. George Roberts* . . . (London, 1726). See also the *Boston News-Letter*, Aug. 4–11, 1718.
73 For a searing denunciation, see *Barlow's Journal*, 553.
74 *Ramblin' Jack*, 84.
75 John Flavel, *Navigation Spiritualized; Or, a New Compass for Sea-Men* (Boston, 1725), 97.

some form or another."[76] But his words, when applied to seamen, suggest a curious irony. Seamen were always perched on the curling lip of disaster; they were ever at the mercy of nature. Yet the very potency of the elements and the consequent need to battle them were key features in promoting a less religious view of the world among seamen. Self-help and solidarity, so utterly essential to survival, eclipsed religion in cultural importance and value. Irreligion became a basis for community, a triumph of sorts over a menacing natural situation.

Although wrong in one respect, William Byrd's comments on the beliefs of "helpless man" were right in another. The omnipotence of the elements forcefully affected the seaman's worldview, intensifying, however, not his attachment to formal religion but to beliefs and practices frequently denigrated as "superstition." The tar's worldview combined the natural, the supernatural, the magical, and the material.

The seaman's work required a precise sensitivity toward nature, an awareness that allowed him to create reliable knowledge from the observation of natural signs. Nature, so central to his labor, was no less central to his consciousness. A man of the sea, Ned Ward pointed out, "trusts much more to the Sun for his Guide, than to the Creator of it."[77] Seamen created a rich store of knowledge, much of it genuinely scientific and reliably predictive, from the heavens and the earth. They studied and interpreted the movements and characteristics of the sun, moon, and stars, the clouds, winds, and waters, and even the wildlife of the seas.

A ring around the sun portended ill for a deep-sea vessel and its crew. As a passenger at sea wrote in his journal in 1715:

---

[76] Byrd quoted in Patricia Bonomi and Peter Eisenstadt, "Church Adherence in the Eighteenth-Century American Colonies," *WMQ* ser. 3, 39 (1982), 245. The present argument holds that plebeian disbelief was not as impossible or unlikely as suggested by Lucien Febvre, *The Problem of Unbelief in the Sixteenth Century: The Religion of Rabelais*, trans. Beatrice Gottlieb (Cambridge, Mass., 1982), and James F. Turner, *Without God, Without Creed: The Origins of Unbelief in America* (Baltimore, 1985), 3. For an interesting critique of Febvre, see David Wootton, "Unbelief in Early Modern Europe," *History Workshop Journal* 20 (1985), 82–100.

[77] Ward, *Wooden World*, 37.

"We see a hazy ring about the sun which the sailors say is an infallible sign of bad or blowing weather." A "great Circle about the Sun," explained William Dampier, one of the wisest men of early modern seafaring, meant "storms of Wind, or much Rain." A breach in the circle, furthermore, indicated the direction from which the winds would gust. Another piece of wisdom about the sun was contained in the "common Saying," "a *high Dawn* will have *high winds,* a *low Dawn small Winds.*"[78]

Seamen also fixed their gaze upon the moon, which influenced the tides and the currents. A ring around the moon, like the sun, suggested a storm. Dampier believed that "if there is any very bad Weather in the Month, it is about two or three Days before or after the Full or Change of the Moon." A greenish tint to the moon might indicate "some days of fair weather." The relationship between moon and stars also came under strict scrutiny. "At the rising of the moon," commented John Fontaine, "a star rose after and followed the moon, which the sailors said was a great sign of tempest and [that] upon the like occasions [a storm] commonly happens."[79]

Other elements carried their own messages. It was "a Proverb among Seamen, Up Wind, up Sea, Down Wind, down Sea." In the warm climates seamen took careful notice of the winds, which often raised sudden swells all about them. In certain regions the direction of wind revealed climatic probabilities. In the tropics, clouds gathered on the horizon were "a great sign or token of Land." It was almost always "foggy or cloudy over the land; although it be never so clear at Sea." Some sailors believed that sea animals conveyed information about the weather.[80] Porpoises "come in herds on both sides of the ship: a sign of a storm as the seamen say." Bonitas "running beside the ship were a sign of change in the wind." Seahogs were thought to be "the forerunner of a gale of wind, and that they swim

---

[78] *Journal of John Fontaine,* 71; Dampier, "New Voyage," 295–6, 498.

[79] *The Journal of James Yonge,* ed. F. N. L. Poynter (Hamden, Conn., 1963), 113; Dampier, "New Voyage," 416; Jeremy Roch, "The First Journal," in Ingram, ed., *Three Sea Journals,* 63; *Journal of John Fontaine,* 49. See also *Journal of James Yonge,* 62; "The Journal of Francis Rogers," 151.

[80] Dampier, "New Voyage," 217; *Journal of John Fontaine,* 71; Funnell, *Voyage,* 225–6.

against the gale, or that the wind will come out of the quarter towards which they went."[81]

The sign that indicated natural probability was not radically different from the sign that functioned as an omen of future fortune. Seamen shared the belief, present in high culture and low, that it was possible to predict the future from the signs of the present. This belief took on an extraordinary significance among seamen, who urgently needed to make an almighty nature seem more comprehensible and hence controllable. The seaman, whose life might be threatened on any given day, made omens central to his outlook, seeking mastery over his surroundings not only through natural observation but also through magic, ritual, and supernatural interpretation. Jack Tar relentlessly searched for the sign, knowing all the while that life itself might depend upon it. At sea as on land, the sign was often a crystallization of fear.[82]

Omens appeared to seamen in an abundance of ways. Some came from the heavens. Comets and falling stars, for instance, suggested fortunes good or ill. Another omen was St. Elmo's fire, the "corposant" or glowing starlike mass of material that sometimes appeared after a storm at sea. St. Elmo, a diminutive of St. Erasmus, the patron saint of Mediterranean sailors, appeared "like a Great Ball of fire," as if "a small star" or "a small light" usually affixed to a mast.[83] St. Elmo's fire was variously interpreted as the embodiment of Christ, the Holy Spirit, or Castor and Pollux, the argonauts who in ancient mythology searched for the golden fleece. Some saw in the fire the fugitive soul of a dead comrade who had returned to warn of impending danger. In the seventeenth century, the more religious and supernatural interpretations of St. Elmo's fire seem to have prevailed. Upon sighting the corposants, wrote Dr.

---

[81] Teonge, *Diary*, 30; *Barlow's Journal*, 442; "The Journal of Francis Rogers," 144.

[82] Thomas, *Religion and the Decline of Magic*, 89–91, 623–8; Robert Muchembled, *Popular Culture and Elite Culture in France, 1400–1750*, trans. Lydia Cochrane (Baton Rouge, La., 1985), 80.

[83] Captain Edgar K. Thompson, "The Tradition of St. Elmo's Fire," *American Neptune* 24 (1964), 213–14. "Simsons Voyage," f. 52; "Voyage to Guinea, Antego, Bay of Campeachy, Cuba, Barbadoes, &c., 1714–1723," BL, Add. Ms. 39946, f. 5; George G. Carey, "The Tradition of St. Elmo's Fire," *American Neptune* 23 (1963), 29–38. On comets, see *Journal of James Yonge*, 70.

John Covel in 1670, our men "would hardly be persuaded but that they were not some *Hobgoblins* or *Fairies,* or the inchanted Bodyes of witches and we had many a fine story told to that purpose." Such supernatural meanings faded in the eighteenth century.[84]

St. Elmo's fire was also an omen about the weather. The appearance of only one corposant indicated an imminent tempest or perhaps some vague "dismal future." Two corposants – Castor *and* Pollux – suggested fair weather or good fortune. "The seamen," wrote a seafarer, "have an observation that when the Meteors called Castor and Pollux come not together, that it was a bad Omen." A corposant on the maintopmast was a good sign, but when "they are seen lying on the Deck" – resembling "a great Glow-worm" – "it is generally accounted a bad Sign."[85]

Other omens included birds known as the "Devil's imps," the grampus that promised "mischief," or something as intangible as the feeling experienced by the jittery seaman "not well satisfied in [his] mind." Perhaps not surprisingly in an all-male environment, women were sometimes considered ill omens. On February 14, 1683, a group of seamen were "chusing of Valentines, and discoursing on the Intrigues of Women" when "there arose a prodigious Storm" that lasted for almost two weeks. The seamen "concluded that the discoursing of Women at Sea was very unlucky, and occasioned the storm."[86] Some seamen apparently believed that women, like the adherents of orthodox religion, were potential sources of conflict and perhaps an eventual breach in the solidary order of the ship.

---

[84] J. Theodore Bent, ed., "Extracts from the Diaries of Dr. John Covel, 1670–1679," in *Early Voyages and Travels in the Levant* (New York, 1893), 127. On the progress of more secular meanings in the eighteenth century, see Carey, "St. Elmo's Fire," 37, 29.

[85] "Simsons Voyage," f. 52; Dampier, "New Voyage," 414; *Journal of John Fontaine,* 76; Carey, "St Elmo's Fire," 35; Thompson, "St. Elmo's Fire," 214. To my knowledge, no one has studied Castor and Pollux as symbols among seamen of male or brotherly love.

[86] "The Third Journal of Jeremy Roch," 103; "Simsons Voyage," f. 47; *Adventures by Sea of Edward Coxere,* 45; "Cowley's Voyage Round the Globe," in William Hacke, ed., *A Collection of Original Voyages* (London, 1699), 6. On women, see also *Barlow's Journal,* 171, 257. On omens, see Fletcher S. Bassett, *Sea Phantoms: Or Legends and Superstitions of the Sea and Sailors in All Lands and at All Times* (Chicago, 1885), 126–32, 274–81.

Belief in omens often implied belief in spirits. Seamen sometimes felt the spiritual presence of their deceased comrades.
Spirits took visible forms. As "Ramblin' Jack" Cremer pointed
out, "I have observed *that* Sailors in generall have Noshern
[notion] of fear of Aperishons."[87] Francis Rogers, a man not
the least inclined to believe in phantoms, described an incident
aboard the *William Galley* in 1705. A seaman working his watch
around nine in the evening spotted a boat off the starboard
side. "At first I did not [see it]," declared Rogers, "but presently
did (as I thought) very plain, and it seemed so near us, I was
somewhat surprised, not expecting a boat in the middle of the
ocean, as it were." Astonished by the presence of this tiny craft
upon the high seas, the seaman fetched the captain, who was
no less perplexed, since his calculations also indicated that land
was nowhere near. "We haled it several times, when it was near
us," Rogers continued, "but no answer. Sometimes we imagined we saw the men rowing very plain and then again [later]
could not tell what to make of them." Matters continued thus
"near half an hour. Sometimes we thought it almost on board
and then gone again of a sudden. I fired a pistol at it; it continued the same a very little while, and then we saw no more of
our boat." Mr. Pugh, the chief mate, had "it to be Charon's
boat for Mr. Nesbitt (who was then very ill), saying he believed
he would die, as indeed he did, I think the next night." Everyone aboard who saw the boat "concluded it was an apparition
forerunning Mr. Nesbitt's death." Rogers added a postscript: "I
cannot tell how to resolve within myself about it, not being very
ready to credit the stories of apparitions, but such we thought it
then."[88] Such spirits appeared to seamen in the context of
natural or social dangers, to warn of death or to avenge someone treated unjustly. Early and unnatural death reinforced a
belief in spirits and expanded its social function.

To an extent unknown, seamen also believed in the power of
magicians, though such belief was more pronounced in the

[87] *Ramblin' Jack,* 90.
[88] "The Journal of Francis Rogers," 223–4. There is not enough evidence to
suggest that the dead functioned as an age group in seafaring society. See
Natalie Zemon Davis, "Some Tasks and Themes in the Study of Popular
Religion," in C. Trinkhaus and H. A. Oberman, eds., *The Pursuit of Holiness
in Late Medieval and Renaissance Religion* (Leiden, 1974), 327–35.

seventeenth than in the eighteenth century. Edward Barlow, for one, could not make up his mind about conjuring and witchcraft. He reported that one of his captains thought himself bewitched by an old woman. The captain's fears grew when they found "a black cat on board, which had not long been seen before, and none of our ship's company did know how she came aboard." The ship was later sunk, prompting Barlow to say, yes, they had been bewitched, but to add a qualifier: "Whether there be any such things as witches I know not, yet there were great signs of no better luck to our master as it proved, all things falling out so unlucky in this our late passage, and he being so affrighted and troubled in his mind."[89] Edward Coxere, like Barlow a late-seventeenth-century seaman, described a man made "lame with his shoulder" when his "bed was suddenly pulled from under him, and he hove on the floor by an evil spirit." The same man later accused another of being "the sorcerer that had bewitched him" and proceeded to enact a ritualistic exorcism, driving a hot marlinspike into the foremast "to punish or kill the sorcerer." Coxere described these "whimsies" with detachment and skepticism.[90] It is probably safe to assume that seafarers like Barlow and Coxere lost faith in the power of cunning men and women because the social web upon which magicians depended for knowledge and effective advice could not be replicated in the dispersed and mobile world of maritime labor. By the eighteenth century it would seem that practitioners of magic held almost as little attraction for seamen as official agents of religion.[91]

The seaman's worldview combined Christian and pre-Christian beliefs, referents, and orientations. Seamen used classical mythology, biblical tales, and traditional yarns as they created their lore and their pantheon of meaningful figures. Castor and Pollux appeared with St. Elmo's fire; Charon and the River Styx appeared before dying seamen; Neptune figured with increas-

---

[89] *Barlow's Journal*, 259, 261; see also 471. Early seafaring beliefs in "storm raisers" or conjurers are detailed in Bassett, *Sea Phantoms*, 101–20.

[90] *Adventures by Sea of Edward Coxere*, 44, 45.

[91] Thomas, *Religion and the Decline of Magic*, 172. The argument advanced here does not fully explain the failing confidence in cunning men and women, because by this logic seamen would not have held them in regard in the sixteenth and seventeenth centuries. Perhaps the internationalization of trade helped to break down the older beliefs.

ing prominence in seafaring rituals. Pagan notions such as "luck" took on special meaning among seamen, underpinning a variety of beliefs. Seamen placed coins "under the mast" for luck, for wealth, quick speed, a safe return, or as protection against evil spirits. Some tars believed the coin to be payment to the ferryman Charon to cross the River Styx.[92] The notion of luck, as Keith Thomas has argued, was popular among common Englishmen and women in the early modern era, especially because their fortunes often bore little relation to merit and effort.[93]

The seaman's worldview was an amalgam of religion and irreligion, magic and materialism, superstition and self-help.[94] Seamen used basic empirical observation of nature and its regularities in order to act as successfully as possible within given limits. Yet it must be stressed that the tar did not regard nature in a mystical way. The sea seldom, if ever, took on the character of an omnipotent imaginary being. Nor did sailors make sacrifices to the sea and its special array of deities, as their pagan ancestors had. Anglo-American men of the sea rarely appealed to saints for protection.[95] They studied the "wonders of the deep" but they did not, as ministers never grew weary of repeating, appreciate God's authorship of those wonders.[96] Further, seamen did not commonly invoke "God's will" as an all-embracing explanation of their situation. Still less did they submit to "fate." Their outlook, fundamentally shaped by the nature and the setting of their work, was based upon an essentially materialistic view of nature, a desire to make an omnipotent nature seem orderly and comprehensible, and a

[92] "The Second Journal of Jeremy Roch," 98; Henning Henningsen, "Coins for Luck Under the Mast," *Mariner's Mirror* 51 (1965), 205–10. See also Bassett, *Sea Phantoms*, 437–9.

[93] Thomas, *Religion and the Decline of Magic*, 111–12.

[94] Keith Thomas has written, "What we are faced by in this period is not one single code but an amalgam of the cultural debris of many different ways of thinking, Christian and pagan, Teutonic and classical; and it would be absurd to claim that all these elements had been shuffled together to form a new and coherent system." See *Religion and the Decline of Magic*, 627.

[95] Catholics, of course, made such supplications more often than Protestants, though the extent of such efforts is unknown. One example of praying to a saint as a protector can be found in the seventeenth-century *Journal of James Yonge*, 78. On the early history of sacrifice to pagan deities at sea, see Bassett, *Sea Phantoms*, 379–92.

[96] *Barlow's Journal*, 410; *Whitefield's Journals*, 107.

need to entrust to each other their prospects for survival. But the very forces that created these tendencies also produced obstacles to their extension and ultimate realization. The uncontrollable vicissitudes of nature, the extreme vulnerability of seamen, and the frequency of death at sea gave a special power to superstition, omens, personal rituals, and belief in luck.[97]

The genesis and perpetuation of maritime culture were closely related to the "life cycle" of seafaring workers, particularly to the rituals and activities that marked the stages of life at sea. Cultural life was central both to the seaman's individual identity and to his collective consciousness. After all, a man became a seaman not only by learning the work and language of the sea but by ritual initiation. The "sailor's baptism," a classical rite of passage, was enacted when novices first "crossed the line," that is, the equator. Practiced by all seafaring nationalities and therefore part of an international maritime culture, the seaman's baptism was essentially an initiation ceremony that marked the passage into the social and cultural world of the deep-sea sailor. Appearing among English seamen in the late seventeenth century, the ritual of crossing the line corresponded almost perfectly to the decisive growth in the number of men mobilized for deep-sea work. The rites expressed and reinforced a new occupational identity among these men. The festivities at the line were a lively and meaningful part of every voyage.[98]

Upon crossing "into the Southern part of the World," every sailor – and later, every passenger – was required to pass through the initiation. The novice had a choice: to be ducked in the ocean or to pay a fine. Francis Rogers provided a de-

---

[97] C. John Somerville, *Popular Religion in Restoration England* (Gainesville, Fla., 1977), 73, discusses the general decline of belief in supernatural agency in the late seventeenth century.

[98] I am heavily indebted in this section to the fine study by Henning Henningsen, *Crossing the Equator: Sailors' Baptism and Other Initiation Rites* (Copenhagen, 1961). See also Bassett, *Sea Phantoms*, 416–20. On the origin of the ritual, see Henningsen, *Crossing the Equator*, 88, 84, 245, 266, and Weibust, *Deep Sea Sailors*, 213. Edward Barlow, a late-seventeenth-century mariner, suggested an earlier origin when he called the rite "an old custom among seamen," "an old sea custom." See *Barlow's Journal*, 181, 344.

tailed description of the activities: "Five of our men, not being willing to pay a bottle of brandy and pound of sugar, were ducked according to custom, it being the first time they had passed [the equator]. The manner of ducking is this; there is a block made fast to the main yard arm, through which is reeved a long rope, one end whereof comes down on the Quarter Deck, the other to the water, at which end is made fast a stick about a foot and a half long thwartways, on which the person sits across, holding fast with his hands the rope as it goes up having a running knot about him; when being ready he is hoisted up close to the yard arm, by the people on the Quarter Deck, and at once let run. His own weight from that height plunges him under the water as low as the ship's keel; then they run him up again as fast as they can and so serve him three times, then he is free and may drink with the others that paid." A breathtaking plunge, a crash into the sea, a deep immersion: these were the elements of the sailor's baptism.[99] (See Figure 12.)

The ceremony was not unlike the charivari, the popular pageant of landed society. Shipboard discipline was momentarily relaxed, though a few barriers between captain and crew remained. Some captains probably stood apart from the festivities in the interest of maintaining distance and authority. Others thought the ritual too "heathen."[100] But there were other reasons for disapproval. The ceremony temporarily reversed the ship's official hierarchy, and many a captain was treated with

---

[99] "The Journal of Francis Rogers," 152; Henningsen, *Crossing the Equator*, 103. Other descriptions and mentions of seamen's initiation rites are contained in Rogers, *Cruising Voyage*, 17–18; Esquemeling, *Buccaneers of America*, 10; Harvey v. Barry, SC ADM (1729), f. 716; Teonge, *Diary*, 47; Cooke, *Voyage*, 12; "Voyage to Guinea," BL Add. Ms. 39946, ff. 1, 5, 27; Alexander Hamilton, *Gentleman's Progress: The Itinerarium of Dr. Alexander Hamilton, 1744*, ed. Carl Bridenbaugh (Chapel Hill, N.C., 1948), 56; "Captain Pennycook's Journal," BL, Add. Ms. 40796; *Life and Adventures of Matthew Bishop*, 16; "Diaries of Covel," 105. Some seamen enacted these rites upon crossing the Tropic of Cancer, passing through the Straits of Gibralter, and traveling in other places. There is an excellent description of baptism as practiced by French seamen in Robert Challe, *Journal d'un Voyage fait aux Indes Orientales, 1690–1691* (Paris, 1979), 189–93, where it is noted that the ritual "is customary and not to be denied" by the captain. I owe this reference to Roy Ritchie.

[100] Rogers, *Cruising Voyage*, 18.

Figure 12. The ceremonies upon crossing the line. Note the three seamen, dangling from the yardarm, to be ducked in the ocean as part of their initiation into the brotherhood of deep-sea sailors.

scorn and derision.[101] The church was also lampooned. Crossing the line, as Henning Henningsen has insisted, was not a Christian ritual. In the early eighteenth century, the pagan god

[101] Henningsen, the author of the most learned and comprehensive study of sailors' baptism, has noted: "It is hardly likely that in early times the captain took part in the celebrations that followed the baptism, as that would have been bad for discipline." Some captains apparently found the ceremonies offensive and discouraged them altogether. See *Crossing the Equator*, 108, as well as 15, 60, 62, 110. I have found one piece of evidence to contradict Henningsen's claim about the nonparticipation of captains. It comes from "Captain Pennycook's Journal" (Add. Ms. 40796) of 1698[?]. "This morning we passed the Tropick of Cancer. I caused perform the usuall Ceremonies, by ducking Such as had not past it before, and would not pay the usuall Forfeit viz a Bowl of Punch."

Neptune appeared as a symbolic figure who oversaw the grand occasion. Yet seamen did not worship Neptune, nor did they believe in his natural or supernatural powers. Sailor's baptism had little or nothing to do with Christian baptism.[102] True to their tradition of irreligion, seamen stripped baptism of its religious meanings and used it to serve the ends of occupational solidarity. The rites not only expressed a shared consciousness among seamen but simultaneously dramatized divisions within the social order of the ship.

Once seamen were initiated into the brotherhood of the deep, maritime culture and community were expanded and sustained by a variety of activities – singing, dancing, telling tales, and drinking. The rituals of sociability were crucial in the isolated wooden world. Probably the most important cultural form for creating bonds among men of the sea was song. Indeed, maritime culture has long and justly been famous for its song; seamen have been celebrated for their music, their voices, their lyrics, and their ballads. The late seventeenth century, writes C. H. Firth, witnessed "a great increase in the number of ballads describing the lives, adventures, loves, marriages, meetings, and partings of sailors."[103] These ballads reflected many of the themes discussed earlier. The "sailors' lament," an early form of the blues, consisted of wistful songs of separation from wife, children, parents, friends, and home. Seamen also sang ballads of danger and adventure, tragedy and struggle, of sea battles, storms, impressment, and shipwrecks.[104] The shanty or work song was designed to accompany, even assist, manual labor. Shanties were half-sung, half-chanted, in a call–response pattern most likely adapted from African culture; they were usually sparing in rhyme and generous in profanity. The leader of the shanty was "traditionally licensed to improvise as he wished and insult the officers with impunity." Capstan

---

[102] Henningsen, *Crossing the Equator*, 298: "Baptism at sea has nothing to do with Christian baptism, though this is usually thought to be the case." Henningsen also notes that seamen did not worship Neptune and that they did not believe in his natural or supernatural powers (120, 124).

[103] The analysis of sea songs is rendered difficult by the problem of dating. Since the songs were part of an oral tradition, in which they were continually modified, it is difficult to use them as specific evidence of maritime life in the early eighteenth century. See Firth, *Naval Songs and Ballads*, lix, xliv.

[104] Robinson, *British Tar*, 348–59, 405, 429; Weibust, *Deep Sea Sailors*, 129–43.

shanties were sung when weighing anchor, hoisting topsails, or lading or unlading cargo. There were long-drag shanties, hoisting songs in which a long pull was followed by a short pull; short-drag shanties, usually for the one strong pull to haul sheets in the wind; and finally, hand-over-hand shanties for hoisting light sails. Such songs, in all their variety, were the very vessels of a collective consciousness at sea, the media through which tars expressed their common fears, hopes, needs, and social realities. The bonds that slowly and fitfully emerged from shipboard cooperation often found their way into song.[105]

Dancing was another crucial part of the cultural life of the ship. As John Baltharpe wrote in verse:

> Sometimes to passe sad Cares Away
> On Fore-castle we dance the Hay;
> Sometimes dance nothing, only hop about
> It for good dancing passes amongst the rout;
> .Yet on my word, I have seen Sailors,
> More Nimbler Dance, than any Taylors.[106]

One of these nimble-footed folk was John Thacker, "a Seaman bred, and could neither read nor write; but had formerly learnt to dance in the Musick-houses about Wapping," the sailor's district in East London. Sometimes, as John Covel said, seamen "dance about the mainmast instead of a maypole, and they have a variety of forecastle songs, ridiculous enough."[107]

Seamen sang and danced; they also spent endless hours telling tales. As Jeremy Roch wrote:

> Thus after Dangers past, now safe and well
> The Story to our Friends we often tell,
> And they to Recompense us for our Tale
> Do Strive to Drown us in a Cup of Ale![108]

---

[105] Peter Burke, *Popular Culture in Early Modern Europe* (New York, 1978), 44; Frederick Pease Harlow, "Chanteying Aboard American Ships," *American Neptune* 8 (1948), 81–9. L. G. Carr Laughton, in "Shantying and Shanties," *Mariner's Mirror* 9 (1923), 48–55, 66–74, notes the "sad dearth of evidence" for work songs of the seventeenth and eighteenth centuries.

[106] Baltharpe, *The Straights Voyage*, 22.

[107] Dampier, "New Voyage," 361; "Diaries of Covel," 104. See also R. Campbell, *The London Tradesman* (London, 1747), 325; Defoe, *History of the Pyrates*, 212.

[108] "The Third Journal of Jeremy Roch," 105.

Such tales chronicled the adventurous, the dangerous, and even the miraculous. Seamen also recited, or created, poetry. They were, as one grumbling authority put it, quite adept at "roaring bad verses." They told tales of heroism, glory, and courage. It was widely understood that only some small part of these yarns had to be true. Some seamen enjoyed reading, though they were no doubt frustrated by the dampness that mildewed and destroyed many books. Seamen also performed plays – "homely drolls and *Farses,* which in their corrupt language they nickname Interlutes." Their plays ranged from spoofs of high culture to dramas of naval battles.[109] Gambling was another preferred pastime of seamen, if not always of their "betters." Mariners "rattled the dice," dealt the cards, and played backgammon.[110]

Drinking occupied a central place in seafaring culture, so central, in fact, that Barnaby Slush was moved to say that "liquor is the very cement that keeps the mariner's body and soul together."[111] Not only was drinking common; drinking to deadening excess was common. Religious pamphlets for seamen always denounced with special intensity the "beastly sin" of drunkenness that transformed the seaman into a "stupifyed Atheist."[112] Many was the time when a seaman appeared so "Disguised in Liquor . . . that he could not speake a plain word"; so drunk that he "was entirely deprived of his senses"; or so intoxicated that he was "fast lockt in the arms of Deaths younger Brother."[113] Woodes Rogers once remarked that "good Liquor to Sailors is preferable to Clothing," and his

---

[109] Falconer, *Universal Dictionary,* 196; "Diaries of Covel," 104; Hamilton, *Gentleman's Progress,* 128; Weibust, *Deep Sea Sailors,* 127–43; Henningsen, *Crossing the Equator,* 114.

[110] Falconer, *Universal Dictionary,* 196; Ward, *Wooden World,* 71; John Franklin Jameson, ed., *Privateering and Piracy in the Colonial Period: Illustrative Documents* (New York, 1923), 132; Rogers, *Cruising Voyage,* 267; Cooke, *Voyage,* 121, "Simsons Voyage," f. 38; Defoe, *History of the Pyrates,* 211, 308; Clive Senior, *A Nation of Pirates: English Piracy in Its Heyday* (London, 1976), 37–8.

[111] Slush cited in Robinson, *British Tar,* 107. See also *Barlow's Journal,* 142; Rogers, *Cruising Voyage,* 286.

[112] Flavel, *Pathetical and Serious Disswasive,* 140, 151; *Mariner's Divine Mate,* 48, 49, 50.

[113] Dickinson v. Dawkins, HCA 24/133 (1721); Redwood v. Studley, HCA 24/135 (1726); "The Journal of William Black, 1744," *Pennsylvania Magazine of History and Biography* 1 (1877), 239.

words were not merely the cool and condescending judgment of a "Gentleman Captain."[114]

Some sailors firmly believed that alcoholic beverages were necessary, especially in certain parts of the world, to "support Nature." Beer was, after all, a crucial source of nutrition. Further, liquor permitted an escape from harsh and unrelenting conditions, serving as an opiate of sorts. Edward Barlow believed that seamen incessantly searched for good drink because "they seldom get good victuals." John Woolman echoed and extended this judgment. Seamen, "in the wet and cold, seem to apply at times to strong drink to supply the want of other convenience."[115] But perhaps John Baltharpe put the matter most clearly:

> So that when Saylors get good Wine
> They think themselves in Heav'n for th' time;
> It Hunger, cold, all Maladies expels,
> With cares oth' world, doe trouble not our selves.[116]

Drink offered a momentary respite from the rigors of an often punishing life. Too much plain dealing, with the elements and with the conditions of life at sea, led to a lot of plain old drinking.

Drinking also served crucial social functions in the work culture of the sea. Seamen drank together, got to know each other, and frequently formed enduring friendships. Barlow, who "never had any great fancy for fuddling," did it more "for the love of my company than for the drink."[117] Liquor was also used in ritualized ways as part of daily social intercourse. Seamen, like aristocrats, continually drank toasts – to their "wives and mistresses," their friends, their comrades, their voyage, their good luck, and their safe return. Some drank to the king of England, some to the pope, some to William Penn. Pirates, contrary creatures that they were in almost every regard, drank

---

[114] Rogers, *Cruising Voyage*, 8. According to Tobias Smollett, men in the Royal Navy called their allotment of rum "*Necessity*." See *Roderick Random*, 187.

[115] Petition of John Massey and George Lowther, CO 28/17 (July 22, 1721), f. 199; *Barlow's Journal*, 152; *Journal of John Woolman*, 193. See also the Information of William Steele, HCA 1/58 (1750), f. 7.

[116] Baltharpe, *The Straights Voyage*, 59.

[117] *Barlow's Journal*, 32; Examination of Phillip Roch, HCA 1/55 (1723), f. 36.

to "the Pretender's Health, and hoped to see him King of the *English* Nation." When part of a larger occasion, drinking was attended by relaxed discipline, celebration, a feast, and perhaps the firing of the great guns.[118] Drinking rituals also helped to resolve disputes. Drinking thus reduced, at least temporarily, some of the burdens and stresses of the sailor's lot, helping all the while to create social bonds. Alcohol was "preferable" to clothing because its social and psychological uses were vastly more complex.[119] Like singing, dancing, and storytelling, drinking was a diversion from monotony, an entertainment, and a source of community amons men in the wooden world.

The life cycle of seafaring employment ended, often suddenly and prematurely, with death, which at sea was visible, poignant, commonplace, and never impersonal. No matter which captain a sailor signed on with at the beginning of his voyage, he never for a moment believed he did not have another, as suggested in popular verse:

> I am the chief Commander Captain Death,
> I fight against all Mortals upon Earth;
> When I amongst them chance to have a care,
> I conquer all, none dare with me hold War.

[118] Rogers, *Cruising Voyage*, 210, 78, 182, 32; John Baptiste Labat, *The Memoirs of Pere Labat, 1693–1705* (London, 1931), 56; "Simsons Voyage," f. 23; *Barlow's Journal*, 256; Quotation on the Pretender: *The Tryals of Stede Bonnet and Other Pirates* (London, 1719), 13. See also Roberts, *Four Years Voyages*, 74; Information of William Swale, HCA 1/54 (1721), ff. 130–1; *American Weekly Mercury*, June 13–20, 1723; William Snelgrave, *A New Account of Some Parts of Guinea and the Slave Trade* (1734; reprint London, 1971), 216; E. P. Thompson, "Patrician Society, Plebeian Culture," *Journal of Social History* 7 (1974), 400; Les Cleveland, "Soldiers' Songs: The Folklore of the Powerless," *New York Folklore* 11 (1985), 79–97 (I would like to thank Susan G. Davis for this last reference). There are a few fascinating bits of evidence that seamen, and particularly pirates, engaged in a sort of totemistic drinking. Philip Gosse, *The History of Piracy* (New York, 1932), 238, and Charles Hill, "Notes on Piracy," *Indian Antiquary* 56 (1927), 153, note that some pirates mixed drinks of rum and gunpowder. The same drink was apparently drunk by pirates with John MacPherson; see the *American Weekly Mercury*, Oct. 25–Nov. 4, 1731, 3. Another seaman told stories of drinking from a "Musket Barrel": Information of Henry Hull, HCA 1/56 (1729), f. 29. Perhaps seafarers believed that these drinks gave them special potency.

[119] Rely v. Moulton, HCA 24/130 (1711). See also Malcolmson, *Life and Labour*, 99–102; Rule, *Experience of Labour*, 201.

> I fear not the bravest Champions that be,
> Though they are stout, yet they can't Conquer me;
> 'Tis not Manhood nor Valour can them save
> I make them stoop and yield unto the Grave.[120]

The frailty of life at sea was always evident: "The life of Man is but a bubble/As before the Plough the Stubble," wrote John Baltharpe.[121]

As callous as the seaman appeared toward the death that took so many shapes around him, he could not escape its shadows. William Dampier, who had endured all manner of black and blustering weather, said that one particularly terrifying storm resembled nothing so much as "approaching Death." Even in calm seas the sailor could not escape the reminders of his own mortality. Jack Cremer had special interest in obtaining "a good hammock, or coffin you may call it, for [at sea] they always bury their dead in theair hammocks."[122]

The shadows of death darkened with the grim realization that "Captain Death" and the seaman's actual captain were all too often one and the same. Captain Rice Harris, after beating a seaman lifeless, ordered his corpse to be "put into some old hamack & put into the life boat & be carryed a good way from the ship & thrown over board." Adding insult to mortal injury, Harris "refused to have him buryed in the usual form," that is, with the proper ceremonies. He "refused to let him have Christian Buryal." After seaman Robert Mayor was clubbed to death by Captain John Shepheard, his body – on the master's orders – was immediately sewn up into his hammock so that its wounds might be hidden from the crew. And Samuel Naylor, whose murder of a crewman is detailed in the next chapter, "would not suffer the office for the Buryal of the Dead to be read" over his victim. Such raw assertions of power violated values deeply held by common sailors.[123]

---

[120] "A Description of Plain-Dealing, Time, and Death," by Thomas Lansing, c. 1690, *English Ballads*, BL. See also Ward, *Wooden World*, 69.

[121] Baltharpe, *The Straights Voyage*, 33; Gilbert, "Buggery and the British Navy," 89.

[122] Dampier, "New Voyage," 496–7; *Ramblin' Jack*, 44. See also *Barlow's Journal*, 61; *Voyages and Travels of Captain Nathaniel Uring*, 178.

[123] Smollett, *Roderick Random*, 145, 152; Information of John Daftor, HCA 1/56 (1733), f. 75; Information of Anthony Gwynne, HCA 1/56 (1733), f. 77; Information of David Weems, HCA 1/56 (1733), f. 80; Information of John

Such values were apparent in seamen's ideals concerning the treatment of those who had "come to port," "struck" their colors, or been "boarded" by the grim reaper. Seamen sought for themselves a secure resting place, a proper grave. Everyone, it would appear, preferred burial on land to being "flunge over board" at sea. Yet this most basic desire was contradicted by the central reality of work at sea. Land was usually nowhere to be found. Whenever it was at hand, the bodies of seamen were usually buried ashore. William Dampier noted that when his captain passed away, the body was carried to a nearby island so that they could "give him a Christian Burial." A marked grave was considered essential to peace and eternal rest.[124] Edward Barlow wrote of the unpeaceful end of a wealthy English merchant: "all his riches [afforded] him no better grave than the wide ocean, to be tossed from one place to another." Efforts were sometimes made to tie some cannonshot to the corpse to secure it at the bottom of the sea. It was the best grave the circumstances permitted.[125]

Seamen hoped to protect the body of the dead, but of course this was impossible once the corpse was committed to the deep.[126] Francis Rogers wrote of a shipmate, a cook, who expired: "Having sewn him up in a blanket, we heaved him overboard." The next day "10 or 12 sharks hankered about the ship for another such meal, they having met with the poor greasy cook." The seaman, by Edward Braithwaite's account, "goes not the way of all Flesh, but the way of all fish, whose fry feedes on him, as their forefathers fed him." Many thousands of tars were thrown into "a grave many times wide and big enough," where they became "meat for the fishes of the sea." To see a

---

Hill and James Jones, HCA 1/30 (1721), f. 123; Information of John Hill, HCA 1/54 (1721), ff. 126–7; Information of James Tindall, HCA 1/56 (1732), f. 63.

[124] Journal of a Mid-Shipman in voyage of H.M.S. *Happy Neptune*, 1678–80, BL, Sloane Ms., 978, ff. 30, 26; Dampier, "New Voyage," 113; Teonge, *Diary*, 246. See also Betagh, *Voyage*, 83, who described the marking of a comrade's grave: They "had an end of a strong plank drove down at the head of his grave, inscribed with his name, the ship's name, with the month and year."

[125] *Barlow's Journal*, 273.

[126] Peter Linebaugh, "The Tyburn Riot against the Surgeons," in Douglas Hay et al., eds., *Albion's Fatal Tree: Crime and Society in Eighteenth-Century England* (New York, 1975), 104–10.

shipmate's corpse "devoured by sharks and carrion crows" must have been a grisly and chilling sight.[127]

The rituals of death at sea were characterized, perhaps above all else, by simplicity. Burials took place with little ceremony and usually immediately, because seamen did not like to carry dead men on board. Bodies could not be preserved, and the stench was unbearable. Usually the ritual included "Prayers for the Dead" – a brief supplication – followed by "the usual Ceremony of firing the Guns."[128] Someone offered a few words in memory of his departed brother tar. Others paid their respects, but apparently with little display of emotion. Lingering grief, which would have turned some voyages into an endless rite of mourning, could hardly have been tolerated.

Parts of the ritual were organized according to class and status distinctions. The ceremonies for captains and mates were always careful and elaborate, and extra effort was made to find them proper places for burial. The highest-ranking men were often buried in specially constructed and weighted coffins rather than hammocks and blankets. The ship's colors were placed at half-mast, and more and bigger guns, often the greatest cannons, were fired to solemnize the occasion. The basic relations of authority in daily life were expressed, even reinforced, in the rituals that marked entrance into the afterlife.[129]

Edward Barlow, in a resentful and sarcastic aside, described the circumstances that usually surrounded the death of a seaman, and in the process he indicated by implication a positive vision most likely shared by his fellow workers: "And when [the seaman] is dead, he is quickly buried, saving his friends and acquaintance that trouble to go to church and have his passing bell rung, nor to be at the charges of making his grave and coffin, or to bid his friends or acquaintance to his burial, or to

---

[127] "The Journal of Francis Rogers," 163; Braithwaite quoted in Robinson, *British Tar*, 99; *Barlow's Journal*, 214; Slush, *Navy Royal*, 214; Smollett, *Roderick Random*, 190–1.

[128] Rogers, *Cruising Voyage*, 118; Funnell, *Voyage*, 12; John Esquemeling, *The Buccaneers of America* (1684; reprint New York, 1951), 366, 392, 397, 420, 448.

[129] Dampier, "New Voyage," 113; *Barlow's Journal*, 477, 437; Journal of a Midshipman, Sloane Ms. 978, f. 33; Rogers, *Cruising Voyage*, 118; Bartholomew Sharp "Captain Sharp's Journey over the Isthmus of Darien," in Hacke, *Collection*, 45; BL, Sloane Ms. 2296, 15, 18; "The Journal of Francis Rogers," 169.

buy wine or bread for them to drink or eat before they go to the church, and none of all this trouble, but when he is dead to sew him up in an old blanket or piece of old canvas, and tie to his feet two or three cannon bullets, and so to heave him overboard, wishing his poor soul at rest, not having a minister to read over his grave, nor any other ceremonies." Barlow was more religious than most seamen, but his preferences would probably have been affirmed by his comrades. A proper occasion would have included a gathering of friends and loved ones, perhaps a feast in honor of the dead, a good coffin, a secure and well-marked grave, and a decent and respectful set of ceremonies. It was a plea for dignity, a modest request. But it was equally an impossible one. The very conditions, geographical and social, of life and work at sea overwhelmed these most basic human needs.[130]

Seamen did the best they could within limits. One of the most touching rituals of death took place several days after a man had passed away. The dead man's goods – his chest, bedding, clothes, and the few other items he possessed, perhaps a book or two, cards, or a musical instrument – were auctioned off as everyone gathered round the mainmast. Seeking to honor the dead and to provide for his family, seamen purchased all of the goods at an "extreme dear rate." William Funnell wrote of an auction at the mast in 1704: "one of our Men being dead, his things were sold as follows. A chest, value five Shillings, was sold for three Pounds; a pair of shooes, value four Shillings and six pence, sold for thirty one Shillings; half a pound of Thread, value two Shillings, sold for seventeen Shillings and six pence." Richard Simson likewise noted that when the effects of a dead man "were sold at the Mast according to Custome," the goods "of the deceased not intrinsically worth above 30s were sold for 9lb Sterl 10s." Seamen sought to give value to a life that after years of toil had found no better end than a death in the middle of nowhere and an unceremonious burial in the briny deep.[131]

It is revealing that seamen, notoriously poor and underpaid,

---

[130] *Barlow's Journal,* 214; see also Linebaugh, "Tyburn Riot," 115.
[131] Teonge, *Diary,* 109; Funnel, *Voyage,* 15; "Simsons Voyage," f. 16; Betagh, *Voyage,* 133; McNamara v. Barry, SC ADM (1729), f. 648; Parker v. Boucher, HCA 24/137 (1719).

responded to the death of a comrade by redistributing their meager wealth to help his family. Their actions suggest both a consciousness of kind and an understanding of the struggles of poor families frequently dependent upon a male wage earner. The ritual also indicates something of the sense of responsibility that seamen felt toward each other. Their sentiments and responses may be seen as a forerunner – albeit in different and constrained circumstances – of later working-class efforts in friendly societies to see that the dead and their survivors received proper care. The ritual of redistribution expressed in yet another, particularly poignant, way the incipient collectivism of seafaring culture.

Mobility, dispersion, and social diversity governed the sailor's life and conditioned his cultural practices. His rituals were generally simple, unaffected, and straightforward; the seaman, "a Man of no Ceremony," made the best he could of necessity. Jack Tar scarcely had the props and materials for elaborate ritual at sea. Yet the lack of ceremony and the simplicity of ritual and ceremony expressed more than necessity. They were yet another part of plain dealing, and their function was vital. Maritime rituals were broadly accessible to and understood by an extremely diverse group of working men who came from many nations and almost all parts of the British Empire. Such rituals and festivities served to integrate, to create cohesion, to incorporate individuals of differing backgrounds into a new and meaningful collectivity. Rituals, organized according to the life cycle, created bonds, a common or at least overlapping identity, notions of reciprocity, responsibility, and mutuality.[132] They helped, in short, to create community at sea and to dramatize class divisions within it.

The formative influences upon maritime culture were essentially threefold: the nature, conditions, and social relations of work; the physical setting of the ship; and the social characteristics of the producers. Maritime culture was not static, but rather developed over time in response to changes in work, the workplace, and the nature of the workers themselves. Maritime

---

[132] The quotation is from Ward (*Wooden World*, 29), who intended to satirize naval surgeons.

culture was continually formed and reformed within the wooden world.

Work lay at the heart of the seaman's complex cultural experience. The changing character of maritime labor – particularly its intensification, its growing collectivism, and its increasingly mass character – initiated changes in the cultural order of the wooden world. Cultural forms such as the work song and the specialized language of the sea developed apace, and ritual and cultural activities took on more integrative roles, helping to forge occupational identity and solidarity. Other elements of the culture changed slowly, if at all, because the fundamental relationship between the seamen and nature changed relatively little during the first half of the eighteenth century. Extensive changes lay ahead in the nineteenth century, with the shift to steam power and the increasing substitution of seamen from underdeveloped countries for tars from England and America.

In the eighteenth century, many were the ways in which maritime life and culture were organized along the lines of a craft. This, at least, was how most captains saw the matter. The merchant ship in several ways resembled the traditional workshop. It had a master (the captain), a few journeymen (the mates who aspired, and sometimes managed, to become masters), apprentices (the lesser officers), and day laborers (the common tars). The organizational whole was held together by a corporate collectivism based on principles of hierarchy, paternalistic authority, and deference. Vertical solidarities linked the bottom and the top of the division of labor. Cultural life at sea expressed these basic principles and relations in a variety of ways.[133]

Yet there were numerous ways in which the ship did not – indeed, could not – resemble a workshop. Sailors, unlike craftsmen, did not own the tools of their trade. They possessed no property in artisanal skills. They depended upon the money wage. They did not labor within a regulated craft; rather, they were fully integrated into an international market economy.

[133] See Chapter 5 of this book for an elaboration of these ideas. See also Slush, *Navy Royal*, 48; Gary B. Nash, *The Urban Crucible: Social Change, Political Consciousness, and the Origins of the American Revolution* (Cambridge, Mass., 1979), 382–3; John Rule, *The Experience of Labour in Eighteenth-Century English Industry* (New York, 1981), 208–13.

They lost and found work according to the violent shifts of war and peace and the anarchic swings of economic cycles. Free of property and skills, unprotected from fluctuating market forces, and living lives shaped by mobility, dispersion, and high mortality, seamen largely failed to develop craft traditions or a craft consciousness.

Some of the ways in which the ship did *not* resemble a workshop were ways in which it *did* resemble a factory. The seaman's relationships to tools and wages are cases in point. If, as E. P. Thompson has argued, the eighteenth-century artisan experienced work as but one part of life, then seamen, like later proletarians, saw life ruthlessly subordinated to work.[134] To a far greater extent than most of his contemporaries, the seaman confronted his labor as something external, something alien. His incarceration on a deep-sea vessel resulted in a radical loss of social ties, liberty, and personal autonomy and an intensification of emotional strain. Jack Tar, one of the first collective laborers, was also one of the first alienated laborers. His ready resort to strong drink must be viewed in this light.[135]

The craft model, though popular among captains and some officers, was increasingly inappropriate to the social realities of the sailor's life. There was in fact a deepening rupture within the craft, a structural and cultural transformation taking place from within. Paternal obligations were eroded by the mobile seaman's quick, easy, and regular changes of masters, as well as by the depersonalized nature of the monetary wage. Seamen made many fewer appeals to custom than their counterparts in other occupations, because laissez-faire arrangements had all but banished the paternalistic responsibilities invoked by such appeals. The hoary triad of master-journeyman-apprentice had less relevance to the sailor's world than did the stark dichotomy of boss and waged worker, the corporate whole often less than the stratified part. As the vertical ties that bound together the corporate whole began to unravel, the horizontal links between common seamen grew in strength and number. The captain's preference for hierarchy and deference met the seaman's chal-

---

[134] E. P. Thompson, "Time, Work-Discipline, and Industrial Capitalism," *P&P* 38 (1967), 60.
[135] This has obvious links to Karl Marx's theory of alienation. See his *Economic and Philosophic Manuscripts of 1844* (Moscow, 1959), 61–74.

lenges of equality and autonomy. Perhaps the most telling proof of this broad transformation – and this we shall discuss in the next chapter – lay in the fact that merchant capitalists and captains did not bank upon the seaman's voluntary acceptance of capitalist relations of production in shipping. The increasingly vicious, even terroristic, methods of maintaining discipline and obedience were bloody testimony to the absence of a shared conception among master and men. Maritime culture in the early eighteenth century was undergoing a long and uneven transition in which something similar to craft organization was being eclipsed by that of class.[136]

A related transition was taking place in the larger societies of which seamen were a part. Richard Bushman has observed that "Cultural evolution in England and America was a single integrated process." A major part of the process was "cultural dissociation based on class." Each society during the eighteenth century divided into "gentle" and "simple" ways of life, patrician and plebeian cultures.[137] As seamen and other working people developed common cultural practices, their class counterparts, urban merchants – though on different scales and at different speeds in England and America – evolved shared notions of gentility and refinement.[138]

Maritime culture was an important part of plebeian culture and, in fact, shared many features with it. There were, as we have seen, commonalities in the realm of language, the use of curses, oaths, and swearing; in the realm of religion and irreligion; in the realm of perception and belief, particularly as each related to nature; and in the realm of cultural forms and activi-

---

[136] See Thompson, "Patrician Society, Plebeian Culture," 383, 388, 391, 396; Thompson, "Eighteenth-Century English Society: Class Struggle Without Class?" *Social History* 3 (1978), 134, 145; Malcolmson, *Life and Labour*, 132, 151, 147; Nash, *Urban Crucible*, 382–3.

[137] Richard Bushman, "American High Style and Vernacular Cultures," in Jack P. Greene and J. R. Pole, eds., *Colonial British America: Essays in the New History of the Early Modern Era* (Baltimore, 1984), 366, 373; Malcolmson, *Life and Labour*, 148; Thompson, "Patrician Society, Plebeian Culture," 382, 385, 396, and "Eighteenth-Century English Society," 149–50, 154. See also Alfred F. Young, "English Plebeian Culture and Eighteenth-Century American Radicalism," in Margaret and James Jacob, eds., *The Origins of Anglo-American Radicalism* (London, 1983), 185–213.

[138] Bushman, "American High Style," 350, 352, 357, 359; Nicholas Rogers, "Money, Land, and Lineage: The Big Bourgeoisie of Hanoverian London," *Social History* 4 (1979), 437–54.

ties: rituals, songs, ballads, dances, and tales. Maritime culture prominently featured many of the profane and rebellious ways of its parent culture.[139]

Many scholars have emphasized that plebeian culture was characterized, perhaps above all else, by diversity. "Plebeians" were those who made a living by their hands – farmers, artisans, laborers, even small traders; they made up the great bulk of the population in England and America in the eighteenth century. A heterogeneous array of social groups and types inhabited the terrain of plebeian culture. But there was unity within the diversity, especially since, as Hans Medick has recently argued, the dispossessions, breakdowns, and uncertainties occasioned by capitalist development in the early modern period gave plebeian culture a defensive but eminently supportive character.[140]

A second defining feature of this culture was in fact yet another instance of diversity: locality. "Folk culture," according to Henry Glassie, has always been in essence spatial. Locale and region have been its basic units. In England and in America geographical diversity, no less than social diversity, gave specific content and shape to the culture of working people.[141]

The diversity within plebeian culture owed much to the different ways in which its constituent groups experienced the process of capitalist development. Structural transformation took place within folk culture, and seamen were among the first to experience it. The increasingly rapid polarization of capital and labor in shipping pointed the way toward the future. Maritime culture, or at the very least its class subculture, represented a proletarian particle within the larger plebeian culture. Maritime employments thus not only perpetuated certain plebeian cultural activities but subtly and decisively modified them. They extinguished others. There was a process of culture stripping within that of becoming a "true bred sailor,"

---

[139] In general, see Malcolmson, *Life and Labour*. No comparable synthetic study yet exists for early American cultural and social history.

[140] Ibid., 12; Hans Medick, "Plebeian Culture in the Transition to Capitalism," in Raphael Samuel and Gareth Stedman Jones, eds., *Culture, Ideology, and Politics: Essays for Eric Hobsbawm* (London, 1982), 108.

[141] Glassie quoted in Bushman, "American High Style," 370; Malcolmson, *Life and Labour*, 94.

for the imperatives of work and survival left little room for incompatible cultural forms. As men moved from the social and cultural worlds of the farm, workshop, and household to that of the ship, attachments to previous ways of life were in crucial ways weakened. The processes of language acquisition and dechristianization illustrate the point. So, while integration into maritime culture created new bonds to replace the old, it also helped to create cultural distance between maritime workers and the rest of plebeian culture. The fear of proletarianization made many skilled and landed workers regard their seafaring brothers at a distance, sometimes with hostility and condescension.[142]

Yet on the other hand, seamen were among the most footloose of workers, and they helped to link the various social and geographical particles of plebeian culture. They transcended plebeian localism; they were bearers of culture and information among far-flung groups and places. They contributed to processes of cultural standardization and communication among working people. Since service in maritime employments, whether merchant shipping, the Royal Navy, privateering, or piracy, was relatively common among workingmen, even if only for a year or two at a time, commonalities of cultural experi-

---

[142] Malcolmson, *Life and Labour*, 149, 23. As the uneven process of proletarianization created distance between seamen and other working people, it placed obstacles between seamen and various social movements. Such appears to have been the case in the Great Awakening. Some sailors, especially those in depression-laden Boston, were touched by the messages of equality and fraternity, by the critique of traditional authority, and by the simplicity, the plain dealing, of the revival. In these general ways, maritime culture was congruent with the Great Awakening. Yet serious incongruities also existed, and these would have limited the appeal of religious rhetoric to seamen. Irreligion and dechristianization posed problems, as did the seaman's emphasis upon self-help over transcendent faith. The sailor's culture, formed in the context of extreme exploitation, was difficult to shed, not least because doing so would have created many new and dangerous vulnerabilities. "Love and Christian charity," as John Woolman painfully learned, often met their match in the class relations of life at sea. Daniel Vickers notes that the Great Awakening had little effect on most of the fishing communities of Massachusetts (see "Maritime Labor in Colonial Massachusetts," 236–7). But Christine Heyrman, in *Culture and Commerce: The Maritime Communities of Colonial Massachusetts, 1690–1750* (New York, 1984), detects a rising religiosity among the fishermen of Gloucester and Marblehead during the eighteenth century. The matter needs further study.

ence, and hence bases for shared consciousness, were established among the broader population of working people. In the domain of culture as in others, seamen were enmeshed in the momentous transition in which the world came to be governed by capitalism and class.

5

THE SEAMAN AS THE "SPIRIT OF REBELLION"

Authority, Violence, and Labor Discipline

Through the ages, sailors have built an extraordinary tradition of labor militancy. In the eighteenth century they were one of the most likely groups of British workers to strike. Indeed, as we have seen, the very term "strike" evolved from the collective decision of London seamen to strike the sails of their ships in 1768, halting the flow of commerce and the accumulation of capital.[1] Seamen frequently took to the streets in rowdy and rebellious demonstration, involving themselves in almost every port-city demonstration in England and America in the early modern period. Richard B. Morris has noted that "mariners were among the more radical and obstreperous element" in the early American working class. Eric Foner has echoed this judgment, describing sailors as "a particularly volatile element in

[1] See C. R. Dobson, *Masters and Journeymen: A Prehistory of Industrial Relations, 1717–1800* (London, 1980), 154–170, 25, who calls seamen one of the "three most conspicuously militant groups" of eighteenth-century English workers. See *Oxford English Dictionary,* s.v., "strike." For seamen's activism, see Max Beloff, *Public Order and Popular Disturbances in England, 1660–1714* (London, 1938), 127; John Stevenson, *Popular Disturbances in England, 1700–1870* (London, 1979), 71–2, 123–33; George Rude, "The London 'Mob' of the Eighteenth Century," in his *Paris and London in the Eighteenth Century* (New York, 1970), 300; R. B. Rose, "A Liverpool Sailors' Strike in the Eighteenth Century," *Transactions of the Lancashire and Cheshire Antiquarian Society* 68 (1958), 86; Peter Linebaugh, "The Tyburn Riots Against the Surgeons," in Douglas Hay et al., eds., *Albion's Fatal Tree: Crime and Society in Eighteenth-Century England* (New York, 1975), 85, 89–91; Carl Bridenbaugh, *Cities in the Wilderness: The First Century of Urban Life in America, 1625–1742* (London, 1938), 223, 224, 383, and *Cities in Revolt: Urban Life in America, 1743–1776* (New York, 1955), 114, 118, 305–14; Dirk Hoerder, *Crowd Action in Revolutionary Massachusetts, 1765–1780* (New York, 1977), 374–5; Bernard Bailyn, ed., *Pamphlets of the American Revolution, 1750–1765* (Cambridge, Mass., 1965), 581–3.

the [early American] urban population." John Stevenson, speaking of England, says: "During the course of the eighteenth century sailors became prominent in strikes and the disturbances associated with them; the middle years of the century, in particular, led to a number of disputes."[2]

This militancy represented only one side of a complex process, the flip side of which was the expansion of the world capitalist economy and its need for new types of authority and discipline. We saw in Chapter 2 that any worker who came from a workshop, a farm, or an estate to the ship entered not only one of the great technological wonders of the day but a new set of productive relations as well. The seaman was confined within a spatially limited laboring environment, forced to cultivate regular habits and keep regular hours, and placed in cooperative relationships with both other workers and the supervisors of his labor. In all of these ways, the seaman's experience foreshadowed that of the factory worker during the Industrial Revolution. New patterns of authority and discipline were crucial to the process of industrialization.[3]

This chapter explores the relationships among maritime authority, discipline, and militance during the early stage of capitalist expansion. The timing is crucial, for questions of authority and labor discipline at sea took on special significance after 1690 when, for the first time in Great Britain, the growth of shipping and the increased needs of the Royal Navy during years of war outstripped population growth and capacity.[4] The

---

[2] Richard B. Morris, *Government and Labor in Early America* (New York, 1946), 189; Eric Foner, *Tom Paine and Revolutionary America* (New York, 1976), 54; Stevenson, *Popular Disturbances*, 123.

[3] As Karl Marx noted, "The work of directing, superintending, and adjusting becomes one of the functions of capital, from the moment that the labour under capital's control becomes cooperative." See Marx, *Capital: A Critique of Political Economy*, trans. Ben Fowkes (New York, 1977), 448. See also Sidney Pollard, "Factory Discipline in the Industrial Revolution," *EHR* 16 (1963–4), 254–71; Neil McKendrick, "Josiah Wedgewood and Factory Discipline," *Historical Journal* 4 (1961), 30–55. The seminal article on the subject is E. P. Thompson, "Time, Work-Discipline, and Industrial Capitalism," *P&P* 38 (1967), 56–97.

[4] Ralph Davis, *The Rise of the English Shipping Industry in the Seventeenth and Eighteenth Centuries* (London, 1962), 391; J. H. Parry, *Trade and Dominion: The European Overseas Empires in the Eighteenth Century* (New York, 1971), 56; Christopher Lloyd, *The British Seaman, 1200–1860: A Social Survey* (Rutherford, N.J., 1970), 115.

establishment of authority and discipline was also crucial to the stabilization of the merchant shipping industry and even the empire itself in the first half of the eighteenth century. We shall examine the sources, types, and nature of maritime authority as negotiated between the captain and the crew, and conclude with a discussion of why, in the light of his experience, Jack Tar was so willing to take to the streets.

Eighteenth-century Britain and America, as suggested in the previous chapter, experienced the erosion of paternalist forms of labor control and the emergence of a new reality, and hence psychology, of free wage labor. Older social authority, organized around the family, the household, and the manorial village, was breaking down, and economic rationalization nibbled through the bonds of paternalistic discipline.[5] The older system of authority characterized by mutual obligations, reciprocity, and deference gave way to a system geared to market realities – supply, demand, and the business cycle. Tension and conflict marked relations of authority during the transition; they were especially evident in the interaction of the captain and crew in the merchant shipping industry between 1700 and 1750.

Maritime industries, at least from the point of view of legislators, merchants, ship owners, and captains, addressed this transitional dilemma with a flexible program best described as "disciplinary paternalism." The sea captain made symbolic use of the dominant institutions of the period, attempting to legitimate his authority by reference to the workship, the family, and the nation. Merchant captains variously referred to themselves as masters (of servants or apprentices), fathers (of children), and kings (of subjects). The very profusion of metaphors suggests the novelty and the uncertainty of the increasingly stark opposition between boss and wage worker. One captain told his crew that he was the "Head" of the ship and "they were the body." Captain William Kennett testified in 1730 that he "generally used his Marriners in so kind & tender a Manner that when he

---

[5] E. P. Thompson elaborated these views in two important articles: "Patrician Society, Plebeian Culture," *Journal of Social History* 7 (1974), 382–405, and "Eighteenth-Century English Society: Class Struggle without Class?" *Social History* 3 (1978), 133–65.

speaks to or of his Ships Company he calls them Children."
The law supported the captain in his familial fiction, calling his
authority "analogous to that of a parent over his child, or of a
master over his apprentice or scholar." Another captain, in
contrast, apparently considered it his duty to enforce "Martial
Law" on board his ship. Maritime officers thus adopted a variety of leadership strategies. Their transposition of the traditional, the familiar, and the familial to a relatively new factory-
like setting foreshadowed the industrial paternalism of the
nineteenth century and was designed, like later efforts, to "rob
industrialism of its sting."[6]

Maritime authority was organized around the formal roles
designated in the shipboard division of labor. The organization
was essentially hierarchical, though there was some overlap of
functions, and the ship's captain stood mightily at the apex of
the system of authority. Captains "had absolute authority over
the mates, the carpenters and boatswains, and the seamen" of
their ships, and they "could make life tolerable or unbearable
as they wished."[7] Their authority was guaranteed by law, upheld in the admiralty courts, and embodied in the wage contract negotiated with the individual seaman. Some thought that
"a Captain is like a King at Sea, and his Authority is over all
that are in his Possession."[8] He was to

show a laudable example of honour and virtue to the officers and
men, and to discountenance all dissolute, immoral, and disorderly
practices, and such as are contrary to the rules of discipline and subordination, as well as to correct those who are guilty of such offenses, as
are punishable according to the usage of the sea.[9]

---

[6] For a discussion of the concept in a later period, see E. P. Hohman, *The
History of American Merchant Seamen* (Hamden, Conn., 1956), 20–1. See also
Longust v. Youron, HCA 24/130 (1714); Brazier v. Kennett, HCA 24/136
(1730); Trumbull v. Jesse, HCA 24/133 (1722); Richard Sennett, *Authority*
(New York, 1980), 59; J. P. Aspinall, B. Aspinall, and H. S. Moore, eds., *A
Treatise of the Law Relative to Merchant Ships & Men by Charles, Lord Tenterden*
(London, 1901), 14th ed., 238.

[7] Davis, *English Shipping*, 131–2.

[8] *The Life and Adventures of Matthew Bishop* (London, 1744), 78.

[9] William Falconer, *An Universal Dictionary of the Marine* (1769; reprint New
York, 1970), 77. Both of these last two quotations described naval captains,
but they apply as well to masters and commanders in the merchant service.

The definition of the "usage of the sea" was, as we shall see, very much a matter of contention.[10] The captain, however, was enjoined not only to run his ship but to reform the character of his men. Work discipline required it.

The nature of customary usage changed with the passage of time. The captain's authority expanded in response to shifts in the British economy, which saw the coastal and luxury trades of the fifteenth, sixteenth, and early seventeenth centuries give way in importance to the deep-sea bulk trade of the late seventeenth and early eighteenth centuries. A voyage in medieval times, when all on board often held shares as "associates," was a relatively communal and egalitarian undertaking. The Ordinance of Trani (1063), central to Mediterranean shipping, specified that "the master of a ship may not strike a mariner and . . . the mariner may defend himself if the master persists in striking him." As deep-sea sailoring became more central to the economy, the captain's powers became more autocratic, and his disciplinary activities became a crucial part of the international movement of commodities.[11]

[10] In addition to the influences of war and peace to be discussed, the size of the crew affected authority relations. Many different emphases were possible within "disciplinary paternalism." In general, the smaller the crew, the less the need for discipline and the greater the tendency toward paternalistic relations. This formulation predicts that coercive discipline would have been least important on small coastal traders and greatest on East India Company vessels, which were frequently as large as a man-of-war, and this appears to have been the case. American-owned and -operated ships, generally smaller than the British but increasing in size over time, probably had less need for physical discipline. See Marx, *Capital*, 449: "As the number of co-operating workers increases, so too does their resistance to the domination of capital, and, necessarily, the pressure put on by capital to overcome this resistance." This statement makes it possible to see increases in discipline and decreases in crew sizes (discussed in Chapter 2), both prominent throughout the eighteenth century, as complementary parts of the same broad process and strategy.

[11] F. R. Sanborn, *Origins of the Early English Maritime and Commercial Law* (New York, 1930), 49; William McFee, *The Law of the Sea* (Philadelphia, 1950), 50, 54, 72; C. Ernest Fayle, *A Short History of the World's Shipping Industry* (London, 1933), 72; Immanuel Wallerstein, *The Modern World-System II: Mercantilism and the Consolidation of the European World-Economy, 1600–1750* (New York, 1980), 102–5; Sir Evan Cotton, *East Indiamen: The East India Company's Maritime Service*, ed. Sir Charles Fawcett (London, 1949), 91. The master's general authority increased in the eighteenth century as he took over the tasks previously reserved to the supercargo and gunner. For a colonial legislature's efforts to extend the captain's punitive powers, see "An Act for

The admiralty court system, vastly expanded in the late seventeenth century, served as an institutional base of the captain's authority, defining it in ways that prevented gross abuses and acting frequently as the interpreter of the wage contract, or articles, between captain and seaman. The wage contract, fully formalized in 1729 with the Act for the Better Regulation and Government in the Merchants Service, specified the principals of the agreement, wages, date of signing on, and advance pay. The seaman promised obedience, duty, and service. Articles represented the foundation of authority in the shipping industry. Yet their power to constrain behavior was strictly limited, and both captains and seamen broke them often and with relative impunity.[12]

Mates, carpenters, boatswains, gunners, stewards, and surgeons each had specific types of authority inherent in their formal roles. Taken together these officers constituted a second line of authority on the ship, vastly inferior to the captain but exercising specific, although considerable, powers over the crew. The chief mate, though a supervisor himself, remained a worker "perpetually supervised" by the captain, who was, by contrast, "the employer's representative working, usually, beyond the range of easy control."[13] All officers had some supervisory duties, and the small hierarchy served at times to mediate the extraordinary powers possessed by the captain.

Apart from, sometimes overlapping with, and frequently conflicting with the formal division of labor was another primary source of authority at sea: maritime experience. In a dangerous laboring environment, substantial authority accrued to those who had accumulated extensive practical knowledge and skills. Among the experiences and characteristics that

Footnote 11 (*cont.*):
Punishing mutinous and disobedient Seamen and for the more speedy determination of controversies arising between Masters of Ships and their Crews," CO 412/22 (Virginia, 1722).

[12] L. Kinvin Wroth, "The Massachusetts Admiralty," in George Athan Billias, ed., *Law and Authority in Colonial America* (Barre, Mass., 1965), 38, 57; Helen J. Crump, *Colonial Admiralty Jurisdiction in the Seventeenth Century* (London, 1931), 1, 2, 91; T. L. Mears, "The History of Admiralty Jurisdiction," in *Selected Essays in Anglo-American Legal History* (Boston, 1908), vol. II, 343–9. See also Partridge v. Pine, HCA 24/127 (1702); Linam v. Chapman, HCA 24/136 (1730).

[13] Davis, *English Shipping*, 126.

earned a seaman – of whatever formal role – authority and esteem were an understanding of the techniques and technicalities of the workplace, knowledge of the trade routes, the
world's geography, the language of the sea, having survived a
shipwreck or two, a good singing voice or a nimble dancing
step, physical strength and courage, good humor, and, among
the men at the bottom of the laboring hierarchy, scars on the
back from the cat-of-nine-tails, telltale symbols of endurance
and defiance. Having been stung and scarred by the cat-of-
nine-tails, many a tar was "as proud of the Wales on his Back,
as a *Holy-Land* Pilgrim is of a Jerusalem print." This informal,
collectively defined system of authority was based upon the
social and cultural relations of the workplace. It arose from the
daily experience of labor, had little or nothing to do with profits and productivity, and frequently stood in opposition to the
structural, hierarchical system of authority based upon the division of labor.[14]

The key to understanding maritime authority was offered,
tongue in cheek, by an experienced late-eighteenth-century mariner who explained the social logic of life at sea to a "green
hand": "There is no justice or injustice on board ship, my lad.
There are only two things: duty and mutiny – mind that. All that
you are ordered to do is duty. All that you refuse to do is
mutiny."[15] Many captains apparently set up command along
precisely these lines. They were aided in their efforts by the fact
that "once the ship had passed beyond the confines of the port it
became difficult for anyone to control the master's actions."[16]
The captain possessed extensive formal control through the
rigid definition of duty, and he enacted that control in eerie
isolation. The power relation between captain and seaman, set
apart from most agencies of social regulation and control, was
stripped to its essentials and depended as much on coercion as
on persuasion. The ship was a "total institution" in which the
captain had formal powers over the labor process, the dispens-

[14] See Peter Kemp, *The British Sailor: A Social History of the Lower Deck* (London,
1970), 70; Ned Ward, *The Wooden World Dissected: In the Character of a Ship of
War* (1708; reprint London, 1756), 71.
[15] Quoted in Knut Weibust, *Deep Sea Sailors: A Study in Maritime Ethnology*
(Stockholm, 1969), 372.
[16] Davis, *English Shipping*, 168.

ing of food, the maintenance of health, and general social life on board the ship.[17] Such formal and informal controls invested the captain with near-dictatorial powers and made the ship one of the earliest totalitarian work environments.

The tactics of authority and discipline employed by the merchant captain must be seen as part of a class relationship between the seaman who provided labor power and the captain who directed that labor power within a productive, profit-oriented enterprise. Between the two, authority was incessantly negotiated. Though the captain formally possessed dictatorial powers, the extent to which he could impose his will depended firmly upon the kind and amount of resistance he received from his crew. The captain's authority was an ever-contested reality that rested upon the often fragile "principle of obedience."[18]

One of the main enforcers of the principle of obedience, and an essential component of the master's authority, was the cat-of-nine-tails, the legendary emblem of maritime brutality. The captain's armory was also well stocked with canes, ropes, belts, sticks, and numerous other objects that could be made to function as weapons. Some captains administered whippings on "market day," usually a Monday set aside for discipline, whereas others did so at any time in response to specific events. Some seamen "endured their chastisem[en]t with greate presence of minde; others shrunk and roared like lusty fellows." Some masters saw the need to "tame" the men who came aboard, and the law encouraged them to the task. (See Figure 13.) Discussing medieval maritime law, William McFee claims that "None of the codes includes what became in the eighteenth century an almost universal feature of the life of a sailor, the unrestricted power of the captain to treat his men with the utmost cruelty without redress."[19] The captain's power was not unlimited, for the vice-

---

[17] The original and lasting conceptualization of the total institution was provided by Erving Goffman in *Asylums* (New York, 1962), xiii: "a place of residence and work where a large number of like-situated individuals, cut off from the wider society for an appreciable period of time, together lead an enclosed, formally administered round of life."

[18] Morris, *Government and Labor*, 225.

[19] "Richard Simsons Voyage to the Straits of Magellan and S. Seas in the year 1689," BL, Sloane Ms. 86, f. 24. See also *Ramblin' Jack: The Journal of Captain John Cremer*, ed. R. Reynall Bellamy (London, 1936), 45; McFee, *Law of the*

admiralty courts occasionally punished a brutal master. But the largely unchecked nature of the captain's legal powers cannot be denied. Most checks, such as they were, came not from the law but rather from the seamen themselves.

Edward Barlow, a late-seventeenth-century mate who was "reckoned rather too mild ... to bear [captain's] command over a parcel of seamen," summed up the rationale for discipline clearly:

> many seamen are of that lazy, idle temper, that, let them alone and they never care for doing anything they should do, and when they do anything it is with a grumbling unwilling mind, so that they must be forced and drove to it, which is a great trouble and vexation to those men that overlook them, and many times are forced to strike them against their will when fair means will not do it.[20]

Edward Barlow was doubtless a more humane mate than many of those who supervised labor at sea, for some "drove men to it" with such passion that they seemed far from troubled or vexed about it. Indeed, the East India Company maintained such severe discipline in its ships that a quarterdeck where floggings were administered resembled at times a "slaughter-house."[21]

A general, though by no means fully reliable, picture of the trends of discipline and violence at sea can be constructed from the cases of alleged excessive violence in the High Court of

Sea, 49; Lowther v. Rutlidge, HCA 15/43 (1744). One admiralty judge apparently considered any punishment that drew blood to be excessive: See Lawler v. Forrest, MASS ADM (1725), f. 276; Hooper v. Harris, MASS ADM (1725), f. 266. This appears to have been a dissenting opinion within admiralty law. When Karl Marx noted that the modern wage labor system could not have emerged without the bloody assistance of the lash, he may well have had the early modern shipping industry in mind. It is not without significance, therefore, that the Levellers were the first group in a political movement to oppose whipping, which they considered "only fit for bondmen" and not for free-born Englishmen. See Christopher Hill, "Pottage for Freeborn Englishmen: Attitudes to Wage Labour," in his *Change and Continuity in Seventeenth-Century England* (Cambridge, Mass., 1974), 227. For a discussion of the ways in which the critique of flogging became part of a later radical movement, abolitionism, see Myra C. Glenn, "The Naval Reform Campaign Against Flogging: A Case Study of Changing Attitudes toward Corporal Punishment, 1830–1850," *American Quarterly* 35 (1983), 408–25.
[20] *Barlow's Journal,* 453, 452.
[21] Cotton, *East Indiamen,* 60.

Figure 13. William Hogarth depicts Tom Idle, "the Idle 'Prentice," as he is "sent to sea." Several seamen introduce poor Tom to the social realities of life at sea. The seaman to the left dangles before him a cat-of-nine-tails, and another points to the distant corpse of a pirate hanging in chains. Hogarth anticipated Karl Marx's claim that the gallows and whip lined the road to wage labor.

Admiralty between 1700 and 1750. Such allegations were, first of all, 3.1 times more likely to be made in times of peace, periods of low wages and high unemployment, than during war years. They were also more likely to occur between the years 1715 and 1737, when four of every five charges were registered. More than half of the allegations of excessive violence were made between 1725 and 1736. Similar patterns and periodizations emerge from an analysis of the charges of murder made in the High Court of Admiralty at this time. Whether committed by a captain against a seaman or vice versa, murder was 3.3 times more likely to occur during years of peace than in war. Again the years 1715–37 stand out as especially brutal, containing three-quarters of all murders. The period 1723–35 conspicuously featured 60 percent of the homicides. It is difficult to know how much stock to place in these figures, since they are constructed from unsystematic and fragmentary data. They do, however, represent the only statistical measures available. But as E. P. Thompson has noted, "Neither terror nor counter-terror can disclose their meaning under purely quantitative examination. For the quantities must be seen within a total context, and this includes a symbolic context which assigns different values to different kinds of violence." Other data, in the form of descriptions, permit an ethnographic approach to the problems of authority and discipline.[22]

John Pattison, foremastman on the *Unity* sailing to the West Indies in 1708, failed to remember a chore. He was seized "by the hair of his head" by Captain Matthew Beesley, who forced his head "under the 2nd Gun on the Larboard side" and beat him with "a great Roap . . . so long and in such a barbarous & Cruel manner that . . . Pattison for sometime after was scarcely able to lift his Arms or hands to his head." Beesley, Pattison deposed, "would then have certainly murdered or crippled" him "had not the Gunner or some other persons cryed out Shame on it" and thereby "prevented him." On other occasions Beesley beat Pattison, causing "almost a pinte of Blood" to flow from his nose, made him serve a late night watch "bareheaded" in the rain, threatened to stab him with a knife and flog him "til the skin was all of[f] his Bones," and once tied him to the gangway. In 1736 Nathan Drew was severely whipped with a rope for using the wrong cloth to make a sail, and in 1726 John

---

[22] There is no evidence of changes in the internal operation of the High Court of Admiralty that would have affected these figures. There is, however, a bias against the later period, since complete documentation of allegations of excessive violence is available only for the 1700–39 period. The cases from late 1739 to 1744 (mostly wage disputes) are missing from the PRO, and after 1744 the court began to use a less systematic filing arrangement that makes it impossible to know how reliable the records are. These data are taken from HCA 24/127–24/139 and from the HCA 15 series. Data on murder, also fragmentary, come from the HCA 1 series. In allegations of excessive violence, $N = 163$, and for murders, $N = 50$. Quotation: E. P. Thompson, "Folklore, Anthropology, and Social History," *Indian Historical Review* 3 (1977), 255.

Salter was given several "stripes" for "loosing a new oare out of the Yaul." Captain Thomas Barry in 1729 lashed Richard Sargeant for the "irregular steering" of the vessel. Gilbert Lamb, returning late to his ship from shore, was smashed "several blows on the head" by his captain with a "peice of Oak"; he was "so much hurt that he could not for some time swallow any victualls" other than those tenderly fed to him by his comrades below deck. Thomas Wood, accused in 1729 of stealing wine, was beaten by his captain with a large broomstick until it "was broke into severall Splinters and small peices by the blow."[23]

Some of the beatings given sailors by captains or, in a few cases, by mates, were vicious almost beyond belief. Captain William Newcomin in 1733 beat John Jones with a stone mug and "broke four of his teeth quite out of his head." George Winter, a master accused of having a "very sower Morose temper," punched Thomas Waterson "until his Cheeks were very much swell'd and his Eyes beat almost out of his head." Still, Waterson fared better than Richard Desbrough, who claimed that his captain beat him with "his fist, Roaps, Sticks, & Canes," as well as a "maintopsail brace," and "beat & cut out one of his Eyes." James Conroy testified in 1707 that his captain, a Mr. Wherry, "catched him fast by the Nose with his left hand & thrust his thumb" into his "left Eye & with his right hand struck three Blows on his said Thumb & in that manner wilfully, designedly, & malitiously maimed & put out" his eye.[24]

In 1721 Master Richard Haskins of the *Laventon* galley allegedly attacked John Phillips in his sleep, punching him several times and then giving him ten to twelve blows with a marlinspike. Phillips began to convulse. Then, "with a design of having him fall over board," Haskins compelled Phillips by "force & violence" to go aloft in a hard, cold rain "to loose the fore top Gallant saile," even though the seaman was "all over

[23] Pattison v. Beesley, HCA 24/129 (1709); Powell v. Hardwicke, HCA 24/139 (1738); Examination of John Salter, HCA 24/135 (1727); Deposition of Daniel McNamera, SC ADM (1729), f. 733; Lamb v. Murrin, HCA 24/129 (1707); Wood v. German, HCA 24/136 (1729).
[24] Jones v. Newcomin, HCA 24/138 (1735); Waterson v. Winter, HCA 24/130 (1712); Desbrough v. Christian, HCA 24/132 (1720); Deposition of James Conroy, HCA 1/16 (1707), f. 133. See also Macknash v. Wood, HCA 24/134 (1724); Parker v. Boucher, HCA 24/132 (1717); Long v. Powell, HCA 24/134 (1723).

bloody" and had "nothing on but his shirt & breeches." While aloft, Phillips was "taken with another Fitt," but Haskins would not "suffer any of the Men to go to his assistance tho several offer'd ye same but swore he would shoot any body that should offer to go to assist or help him." Phillips somehow managed to hang on, but later claimed that he suffered permanent disability from the beatings.[25]

Some captains demonstrated great creativity in administering beatings. Samuel Matthews in 1733 said he was battered with a bull's foot, then with a "Manyocker (which is a tough root as thick as a Mans Legg)"; later he got a more conventional thrashing with 100 stings from the cat. Andrew Andrewson described a piece of oppression scarcely to be imagined when he claimed in 1736 that he had been beaten "upon the head with an Elephant's dry'd Pizle."[26] Practically anything, it would seem, could be made to serve as a weapon in the imposition of discipline.

Cruelties such as these represented a tactic of authority utterly central to maritime discipline – intimidation. As Richard B. Morris wrote, "Masters frequently drove their crews to the limit of endurance by bullying, profane threats, and the unsavory practice of hazing or 'working up,' which consisted of assigning dirty, disagreeable, and dangerous tasks to a particular seaman, too often as a means of settling personal grudges."[27]

[25] Phillips v. Haskins, HCA 24/133 (1722).
[26] Arnold v. Ranson, HCA 24/129 (1706).
[27] Matthews v. Tripland HCA 24/137 (1733); Andrewson v. Blinston, HCA 24/139 (1736). Another torture was to "whip and pickle" a sailor, the "manner whereof is to fasten or tye a Man with his Hands and Legs extended to the Blackstakes, Capston, or Jeers of the Ship, and strip him to the Waste, and with Whips of Cords, called Cats of Nine Tails, divers have had so many Lashes, as have made the Punishment worse than Death (as some Inflictors have told them before-hand), and being thus whipped or rather flead [flayed], a Tub of Brine or Pickle from their Salt Meat has been prepared; into which some (to make the Punishment the Greater) have caus'd more Salt to be put; with which they have washed their flead Bodies, and whipt and pickled them again: The dread of which Punishment has not only caus'd many to desert the Service, but also to indeavour to destroy themselves. And this punishment (how cruel soever it is) is now become so common, that Men are often thus treated on frivolous Occasions." See John Dennis, *An Essay on the Navy* (London, 1702), 8–9. See also Edward Cooke, *A Voyage to the South Seas* (London, 1712), 334; and Chapter 6 of this book for the use of this form of discipline by pirates. James Yonge reported that slaves on seventeenth-century Spanish galleys were whipped by the boatswain "with a bull's pizzle." See *The Journal of James Yonge*, ed. F. N. L. Poynter (Hamden, Conn., 1965), 69.

This last observation is crucial: authority at sea was intensely personal, which in turn was the very basis of intimidation. Undoubtedly many of the men described previously were used as "a publick Example" to the rest of the crew, as something of a medium for the dramatic and symbolic enactment of awesome authority. Captain Woodes Rogers had one seaman "severely whipt before the whole Company as a Terror to the rest." Intimidation, of course, was often effective even when no actual violence was necessary. Edward Kinney, for example, did something to rankle his chief mate, who responded with a promise "to wring off his Noase." Kinney, according to a fellow tar, "was afraid to be defaced, and began to be more Complasent." Other such threats and blusterings were common. David Wills, seaman of the inaptly named *Olive Branch,* was roughed up by Captain Nicholas Legau, who told "him that if ever he came [back] on board he would Cutt his Ears off."[28]

In 1727 Master Abraham Harris drubbed John Hamilton, making him lame in one arm in the process. Later in the voyage Harris threatened, "I will break your other arm." Captain Samuel Hayes told Amos Merritt in 1725 that he would "split his Soul or Stab him and eat a piece of his Liver." Francis Rogers, master of the *Crown,* told several of his crew that he was tempted to "skin them alive," and later informed "his Officers that if they should break the leggs and Arms of his Sailors" he would "justifye them" if the matters were taken to court. Calculated viciousness was often a foundation of authority, a stellar part of a larger economy of discipline.[29]

Even though the merchant ship master was empowered to administer only "moderate" correction, discipline occasionally lapsed, as we have seen, into cruelty and beyond, into torture and murder. Richard Edmondson, a member of the East India Company's *Union,* claimed that John Franklin ordered his "hands to be tied to the Capstan Barrs" and then hung a basket containing several hundred pounds of shot around his neck, "which caused him a great deale of pain, Misery, and Torture and forced his blood to gush out of his Nose and Mouth in

[28] Morris, *Government and Labor,* 265.
[29] Woodes Rogers, *A Cruising Voyage Round the World,* ed. G. E. Manwaring (1712; reprint London, 1928), 122; Dennison v. Toben, HCA 24/132 (1719); *Ramblin' Jack,* 95; Wills v. Legau, MASS ADM (1728), f. 36.

great Quantities & abundance." In 1746 John Cressey was made to place his "Middle Finger" in the hole of a specially bored block of wood. Captain Thomas Brown then drove wedges into the hole "with great force and violence," crushing his finger and causing "his hand and Arm then very much to swell." Brown then forced Cressey to tote the block of wood, which weighed near "Fifty pounds," around with him for "upwards of half an hour," and occasionally gave the block a kick for good measure.[30]

It is impossible to know how many seafaring men were murdered between 1700 and 1750, primarily because the available records are profoundly incomplete. But there are further problems in considering the question of murder on the high seas. The crime was rather easily concealed, given its often distant setting. Moreover, when was a death a murder? Many men were bludgeoned to death and obviously qualified as victims of homicide. But what of those who were "pinched in their provisions" by a captain trying to save on the costs of a voyage, men who grew weak, caught a fever, and died? And what of those flogged or mauled and then denied adequate medical assistance? In any case, many examples exist to show that, whatever the definition, murder was clearly a part of the social relations of work at sea.

Richard Baker signed on the *Europa* in 1734 for the run from St. Kitts to London, but soon grew sick and weak with the flux. His commander, James Blythe, ordered him to duty but he was unable to comply. Blythe then made him "hold the Helm ffour hours which is two Men's turns." He then whipped Baker, but concluded, "damn the Dog, the Rope will make no Impression on him." Blythe then ordered the boatswain to strap Baker to the mizenmast, was refused, and strapped him up himself, leaving him dangling for an hour and a half. Baker died four days later, his corpse "very much mark'd by the Beating with the Rope." Charles Ellis on the *Welfare* "refused to work for so long a time on a Sunday as the Mate of the Ship ordered him to work," and said that the labor was unnecessary since the vessel "was not in any manner of distress." He was

---

[30] Hamilton v. Harris, HCA 24/135 (1728); Merritt v. Hayes, HCA 24/135 (1727); Nairn v. Rogers, HCA 24/130 (1712). See also Pattison v. Beesley, HCA 24/129 (1709); Redwood v. Studly, HCA 24/135 (1726).

beaten by Captain Peter Dorbing, and his body was soon "very black from his Breast to his Throat." He died a few days thereafter. Master Robert Hartley made one of his sailors go "up to the main top to grease the Halyards" without a shirt, and when the man, weakened from a drubbing, fell into the sea, Hartley permitted no one to save him. In 1719 Captain John Shepheard of the *Borneo* dispensed discipline to Robert Mayor, vowing that he would bring him to "better manners" by a pummeling with a tar brush. Mayor died from his wounds, and "a few Minutes after the Breath was out of his Body he was [on the captain's orders] sewed up in his hamack" in order "to prevent any persons from seeing the Marks" left by the battering. Anthony Comerford was accused by Commander John Pinkethman of the *Ridge* of stealing a fowl, and was lashed to the shrouds to receive two stings of the whip from each member of the ship's company. During the punishment Pinkethman "stood by with his Blunderbuss & swore that he would shoot that Man that refused to lash the said Comerford." Just before his death, Comerford said that "he freely forgave all the Ships Company except the Captain & Mate."[31]

Valentine Arrisson stood his watch as the *Thomas and John* in 1706 sailed toward Virginia with a human cargo of slaves. Captain Robert Ranson "saw the Negros drinking some water they ought not to drink" and growled at Arrisson, "You dog, what do you let the Negros drink this water for, and took the Cutlass out of his [Arrisson's] hand and struck him sev[era]ll blows with it, and said, you Dog I will murther you if you do." Joseph Bottick, the caulker of the ship, heard Arrisson claim that the captain had given him his death's wound; "the Captain hearing him said . . . what did the Dog grumble at[?]" Bottick relayed, "he saith that you have killed him," to which Ranson replied, "God damn him, if I han't, I will," and quickly ran after Arrisson over on the "Larboard side and struck him two or three blows with his hand in the face." Arrisson, just before he died six days later, told Samuel Miller, the cook's mate, that "he had been a slave in Turkey and had never received so great an abuse as he had done by this Rogue meaning Captain Ranson."

[31] Morris, *Government and Labor*, 230; Edmondson v. Franklin, HCA 24/129 (1708); Cressey v. Brown, HCA 15/45 (1747).

In self-defense, Arrisson's mates kept alive the memory of his death. Later, "when the Capt[ain] struck one of the Men a box on the Ear, he ask'd him if he would kill him as he did Valentine." And when Ranson struck James Bradford, this seaman defiantly "told the Captain he had a mind to serve him as he had done Valentine."[32] The "cruel and barbarous" captain proceeded to kick Bradford "in such a manner that the blood run down his head & [then] prick[ed] him with a Cutlass in several places of [his] Body & beat out one or two of his teeth & cut his lip & beat him with a broomstick till he was black & blew & bruised all over his body."[33] Many seamen came away from such confrontations with both swollen backs and swollen hearts.

These incidents reveal how far the imposition of maritime discipline sometimes went. These, of course, were extreme cases, and in fact are preserved among admiralty records because they represented transgressions of both custom and law. Yet they were highly visible and well-remembered events, part of what Jesse Lemisch has called the "folk memory of ty-

---

[32] Information of Barkley Gould, HCA 1/56 (1736), ff. 94–5; Deposition of Barkley Gould, John Mackneal, James Kane, Richard Gell, and Robert Carter, HCA 1/19 (1735), f. 4; Information of Thomas Blood, HCA 1/54 (1715), f. 26; Information of Albert Ricsters, HCA 1/56 (1731), ff. 39–40; Information of John Hill and James Jones, HCA 1/30 (1721), f. 123; Information of John Hill, HCA 1/54 (1721), ff. 126–7; Information of Michael Clancy and Nathaniel Jelly, HCA 1/56 (1734), ff. 90–1. For similar cases, see Information of John Irwin, HCA 1/57 (1743), f. 81; Information of Francis Jarrott, HCA 1/53 (1702), f. 112; Memorandum of Francis Jarrott, HCA 1/29 (1701), f. 319; Examination of Rice Harris, HCA 1/56 (1733), f. 79; Information of John Daftor, Anthony Gwynne, and John Seirs, HCA 1/56 (1733), ff. 75–8; Information of William Granger and Robert Christion, HCA 1/56 (1731), ff. 45–9; Information of Edward Shoult, HCA 1/56 (1728), f. 22; Information of Thomas Summers, HCA 1/55 (1723), f. 48; Information of Benjamin Bush, HCA 1/55 (1724), ff. 91–2; Deposition of William Bennett, HCA 1/55 (1730), f. 140; Information of Henry Hall, HCA 1/56 (1729), ff. 29–31; Information of John Simons, HCA 1/56 (1736), f. 121; Information of Robert Howard, HCA 1/54 (1713), f. 17; Information of John Jackson, HCA 1/56 (1725), f. 1; Information of John Brockham, HCA 1/57 (1745), ff. 103–4; Information of Robert Fanning, HCA 1/58 (1751), f. 11; Deposition of Richard Carter, HCA 1/16 (1708), f. 165; Deposition of Edward Perry, HCA 1/29 (1701), f. 345; Deposition of Samuel Watson, HCA 1/19 (1735), f. 21; Information of Hector McNeal, HCA 1/56 (1731), f. 44; Information of Peter King, HCA 1/54 (1716), f. 36.

[33] Depositions of the Seamen [Jonathan Yates, Joseph Bottick, William Hurnard, Samuel Miller, Henry King] of the Ship *Thomas and John* relating to the Murder of Valentine Arrisson by the Master of the said Ship, CO 5/1315 (1706).

ranny."[34] They also served to define and establish the context for the social relations of work and authority in the merchant shipping industry, and they had potent social and symbolic functions. Physical discipline was probably the most powerful tactic in the system of maritime authority; it was, however, supplemented by many other initiatives from above.

Another important tactic was the unlawful and premature discharge of seamen. Many captains did not hesitate to turn a sailor ashore, especially in times of peace and high unemployment when replacements were easily found. In 1740 William Coates marooned John Monson in the Orkney Islands, telling him to "starve and be damned." John Baker of the *Portsmouth* was left by his master on "a desolate Island." Amos Merrit in 1725 was turned ashore "naked," without his chest, clothes, and bedding. And John Moodie, injured aboard the *Constant Anne* in 1725, was told by his captain, "you Dogg, be gone out of my Ship. You have no business here. I have discharged you this month & I will not give you any more Victuals, therefore be gone out of my Ship."[35]

Responsibility for the rationing of food was an important part of the captain's near-dictatorial control over the ship as a working and social environment. Withholding victuals from the crew was used as a means of discipline, and was especially important since any money saved on this account increased the profitability of the voyage for the owners. As Richard B. Morris noted, "It is perhaps significant that complaints on the score of food seem to have occurred most frequently when the master of a vessel was also a part owner." Since a great many masters in this period were indeed small part owners, bitter conflict often centered on the access to proper food.[36]

Although the captain was enjoined by law "to provide his seamen aboard ship with good food and living conditions," such an injunction was often disregarded. William Robuds in

[34] Jesse Lemisch, "Jack Tar vs. John Bull: The Role of New York's Seamen in Precipitating the Revolution," Ph.D. diss., Yale University, 1962, 51.

[35] Morris, *Government and Labor,* 264; Mowson v. Coates, HCA 15/42 (1741); *Rex* v. Winkley, MASS ADM (1728), f. 71; Merritt v. Hayes, HCA 24/135 (1727); Moodie v. Hogg, HCA 24/134 (1725).

[36] Morris, *Government and Labor,* 257, 263; Davis, *English Shipping,* 127. Peter Kemp, speaking of the Royal Navy in about 1700, remarks, "all captains and pursers were widely believed to be dishonest" (*British Sailor,* 57).

1710 complained that the crew of the *Selby*, commanded, not surprisingly, by Ralph Selby, had been kept "very short of Provisions" – they grew "weak & almost starved" – when in fact sufficient provisions for the seamen were on board the ship. The seamen of the *Wanstead*, at anchor in Maryland, were "almost starved on board the ship tho in a very plentifull Country where provisions and victuals are very reasonable." One of the men, John Redish, died because his captain "did not allow victualls & liquor enough to support them & used them very barbarously in their diett." Captain Thomas Barry of the *William* in 1729 began to pinch provisions, even though, his sailors insisted, "wholesome provisions [were] on board Sufficient to Entertain the Ships Company." William Biron charged in 1729 that Master Stephen Pamphlett did not allow enough food, "notwithstanding he had sufficient provisions on board but [instead] stinted them of the usual and accustomed allowance of provisions allowed by other Masters [in] the like Voyages." The seamen of the *Norfolk* in 1718 complained that their food was "full of maggots and not fit for use," but were told by their captain that they should eat them or "starve," for "he would provide no other." Perhaps this problem of food was best summed up by Dr. James Houston, who surveyed the conditions and prospects of health on the African coast for the merchants who traded with that part of the world. Two of the major "Diseases epidemical in this Country," he wrote, "are Tyrannical Oppression and Want of Necessaries of Life." Many seamen would have heartily agreed, since they often charged their masters with refusing them "the comon necessaries of life."[37]

Control over physical punishment and food equaled a measure of control over health, a matter of special importance among men who notoriously suffered from yellow fever, ma-

---

[37] Morris, *Government and Labor*, 230; Robuds v. Selby, HCA 24/129 (1710); Parker v. Boucher, HCA 24/132 (1719); Petition of Richard Sargeant and Christopher Harvey, SC ADM (1729), f. 713; Biron v. Pamphlett, HCA 24/136 (1729); Shackleton v. Swan, HCA 24/132 (1719); James Houston, *Some New and Accurate Observations . . . of the Coast of Guinea* (London, 1725), 57; Wistridge v. Chapman, HCA 24/135 (1727). See also Gray v. Travis, MASS ADM (1728), f. 106; Earle v. Odar, MASS ADM (1728), f. 65; Coulter v. Pitt, HCA 24/137 (1732); Jacob v. Hubbard, HCA 24/129 (1709); Astill v. Baggatt, HCA 24/139 (1735).

laria, dysentery, and scurvy.[38] A fully documented case from 1731 reveals how these issues of discipline, food, and health intertwined in an intricate spiral of power and authority. Rumors of mutiny began to circulate on board the *Hunter,* captained by Samuel Naylor. The master called for arms to protect himself against the revolt, but the gunner, a man by the name of Potter, "went down between Decks & locked the Arm Chest that the Captain might not have any of the Arms." Once aware of Potter's actions, Naylor "with all his strength struck him with his . . . larg walking Cane upon his head which broak his head in such a manner that the Blood gushed out in a great Quantity & flew upon the Cloaths of George Taylor," who was standing on the other side of the vessel. Several seamen apparently rushed to Potter's aid, attempting to provide medical attention, but Naylor quickly intervened, saying that the only dressing Potter was to receive for his wound was one made of brine. Further, he threatened the crew that "if any Man gives him a drink of Water he had better jump over board." Anyone offering food would be served "as bad or worse." Potter later died in the arms of George Taylor: "his last words were ffor God's Sake don't conceal my Murther for that Turk (meaning . . . Capt[ain] Naylor) has murthered me."

As the crew prepared to throw Potter's blackened and bruised corpse overboard, Naylor once more asserted his authority. He "would not suffer the Office for the Buryal of the dead to be read over him." As the ship came into port, Naylor sought out foremastman William Dixon and offered him money to testify that Potter's wounds were not severe, that the wounds had healed by the time of his death, and that Potter had returned to active duty. Naylor promised Dixon that he "should not soon have Occasion to go to sea again." On behalf of the captain, surgeon John Comrie contacted a Mr. Morecraft, "reputed to be the Crimp that shipped the Saylors" on the voyage, in an effort to contact other seamen to whom he would offer similar bribes in return for false testimony.[39] The cover-up failed, and Naylor was unable to conceal Potter's murder.

[38] Lloyd, *British Seaman,* 258–64.
[39] Information of James Tindall, George Taylor, Christopher Briggs, Matthew Hale, William Dixon, and Elizabeth Beal, HCA 1/56 (1732), ff. 63–9.

Struggles over health posed further problems of discipline, since seamen at times feigned illness to avoid working. Mariners realized that a "master had no legal right to administer corporal punishment to a sick mariner." Undoubtedly some captains dealt ferocious thrashings when they felt that their crewmen "dissembled" or "shammed." Jonathan Summers apparently felt that way about Richard Sandhill, whom he pulled from his hammock "by the hair of the head & told him he would be his Doctor & with great violence gave him upwards of sixty blows over his head, eyes, face, mouth & breast & knock'd & beat his head against the cable." Sandhill was injured so severely that he was unable to work for two months. In 1721 Jacob Bigelow turned out John Povey as chief mate of the *Shirley*. Povey fell ill, and Bigelow instructed his officers and seamen not to assist him so that he might "dye & be damned."[40]

Captains also used confinement as a means of maintaining order. William Toson was beaten by James Steed in 1718, then confined for twenty hours with no "manner of subsistence." In 1720 Edward Hamlin was thrashed and placed in irons for eight days and nights on the deck "without any Covering & was exposed to ye Wind & rain & dues [dews] which are very great" in Cádiz, all of which worked "to ye great hazard of his Life." Related to this tactic was the practice of lashing seamen to the shrouds or masts. William Squier, after a harsh walloping with a fifteen- to twenty-pound iron stanchion, was tied to the shrouds and forced to hang with all of his weight on his arms for five or six hours. James Pringle in 1727 was also hung up on the shrouds, a discipline "usually inflicted on Sailors when drunk or mutinous."[41]

Masters regularly disciplined their men by discharging and incarcerating them aboard a man-of-war, in jail, or in prison.

[10] Morris, *Government and Labor*, 267; Information of William Wham, HCA 1/58 (1751), ff. 22–4; Sandhill v. Summers, HCA 24/134 (1724); Povey v. Bigelow, HCA 24/134 (1722). Authority over physical discipline, food, and health by no means exhausted the captain's controls, for he also acted frequently as a merchandiser on the longer voyages, as discussed in Chapter 3 of this book. See Jonathan Press, *The Merchant Seamen of Bristol, 1747–1789* (Bristol, 1976), 8.

[1] Morris, *Government and Labor*, 264; Toson v. Steed, HCA 24/132 (1719); Eastes v. Winnicot, HCA 24/133 (1721); Squier v. Arnold, HCA 24/132 (1720); Pringle v. Pett, HCA 24/136 (1730).

Captain Thomas Barry, sailing into Charleston aboard the *William* in 1729, asked a local seafaring man "if there was any of the Kings ships in the Harbour." Told that there were, Barry explained that he "had a troublesome man on board and that he'd put [him] on board one of the said Ships as soon as he arrived in the Harbour." Bernard Chalkley of the *Worcester* did the same with Robert Hay and John Mason, who claimed that they were only "being merry and singing and dancing." Chalkley told the commander of the warship that they had been "mutinous." Other captains during wartime boarded the king's ships and, much to the anger of their crews, "voluntarily offered" the services of some of their men, frequently specifying by name those who might be the most "serviceable." Some masters, rather than seek a floating prison, immediately slapped their men into a regular prison or jail once they docked in port.[42]

These were the tactics most frequently employed in a system of authority best described as violent, personal, and arbitrary. The system placed violence and discipline at the heart of the social relations of work and reproduced that violence by creating a powerful dynamic of aggression and counteraggression, a strong tendency toward personal vengeance. Discipline in the service of efficiency and productivity was directed at "lazy," "obstinate," "obdurate," "unwilling," "disobedient," "insolent," and "uncooperative" workers, for apparently many captains believed, with Nathaniel Uring, that seamen were "unthinking, ungovernable Monsters . . . when once from under Command," and that men were "wretched ungovernable Creatures . . . when there is no power nor Laws to restrain them." Or, as three ship masters put it in their petition to the Virginia legislature in 1722, "That as no Society can be long kept in Order, without discipline, so it is but too well known that common sailors are of all men least Capable of Submitting to the authority of their Commanders, when they find themselves under no fear of correction." Such figures of authority could

---

[42] Deposition of John Raper, SC ADM (1729), f. 676; Domanns v. Chalkley, HCA 24/127 (1701); Shimins v. Pitch, HCA 24/128 (1704); Vesey v. Yoakley, HCA 24/129 (1707). See also Longust v. Youron, HCA 24/130 (1714); Banks v. Christian, HCA 24/134 (1724); Battin v. Billup, HCA 24/127 (1704); Hays v. Moses, HCA 24/129 (1708).

scarcely afford to see matters otherwise, lest they call into question the moral foundation of their own extraordinary, often
brutally used, powers.[43]

Yet the masters' petition, even though self-serving, contains
an insight as vitally important as it was unintentional. Why
should seamen – "of all men" – be least capable of submitting to
authority unarmed with disciplinary violence? If we substitute
"least willing" for "least capable," the masters' words suggest
that "common sailors" had developed oppositional practices
and values quite distinct from and often violently at odds with
those imposed by the disciplinary regime of the capitalist merchant shipping industry. These practices and values constituted
the other side of the system of maritime authority, the welter of
initiatives, resistances, and negotiations that grew out of the
need for collective self-defense on the lower deck. Many countertactics, forms of organization, and bases of power emerged
as part of the creative self-activity of common maritime working people.

The most powerful countertactic of authority was the mutiny, the collective effort, planned or spontaneous, to curtail
the captain's power and, in the most extreme cases, to seize
control of the ship. Before looking at mutiny full face and in
action, let us look at its profile. Although there is no systematic
record of mutinies for the first half of the eighteenth century,
documentation exists for sixty such rebellions, and certainly
this must represent only a small portion of those that occurred.
The timing of the mutinies is instructive. Only nine took place
during the war years 1702–13, 1727, and 1740–8, twenty-one
years in all. Forty-nine outbreaks appeared during times of
peace, making such upheaval 3.9 times more likely to have

---

[43] Twine v. Barnes, HCA 24/139 (1736); *Ramblin' Jack*, 84; Jenkinson v. Cleeland, HCA 24/135 (1729); *The Voyages and Travels of Nathaniel Uring*, ed.
Alfred Dewar (1726; reprint London, 1928), 234–5, 132; Petition of Randolph, Cane, and Halladay, 1722, in William P. Palmer, ed., *Calendar of
Virginia State Papers . . .* (Richmond, Va., 1875), vol. I, 202. William Betagh,
in *A Voyage Round the World* (London, 1728), 37, notes that "landsmen" at sea
always protested "in a more submissive manner." For an evocation of the
way in which a ship acted as a hothouse, transforming petty conflicts and
jealousies into affairs of honor and revenge, see the treatment of the feud
between Random and Crampley in Tobias Smollett's *Roderick Random* (1748;
reprint London, 1927). On vengeance and piracy, see Chapter 6 of this
book.

occurred between 1700–1, 1713–26, 1728–39, and 1749–50, twenty-nine years total. Forty-eight mutinies erupted between 1715 and 1737, suggesting once again that this was a period of bitter conflict; more specifically, 1718–23 witnessed twenty-one mutinies. These rebellions usually broke out on African and West Indian voyages, though several occurred on voyages to North American and Mediterranean ports, and four mutinies took place on privateers. All deep-sea voyages were vulnerable to insurrection at sea.

Mutinies were usually violent. No fewer, and probably a great many more, than half of these risings used or threatened violence against the ship's officers. About one in five – probably a fairly reliable statistic – featured the killing of one or more officers by the crew. Of the fifteen officers known to have been killed, thirteen died between 1725 and 1737. One-half of the rebellions actually succeeded in taking control of the ship, and roughly one-third moved into piracy.[44]

Mutiny had many causes. Some mutinies were straightforward responses to oppression and mistreatment. As William Mething said of life on board his ship in 1719, "damn it, it was better to be hanged than live so." Others claimed that their ships were too leaky, had too few hands, too many officers, inadequate provisions, or too much work. Other crews complained of poor health care, a "mad" captain, or a breach of the wage contract. Many mutinies came about because seamen wanted "ready money," and thought that they might get it as pirates. Mutinies were rarely a response to a single incident, but rather to an overall pattern of abuse, and most revolts contained multiple grievances and causes.[45]

Mutinies took shape as common or overlapping complaints were identified among some portion of the crew, usually three

----

[44] It should be stressed that every charge of mutiny in the admiralty court records has not been included in this file. Captains often applied the term to the most minimal disobedience. Mutiny as used here is an organized, self-conscious revolt against constituted authority, aimed at curtailing the captain's powers or seizing control of the ship. It is remarkable that historians have devoted so little attention to mutinies in the merchant shipping industry.

[45] See, for examples, *The Tryals of Captain John Rackam and other Pirates* (Jamaica, 1721) in CO 137/14, 29; *Ramblin' Jack*, 144; Information of Alexander Thompson, HCA 1/55 (1723), ff. 23–4; Examination of John Peterson, HCA 1/55 (1725), f. 116; Tatum v. Wilson, HCA 24/137 (1732).

or four men initially, who formed a nucleus and began to enlist the solidarity of others for their cause. Support usually co-alesced around a particularly bold, daring, and defiant member of the crew, often a minor officer who possessed the requisite skills for sailing the ship. Navigational knowledge was essential to a band of mutineers. A mutiny could be put into effect with the support of only 20–30 percent of the crew so long as the majority of the seamen could be counted upon to remain neu-tral or to join up once the seizure of power was underway.

At sea in 1700, James Man, captain of the *Happy Return*, changed his original voyage in an effort to respond more profit-ably to changing markets. Tension on the ship ran high, and Man must have known that a confrontation was near when he ordered his sailors to weigh anchor, and several "jeeringly told him if he [himself] would weigh the anchor they did not hinder him." One seaman claimed that the crew should "goe with the Shipp where they pleased." Man, angered by such imperti-nence, said, "What, without my command?" Richard Dyer, sec-ond mate and apparent ringleader of the revolt, gave a sharp reply: "wee do not value you nor your command." Other sea-men of the *Happy Return* said they would "Stick by . . . Dyer and stand by him one another to the last drop of their blood . . . and the general words amongst them were 'one and all.' "[46]

Captain Nathaniel Uring, "apprehensive that [his] Seamen had a mind to turn Pirates," in 1712 expected a mutiny to erupt at any moment. So much so, Uring declared, that "I loaded my Pistols, and kept them upon my Pillow by me" when sleeping. One morning Uring called out his entire crew and asked each man for the key to his chest in hope of finding the petition, or "Round Robin," drawn up by the seamen stating their grievances and demands. Uring said, "I began with one of the Men whom I knew to be a seditious Fellow, which I sus-pected to be the Cheif Conspirator"; the man had formerly been the ship's gunner, but had been removed from his post for "Negligence and Disobedience." Uring then proceeded to enact a gutsy drama. Taking off his hat and bowing low to the suspected mutineer, Uring called him "Captain" and asked to

[46] Morgan v. Man, HCA 24/127 (1700).

see the Round Robin. The former gunner responded with a "snearing Laugh," and Uring gave him several sharp strokes with his cane until "the Blood" came "running about his Ears." Another seaman stepped up and "began to speak some seditious Words," and even though Uring must have feared that his power play was failing and that he might be tossed overboard at any instant, he quickly gave this man a drubbing and, seemingly still undaunted, faced the rest of the crew. A "third Fellow of the Clan said, he thought it was very hard to be so beat for nothing," and he swiftly took some licks for his suggestion. Finally, someone who had not signed the petition said that he knew its whereabouts and fetched it. Uring reported that fewer than one-half of the crew had signed, "they not having had time to compleat it, some of them being as yet not so hardy to enter into it." Uring claimed that all of those beaten had signed the instrument, but also found, much to his consternation and surprise, that "some of the honestest Men I had" had likewise endorsed the protest. With the mutiny effectively squashed and the possible legal charge of piracy hanging over their heads, "the seamen were exactly diligent and obedient during the rest of the Voyage."[47]

Robert Sparks, seaman of the *Abington,* told several of his comrades that their ship "would make a good Pirate Ship, for," he insisted, "they had better be dead than live in Misery." The conspiracy for mutiny began. Ten stout sailors agreed that the chief mate was to be thrown overboard, that the doctor and captain were to be seized and confined, "and as for the rest, they would soon yield themselves and consent." One man argued that there should be "no Occasion for committing Murder"; but John Whitcomb replied, "it was much better to Murder, when they had begun, than not to go through with it." The mutineers then, in an oath, pledged "to spend their dearest blood for each other." James Ogelsby plotted some personal revenge: "as for those blows, which he had received [from the captain], they were but lent; and as for those Threats, which he had received from the Boatswain, he would requite them with a Ball through his Body." Others also vowed to get their "Revenge on those Dogs," but they never managed to do so be-

[47] *Voyages and Travels of Nathaniel Uring,* 176–8.

cause the plot was uncovered. The case came to court and at least two of the rebels were sentenced to the gallows.[48]

Off the African coast in 1721 the *Gambia Castle,* a Royal African Company vessel captained by Charles Russell, was seized by mutineers under the leadership of second mate George Lowther. Lowther claimed that the Royal African Company had criminally neglected the seamen's health. The men had arrived in Africa "in perfect Health" but soon found themselves in a "miserable" state. Some difficulties apparently arose over procuring a cargo of slaves, and Lowther maintained that the merchants said that the seamen should stay on the coast "till they Rotted." The tars considered their plight to be one of "bondage," in which they endured "Barbarous & Unhumane Usage from their Commander." Lowther and John Massey, leader of the mutiny among the soldiers on board the ship, felt "bound in Duty to Relieve those poor wretches from a Vissable & Tyrannical Calamity." Their "Designes was only to fly away from ye Death of Perishing as the Rest of our Country Men did for want of Necessary Subsistence." The mutineers renamed their vessel the *Delivery* and took to the seas. Clearly, Lowther saw "Duty" more in terms of people than profits. He and his men went on to become pirates; John Massey surrendered and was hanged at Albion's fatal tree.[49]

Conflict broke out on board the *Zant* in 1721, instigated and led in this case by a "free Negro," a common tar who lived at Deptford, who "bred a Mutiny that we had too many Officers, and that the work was too hard, and what not." Several seamen "muttered" at the captain and "often wished that the said Ship was in the hands of the Pyrates." Michael Wilkinson, gunner of the vessel, showed the strategic importance of his station to any revolt when he claimed he could make a mutiny anytime he wanted, since he "had under his Care the powder and small Arms" that belonged to the ship. Wilkinson's words help to explain why gunners were increasingly eliminated from ship's crews after 1726, their responsibilities taken over by the captain or chief mate. In any case, the captain of the *Zant* moved quickly to get rid of the black seaman, incarcerating him on a

---

[48] *Tryals of Captain John Rackam,* 28–9.
[49] Information of Alexander Thompson, HCA 1/55 (1723), ff. 23–4; Petition of John Massey and George Lowther, CO 28/17 (July 22, 1721), ff. 197–9.

man-of-war and shipping a Venetian seaman, "a Quiate fellow," in his place. But matters soon flared up again, this time with the second mate and some foremastmen demanding their wages. Apparently the captain and some of his loyal officers threatened to fight the mutineers. The chief mate said that the rebels "told us if we Struck one man, overboard we Should all goe." The specific outcome of this confrontation is unknown, but the dispute seems to have been resolved.[50]

The anguish and intensity of the class relations of life at sea were demonstrated in gruesomely vivid form in the mutiny of the *George* in 1725. Five seamen conspired to set up as pirates, claiming that they "had not a sufficient quantity of Provisions allowed them." Michael Moor's task in the revolt was to "make the Sun & Moon shine through" the bodies of the captain, chief mate, surgeon, and supercargo. William Melvin reportedly said to the officers, "Damn you, you Doggs I'le hang you when you are dead." Three of the officers were indeed killed, and Melvin made good his promise, taking the "end of the Whipfall" and putting it "about the Chief Mates Neck," who already lay "dead between Decks & hoysted him upon Deck." John Smith, later known by the alias John Gow, was the only rebel who knew navigation, and he became captain of this new pirate ship, renamed the *Revenge* and set in search of fortune. Smith and several of his men met their end on the gallows.[51]

Other important features of mutiny were illuminated in 1736 when six of the *Dove*'s crew went ashore and conspired to run away with the ship. They allocated new positions among themselves, designating a captain, mate, and boatswain, and agreed that they would all "go equally shares in the cargo." These mutineers self-consciously drew upon the experience of one of their number, Edward Johnson, who was esteemed "a special good fellow for this purpose and has been several times upon the Account," meaning that he had several

---

[50] *Ramblin' Jack*, 144, 158; Gouldin v. Sanders, HCA 24/133 (1721). See also Information of James Tindall, HCA 1/56 (1732), f. 63.
[51] Examinations of John Peterson, Peter Rollson, James Williams, and Robert Read, HCA 1/55 (1725), ff. 103–32. See also Daniel Defoe, *An Account of the Conduct and Proceedings of the Late John Gow, alias Smith, Captain of the Late Pirates . . .* (London, 1725).

times sailed as a pirate.[52] Johnson and his fellow mutineers were not unusual in their choice to divide their shares equally. Captain George Shelvocke of the privateer *Speedwell* denounced his crew as a "Gang of Levellers" when they mutinied, carefully curtailed his powers, implemented a democratic decision-making system, and cut out the shares of the "Gentlemen Adventurers in England" who had financed the voyage. William Betagh described the same leveling instinct. After a band of privateers cut out the shares of their "Gentleman Owners," their "new establishment was more like a Commonwealth than an absolute monarchy."[53]

Mutinies provided perhaps the most clear-cut examples of the way class lines were drawn on board the ship, since self-consciously organized centers of authority and control emerged from below to challenge for power. William Doyle, a mutineer on the *Joseph and Ann* in 1726, tried to get other seamen "to side with him and neglect their Service" and to depose Alexander Cupples as commander. Apparently he met with some success because he soon told Cupples that he "had a stronger party on board . . . and that he w[oul]d speedily disinherit the s[ai]d Master of his wooden world, meaning he would soon take from him the Command of the s[ai]d Ship." Cupples, however, was able to solicit help from other ships nearby to "quell the Mutiny."[54] Thomas Powell of the *Pearl* in 1736 "did endeavour to raise a Mutiny to perswade the Mariners . . . to side with him against" Captain Eustace Hardwicke. Eight sailors vowed to "stand by one another" and began, in an act of deliberate intimidation, to ask everyone if they recalled the fate of a Captain Beard, a master whom everyone knew had been murdered by his crew.[55] These incidents illuminate a deeper meaning of Jack Cremer's words: "As our Master of the Ship

[52] Information of Richard Walker and William O'Mara, HCA 1/57 (1737), ff. 1–8.

[53] George Shelvocke, *A Voyage Round the World* (London, 1726), 157, 42, 219, 218; Betagh, *Voyage*, 186–7. See Rogers, *Cruising Voyage*, 172–3, for another mutiny over the shares of the "Gentlemen." For a discussion of the ways in which this egalitarianism was institutionalized on the pirate ship, see Chapter 6 of this book.

[54] Doyle v. Holland, HCA 24/135 (1728) and HCA 24/136 (1729).

[55] Powell v. Hardwicke, HCA 24/139 (1738).

said – to be of the Captain's way of thinking was best, right or [w]rong." This, obviously, was one point of view. But "to be One of the Strongest Side" must, Cremer held, "be best." Captain Thomas King said of mutineer Peter Lester in 1723, "it was with much diffeculty that wee prevail'd upon" him "to goe ashoar for noe Violence cou'd be use'd where the Major part of the Ships Company were inclin'd to favour him." After quelling a mutiny – and an "unlawful Friendship" among its makers – on his privateering voyage, Woodes Rogers said, "The Ship's Company seeming much inclin'd to favour the Mutineers, made me the easier forgive." Just as the logic of discipline was individual, imposed from above by a figure invested with extraordinary formal power, the logic of mutiny was collective, arising from below through shared grievances and informal sanctions.[56]

The collective logic of mutiny and, I would argue, all of social life among common seamen is fully illustrated in the sailors' creation of a cultural form, the instrument of protest known as the Round Robin. This "Mutinous and Seditious paper" was essentially a means of organizing resistance. Nathaniel Uring provided a detailed description:

They take a large Sheet of Paper, and strike two Circles, one a good distance without the other; in the inner Circle, they will write what they have a mind to have done; and between the two Circular Lines, they write their Names, in and out, against the Circles; beginning like the four Cardinal points of the Compass, right opposite to each other, and so continue till the Paper is filled; which appears in a Circle, and no one can be said to be first, so that they are all equally guilty: Which I believe to be contrived to keep 'em all firm to their purpose, when once they have signed it; and if discovered, no one can be excused, by saying, he was the last that signed it, and he had not done it without great Persuasion.[57]

Seamen used the Round Robin "to engage one another" in a plot, "to try ye Strength of their party," while guaranteeing that "it might not be known who were the beginners or Ringleaders." The sailor had to select his forms of protest carefully,

---

[56] *Ramblin' Jack,* 55; Lester v. King, HCA 24/134 (1723); Rogers, *Cruising Voyage,* 10.

[57] Wise v. Beekman, HCA 24/131 (1716); *Voyages and Travels of Captain Nathaniel Uring,* 178.

lest his complaints be "returned upon his back with a Vengeance." The Round Robin was a cultural innovation from below, an effort at collective self-defense in the face of nearly unlimited and arbitrary authority. The Round Robin eloquently expressed the collectivistic ethos of the seamen's oppositional culture, demonstrating how the equal distribution of risks was often essential to survival.[58]

Yet to "be One of the Strongest Side" often meant being one of the captain's side, and frequently seamen were forced to choose quickly. As Jack Cremer's experience as a young seaman indicated:

I soon got in favor with the Master and his Mates, but the Sailors did not like me, but called me "man-of-war's dog," and I youst to watch them Narrowly, and keep everything well-lockt up of my Master's things, Provisions, Bread, etc., to the Great Mortification of the fellows.[59]

The captain's side almost always consisted of the steward and the surgeon, both generally regarded as "tell-Tales to Cap[tai]ns," and some varying number from the lower officers and the men.[60] The boundaries of the sides shifted according to the issues at hand, the nature of discontent, and the degree of power possessed by each side.

The mutiny and the Round Robin represented dramatic and vitally important moments of resistance, but they were only two parts of a complex array of countertactics of authority. Short of mutiny itself, there was always the threat of mutiny. Peter Winnicoate, Robert Hayes, and Edward Edwards complained of a short allowance in 1708 and vowed to "bear away [with the vessel] for the first port" they should come to. Another prac-

---

[58] Smith v. East India Company, HCA 24/127 (1700); Wise v. Beekman, HCA 24/131 (1716). See also Hood v. Jennis, HCA 24/131 (1717); Longust v. Youron, HCA 24/130 (1714); Captain Charles Johnson [Daniel Defoe], *A General History of the Pyrates,* ed. Manuel Schonhorn (1724, 1728; reprint Columbia, S.C., 1972), 290; *Tryals of Captain John Rackam,* 29; Clipperton v. Seamen, SC ADM (1719), f. 495; Information of Henry Bolton (1701) in J. F. Jameson, ed., *Privateering and Piracy in the Colonial Period: Illustrative Documents* (New York, 1923), 248; *Gentlemen's Magazine* (1731); Betagh, *Voyage,* 36; Barnaby Slush, *The Navy Royal; Or a Sea-Cook turn'd Projector* (London, 1709), 82.

[59] *Ramblin' Jack,* 66.

[60] Ibid., 271.

tice, similar to fragging in the Vietnam War, was to get rid of an officer while making his loss appear to be an accident. Some were hit by falling gear, others swept overboard in a storm. It is not hard to imagine the fears of captains such as Robert Berry, who said that his crew was "thretening to hive [heave] me over bord" after a wage dispute, or Durrell Bayley, who after striking Samuel Greenaway for breach of duty was told, "if he struck him again," into the blue he would go.[61]

This use of threat and innuendo shaded imperceptibly into the next countertactic: the use of intimidation. Such matters worked both ways. Frequently seamen attempted to intimidate their captain or officers with the defiant refusal of work. David Macky, of the *Christabella* in 1721, was ordered by his master to set sail and responded: "God damn you, you may come and sett it yourself and be damned for I will not do it." His messmate Mathew Carmichael was told to work on the maintopsail and told the captain that "he might kiss his Arse for by God he would not do it." Their captain, George Jesson, was apparently afraid to discipline the men, but kept himself double-armed in case they should decide to "turn Pyrates." John Ward in 1729 refused to work in "any but his own way" and often insisted, so that the whole crew of the *Lawson* could hear, that if the "Master struck or any ways corrected him for his disobedience he would knock him down and not take a Blow of[f] him."[62]

Many other seamen refused physical discipline. John Scroge, hit by his captain, proclaimed, "I won't be used after so barbarous a rate as this." William Brown swore in 1742 that "no Captain in England should lay hands on or Strike him." And as George Williams announced in 1728: "I never was beat by any Master yet and it will be very hard to be beat now." John Potter of the *St. Quintin* was drenched with water, then struck by Captain Ralph Selby. Potter then "fell upon ye Master and beat him and Swore he would be none of his Slave nor be beat like a

[61] Hays v. Moses, HCA 24/129 (1708); Robert Berry to ?, HCA 24/128 (1702); Sailors v. Alloyn, SC ADM (1730), f. 767; Deposition of William Pricklove, HCA 1/17 (1715), f. 21; Rane v. Clarke, HCA 24/136 (1730); Depositions of Argentown Williams and Thomas Lukeham, HCA 1/57 (1737), ff. 18–19.

[62] King v. Jesson, HCA 24/133 (1721); Ward v. Corne, HCA 24/136 (1730); Sedgewick v. Burroughs, HCA 24/134 (1723); Mason v. Pomeroy, HCA 24/127 (1701); Parker v. Boucher, HCA 24/132 (1719); Murray v. Hyde, HCA 24/135 (1726); Beard v. Hayes, HCA 24/136 (1711).

Dogg." After the scuffle Selby followed Potter, who politely but firmly warned him, "Mr. Selby if you come any Farther by God Ile knock your brains out if I can, or strike you over board." Potter was jailed in Naples but came back aboard for the run home. He announced, as one of the crew relayed, that "he was none of the Masters servant and bid us all take notice that from that very Day he would never serve him more nor doe any thing for him but would goe home in the Ship as a Prisoner and not as his Servant."[63]

Some incidents of counterintimidation were more lurid. Richard Whitman, demanding his wages from Benjamin Eyres in 1715, "threatened to beat him & cut his Ears off and challenged him to go on Shoar and fight him." And in 1717 George Drummond, for reasons unknown, swore to his captain, Richard Norman: "God damn him he'd skin him alive and slit his Nose."[64]

The physical environment of the ship, providing an almost infinite assortment of tools and work-related items that could be used as weapons, was the essential context for the negotiation of authority. Resort to handspikes, boards, hogshead staves, sticks, ropes, cables, marking irons, braces, hooks, adzes, axes, tar brushes, broomsticks, pitch mops, oars, harpoons, cutlasses, knives, or pistols made the possibility and reality of armed struggle ever-present. Many a tar decided to see whether his weapon or his captain's head was harder. But the tar had no monopoly on the use of these objects, and he himself suffered under the impact of many of these improvised weapons. But so too did many seamen use them to fight back. Captain William Kennett "corrected" second mate Robert Hawkes with a leather belt for insolence, but Hawkes picked up a handspike "and swore he would knock out the Capt[ain]s brains." Captain Kennett called for help from the crew, but no one responded. Soon all the men had taken Hawkes's side, downed their tools, and deserted the ship at anchor in a Baltic port. As they departed, they called out in a "rideculeing Man-

---

[63] Examination of Thomas Wood, HCA 24/137 (1731); Information of Andrew Smith, HCA 1/57 (1743), ff. 46–7; Information of Phillip Brand, HCA 1/56 (1729), ff. 32–3; Potter v. Selby, HCA 24/128 (1704).
[64] Whitman v. Eyres, HCA 24/131 (1716); Drummond v. Norman, HCA 24/132 (1718).

ner": "wee wish you well to London." In 1719 Sampson March was drubbed several times by Master James Stadden of the *Satisfaction*. "[A]pprehending himself to be in imminent danger and perill of his life," March "took up a handspike to defend himself, and thereby prevented the farther mischief which the said Master in all probability would have done him."[65]

John Hays in 1722 refused to work and "swoar he would not be ruled or governed or that he would do what he pleased & that he was a better man then [sic] the Master." He backed up his claim by threatening to give the captain a few hacks with his axe. When Captain Stephen Yoakley tried to bully William Garrett in 1705, the seaman picked up his adze "and swore by God that if he offered to strike or come near him hee would have a Limb of him." Yoakley quickly found Garrett a safe spot on board a man-of-war.[66]

Merchant seamen had, of course, built a stout tradition of armed self-defense in their dealings with the Royal Navy. They used all of the weapons listed previously, plus swords, blunderbusses, pistols, and twelve-, six-, and half-pound cannon. Fingers were lopped off, skulls fractured, and bodies pierced with bullets as press gangs in search of labor tried to board merchant vessels. Such resistance was not radically different from that demonstrated in the normal course of social life in the merchant service.[67]

Another countertechnique of authority was direct action, the crew's active contradiction of an order from above. Under admiralty law, "seamen were not permitted to interfere when ships' officers confined or otherwise punished one of the crew for disorderly conduct." Yet since seamen realized that the merchant captains themselves did not keep politely to the rules

---

[65] Brazier v. Kennett, HCA 24/136 (1730); March v. Stadden, HCA 24/133 (1721). See also Information of Robert Beckett and Benjamin Paxton, HCA 1/53 (1701), ff. 91–2; N. Bostorh to Lords of Admiralty, ADM 1/1464 (Mar. 20, 1703).

[66] Hays v. Russell, HCA 24/134 (1724); Vesey v. Yoakley, HCA 24/129 (1707).

[67] Lloyd, *British Seaman*, 143; Jesse Lemisch, "Jack Tar in the Streets: Merchant Seamen in the Politics of Revolutionary America," *WMQ* 25 (1968), 389, and "Jack Tar vs. John Bull," 33. See also George Rude, "Labor Disputes in Eighteenth-Century England," in his *The Crowd in History: A Study of Popular Disturbances, 1730–1848* (New York, 1964), 69; and Information of Randolph Barber, HCA 1/54 (1718), ff. 76–7.

of admiralty law, they likewise defied its strictures, especially when a seaman was receiving harsh or dangerous discipline.

Crews intervened against whippings, beatings, confinements in irons, hangings, maroonings, and efforts to throw men overboard. Captain James Studley would have choked William Bushby to death in 1728 had it not been for the several sailors who "prevented his being kill'd." Captain Maynard Morgan tried to murder Edward Murphett with a "harpoon stock," but the crew intervened. Another captain, Thomas Bows, endeavored to throw James Philipson over the side of his vessel but was prevented by the seaman's comrades.[68]

Seamen also refused to obey orders in order to protect their own. After Captain Edward Tennel had thrashed Christopher Hopkins in 1737, he ordered his men to fling him overboard. His tars offered him not a hand, but defiance. Tennel then ordered them to maroon Hopkins "where he might perish, but the Mariners detesting and abhorring so barbarous an act" responded "contrary to the commands given them" and put the seaman ashore in an inhabited place where he would receive proper care.[69] Seamen used direct action to limit the enormous and arbitrary authority concentrated in the hands of masters and mates, whether used in the dispensation of physical discipline or food. John Babb, a member of the *Worcester,* complained of poor and short provisions – so poor, one tar deposed, that four men died for lack of proper food – and resented the fact that the captain, steward, and surgeon "were allowed . . . their full allowance of provisions and liquors" as if there had been no scarcity of food and drink whatsoever. He resented it so much, in fact, that he proceeded to give the steward "severall blows on his naked back with a catt of nyne tails." Direct action sometimes imposed a discipline of its own.[70]

---

[68] Bushby v. Studley, HCA 24/135 (1728); Murphett v. Morgan, HCA 24/135 (1728); Holland v. Bows HCA 24/132 (1720). See also Adey v. Stiss, HCA 24/136 (1729); Certiss v. Crawford, HCA 24/138 (1734); Pattison v. Beesley, HCA 24/129 (1709); Arnold v. Ranson HCA 24/129 (1706).

[69] Hopkins v. Tennel, SC ADM (1737), f. 98. See also Information of John Daftor, HCA 1/56 (1733), f. 75; Lamb v. Murrin, HCA 24/129 (1707); Examination of Francis Wise, HCA 1/55 (1723), ff. 44–5; *Life and Adventures of Matthew Bishop,* 242; Edwards v. Booth, HCA 24/137 (1732); Jenkinson v. Cleeland, HCA 24/136 (1729); Weibust, *Deep Sea Sailors,* 375.

[70] Babb v. Chalkley, HCA 24/127 (1701); Holland v. Bows, HCA 24/132 (1720); Arnold v. Ranson, HCA 24/129 (1706); Bushby v. Studly, HCA

Another countertactic was the division of command, the deliberate effort to create competing and conflicting centers of authority within the daily operation of the ship. Such efforts, in the words of Jack Cremer, usually split the crew into "Two Divisions. One for the Cap[tai]n, the other for the Mate's side." Bernard Rely in 1711 was accused of trying to "make differences and quarrels" on the *Anne* "between . . . Thomas Moulton the Master and his Mate and other of the s[ai]d Ships Compa[ny]." By fomenting such "mix'd Command," seamen limited the captain's authority and loosened discipline. As Captain Thomas Barry said of his chief mate, Nicholas Worsdale, in 1729, he was "giving out Speeches that he had equal Command of the Vessel thereby encouraging the rest of the Mariners to be negligent & Disobedient."[71]

Seamen used a host of other tactics to protect themselves from the captain. Some seamen used the admiralty courts to fine advantage, even in prosecuting their captains for excessive beatings. When John Coulter, for example, was severely threatened by his master, George Pitt, Coulter retorted that "they should pay for it" when "he came to England," meaning thereby "that he would commence actions against them if they struck him." Many seamen "consented to try the law and see what it would do for us." Yet trying the law was not only time-consuming but expensive, as indicated by Edward Barlow after he was bilked out of his wages:

And thus a poor man is abused with proud and ambitious masters, finding no recompense, having no money to try the law, for if I had, I might have called him to have paid sore for his dealing with me.

And on another occasion:

And so, if I had had money to have spent in law, I might have uncovered some right, but having none, I must sit down with my only patience, praying to God in His good time to revenge my cause, for might did overcome right.

Footnote 70 (*cont.*):
24/135 (1728); Murphett v. Morgan, HCA 24/135 (1728); Jenkinson v. Cleeland, HCA 24/135 (1729); Hopkins v. Tennel, SC ADM (1737), ff. 97–103; Morris, *Government and Labor*, 264–5.
[71] *Ramblin' Jack*, 80; Rely v. Moulton, HCA 24/130 (1711); Barry v. Worsdale, SC ADM (1729), f. 661. See also Clipperton v. Seamen, SC ADM (1719), ff. 490–556; Hawkins v. Blomfall, HCA 24/130 (1711); Examination of John Gardner, HCA 1/57 (1739), f. 30; Rogers, *Cruising Voyage*, 227, 33.

Many seamen, it must be added, did not wait for God to take up their cause, preferring instead to take matters into their own hands, bypassing the legal system altogether.[72]

Some seamen did not share Barlow's optimism about the advantages to be gained in the admiralty courts. When customs agents went to inspect the *Two Brothers* off the Carolina coast in 1730, they were insulted by seamen who swore that "they valued the Gov[ernmen]t no more than they did the Judge of Ad[miral]ty." And in fact they showed just how little they valued the North Carolina judge of admiralty when, less than a year later, a "Mob" – almost surely composed largely of sailors – was raised "in Edenton, to murther the Judge of Adm[iral]ty." But despite the variation in attitudes, it is clear that the admiralty courts could be useful in upholding seamen's rights and that they functioned as one resource among many.[73]

These were the major tactics devised and employed by Jack Tar and his mates when they found themselves dealing with a captain who was

> Lustee in his Limbs and Rustee in his Skin
> A Bear without, And a wers beast within.[74]

The violent captain and the militant seaman defined and shaped the context and relations of authority at sea, but of course all captains were not brutal, nor were all sailors rebellious. Although the system of maritime authority itself was based on violence (or the incessant threat of violence), some masters made sparing use of physical discipline. Given the conditions of life at sea, and in particular the need for some discipline for the sake of survival, what was the best seamen could hope for in a master? They hoped for someone not too "precise," someone not "finding fault with every small occasion," but someone in no way arbitrary; someone who "gave grand entertainment," meaning good victuals and fair wages; some-

---

[72] Coulter v. Pitt, HCA 24/137 (1732); *Barlow's Journal*, 90, 358, 365. See also Morgan v. Steward, HCA 24/139 (1736).

[73] *Rex* v. *Two Brothers*, Minutes of the Vice Admiralty Court of North Carolina, ff. 25, 39, LC, Manuscripts Division. Seamen might also get back at a captain by telling merchants that a vessel was "rotten and unable to fulfill her Voiage"; see Seamen v. *Mary Ann*, Virginia Admiralty, CO 5/1311 (1698), ff. 122–3.

[74] *Ramblin' Jack*, 107.

one "of a kind disposition, and of a complacent and affable temper, and one that always behaved himself towards his Crew with abundance of Justice, tenderness, and meekness, no ways addicted to severity or excess of passion"; someone good-natured "drunk or sober," but usually sober and sedate; someone who "Sung a good song"; someone who was "a Compleate Seaman & Artice."[75] Seamen sought someone who represented the values of a more moral world, someone fair, decent, and able. Unfortunately, such captains seem to have been in relatively short supply in the Royal Navy, as well as the merchant service, in the early eighteenth century.[76] The very nature of life and work at sea created the need for sailors to be always prepared for self-defense and to resist the excesses and injustices they faced.

Ralph Davis pointed out that "life on board [the eighteenth-century merchant] ship was carried on amid a discipline which grew harsher with the passage of time."[77] Those dispensing this discipline, it must be admitted, showed great resourcefulness. But so too did those who resisted, those who built an oppositional culture out of the values that were "rooted in the ties people have to one another in daily life in production."[78] The struggles over authority and labor discipline, especially between 1715 and 1737, can probably be described most accurately as class war: "class" because the setting of conflict was the workplace and because the conflict grew directly out of the social relations of production, manifested between those buying and directing labor power and those selling and providing it; "war" because the hostility and struggle between opposing forces for different ends was armed, violent, and nearly chronic. The struggle took on different forms and intensities at different times, but the essential conflict was always there. Some men on

---

[75] Ibid., 213; Dennison v. Toben, HCA 24/132 (1719); *Barlow's Journal*, 355. The long quotation in this paragraph comes from a captain's self-description at an admiralty hearing in which he was charged with brutality. Even though he probably did not speak the truth about himself, he seemed to be outlining a captain's character that would have been acceptable to many seamen. See also Wilson v. Parsons, HCA 24/129 (1710).

[76] Peter Kemp (*British Sailor*, 51) indicates that complaints about the brutality of captains in the Royal Navy ran especially high between 1688 and 1708.

[77] Davis, *English Shipping*, 154.

[78] Gerald Sider, "The Ties That Bind: Culture and Agriculture, Property and Propriety in the Newfoundland Village Fishery," *Social History*, 5 (1980), 25.

the ship gave their primary allegiance to the owners and their profits, whereas others owed allegiance to each other, to their own ends and interests, diverse though they certainly were, and at bottom, to survival.

We noted in the previous chapter that two distinct kinds of collectivism were taking shape on the early modern merchant ship. The first was the collectivism of the entire ship, constituted in the confrontation with nature and by the need for survival. The second, a prominent theme in this chapter, was the collectivity formed among the common tars, constituted in the confrontation with capital, created over and against the logic of discipline and cooperation for the sake of profit. Collective labor passed easily into collective self-defense as seamen sought to protect themselves from harsh conditions, excessive work, and oppressive authority. Whereas the collectivism of the entire ship depended upon a harmony of wills, a consensus, and a set of paternalistic relations of authority, the collectivism of the common tar, in stark contrast, was formed instead from the conflicts inherent in the social relations of production in shipping and the consequent negotiations of waged work. The collectivism of the ship was vertical, that of the common wage-earning seaman horizontal.[79]

The seaman's collectivism, as we have seen, frequently aimed to limit exploitation, as well as discipline and its often bloody forms. In previous chapters we have explored the dramatic oppositional forms – work stoppages, desertions, strikes, mutinies, and piracies – all of which grew out of the various routines of work and social life. We have noted how seamen referred to each other as "Brother Tar," establishing a system of fictive kinship that provided some sense of unity, and with it mutual

---

[79] See Marcus Rediker, " 'Lets Stand by One Another and Take Care of Ourselves': The Ethos of the Anglo-American Seaman in the Early Age of Empire," paper presented to the Annual Convention of the Organization of American Historians, Cincinnati, 1983. Although the matter has not been studied carefully for the merchant service, it appears that the eighteenth century witnessed a significant decline in social mobility from seaman to officer and captain. For comments on the increasingly stark class divisions in the navy, see Lloyd, *British Seaman*, 76, 89, 90. The decline in mobility and the quantitative growth in the number of merchant seamen would have facilitated the emergence of an oppositional culture at sea.

responsibilities and protections.[80] The seaman's collectivism extended from self-defense to acts of mutual care to a sometimes communal attitude toward property. Common tars were notoriously generous with what little they had, and they developed elaborate codes of hospitality and sharing. They banded together in units of two, three, four, or more – sharing as brothers, as messes, as gangs. They gave a special meaning to the words spoken by Richard Taylor to his fellow pirates in 1722: "lets stand by one another and take Care of ourselves."[81]

A second aspect of the seaman's oppositional culture, closely related to collectivism, was the value of antiauthoritarianism. The source of the value is not hard to locate. It lay in the violent, personal, and arbitrary nature of the authority possessed and discipline dispensed by the merchant captain or his mate. But the antiauthoritarianism of deep-sea tars was not reserved exclusively for captains and mates, no matter how sharply or violently they responded to these men on given occasions. They generously cast their contempt upon many others. Most seamen apparently regarded sea doctors with a loathing bitterly expressed by Edward Barlow: "And the surgeons and doctors of physic in ships many times are very careless of a poor man in his sickness, their common phrase being to come to him and take him by the hand when they hear that he hath been sick two or three days, thinking that is soon enough, and feeling his pulse when he is half-dead, asking him when he was at stool, and how he feels himself, and how he has slept, and then giving him some of their medicines upon the point of a knife, which doeth as much good to him as a blow

---

[80] *Ramblin' Jack*, 117, 125, 131; Deposition of James Lindsey, BL, Add. Ms. 40831, f. 34. On the concept of "fictive kin," see Herbert G. Gutman, *The Black Family in Slavery and Freedom* (New York, 1976), 154, 197, 216–27, 358.

[81] For comments on attitudes toward property among buccaneers, see Esquemeling, *Buccaneers of America*, 61, 75. A less formal version of the shipmates' pact described by Esquemeling (44) was probably quite common among seventeenth- and eighteenth-century seamen: "It is a general and solemn custom amongst [buccaneers] all to seek out for a comrade or companion, whom we may call partner, in their fortunes: with whom they join the whole stock of what they possess, towards a mutual and reciprocal gain. This is done also by articles drawn and signed on both sides, according to what has been agreed between them." See also BL, Add. Ms. 40831, 72–3; Ringrose in Esquemeling, *Buccaneers of America*, 474; *Ramblin' Jack*, 117; Falconer, *Universal Dictionary*, 137, 192; "Simsons Voyage," 22; *Tryals of Captain John Rackam*, 29; Further Information of Clement Downing, HCA 1/55 (1724), f. 93.

upon the pate with a stick." Other, more distant figures and bodies of authority did not escape the seaman's salty denunciations: king, Parliament, governors, royal officials – one and all, various seamen claimed, might be damned.[82]

Judges and courts were sometimes the objects of especially stinging satire. In mock courts, seamen dramatized sneering attitudes toward the state and its legal functionaries. The pirates of Thomas Anstis's crew, ashore in 1721, "appointed a Mock-Court of Judicature to try one another for Pyracy, and he that was a Criminal one Day was made Judge another." The judge himself "got up in a tree" – the elevation enhancing his authority – with a "dirty Tarpaulin hung over his Shoulders"; he had a "Thrum Cap (like a mop) on his Head, and a large Pair of Spectacles upon his Nose." The scene suggests a Hogarth painting with proletarian actors jeeringly strutting about in the leading roles.[83] (See Figure 14.)

One can only wonder how many seamen shared the radical sentiments of pirate Charles Bellamy, who was said to have lectured a merchant thus: "you are a sneaking Puppy, and so are those who submit to be governed by Laws which rich Men have made for their own Security, for the cowardly whelps have not the courage to defend what they get by their Knavery; but damn ye altogether. . . . They villify us, the Scoundrels do, when there is only this Difference, they rob the Poor under the Cover of Law, forsooth, and we plunder the rich under the protection of our own Courage."[84] Antiauthoritarianism that began with a stand against a merchant captain might end with a sweeping condemnation of "rich Men" and the self-made laws by which they ruled.

A third and final core value in the culture of the common seaman was egalitarianism, a belief that, at bottom, held that all sailors benefited from a relatively equal distribution of risks,

---

[82] *Barlow's Journal*, 213–14; *Voyages and Travels of Captain Nathaniel Uring*, 168; Tozer v. Slade, HCA 24/128 (1703); Slush, *Navy Royal*, 36. See also Defoe, *History of the Pyrates*, 217; Note of James Bremer, Deputy Register of Vice-Admiralty Court of North Carolina, Jan. 7, 1731, Minutes of the Vice-Admiralty Court of North Carolina, 30; Rex v. Gale, 1730; North Carolina Vice-Admiralty, 25.

[83] Defoe, *History of the Pyrates*, 292. See also Malcolmson, *Life and Labour*, 105–6; Burke, *Popular Culture*, 180–201; Henningsen, *Crossing the Equator*, 92–3.

[84] Defoe, *History of the Pyrates*, 587.

Figure 14. The pirate crew of Captain Thomas Anstis holds a mock trial. The judge, using an old tarpaulin as a robe and a mop-end as a wig, sits in a tree, overseeing the trial of a pirate. The prisoner hoped that the judge "will hear some Reason," to which his Lordship replied, "D'ye hear how the Scoundrel prates? – What have we to do with Reason? – I'll have you know, Raskal, we don't sit here to hear Reason; – we go according to Law."

resources, and rewards aboard the ship. This value was reflected in a preference for "shares" over "wages" as a means of compensation for labor. The share system, which in medieval times gave each seaman part of the profits of the voyage, lived on in privateering, piracy, and the fishing industry and served to attract men to each.[85]

This egalitarianism emerged, at least in part, as a reaction against the hierarchical social organization of the merchant ship and its attendant privileges and abuses. One seaman testified in 1700 that whereas the ship's people "were att short allowance and wanted bread," the captain, steward, and doctor "had and were allowed in the said Masters Cabbin their full allowance of provisions and liquors as if there had been no want or scarcity of any thing on board."[86] Such offenses against equality of condition rankled many a seaman. Speaking of the unequal and unfair division of shares of prize money in the Royal Navy, Barnaby Slush noted that this "kindles in the Breast of a true bred Sailor, a stronger aversion to the Service, than if such a Bounty had never been granted." Of these same "true bred" men of the sea Slush wrote, "No one grumbles at his Lot in an Engagement, nor Curseth the Bullet that Unlegs him, because all on board, were alike exposed to the Misfortune." Seamen were always more content when everyone shared in "the General Toil and Danger." But, of course, in many areas of shipboard life – food, wages, discipline – all were not "alike exposed," and a leveling sentiment grew up in opposition.[87]

The emphasis on equality also grew from the very scarcity of necessities aboard the ship, from the fact that all too often the seaman faced poverty and deprivation. Matthew Bishop observed: "For when we had whole Allowance, and messes together, some Men would eat as much more as others; but when we came to half Allowance every one took care to have an equal

---

[85] Timothy J. Runyon, "Ships and Mariners in Later Medieval England," *Journal of British Studies* 16 (1977), 1–17; George Shelvocke, *A Voyage Round the World by Way of the Great South Sea* (London, 1726), 221, 223, 235; Betagh, *Voyage*, 186–7.

[86] Babb v. Chalkley, HCA 24/127 (1701).

[87] Slush, *Navy Royal*, 21–7, 28, vii. See also Hamilton v. Wilkinson, HCA 24/136 (1727).

share."[88] Resources had to be carefully and equally dispensed. But notions of equality were not confined merely to situations of scarcity. Pirates, for example, even when sated with goods, were usually careful to observe an extremely egalitarian plan of division.[89]

This ethic of egalitarianism both grew from and was nourished by the manifold vulnerabilities of life at sea. Seamen existed as both a community of suffering and a "brotherhood of peril." The very omnipresence of death acted in certain ways as a leveler. James Yonge quoted *The Agamemnon* in his journal to illuminate the sailor's *mentalité:*

> He that smiling can gaze on
> *Styx* and black wav'd *Acheron,*
> that dares brave his ruin, he
> to Kings, to Gods, shall equal be.

Perhaps this illuminates Daniel Defoe's description of pirates, where every man was "in his own Imagination a Captain, a Prince, or a King." Such positions of authority may not have been so bad as long as everyone could claim a title.[90]

The seaman's egalitarianism was of a piece with other aspects of his culture. It was an essential part of an emphasis on hospitality and cooperation, reciprocity and mutuality, and generosity over accumulation. Everyone's chances for survival and prosperity improved because of such an ethic. Egalitarianism was also congruent with the all-important reality of movement. Since mobility tended to limit accumulation to transportable property, material differences among seamen were relatively limited. Egalitarian forms of social organization and social relations have been commonplace among history's nomadic peoples.[91] They

---

[88] *Life and Adventures of Matthew Bishop,* 33.
[89] See Chapter 6 of this book.
[90] *Journal of James Yonge,* 138; Defoe, *History of the Pyrates,* 224; Robinson, *British Tar,* 213.
[91] P. Bonte, "Non-Stratified Formations among Pastoral Nomads," *The Evolution of Social Systems,* ed. J. Friedman and M. J. Rowland (London, 1977), 173–200; Richard Symanski, Ian R. Manners, and R. J. Bromley, "The Mobile–Sedentary Continuum," *Annals of the Association of American Geographers* 65 (1975), 461–71; Douglas L. Johnson, "Nomadic Organization of Space: Reflections on Pattern and Process," *Dimensions of Human Geography: Essays on Some Familiar and Neglected Themes,* ed. Karl W. Butzer (Chicago, 1978), 25–47.

also help to explain how "justice" came to be a watchword among seamen. As Barnaby Slush said, "Without Justice, there can be no true discipline, no Love, no Followers." The ship in its own way was a school in social and economic democracy. Collectivism,' antiauthoritarianism, and egalitarianism were core values in the common seaman's ethos.[92]

We noted at the outset of this chapter that Jack Tar participated in almost every port-city riot in England and America in the early modern period. Seamen were active in disturbances in Boston in the 1690s and 1740s, in Philadelphia in 1741, 1742, and 1759–69, in Newport in 1719, New York in 1705, Charleston in 1701, and in all of these cities in the 1760s and 1770s. They protested in London and Liverpool throughout the century, particularly in the 1760s and 1770s. And these are but a few of the riots tars joined or instigated. The explanations of their willingness to take to the streets have emphasized circumstances. Seafarers joined these tumults because they were footloose in the port towns between voyages; they were available. Furthermore, seamen were not usually natives of the city where the riot developed; hence they were not tied to the structures of social control and deference in that particular locality. They were outsiders.[93] These arguments contain important insights, but they are incomplete since they do not explore the link between the seaman's militancy and his social experience. Jesse Lemisch deepened the understanding of this problem when he began to examine "rioting as political expression" among seamen, and concluded that the harshness of the sailor's life and his hatred of the Royal Navy brought Jack to the streets, using "purposeful" violence in protest.[94]

Lemisch's view must be broadened by considering the sailor's militancy in relation to his specific work experience. For Jack's major, most enduring, and most formative struggle with authority was not against the Royal Navy, but rather on board his

---

[92] See footnote 1 of this chapter.

[93] Bridenbaugh, *Cities in the Wilderness*, 383–4, and *Cities in Revolt*, 114, 117, 306; Hoerder, *Crowd Action*, 374–5; Bailyn, ed., *Pamphlets*, 582; James G. Lydon, *Pirates, Privateers, and Profits* (Upper Saddle River, N.J., 1970), 18.

[94] Lemisch, "Jack Tar in the Streets," 396, 378–9, 381–7, 393–5, 390. For an example of this purposeful violence, see the Information of Humphrey Downes, HCA 1/54 (1718), f. 80.

own merchant ship. The tradition of armed resistance was not confined to battling the state and the press gang, but was part of a daily conflict in life at sea.

The work experience at sea – the source of an oppositional culture – was in many ways carried ashore. Seamen often brought to the ports a militant attitude toward arbitrary and excessive authority, a willingness to empathize with the grievances of others and to cooperate for the sake of self-defense, and a tendency to use purposeful violence and direct action to accomplish collectively defined goals. As an East India Company captain noted, "seamen being zealous abetters of liberty, will admit of no arbitrary force, and may be easily led, but not drove."[95]

Other aspects of the seaman's experience predisposed him to this sort of undertaking. Life at sea required a great deal of courage. As Matthew Bishop observed in 1744: "a Sailor should never be afraid of any Thing the Sea can produce; for if your Fear once gets the better of your Courage, you will be of no use at all."[96] Or as Ned Ward put it, "No Man can have a Greater contempt for Death. For every day he constantly shits upon his own Grave, and dreads a Storm no more, than He does a broken Head, when drunk."[97] A culturally valued notion of defiance, of daring initiative, was built into life at sea by the perilous environment. It was only a small step to apply Matthew Bishop's admonition to the social relations of work and authority, and then to transform these values of courage, defiance, and antiauthoritarianism into effective protest. The seaman's labor also required a great deal of physical prowess, and masculinity and athletic ability were also highly valued. Fighting and boxing were major sports and pastimes among seamen,

---

[95] Anonymous officer of an East India Company ship, *Piracy Destroy'd, Or, a Short Discourse Shewing the Rise, Growth, and Causes of Piracy of Late, with a Sure Method How to put a Speedy Stop to that Growing Evil* (London, 1701), 12.

[96] *Life and Adventures of Matthew Bishop*, 51; Lloyd, *British Seaman*, 74. See also "Simsons Voyage." Perhaps this matter was explained most poetically by Herman Melville, who wrote about working the sails in a storm: "The truth is, that, in circumstances like these, the sense of fear is annihilated in the unutterable sights that fill all the eye, and the sounds that fill all the ear"; quoted in C. L. R. James, *Mariners, Renegades, and Castaways: The Story of Herman Melville and the World We Live In* (Detroit, 1978), 100.

[97] Ward, *Wooden World*, 69.

and many seem to have liked the idea of joining a brawl for a good cause.[98]

Seamen were not much constrained by legalities, since they witnessed the breach of legal authority on a regular basis and in fact created breaches of their own whenever they seemed necessary. As Lemisch has argued, "Illegality had thus become an accepted part of seamen's daily lives, a means of expression in a society whose institutions and customs seemed in many ways planned to worsen their very difficult lot." Further, "One of the institutions most familiar to seamen was the jail."[99] Seamen had also experienced the double exploitation of life in the wooden world. As producers they labored in an environment where their boss held almost tyrannical powers of discipline and control, and as consumers they lived within a shipboard economy in which food, health, and social life were firmly regulated from above by the very same boss. So seamen risked broken heads by joining and promoting riots, encouraged by their oppositional culture to defiance, activism, and a broader identification with the struggles of others.

The importance of the experience that the seaman lugged ashore must not be underestimated, for by a momentous turn of events this experience, once translated into protest, had a profound impact upon the development of political thought in America and upon the formulation of ideologies of resistance still resonant today. It all began in the Knowles Riots that shook Boston in 1747.[100]

Commander Charles Knowles of HMS *Lark* seized several Bostonians in a hot press. A mob, initially consisting of 300 seamen but ballooning to "several thousand people," quickly seized some officers of the *Lark* as hostages, beat a deputy sheriff and slapped him into the town's stocks, surrounded and attacked the Provincial Council Chamber, and posted squads at all piers to keep naval officers from escaping back to their ship. Armed with "clubs, swords, and cutlasses," the mob was led by men of the working class: laborers and domestic and "foreign

[98] For a later period, see the remarks of Weibust, *Deep Sea Sailors*, 196.

[99] Lemisch, "Jack Tar vs. John Bull," 75, 59.

[100] In the next two paragraphs I am heavily indebted to John Lax and William Pencak, "The Knowles Riot and the Crisis of the 1740s in Massachusetts," *Perspectives in American History* 10 (1976), 163–214.

seamen."[101] The original reason for the sailors' assembly was "self-defense," but there was a positive element to their protest as well. As Knowles himself remarked:

The Act [of 1746] against pressing in the Sugar Islands, filled the Minds of the Common People ashore as well as Sailors in all the Northern Colonies (but more especially in New England) with not only a hatred for the King's Service but [also] a Spirit of Rebellion each *Claiming a Right* to the same Indulgence as the Sugar Colonies and declaring they will maintain themselves in it.[102]

Maintain themselves in it they did. As Ned Ward wrote in 1711 and might have reiterated had he been in Boston in 1747:

> Aspiring in their Noble Thought
> Above the Law as they'd been taught,
> Presum'd to make a Street Convention,
> To Prosecute a New Intention.[103]

As Jesse Lemisch argued about the sailors of a later period, "The seaman who defended himself against impressment felt that he was fighting to defend his 'liberty,' and he justified his resistance on grounds of 'right.' "[104]

This, in fact, was the essential idea embodied in the seamen's *activity*, in their resistance to unjust authority, in their many "class victories" against impressment. Learning and deriving a creative impulse from this active "Spirit of Rebellion," Samuel Adams began the task of explaining, at the level of political discourse, what these working people *were doing*. Adams used the Knowles Riot "to legitimize the right of the public forcibly to resist authority when it had overstepped its bounds." In so doing, Adams moved from the concrete, historical rights of English men and women to the abstract rights of humankind: "The riot was also the immediate cause of Samuel Adams' formulation of an ideology of resistance, in which the natural rights of man were used for the first time to justify mob activity." Further, Adams saw that the mob "embodied the fundamental rights of man against which government itself could be

---

[101] Ibid., 188, 186, 199.
[102] Quoted in ibid., 182, 186; my emphasis.
[103] Ned Ward, *Vulgus Britannicus* (London, 1711), 14.
[104] Lemisch, "Jack Tar in the Streets," 400.

judged."[105] But the self-activity of some common tars, "zealous abetters of liberty," came first. They brought into Boston harbor a potent experience of labor, exploitation, and resistance to authority that soon became a "New Intention." Early American libertarian thought was thus indebted to the "international circulation of workers' experience."[106]

[105] Lax and Pencak, "Knowles Riot," 205, 214; Nash, *Urban Crucible,* 223.
[106] Peter Linebaugh, "Socking: Tobacco Porters, The Hogshead, and Excise," *The London Hanged: Crime and Civil Society in the Eighteenth Century* (forthcoming).

6

THE SEAMAN AS PIRATE

Plunder and Social Banditry at Sea

Writing to the Board of Trade in 1724, Governor Alexander
Spotswood of Virginia lamented his lack of "some safe opportunity to get home" to London. He insisted that he would travel
only in a well-armed man-of-war.

> Your Lordships will easily conceive my Meaning when you reflect on
> the Vigorous part I've acted to suppress Pirates: and if those barba-
> rous Wretches can be moved to cut off the Nose & Ears of a Master
> for but correcting his own Sailors, what inhuman treatment must I
> expect, should I fall within their power, who have been markt as the
> principle object of their vengeance, for cutting off their arch Pirate
> Thatch [Teach, also known as Blackbeard], with all his grand Designs,
> & making so many of their Fraternity to swing in the open air of
> Virginia.[1]

Spotswood knew these pirates well. He had authorized the expedition that returned to Virginia boasting Blackbeard's head
as a trophy. He had done his share to see that many pirates
swung on Virginia gallows. He knew that pirates had a fond-
ness for revenge, that they often punished ship captains for
"correcting" their crews, and that a kind of "fraternity" prevailed among them. He had good reason to fear them.

   Anglo-American pirates created an imperial crisis with their
relentless and successful attacks upon merchants' property and
international commerce between 1716 and 1726. Accordingly,
these freebooters occupy a grand position in the long history of
robbery at sea. Their numbers, near 5,000, were extraordinary,

---

[1] Alexander Spotswood to the Board of Trade, CO 5/1319 (June 16, 1724).

and their plunderings were exceptional in both volume and value.[2] This chapter explores the social and cultural dimensions of piracy, focusing on pirates' experience, the organization of their ships, and their social relations and consciousness. It concludes with observations on the social and economic context of the crime and its culture. Piracy represented "crime" on a massive scale. It was a way of life voluntarily chosen, for the most part, by large numbers of men who directly challenged the ways of the society from which they excepted themselves. The main intent of this chapter is to see how piracy looked from the inside and to examine the kinds of social order that pirates forged beyond the reach of traditional authority. Beneath the Jolly Roger, "the banner of King Death," a new social world took shape once pirates had, as one of them put it, "the choice in themselves."[3] It was a world profoundly shaped and

[2] Studies of piracy include general surveys, descriptive chronicles of exploits, and specific, often monographic examinations of certain features of pirate life. Daniel Defoe was the first historian of these pirates. Under the name Charles Johnson, he published an invaluable collection of mostly accurate information, *A General History of the Pyrates,* ed. Manuel Schonhorn (1724, 1728; reprint Columbia, S.C., 1972), hereafter cited as *History of the Pyrates.* George Roberts (believed by some to have been Defoe), *The Four Years Voyages . . .* (London, 1726), contains believable accounts of pirates. The best recent study is Hugh F. Rankin, *The Golden Age of Piracy* (New York, 1969). More ambitious are Philip Gosse, *The History of Piracy* (New York, 1932); Neville Williams, *Captains Outrageous: Seven Centuries of Piracy* (London, 1961); and P. K. Kemp and Christopher Lloyd, *Brethren of the Coast: Buccaneers of the South Seas* (New York, 1960). Patrick Pringle's *Jolly Roger* (New York, 1953), a piece of popular history, has some fine insights. Charles Grey, *Pirates of the Eastern Seas, 1618–1723: A Lurid Page of History,* ed. George MacMunn (1933; reprint Port Washington, N.Y., 1971); George Francis Dow and John Henry Edmonds, *The Pirates of the New England Coast, 1630–1730* (Salem, Mass., 1923); and John Biddulph, *The Pirates of Malabar; and, An Englishwoman . . . in India . . .* (London, 1907) are somewhat descriptive but contain important data. Stanley Richards, *Black Bart* (Llandybie, Wales, 1966), is a biography of Bartholomew Roberts. See also Shirley Carter Hughson, *The Carolina Pirates and Colonial Commerce, 1670–1740,* Johns Hopkins University Studies in Historical and Political Science, XII (Baltimore, 1894); B. R. Burg, "Legitimacy and Authority: A Case Study of Pirate Commanders in the Seventeenth and Eighteenth Centuries," *American Neptune* 37 (1977), 40–9; James G. Lydon, *Pirates, Privateers, and Profits* (Upper Saddle River, N.J., 1970); and Richard B. Morris, "The Ghost of Captain Kidd," *New York History* 19 (1938), 280–97. The literature on piracy is vast. For the newcomer, these works provide a solid beginning.
[3] S. Charles Hill, "Episodes of Piracy in Eastern Waters," *Indian Antiquary* 49 (1920), 37; Arthur L. Hayward, ed., *Lives of the Most Remarkable Criminals . . .*

textured by the experiences of work, wages, culture, and authority accumulated in the normal, rugged course of maritime life and labor in the early eighteenth century.

Contemporary estimates of the pirate population during the period under consideration placed the number between 1,000 and 2,000 at any one time. This range seems generally accurate. From records that describe the activities of pirate ships and from reports or projections of crew sizes, it appears that 1,800 to 2,400 Anglo-American pirates prowled the seas between 1716 and 1718, 1,500 to 2,000 between 1719 and 1722, and 1,000 to 1,500, declining to fewer than 200, between 1723 and 1726. In the only estimate we have from the other side of the law, a band of pirates in 1716 claimed that "30 Company of them," or roughly 2,400 men, plied the oceans of the globe. In all, some 4,500 to 5,500 men went, as they called it, "upon the account." The pirates' chief military enemy, the Royal Navy, employed an average of only 13,000 men in any given year between 1716 and 1726.[4]

Footnote 3 (*cont.*):
(London, 1735; reprint New York, 1927), 37. Following E. P. Thompson, *Whigs and Hunters: The Origins of the Black Act* (New York, 1975), and Douglas Hay et al., eds., *Albion's Fatal Tree: Crime and Society in Eighteenth-Century England* (New York, 1975), this chapter uses the social history of crime as access to working-class life in the eighteenth century. I define a pirate as one who willingly participates in robbery on the sea, not discriminating among nationalities in the choice of victims. Part of the empirical base of this chapter was accumulated in piecemeal fashion from documents of all varieties. Individual pirates were recorded by name and dates of activity, and information on age, labor, class, family background, and miscellaneous detail was noted. This file (519 men, 2 women) can be replicated only by consulting all of the sources that follow in the footnotes. Since I have found mention of only two female pirates, and since the maritime world was predominantly male, the latter gender is used in references.

[4] James Logan (1717) estimated 1,500 in Hughson, *Carolina Pirates*, 59; Governor of Bermuda (1717) "at least 1,000" in Pringle, *Jolly Roger*, 181, and in HCA 1/54 (1717), f. 113; Woodes Rogers (1718) "near a thousand" in Defoe, *History of the Pyrates*, 615; Daniel Defoe (1720) 1,500, ibid., 132; Governor of South Carolina (1718) "near 2,000" in W. Noel Sainsbury et al., eds., *Calendar of State Papers, Colonial Series, America and the West Indies* (London, 1860–   ), vol. XXXI, 10, hereafter cited as *Cal. St. Papers;* Anonymous (1721) 1,500 in Abel Boyer, ed., *The Political State of Great Britain . . .* (London, 1711–40), vol. XXI, 659. Quotation from Representation from Several Merchants Trading to Virginia to Board of Trade, CO 5/1318 (Apr. 15, 1717). Estimates of the sizes of crews are available for thirty-seven pirate ships: The mean is 79.5. I have found reference to seventy-nine crews

These sea robbers followed lucrative trade and, like their predecessors, sought bases for their depredations in the Caribbean Sea and the Indian Ocean. The Bahama Islands, undefended and ungoverned by the crown, began in 1716 to attract pirates by the hundreds. By 1718 a torrent of complaints had moved George I to commission Woodes Rogers to lead an expedition to bring the islands under control. Rogers's efforts largely succeeded, and pirates scattered to the unpeopled inlets of the Carolinas and to Africa. They had frequented African shores as early as 1691; by 1718, Madagascar served as both an entrepôt for booty and a spot for temporary settlement. At the mouth of the Sierra Leone River on Africa's western coast, pirates stopped off for "whoring and drinking" and to unload goods. Theaters of operation among pirates shifted, however, according to the policing designs of the Royal Navy. Pirates favored the Caribbean's small, unsettled cays and shallow waters, which proved hard to negotiate for men-of-war that offered chase. But generally, as one pirate noted, these rovers were "dispers't into several parts of the World." Sea robbers sought and usually found bases near major trade routes, as distant as possible from the powers of the state.[5]

through mention of the ship or captain. Totals were obtained by arranging ships according to periods of activity and multiplying by the mean crew size. If this mean holds, the total population would have been 6,281. Yet this figure counts some pirates more than once. For example, many who sailed with both Howell Davis and Bartholomew Roberts are counted twice. The range 4,500–5,500 expresses the uncertainty of the calculations. It seems that, in all, some 5,000 men were involved. For estimates of the number of men in the Royal Navy, see Christopher Lloyd, *The British Seaman, 1200– 1860: A Social Survey* (Rutherford, N.J., 1970), 287, and Marcus Rediker, "Society and Culture among Anglo-American Deep-Sea Sailors, 1700– 1750," Ph.D. diss., University of Pennsylvania, 1982, 49, 317.

5 Deposition of John Vickers, CO 5/1317 (1716); Spotswood to Council of Trade and Plantations (hereafter CTP) CO 5/1364 (May 31, 1717); Defoe, *History of the Pyrates*, 31–4; Leo Francis Stock, ed., *Proceedings and Debates of the British Parliaments Respecting North America* (Washington, D.C., 1930), vol. III, 399; Deposition of Adam Baldridge in John Franklin Jameson, ed., *Privateering and Piracy in the Colonial Period: Illustrative Documents* (New York, 1923), 180–7; R. A. Brock, ed., *The Official Letters of Alexander Spotswood . . .* (Virginia Historical Society, *Collections*, N.S., II [Richmond, Va., 1882]), 168, 351, hereafter cited as Brock, *Letters of Spotswood;* William Snelgrave, *A New Account of Some Parts of Guinea and the Slave Trade* (London, 1734), 197; Abbe Rochon, "A Voyage to Madagascar and the East Indies," in John Pinkerton, ed., *A General Collection of the Best and Most Interesting Voyages and Travels . . .* (London, 1814), vol. XVI, 767–71; William Smith, *A New Voyage*

Almost all pirates had labored as merchant seamen, Royal Navy sailors, or privateersmen.[6] The vast majority came from captured merchantmen as volunteers, for reasons suggested by Dr. Samuel Johnson's observation that "no man will be a sailor who has contrivance enough to get himself into a jail; for being in a ship is being in jail with the chance of being drowned. . . . A man in jail has more room, better food, and commonly better company."[7] Dr. Johnson's class condescension aside, he had a point. Incarceration on a ship did not differ essentially from incarceration in a jail. As previous chapters have suggested, merchant seamen had an extremely difficult lot in the early eighteenth century. They got a hard, close look at death. Disease and accidents were commonplace in their occupation, natural disasters threatened incessantly, rations were often meager, and discipline was brutal, even murderous on occasion. Peacetime wages were low, fraud and irregularities in the distribution of pay general. A prime purpose of eighteenth-century maritime laws was "to assure a ready supply of cheap, docile labor."[8] Merchant seamen also had to contend with impressment by the Royal Navy.

Footnote 5 (*cont.*):
to Guinea . . . (London, 1744), 12, 42. On Defoe's credibility, see Schonhorn's introduction to *History of the Pyrates*, xxvii–xl; Gosse, *History of Piracy*, 182; and Rankin, *Golden Age*, 161.

[6] Biographical data indicate that 155 of the 157 for whom labor background is known came from one of these employments; 144 had been in the merchant service. Probably fewer than 5 percent of pirates originated as mutineers. See *History of the Pyrates*, 116, 196, 215–16; Snelgrave, *Account of the Slave Trade*, 203; Deposition of Richard Simes, *Cal. St. Papers*, vol. XXXII, 319; and ibid., vol. XXXIII, 365 on volunteers.

[7] James Boswell, *The Life of Samuel Johnson* . . . (London, 1791), 86.

[8] Jesse Lemisch, "Jack Tar in the Streets: Merchant Seamen in the Politics of Revolutionary America," *WMQ* 25 (1968), 379, 375–6, 406; Richard B. Morris, *Government and Labor in Early America* (New York, 1946), 246–7, 257, 262–8; Defoe, *History of the Pyrates*, 244, 359; A. G. Course, *The Merchant Navy: A Social History* (London, 1963), 61; Samuel Cox to CTP, *Cal. St. Papers*, vol. XXXII, 393; Ralph Davis, *The Rise of the English Shipping Industry in the Seventeenth and Eighteenth Centuries* (London, 1962), 144, 154–5; *The Voyages and Travels of Captain Nathaniel Uring*, ed. Alfred Dewar (1726; reprint London, 1928), xxviii, 176–8; Arthur Pierce Middleton, *Tobacco Coast: A Maritime History of Chesapeake Bay in the Colonial Era* (Newport News, Va., 1953), 8, 13, 15, 18, 271, 281; Lloyd, *British Seaman*, 249, 264; John Atkins, *A Voyage to Guinea, Brasil, and the West-Indies* . . . (London, 1735), 261; G. T. Crook, ed., *The Complete Newgate Calendar* . . . (London, 1926), vol. III, 57–8; S. Charles Hill, "Notes on Piracy in Eastern Waters," *Indian Antiquary* 46 (1927), 130; Hayward, ed., *Remarkable Criminals*, 126.

Some pirates had served in the navy, where conditions aboard ship were no less harsh. Food supplies often ran short, wages were low, mortality was high, discipline severe, and desertion consequently chronic. As one officer reported, the navy had trouble fighting pirates because the king's ships were "so much disabled by sickness, death, and desertion of their seamen."[9] In 1722 the crown sent the *Weymouth* and the *Swallow* in search of a pirate convoy. Royal surgeon John Atkins, noting that merchant seamen were frequently pressed, underlined precisely what these sailors had to fear when he recorded that the "*Weymouth,* who brought out of *England* a Compliment [sic] of 240 Men," had "at the end of the Voyage 280 dead upon her Books." The same point was made by the captain of a man-of-war sent to Jamaica to guard against pirates in 1720–1. He faithfully recorded the names of the thirty-five seamen who died during the year of duty.[10] Epidemics, consumption, and scurvy raged on royal ships, and the men were "caught in a machine from which there was no escape, bar desertion, incapacitation, or death."[11] Or piracy.

Pirates who had served on privateering vessels knew well that such employment was far less onerous than on merchant or naval ships. Food was usually more plentiful, the pay considerably higher, and the work shifts generally shorter.[12] Even so, owing to rigid discipline and other grievances, mutinies were

---

[9] Gov. Lowther to CTP, *Cal. St. Papers,* vol. XXIX, 350; Morris, *Government and Labor,* 247; Lemisch, "Jack Tar," 379; Davis, *English Shipping,* 133–7; R. D. Merriman, ed., *Queen Anne's Navy: Documents Concerning the Administration of the Navy of Queen Anne, 1702–1714* (London, 1961), 170–2, 174, 221–2, 250; Lloyd, *British Seaman,* 44–6, 124–49; Peter Kemp, *The British Sailor: A Social History of the Lower Deck* (London, 1970), chaps. 4, 5; Arthur N. Gilbert, "Buggery and the British Navy, 1700–1861," *Journal of Social History* 10 (1976–7), 72–98.

[10] Atkins, *Voyage to Guinea,* 139, 187; Captain's logbook, "At Jamaica, 1720–1721," Rawlinson Manuscripts A-299, Bodleian Library, Oxford; *The Historical Register, Containing an Impartial Relation of All Transactions . . .* (London, 1722), vol. VII, 344.

[11] Merriman, *Queen Anne's Navy,* 171. Lloyd, *British Seaman,* 44, estimates that one-half of all men pressed between 1600 and 1800 died at sea.

[12] Course, *Merchant Navy,* 84; Lloyd, *British Seaman,* 57; Edward Cooke, *A Voyage to the South Sea* (London, 1712), v–vi, 14–16; Woodes Rogers, *A Cruising Voyage Round the World,* ed. G. E. Manwaring (1712; reprint New York, 1928), xiv, xxv; George Shelvocke, *A Voyage Round the World* (London, 1726), 34–6, 38, 46, 157, 214, 217; William Betagh, *A Voyage Round the World* (London, 1728), 4.

not uncommon. On Woodes Rogers's spectacularly successful privateering expedition of 1708–11, Peter Clark was thrown into irons for wishing himself "aboard a Pirate" and saying that "he should be glad that an Enemy, who could over-power us, was a-long-side of us."[13]

Most men became pirates when their merchant vessels were taken. Colonel Benjamin Bennet wrote to the Council of Trade and Plantations in 1718, setting forth his worries about free-booters in the West Indies: "I fear they will soon multiply for so many are willing to joyn with them when taken." The seizure of a merchant ship was followed by a moment of great confrontational drama. The pirate captain or quartermaster asked the seamen of the captured vessel who among them would serve under the death's head and black colors, and frequently several stepped forward. Many fewer pirates originated as mutineers who had boldly and collectively seized control of a merchant vessel. But regardless of their methods, pirates necessarily came from seafaring employments, whether the merchant service, the navy, or privateering. Piracy emphatically was not an option open to landlubbers, since sea robbers "entertain'd so contemptible a Notion of Landmen."[14] Men who became pirates were grimly familiar with the rigors of life at sea and with a single-sex community of work.

Ages are known for 117 pirates active between 1716 and 1726. The range was 17 to 50 years, the mean 27.4, and the median 27; the 20–24 and 25–29 age categories had the highest concentrations, with thirty-nine and thirty-seven men, respectively. Three in five were 25 or older. The age distribution was almost identical to that of the merchant service as a whole, suggesting that piracy held roughly equal attraction for sailors of all ages.[15] Though evidence is sketchy, most pirates seem not to have been bound to land and home by familial ties or obligations. Wives and children were rarely mentioned in the records

[13] Rogers, *Cruising Voyage*, 205. See also Shelvocke, *Voyage*, 43, 221–5.

[14] Col. Benjamin Bennet to Council of Trade and Plantations, CO 37/10 (May 31, 1718, and July 30, 1717), f. 18; Defoe, *History of the Pyrates*, 228. On volunteers, see footnote 6 of this chapter.

[15] See footnote 3 of this chapter. Ages were taken at the time of the first known piracy. See also Appendix A of this book. In " 'Under the Banner of King Death': The Social World of Anglo-American Pirates, 1716 to 1726," *WMQ* 38 (1981), 208, I mistakenly argued that pirates were older than the seafaring population as a whole.

of trials of pirates, and pirate vessels, to forestall desertion, often would "take no Married Man."[16] Almost without exception, pirates, like the larger body of seafaring men, came from the lowest social classes. They were, as a royal official condescendingly observed, "desperate Rogues" who could have little hope in life ashore.[17] These traits served as bases of unity when men of the sea decided, in search of something better, to become pirates.

These characteristics had a vital bearing on the ways pirates organized their daily activities. Contemporaries who claimed that pirates had "no regular command among them" mistook a different social order – different from the ordering of merchant, naval, and privateering vessels – for disorder.[18] This social order, articulated in the organization of the pirate ship, was conceived and deliberately constructed by the pirates themselves. Its hallmark was a rough, improvised, but effective egalitarianism that placed authority in the collective hands of the crew. A core value in the broader culture of the common tar, egalitarianism was institutionalized aboard the pirate ship.

A striking uniformity of rules and customs prevailed aboard pirate ships, each of which functioned under the terms of written articles, a compact drawn up at the beginning of a voyage or upon election of a new captain, and agreed to by the crew. By these articles crews allocated authority, distributed plunder, and enforced discipline.[19] These arrangements made the cap-

---

[16] Only 23 in the sample of 521 are known to have been married. In pirate confessions, regrets were often expressed to parents, seldom to wives or children. See Cotton Mather, *Useful Remarks: An Essay upon Remarkables in the Way of Wicked Men: A Sermon on the Tragical End, unto which the Way of Twenty-Six Pirates Brought Them; At New Port on Rhode-Island, July 19, 1723 . . .* (New London, Conn., 1723), 38–42; and *Trials of Eight Persons Indited for Piracy . . .* (Boston, 1718), 24, 25. Quotation from John Barnard, *Ashton's Memorial: An History of the Strange Adventures, and Signal Deliverances of Mr. Philip Ashton . . .* (Boston, 1725), 3.

[17] Peter Haywood to CTP, CO 137/12 (Dec. 3, 1716); Lemisch, "Jack Tar," 377; Davis, *English Shipping*, 114. Biographical data show that seventy-one of seventy-five pirates came from working-class backgrounds.

[18] Betagh, *Voyage*, 148.

[19] Defoe, *History of the Pyrates*, 167, 211–13, 298, 307–8, 321; Hayward, ed., *Remarkable Criminals*, 37; Information of Alexander Thompson, HCA 1/55 (1723), f. 23; Snelgrave, *Account of the Slave Trade*, 220; Jameson, ed., *Privateering and Piracy*, 337; Rankin, *Golden Age*, 31. The vast differences between pirate and privateer articles can be seen by comparing the preceding to Rogers, *Cruising Voyage*, xiv, xxv, 22–3; Shelvocke, *Voyage*, 34–6, 159, 218, 223; Cooke, *Voyage*, iv–vi; and Betagh, *Voyage*, 205–6.

tain the creature of his crew. Demanding someone both bold of temper and skilled in navigation, the men elected their captain. They gave him few privileges. He "or any other Officer is allowed no more [food] than another man, nay, the Captain cannot keep his Cabbin to himself."[20] Some pirates "messed with the Captain, but withal no Body look'd on it, as a Mark of Favour, or Distinction, for every one came and eat and drank with him at their Humour." A merchant captain held captive by pirates noted with displeasure that crew members slept on the ship wherever they pleased, "the Captain himself not being allowed a Bed."[21] The determined reorganization of space and privilege aboard the ship was crucial to the remaking of maritime social relations.

The crew granted the captain unquestioned authority "in fighting, chasing, or being chased," but "in all other Matters whatsoever" he was "governed by a Majority."[22] As the majority elected, so did it depose. Captains were snatched from their positions for cowardice, cruelty, or refusing "to take and plunder English Vessels."[23] One captain incurred the class-conscious wrath of his crew for being too "Gentleman-like."[24] Occasionally, a despotic captain was summarily executed. As pirate Francis Kennedy explained, most sea robbers, "having suffered formerly from the ill-treatment of their officers, provided carefully against any such evil" once they arranged their own command. The democratic selection of officers echoed similar demands within the New Model Army in the English Revolution and stood in stark, telling contrast to the near-dic-

[20] Clement Downing, *A Compendious History of the Indian Wars . . .* (1737; reprint London, 1924), 99; Defoe, *History of the Pyrates*, 121, 139, 167–8, 195, 208, 214, 340, 352; Snelgrave, *Account of the Slave Trade*, 199; *Trials of Eight Persons*, 24; Boyer, *Political State*, vol. XXVIII, 152; Roberts, *Four Years Voyages*, 39.

[21] "Proceedings of the Court held on the Coast of Africa upon Trying of 100 Pirates taken by his Ma[jes]ties Ship *Swallow*," HCA 1/99 (1722), f. 59; Snelgrave, *Account of the Slave Trade*, 217; Defoe, *History of the Pyrates*, 213–14.

[22] Defoe, *History of the Pyrates*, 139; Hayward, ed., *Remarkable Criminals*, 37; Boyer, ed., *Political State*, vol. XXVIII, 153; Burg, "Legitimacy and Authority," 40–9.

[23] Jameson, ed., *Privateering and Piracy*, 294; Defoe, *History of the Pyrates*, 139, 67; Dow and Edmonds, *Pirates of New England*, 217; *Trials of Eight Persons*, 23; Morris, "Ghost of Kidd," 282.

[24] Snelgrave, *Account of the Slave Trade*, 199; Burg, "Legitimacy and Authority," 44–8.

tatorial arrangement of command in the merchant service and the Royal Navy.[25]

To prevent the misuse of authority, pirates delegated countervailing powers to the quartermaster, who was elected to represent and protect "the Interest of the Crew."[26] The quartermaster, who was not considered an officer in the merchant service, was elevated to a valued position of trust and authority. His tasks were to adjudicate minor disputes, to distribute food and money, and in some instances to lead the attacks on prize vessels. He served as a "civil Magistrate" and dispensed necessaries "with an Equality to them all," carefully guarding against the galling and divisive use of privilege and preferment that characterized the distribution of the necessaries of life in other maritime occupations.[27] The quartermaster often became the captain of a captured ship when the captor was overcrowded or divided by discord. This containment of authority within a dual and representative executive was a distinctive feature of social organization among pirates.[28]

The decisions that had the greatest bearing on the welfare of the crew were generally reserved to the council, the highest authority on the pirate ship. Pirates drew upon an ancient custom, largely lapsed by the early modern era, in which the master consulted his entire crew in making crucial decisions. Freebooters also knew of the naval tradition, the council of war, in which the top officers in a fleet or ship met to plan strategy. But pirates democratized the naval custom. Their councils usually included every man on the ship. The council determined such matters as where the best prizes could be

---

[25] Hayward, ed., *Remarkable Criminals*, 37; Defoe, *History of the Pyrates*, 42, 296, 337. See Christopher Hill, *The World Turned Upside Down: Radical Ideas in the English Revolution* (New York, 1972).

[26] Defoe, *History of the Pyrates*, 423; Lloyd Haynes Williams, *Pirates of Colonial Virginia* (Richmond, Va., 1937), 19.

[27] Roberts, *Four Years Voyages*, 37, 80; *The Tryals of Major Stede Bonnet and Other Pirates . . .* (London, 1719), 37; Snelgrave, *Account of the Slave Trade*, 199–200, 238–9; Boyer, ed., *Political State*, vol. XXVIII, 153; Defoe, *History of the Pyrates*, 213–25; *Trials of Eight Persons*, 24, 25; *Tryals of Thirty-Six Persons for Piracy . . .* (Boston, 1723), 9; *Boston News-Letter*, July 15–22, 1717; Quotations from Defoe, *History of the Pyrates*, 213; Downing, *Indian Wars*, 99.

[28] Boyer, ed., *Political State*, vol. XXVIII, 151; Snelgrave, *Account of the Slave Trade*, 272; Defoe, *History of the Pyrates*, 138–9, 312. Davis, *English Shipping*, 113, discusses the quite different role of the quartermaster in the merchant service; see also p. 85 of this book.

taken and how disruptive dissension was to be resolved. Some crews continually used the council, "carrying every thing by a majority of votes"; others set up the council as a court. The decisions made by this body were sacrosanct, and even the boldest captain dared not challenge a council's mandate.[29]

The distribution of plunder was regulated explicitly by the ship's articles, which allocated booty according to skills and duties. Pirates used the precapitalist share system to allocate their take. Captain and quartermaster received between one and one-half and two shares; gunners, boatswains, mates, carpenters, and doctors, one and one-quarter or one and one-half; all others got one share each.[30] This pay system represented a radical departure from practices in the merchant service, Royal Navy, or privateering. It leveled an elaborate hierarchy of pay ranks and decisively reduced the disparity between the top and bottom of the scale. Indeed, this must have been one of the most egalitarian plans for the disposition of resources to be found anywhere in the early eighteenth century. The scheme revealingly indicates that pirates did not consider themselves wage laborers but rather risk-sharing partners. If, as a noted historian of piracy, Philip Gosse, suggested, "the pick of all seamen were pirates,"[31] the equitable distribution of plunder and the conception of the partnership were the work of men who valued and respected the skills of their comrades. But not all booty was dispensed this way. A portion went into a "common fund" to provide for the men who sustained injury of lasting effect.[32] The loss of eyesight or any appendage merited compensation. By this welfare system pirates attempted to

[29] Defoe, *History of the Pyrates*, 88–9, 117, 145, 167, 222–5, 292, 595; *Trials of Eight Persons*, 24; Downing, *Indian Wars*, 44, 103; Hill, "Episodes of Piracy," 41–2, 59; Roberts, *Four Years Voyages*, 55, 86; Boyer, ed., *Political State*, vol. XXVIII, 153. Quotation from Betagh, *Voyage*, 148.

[30] Defoe, *History of the Pyrates*, 211–12, 307–8, 342–3; Dow and Edmonds, *Pirates of New England*, 146–7; Hayward, ed., *Remarkable Criminals*, 37; *Tryals of Bonnet*, 22; Morris, "Ghost of Kidd," 283.

[31] See footnote 20, this chapter; Gosse, *History of Piracy*, 103; Biddulph, *Pirates of Malabar*, x, 155; "A Narrative of the Singular Sufferings of John Fillmore and Others on Board the Noted Pirate Vessel Commanded by Captain Phillips," Buffalo Historical Society, *Publications*, 10 (1907), 32.

[32] Defoe, *History of the Pyrates*, 212, 308, 343; Dow and Edmonds, *Pirates of New England*, 147; pirate Jeremiah Huggins, quoted in Morris, "Ghost of Kidd," 292; Hill, "Episodes of Piracy," 57.

guard against debilities caused by accidents, to protect skills, to enhance recruitment, and to promote loyalty within the group.

The articles also regulated discipline aboard ship, though "discipline" is perhaps a misnomer for a system of rules that left large ranges of behavior uncontrolled. Less arbitrary than that of the merchant service and less codified than that of the navy, discipline among pirates always depended on a collective sense of transgression. Many misdeeds were accorded "what Punishment the Captain and Majority of the Company shall think fit," and it is noteworthy that pirates did not often resort to the whip. Their discipline, if no less severe in certain cases, was generally tolerant of behavior that provoked punishment in other maritime occupations. Three major methods of discipline were employed, all conditioned by the fact that pirate ships were crowded; an average crew numbered near eighty on a 250-ton vessel. The articles of Bartholomew Roberts's ship revealed one tactic for maintaining order: "No striking one another on board, but every Man's Quarrels to be ended on Shore at Sword and Pistol." The antagonists were to fight a duel with pistols, but if both missed their first shots, they then seized swords, and the first to draw blood was declared the victor. By taking such conflicts off the ship (and symbolically off the sea), this practice promoted harmony in the crowded quarters below decks.[33] The ideal of harmony was also reflected when pirates made a crew member the "Governor of an Island." Men who were incorrigibly disruptive or who transgressed important rules were marooned. For defrauding his mates by taking more than a proper share of plunder, for deserting or malingering during battle, for keeping secrets from the crew, or for stealing, a pirate risked being deposited "where he was sure to encounter Hardships."[34] The ultimate

---

[33] Defoe, *History of the Pyrates*, 307, 212, 157–58, 339; see footnote 4, this chapter. James F. Shepherd and Gary M. Walton, *Shipping, Maritime Trade, and the Economic Development of Colonial North America* (Cambridge, 1972), 201–3, show that for the ports of Jamaica (1729–31), Barbados (1696–8), and Charleston (1735–9), respectively, merchant seamen in vessels over 150 tons handled 8.6, 10.7, and 12.0 tons of storage per man. Pirates, by more general calculations, handled only 3.1 tons per man; the difference reveals how much more crowded their vessels were.

[34] *Tryals of Bonnet*, 30; Defoe, *History of the Pyrates*, 211, 212, 343; Biddulph, *Pirates of Malabar*, 163–4; Rankin, *Golden Age*, 37.

method of maintaining order was execution. This penalty was exacted for bringing on board "a Boy or a Woman" or for meddling with a "prudent Woman" on a prize ship, but was most commonly invoked to punish a captain who abused his authority.[35]

Some crews attempted to circumvent disciplinary problems by taking "no Body against their Wills."[36] By the same logic, they would keep no unwilling person. The confession of pirate Edward Davis in 1718 indicates that oaths of honor were used to cement the loyalty of new members: "at first the old Pirates were a little shy of the new ones, ... yet in a short time the *New Men* being sworn to be faithful, and not to cheat the Company to the Value of a *Piece of Eight,* they all consulted and acted together with great unanimity, and no distinction was made between *Old* and *New.*"[37] Yet for all their efforts to blunt the cutting edge of authority and to maintain harmony and cohesion, conflict could not always be contained. Occasionally upon election of a new captain, men who favored other leadership drew up new articles and sailed away from their former mates.[38] The social organization constructed by pirates, although flexible, was unable to accommodate severe, sustained conflict. Those who had experienced the claustrophobic and authoritarian world of the merchant ship cherished the freedom to separate. The egalitarian and collective exercise of authority by pirates had both negative and positive effects. Although it produced a chronic instability, it also guaranteed continuity. The very process by which new crews

---

[35] Defoe, *History of the Pyrates,* 212, 343; Snelgrave, *Account of the Slave Trade,* 256; *American Weekly Mercury* (Philadelphia), May 30–June 6, 1723. The discussion of discipline takes into account not only the articles themselves but also observations on actual punishments from other sources.

[36] Jameson, ed., *Privateering and Piracy,* 304; *Trials of Eight Persons,* 19, 21; Brock, ed., *Letters of Spotswood,* 249; Defoe, *History of the Pyrates,* 260. Some men, usually those with important skills, were occasionally pressed; see *Cal. St. Papers,* vol. XXXIII, 365.

[37] *Trials of Eight Persons,* 21; Deposition of Samuel Cooper, CO 37/10 (1718), f. 35; Defoe, *History of the Pyrates,* 116, 196, 216, 228; Boyer, ed., *Political State,* vol. XXVIII, 148; Governor of Bermuda quoted in Pringle, *Jolly Roger,* 181; Deposition of Richard Symes, CO 152/14 (1721), f. 33; *American Weekly Mercury,* Mar. 17, 1720; *New-England Courant* (Boston), June 25–July 2, 1722.

[38] Dow and Edmonds, *Pirates of New England,* 278; Defoe, *History of the Pyrates,* 225, 313; Lt. Gov. Bennett to Mr. Popple, Mar. 31, 1720, *Cal. St. Papers,* vol. XXXII, 19.

were established helped to ensure a social uniformity and, as we shall see, a consciousness of kind among pirates.[39]

One important mechanism in this continuity can be seen by charting the connections among pirate crews. The accompanying diagram, arranged according to vessel captaincy, demonstrates that by splintering, by sailing in consorts, or by other associations, roughly 3,600 pirates – more than 70 percent of all those active between 1716 and 1726 – fit into two main lines of genealogical descent. Captain Benjamin Hornigold and the pirate rendezvous in the Bahamas stood at the origin of an intricate lineage that ended with the hanging of John Phillips's crew in June 1724. The second line, spawned in the chance meeting of the lately mutinous crews of George Lowther and Edward Low in 1722, culminated in the executions of William Fly and his men in July 1726. It was primarily within and through this network that the social organization of the pirate ship took on its significance, transmitting and preserving customs and meanings and helping to structure and perpetuate the pirates' social world.[40] (See Diagram.)

Pirates constructed that world in defiant contradistinction to the ways of the world they left behind, in particular to its salient figures of power, the merchant captain and the royal official, and to the system of authority those figures represented and enforced. When eight pirates were tried in Boston in 1718, merchant captain Thomas Checkley told of the capture of his ship by pirates who "pretended," he said, "to be Robbin

---

[39] Hayward, ed., *Remarkable Criminals*, 37; Defoe, *History of the Pyrates*, 226, 342.

[40] The total of 3,600 is reached by multiplying the number of ship captains shown in the figure by the average crew size of 79.5. See Defoe, *History of the Pyrates*, 41–2, 72, 121, 137, 138, 174, 210, 225, 277, 281, 296, 312, 352, 355, 671; *New-England Courant*, June 11–18, 1722; *American Weekly Mercury*, July 6–13, 1721, Jan. 5–12 and Sept. 16–23, 1725; Pringle, *Jolly Roger*, 181, 190, 244; Biddulph, *Pirates of Malabar*, 135, 187; Snelgrave, *Account of the Slave Trade*, 196–7, 199, 272, 280; Hughson, *Carolina Pirates*, 70; *Boston News-Letter*, Aug. 12–19, 1717, Oct. 13–20 and Nov. 10–17, 1718, Feb. 4–11, 1725, June 30–July 7, 1726; Downing, *Indian Wars*, 51, 101; Morris, "Ghost of Kidd," 282, 283, 296; *Tryals of Bonnet*, iii, 44–5; Dow and Edmonds, *Pirates of New England*, 117, 135, 201, 283, 287; *Trials of Eight Persons*, 23; Jameson, ed., *Privateering and Piracy*, 304, 341; Boyer, ed., *Political State*, vol. XXV, 198–9; Hill, "Notes on Piracy," 148, 150; Capt. Matthew Musson to CTP, *Cal. St. Papers*, vol. XXIX, 338; ibid., vol. XXXI, 21, 118; ibid., vol. XXXIII, 274; John F. Watson, *Annals of Philadelphia and Pennsylvania . . .* (Philadelphia, 1844), vol. II, 227; *Boston Gazette*, Apr. 27–May 4, 1724; BL, Add. Mss. 40806, 40812, 40813.

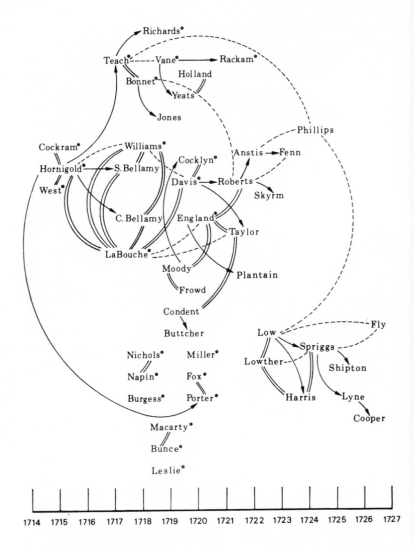

Connections among Anglo-American pirate crews, 1714–26.
[Key to symbols: (→) Direct descent – crew division because of dispute,
overcrowding, or election of a new captain; (═) sailed in consort; (— —
—) other connection – common crew members, contact without sailing
together; (○) used the Bahama Islands as rendezvous.]

Hoods Men."[41] Eric Hobsbawm has defined social banditry as a "universal and virtually unchanging phenomenon," an "endemic peasant protest against oppression and poverty: a cry for vengeance on the rich and the oppressors." Its goal is "a traditional world in which men are justly dealt with, not a new and perfect world"; Hobsbawm calls its advocates "revolutionary traditionalists."[42] Pirates, of course, were not peasants, but they fit Hobsbawm's formulation in every other respect. Of special importance was their "cry for vengeance."

Spotswood told no more than the simple truth when he expressed his fear of pirate vengeance, for the very names of pirate ships made the same threat. Edward Teach, whom Spotswood's men cut off, called his vessel *Queen Anne's Revenge;* other notorious craft were Stede Bonnet's *Revenge* and John Cole's *New York Revenge's Revenge.*[43] The foremost target of vengeance was the merchant captain. Frequently, "in a far distant latitude," as one seaman put it, "unlimited power, bad views, ill nature and ill principles all concur [red]" in a ship's commander. Here was a man "past all restraint" who often made life miserable for his crew.[44] Spotswood also noted how pirates avenged the captain's "correcting" of his sailors. In 1722, merchant captains Isham Randolph, Constantine Cane, and William Halladay petitioned Spotswood "in behalf of themselves and other Masters of Ships" for "some certain method . . . for punishing mutinous & disobe-

---

[41] Testimony of Thomas Checkley (1717) in Jameson, ed., *Privateering and Piracy*, 304; *Trials of Eight Persons*, 11.

[42] E. J. Hobsbawm, *Primitive Rebels: Studies in Archaic Forms of Social Movements in the 19th and 20th Centuries* (New York, 1959), 5, 17, 18, 27, 28; see also his *Bandits* (New York, 1969), 24–9.

[43] *The Tryals of Sixteen Persons for Piracy . . .* (Boston, 1726), 5; *Tryals of Bonnet*, iii, iv; Crook, *Newgate Calendar*, 61; Hughson, *Carolina Pirates*, 121; Rankin, *Golden Age*, 28; Defoe, *History of the Pyrates*, 116, 342; Downing, *Indian Wars*, 98. An analysis of the names of forty-four pirate ships reveals the following patterns: eight (18.2 percent) made reference to revenge; seven (15.9 percent) were named *Ranger* or *Rover*, suggesting mobility and perhaps, as discussed subsequently, a watchfulness over the way captains treated their sailors; five (11.4 percent) referred to royalty. It is noteworthy that only two names referred to wealth. Other names indicated that places (*Lancaster*), unidentifiable people (*Mary Anne*), and animals (*Black Robin*) constituted less significant themes. Two names, *Batchelor's Delight* and *Batchelor's Adventure*, tend to support the probability (footnote 16, this chapter) that most pirates were unmarried; see Defoe, *History of the Pyrates*, 220, 313; William P. Palmer, ed., *Calendar of Virginia State Papers . . .* (Richmond, Va., 1875), vol. I, 194; and *Cal. St. Papers*, vol. XXX, 263.

[44] Betagh, *Voyage*, 41.

dient Seamen." They explained that captains faced great danger "in case of meeting with Pyrates, where we are sure to suffer all the tortures w[hi]ch such an abandoned crew can invent, upon the least intimation of our Striking any of our men."[45] Pirates acted the part of a floating mob with its own distinctive sense of popular justice.

Upon seizing a merchantman, pirates often administered the "Distribution of Justice," "enquiring into the Manner of the Commander's Behaviour to their Men, and those, against whom Complaint was made" were "whipp'd and pickled."[46] Bartholomew Roberts's crew considered such inquiry so important that they formally designated one of their men, George Willson, as the "Dispencer of Justice." In 1724 merchant captain Richard Hawkins described another form of retribution, a torture known as the "Sweat": "Between decks they stick Candles round the Mizen-Mast, and about twenty-five men surround it with Points of Swords, Penknives, Compasses, Forks &c in each of their hands: *Culprit* enters the Circle; the Violin plays a merry Jig; and he must run for about ten Minutes, while each man runs his Instrument into his Posteriors."[47] Many captured captains were "barbarously used," and some were summarily executed. Pirate Philip Lyne carried this vengeance to its bloodiest extremity, confessing when apprehended in 1726 that "during the time of his Piracy" he "had killed 37 Masters of Vessels."[48] The search for vengeance was

[45] Petition of Randolph, Cane, and Halladay (1722) in Palmer, ed., *Virginia State Papers*, 202.

[46] "Proceedings of the Court held on the Coast of Africa," HCA 1/99 (1722), f. 101; Defoe, *History of the Pyrates*, 338, 582; Snelgrave, *Account of the Slave Trade*, 212, 225; Dow and Edmonds, *Pirates of New England*, 301; *Voyages and Travels of Captain Nathaniel Uring*, xxviii. See p. 217 (n. 27) of this book.

[47] Hawkins in Boyer, ed., *Political State*, vol. XXVIII, 149–50; *History of the Pyrates*, 352–3; Dow and Edmonds, *Pirates of New England*, 278; Betagh, *Voyage*, 26. This torture may have exploited that meaning of the verb "to sweat," which was to drive hard, to overwork: The construction of a literally vicious circle here seems hardly coincidental. See *Oxford English Dictionary*, s.v. "sweat"; *Tryals of Sixteen Persons*, 14. Knowledge of this ritualized violence was evidently widespread. In 1722, Bristol merchants informed Parliament that pirates "study how to torture"; see Stock, ed., *Proceedings and Debates of Parliaments*, 453. Torture was also applied to captains who refused to reveal the whereabouts of their loot. It seems that Spanish captains received especially harsh treatment.

[48] Crook, ed., *Newgate Calendar*, 59; Boyer, ed., *Political State*, vol. XXXII, 272; *Boston Gazette*, Oct. 24–31, 1720; Rankin, *Golden Age*, 35, 135, 148; Cotton

in many ways a fierce, embittered response to the violent, personal, and arbitrary authority wielded by the merchant captain.

Still, the punishment of captains was not indiscriminate, for a captain who had been "an honest Fellow that never abused any Sailors" was often rewarded by pirates.[49] The best description of pirates' notions of justice comes from merchant captain William Snelgrave's account of his capture in 1719. On April 1, Snelgrave's ship was seized by Thomas Cooklyn's crew of rovers at the mouth of the Sierra Leone River. Cooklyn was soon joined by men captained by Oliver LaBouche and Howell Davis, and Snelgrave spent the next thirty days among 240 pirates.[50]

The capture was effected when twelve pirates in a small boat came alongside Snelgrave's ship, which was manned by forty-five sailors. Snelgrave ordered his crew to arms. They refused, but the pirate quartermaster, infuriated by the command, drew a pistol and then, Snelgrave testified, "with the but-end [he] endeavoured to beat out my Brains" until "some of my People . . . cried out aloud 'For God sake don't kill our Captain, for we never were with a better Man.'" The quartermaster, Snelgrave noted, "told me, 'my Life was safe provided none of my People complained against me.' I replied, 'I was sure none of them could.'"[51]

Snelgrave was taken to Cocklyn, who told him, "I am sorry you have met with bad usage after Quarter given, but 'tis the Fortune of War sometimes. . . . [I]f you tell the truth, and your Men make no Complaints against you, you shall be kindly used." Howell Davis, commander of the largest of the pirate ships, reprimanded Cocklyn's men for their roughness and, by Snelgrave's account, expressed himself "ashamed to hear how I had been used by them. That they should remember their reasons for going a pirating were to revenge themselves on base

Mather, *The Vial Poured Out upon the Sea: A Remarkable Relation of Certain Pirates* . . . (Boston, 1726), 21; Watson, *Annals of Philadelphia,* 227: Quotation from *Boston Gazette,* Mar. 21–8, 1726. It should be stressed that Lyne's bloodletting was exceptional.

[49] *Boston News-Letter,* Nov. 14–21, 1720.

[50] Snelgrave, *Account of the Slave Trade,* 196, 199. This is a marvelous work written by an intelligent and perceptive man of long experience at sea. The book mainly concerns the slave trade, was addressed to the merchants of London, and apparently was not intended as popular reading.

[51] Ibid., 202–8.

Merchants and cruel commanders of Ships. . . . [N]o one of my People, even those that had entered with them gave me the least ill-character. . . . [I]t was plain they loved me."[52]

Snelgrave's men may not have loved him, but they surely did respect him. Indeed, Snelgrave's character proved so respectable that the pirates proposed to give him a captured ship with full cargo and to sell the goods for him. Then they would capture a Portuguese slaver, sell the slaves, and give the proceeds to Snelgrave so that he could "return with a large sum of Money to London, and bid the Merchants defiance."[53] Pirates hoped to show these merchants that good fortunes befell good captains. The proposal was "unanimously approved" by the pirates, but fearing a charge of complicity, Snelgrave hesitated to accept it. Davis then interceded, saying that he favored "allowing every Body to go to the Devil in their own way" and that he knew that Snelgrave feared for "his Reputation." The refusal was graciously accepted, Snelgrave claiming that "the Tide being turned, they were as kind to me, as they had been at first severe."[54]

Snelgrave related another revealing episode. While he remained in pirate hands, a decrepit schooner belonging to the Royal African Company sailed into the Sierra Leone and was taken by his captors. Simon Jones, a member of Cocklyn's

---

[52] Ibid., 212, 225. Piracy was perceived by many as an activity akin to war. See also Defoe, *History of the Pyrates*, 168, 319. Francis R. Stark, *The Abolition of Privateering and the Declaration of Paris* (New York, 1897), 14, 13, 22, claims that war in the seventeenth and early eighteenth centuries was understood more in terms of "individual enmity" than national struggle. Victors had "absolute right over (1) hostile persons and (2) hostile property." This might partially explain pirates' violence and destructiveness. Rankin, *Golden Age*, 146, correctly observes that "as more pirates were captured and hanged, the greater cruelty was practiced by those who were still alive."

[53] Snelgrave, *Account of the Slave Trade*, 241. For other examples of giving cargo to ship captains and treating them "civilly," see Deposition of Robert Dunn, CO 152/13 (1720), f. 26; Deposition of Richard Symes, CO 152/14 (1721), f. 33; Biddulph, *Pirates of Malabar*, 139; Brock, ed., *Letters of Spotswood*, 339–43; *Boston Gazette*, Aug. 21, 1721; Hill, "Episodes of Piracy," 57; Morris, "Ghost of Kidd," 283; Elizabeth Donnan, ed., *Documents Illustrative of the History of the Slave-Trade to America* (Washington, D.C., 1935), vol. IV, 96; *Tryals of Bonnet*, 13; Boyer, ed., *Political State*, vol. XXVII, 616; Deposition of Henry Bostock, *Cal. St. Papers*, vol. XXX, 150–1; *Boston News-Letter*, Nov. 14–21, 1720; and Spotswood to Craggs: "it is a common practice with those Rovers upon the pillageing of a Ship to make presents of other Commodity's to such Masters as they take a fancy to in Lieu of that they have plundered them of": CO 5/1319 (May 20, 1720).

[54] Snelgrave, *Account of the Slave Trade*, 241, 242, 243.

crew, urged his mates to burn the ship, since he had been poorly treated while in the company's employ. The pirates were about to do so when another of them, James Stubbs, protested that such action would only "serve the Company's interests," since the ship was worth but little. He also pointed out that "the poor People that now belong to her, and have been on so long a voyage, will lose their Wages, which I am sure is Three times the Value of the Vessel." The pirates concurred and returned the ship to its crew, who "came safe home to England in it." Captain Snelgrave also returned to England soon after this incident, but eleven of his seamen remained behind as pirates.[55] Snelgrave's experience revealed how pirates attempted to intervene against – and modify – the standard brutalities that marked the social relations of production in merchant shipping. That they sometimes chose to do so with brutalities of their own shows how they could not escape the system of which they were a part.

Snelgrave seems to have been an exceptionally decent captain. Pirates like Howell Davis claimed that abusive treatment by masters of merchantmen contributed mightily to their willingness to become sea robbers. John Archer, whose career as a pirate dated from 1718 when he sailed with Edward Teach, uttered a final protest before his execution in 1724: "I could wish that Masters of Vessels would not use their Men with so much Severity, as many of them do, which exposes us to great Temptations."[56] William Fly, facing the gallows for murder and piracy in 1726, angrily announced, "I can't charge myself, – I shan't own myself Guilty of any Murder, – Our Captain and his Mate used us Barbarously. We poor Men can't have Justice done us. There is nothing said to our Commanders, let them never so much abuse us, and use us like Dogs."[57] To pirates revenge was justice; punishment was meted out to barbarous captains, as befitted the captains' crimes.

Sea robbers who fell into the hands of the state received the full force of penalties for crimes against property. The official view of piracy as crime was outlined in 1718 by Vice-Admiralty

---

[55] Ibid., 275, 276, 284.
[56] Defoe, *History of the Pyrates*, 351; Jameson, ed., *Privateering and Piracy*, 341.
[57] Mather, *Vial Poured Out*, 21, 48; Boyer, ed., *Political State*, vol. XXXII, 272; Benjamin Colman, *It is a Fearful Thing to Fall into the Hands of the Living God* . . . (Boston, 1726), 39.

Judge Nicholas Trott in his charge to the jury in the trial of Stede Bonnet and thirty-three members of his crew at Charleston, South Carolina. Declaring that "the Sea was given by God for the use of Men, and is subject to Dominion and Property, as well as the Land," Trott observed of the accused that "the Law of Nations never granted to them a Power to change the Right of Property." Pirates on trial were denied benefit of clergy, were "called *Hostis Humani Generis,* with whom neither Faith nor Oath" were to be kept, and were regarded as "*Brutes,* and *Beasts of Prey.*" Turning from the jury to the accused, Trott circumspectly surmised that "no further Good or Benefit can be expected from you but by the Example of your Deaths."[58]

The insistence on obtaining this final benefit locked royal officials and pirates into a system of reciprocal terror. As royal authorities offered bounties for captured pirates, so too did pirates "offer any price" for certain officials.[59] In Virginia in 1720, one of six pirates facing the gallows "called for a Bottle of Wine, and taking a Glass of it, he Drank Damnation to the Governour and Confusion to the Colony, which the rest pledged." Not to be outdone, Governor Spotswood thought it "necessary for the greater Terrour to hang up four of them in Chains."[60] Pirates demonstrated an antinomian disdain for state authority when George I extended general pardons for piracy in 1717 and 1718. Some accepted the grace but refused to reform; others "seem'd to slight it," and the most defiant "used the King's Proclamation with great contempt, and tore it into pieces."[61] One

[58] *Tryals of Bonnet,* 2, 4, 3, 34. See also Hughson, *Carolina Pirates,* 5; Defoe, *History of the Pyrates,* 264, 377–9; Dow and Edmonds, *Pirates of New England,* 297; Brock, ed., *Letters of Spotswood,* 339.

[59] Boyer, ed., *Political State,* vol. XIV, 295; vol. XXI, 662; vol. XXIV, 194; *History of the Pyrates,* 79; *Cal. St. Papers,* vol. XXXII, 168; Hill, "Episodes of Piracy," 39; *American Weekly Mercury,* July 13–20, 1721.

[60] *American Weekly Mercury,* Mar. 17, 1720; Brock, ed., *Letters of Spotswood,* 338. For other cases of hanging in chains, see *Letters of Spotswood,* 342; Jameson, ed., *Privateering and Piracy,* 344; *Tryals of Sixteen Persons,* 19; Defoe, *History of the Pyrates,* 151; *Boston Gazette,* Aug. 27–Sept. 3, 1722; Boyer, ed., *Political State,* vol. XXIV, 201; and Gov. Hart to CTP, *Cal. St. Papers,* vol. XXXIII, 275. For an analysis of this type of terror, see Michel Foucault, *Discipline and Punish: The Birth of the Prison,* trans. Alan Sheridan (New York, 1977), chap. 2.

[61] Deposition of Henry Bostock, CO 152/12 (1717); Snelgrave, *Account of the Slave Trade,* 253; Defoe, *History of the Pyrates,* 217; Spotswood to Board of Trade, CO 5/1318 (May 31, 1717); Jameson, ed., *Privateering and Piracy,* 315.

pirate crew downed its punch, proclaiming, "Curse the King
and all the Higher Powers."[62] The social relations of piracy
were marked by vigorous, often violent, antipathy toward traditional authority. The pervasive antiauthoritarianism of the culture of the common seafarer found many expressions beneath
the Jolly Roger.

At the Charleston trial over which Trott presided, Richard
Allen, attorney general of South Carolina, told the jury that
"pirates prey upon all Mankind, their own Species and Fellow-Creatures without Distinction of Nations or Religions."[63]
Allen was right in claiming that pirates did not respect nationality in their plunders, but he was wrong in claiming that
they did not respect their "Fellow-Creatures." Pirates did not
prey on one another. Rather, they consistently expressed in
numerous and subtle ways a highly developed consciousness
of kind. Here we turn from the external social relations of
piracy to the internal in order to examine this consciousness
of kind – in a sense, a strategy for survival – and the collectivistic ethos it expressed.

Pirates showed a recurrent willingness to join forces at sea
and in port. In April 1719, when Howell Davis and crew sailed
into the Sierra Leone River, the pirates captained by Thomas
Cocklyn were wary until they saw on the approaching ship "her
Black Flag"; then "immediately they were easy in their minds,
and a little time after," the crews "saluted one another with
their Cannon." Other crews exchanged similar greetings and,
like Davis and Cocklyn who combined their powers, frequently
invoked an unwritten code of hospitality to forge spontaneous
alliances.[64]

This communitarian urge was perhaps most evident in the
pirate strongholds of Madagascar and Sierra Leone. Sea robbers occasionally chose more sedentary lifeways on various
thinly populated islands, and they contributed a notorious
number of men to the community of logwood cutters at the
Bay of Campeche in the Gulf of Mexico. In 1718 a royal official complained of a "nest of pirates" in the Bahamas "who

---

[62] Deposition of Edward North, CO 37/10 (1718).
[63] *Tryals of Bonnet*, 8.
[64] Snelgrave, *Account of the Slave Trade*, 199; Defoe, *History of the Pyrates*, 138,
174; Morris, "Ghost of Kidd," 282.

already esteem themselves a community, and to have one common interest."[65]

To perpetuate such community, it was necessary to minimize conflict not only on each ship but also among separate bands of pirates. Indeed, one of the strongest indicators of consciousness of kind is the manifest absence of discord between different pirate crews. To some extent, this was even a transnational matter: French, Dutch, Spanish, and Anglo-American pirates usually cooperated peaceably, only occasionally exchanging cannon fire. Anglo-American crews consistently refused to attack one another.[66]

In no way was the pirate sense of fraternity, which Spotswood and others noted, more forcefully expressed than in the threats and acts of revenge taken by pirates. Theirs was truly a case of hanging together or being hanged separately. In April 1717, the pirate ship *Whidah* was wrecked near Boston. Most of its crew perished; the survivors were jailed. In July, Thomas Fox, a Boston ship captain, was taken by pirates who "Questioned him whether anything was done to the Pyrates in Boston Goall," promising "that if the Prisoners Suffered they would Kill every Body they took belonging to New England."[67] Shortly after this incident, Teach's sea rovers captured a merchant vessel and, "because she belonged to Boston, [Teach] alledging the People of Boston had hanged some of the Pirates, so burnt her." Teach declared that all Boston ships deserved a similar fate.[68] Charles Vane, reputedly a most fearsome pirate, "would give no quarter to the Bermudians" and punished them and "cut away their masts upon account of one Thomas Brown who was (some time) detain'd in these Islands upon suspicion

[65] James Craggs to CTP, *Cal. St. Papers,* vol. XXXI, 10; Board of Trade to J. Methuen, CO 23/12 (Sept. 3, 1716); Defoe, *History of the Pyrates,* 315, 582; Downing, *Indian Wars,* 98, 104–5; *Voyages and Travels of Captain Nathaniel Uring,* 241; Shelvocke, *Voyage,* 242; H. R. McIlwaine, ed., *Executive Journals of the Council of Colonial Virginia* (Richmond, Va., 1928), vol. III, 612; Dow and Edmonds, *Pirates of New England,* 341; Deposition of R. Lazenby in Hill, "Episodes of Piracy," 60; "Voyage to Guinea, Antego, Bay of Campeachy, Cuba, Barbadoes, &c, 1714–1723," BL, Add. Ms. 39946.

[66] *Boston News-Letter,* Aug. 15–22, 1720; *American Weekly Mercury,* Sept. 6–13, 1722.

[67] Trial of Thomas Davis (1717) in Jameson, ed., *Privateering and Piracy,* 308; *Boston News-Letter,* Nov. 4–11, 1717.

[68] *Tryals of Bonnet,* 45.

of piracy." Brown apparently planned to sail as Vane's consort until foiled by his capture.[69]

In September 1720, pirates captained by Bartholomew Roberts "openly and in the daytime burnt and destroyed . . . vessels in the Road of Basseterre [St. Kitts] and had the audaciousness to insult H.M. Fort," avenging the execution of "their comrades at Nevis." Roberts then sent word to the governor that "they would Come and Burn the Town [Sandy Point] about his Ears for hanging the Pyrates there."[70] In 1721 Spotswood relayed information to the Council of Trade and Plantations that Roberts "said he expected to be joined by another ship and would then visit Virginia, and avenge the pirates who have been executed here."[71] The credibility of the threat was confirmed by the unanimous resolution of the Virginia Executive Council that "the Country be put into an immediate posture of Defense." Lookouts and beacons were quickly provided and communications with neighboring colonies effected. "Near 60 Cannon," Spotswood later reported, were "mounted on sundry Substantial Batteries."[72]

In 1723 pirate captain Francis Spriggs vowed to find a Captain Moore "and put him to death for being the cause of the death of [pirate] Lowther," and, shortly after, similarly pledged to go "in quest of Captain Solgard," who had overpowered a pirate ship commanded by Charles Harris.[73] In January 1724, Lieutenant Governor Charles Hope of Bermuda wrote to the Board of Trade that he found it difficult to procure trial evidence against pirates because residents "feared that this very execution wou'd make our vessels fare the worse for it, when they happen'd to fall into pirate hands."[74] The threats of revenge were sometimes effective.

[69] Lt. Gov. Benjamin Bennet to CTP, *Cal. St. Papers*, vol. XXX, 263; *Tryals of Bonnet*, 29, 50; Defoe, *History of the Pyrates*, 195. ·
[70] Gov. Walter Hamilton to CTP, *Cal. St. Papers*, vol. XXXII, 165; *American Weekly Mercury*, Oct. 27, 1720; *Boston Gazette*, Oct. 24–31, 1720.
[71] Spotswood to CTP, *Cal. St. Papers*, vol. XXXII, 328.
[72] Council Meeting of May 3, 1721, in McIlwaine, ed., *Council of Colonial Virginia*, 542; abstract of Spotswood to Board of Trade, CO 5/1370 (June 11, 1722); Spotswood to Board of Trade, CO 5/1319 (May 31, 1721).
[73] Dow and Edmonds, *Pirates of New England*, 281–2; Defoe, *History of the Pyrates*, 355; *American Weekly Mercury*, May 21–8, 1724.
[74] Hope to CTP, CO 37/11 (Jan. 14, 1724), f. 37. See also Treasury Warrant to Capt. Knott, T52/32 (Aug. 10, 1722), P.R.O. Captain Luke Knott, after turning over eight pirates to authorities, prayed relief for "his being obliged

Pirates also affirmed their unity symbolically. Some evidence indicates that sea robbers may have had a sense of belonging to a separate, in some manner exclusive, speech community. Philip Ashton, who spent sixteen months among pirates in 1722–3 noted that "according to the Pirates usual Custom, and *in their proper Dialect,* asked me, If I would sign their Articles."[75] Many sources suggest that cursing, swearing, and blaspheming may have been defining traits of this style of speech, perhaps to an even greater extent than among the larger population of seafaring men. For example, near the Sierra Leone River, a British official named Plunkett pretended to cooperate with, but then attacked, the pirates with Bartholomew Roberts. Plunkett was captured, and Roberts

upon the first sight of Plunkett swore at him like any Devil, for his Irish Impudence in daring to resist him. Old Plunkett, finding he had got into bad Company, fell a swearing and cursing as fast or faster than Roberts; which made the rest of the Pirates laugh heartily, desiring Roberts to sit down and hold his Peace, for he had no Share in the Pallaver with Plunkett at all. So that by meer Dint of Cursing and Damning, Old Plunkett . . . sav'd his life.[76]

We can see only outlines here, but it appears that the symbolic connectedness, the consciousness of kind, extended to the domain of language.

Certainly the best-known symbol of piracy is the flag, the Jolly Roger. Less known and appreciated is the fact that the flag was very widely used. No fewer, and probably a great many more, than 2,500 men sailed under it.[77] So general an

Footnote 74 (*cont.*):
to quit the Merchant Service, the Pirates threatning to Torture him to death if ever he should fall into their hands." Robert Walpole personally awarded Knott £230 for the loss of his career.
75 Barnard, *Ashton's Memorial,* 2, 4; emphasis added. Perhaps this was what M. A. K. Halliday has called an anti-language. This is "the acting out of a distinct social structure [in speech]; and this social structure is, in turn, the bearer of an alternative social reality." An anti-language exists in "the context of *resocialization.*" See Halliday's "Anti-Languages," *American Anthropologist,* 78 (1976), 572, 575.
76 Smith, *New Voyage,* 42–3. See also Morris, "Ghost of Kidd," 286.
77 Anthropologist Raymond Firth argues that flags function as instruments of both power and sentiment, creating solidarity and symbolizing unity. See his *Symbols: Public and Private* (Ithaca, N.Y., 1973), 328, 339; Hill, "Notes on Piracy," 147. For particular pirate crews known to have sailed under the Jolly Roger, see *Boston Gazette,* Nov. 29–Dec. 6, 1725 (Lyne); *Boston News-Letter,*

adoption indicates an advanced state of group identification. The Jolly Roger was described as a "black Ensign, in the Middle of which is a large white Skeleton with a Dart in one hand striking a bleeding Heart, and in the other an Hour Glass."[78] Although there was considerable variation in particulars among these flags, there was also a general uniformity of chosen images. The flag's background was black, adorned with white representational figures. The most common symbol was the human skull, or "death's head," sometimes isolated but more frequently the most prominent feature of an entire skeleton. Other recurring items were a weapon – cutlass, sword, or dart – and an hour glass.[79]

The flag was intended to terrify the pirates' prey, but its triad of interlocking symbols – death, violence, limited time – simultaneously pointed to meaningful parts of the seaman's experience and eloquently bespoke the pirates' own consciousness of themselves as preyed upon in turn. Pirates seized the symbol of mortality from ship captains who used the skull "as a marginal sign in their logs to indicate the record of a death."[80] (See Figure 15.) Seamen who became pirates escaped from one closed system only to find themselves encased in another. But as pirates – and, some believed, only as pirates – these men were able to fight back beneath the somber colors of "King Death"

Sept. 10–17, 1716 (Jennings? Leslie?); ibid., Aug. 12–19, 1717 (Napin, Nichols); ibid., Mar. 2–9, 1719 (Thompson); ibid., May 28–June 4, 1724 (Phillips); ibid., June 5–8, 1721 (Rackam?); Jameson, ed., *Privateering and Piracy*, 317 (Roberts); *Tryals of Sixteen Persons*, 5 (Fly); Snelgrave, *Account of the Slave Trade*, 199 (Cocklyn, LaBouche, Davis); *Trials of Eight Persons*, 24 (Bellamy); Hughson, *Carolina Pirates*, 113 (Moody); *Tryals of Bonnet*, 44–5 (Bonnet, Teach, Richards); Dow and Edmonds, *Pirates of New England*, 208 (Harris), 213 (Low); Boyer, ed., *Political State*, vol. XXVIII, 152 (Spriggs); Biddulph, *Pirates of Malabar*, 135 (Taylor); Donnan, ed., *Documents of the Slave Trade*, 96 (England); and Defoe, *History of the Pyrates*, 240–1 (Skyrm), 67–8 (Martel), 144 (Vane), 371 (captain unknown), 628 (Macarty, Bunce), 299 (Worley). Royal officials affirmed and attempted to reroute the power of this symbolism by raising the Jolly Roger on the gallows when hanging pirates. See Defoe, *History of the Pyrates*, 658; *New-England Courant*, July 22, 1723; and *Boston News-Letter*, May 28–June 4, 1724. The symbols were commonly used in the gravestone art of this period and did not originate with piracy. The argument here is that new meanings, derived from maritime experience, were attached to them.

[78] Boyer, ed., *Political State*, vol. XXVIII, 152. Pirates also occasionally used red or "bloody" flags.

[79] Ibid.   [80] Hill, "Episodes of Piracy," 37.

Figure 15. Captain Jacob Bevan drew these skulls and cross-bones in his ship's log to indicate the death of two of his seamen. On Feb. 22, 1686, Bevan noted that a storm "kild 2 of our men out Right and broke our 3d Mat[e]s arme, our mans thigh and 5 more men brused." The symbol of the death's head was appropriated by pirates and used to emblazon the Jolly Roger, the notorious pirate flag.

against those captains, merchants, and officials who waved banners of authority.[81] Moreover, pirates self-righteously perceived their situation and the excesses of these powerful figures through a collectivistic ethos that had been forged in the struggle for survival.

The self-righteousness of pirates was strongly linked to a world—traditional, mythical, or utopian—"in which men are justly dealt with," as described by Hobsbawm.[82] It found expression in their social rules, their egalitarian social organization, and their notions of revenge and justice. By walking "to the Gallows without a Tear," by calling themselves "Honest Men" and "Gentlemen," and by speaking self-servingly but proudly of their "Conscience" and "Honor," pirates flaunted their certitude.[83] When, in 1720, ruling groups concluded that "nothing but force will subdue them," many pirates responded

---

[81] Ibid.; Snelgrave, *Account of the Slave Trade,* 236.
[82] See footnote 42 of this chapter.
[83] Defoe, *History of the Pyrates,* 28, 43, 244, 159, 285, 628, 656, 660; Hayward, ed., *Remarkable Criminals,* 39; Rankin, *Golden Age,* 155; Mather, *Vial Poured Out,* 47; Jameson, ed., *Privateering and Piracy,* 341; Lt. Gen. Mathew to Gov. Hamilton, *Cal. St. Papers,* vol. XXXII, 167; Bartholomew Roberts, the pirate, to Lt. Gen. Mathew, *ibid.,* 169.

by intensifying their commitment.[84] Edward Low's crew in 1724 swore "with the most direful Imprecations, that if ever they should find themselves overpower'd they would immediately blow their ship up rather than suffer themselves to be hang'd like Dogs." These sea robbers would not "do Jolly Roger the Disgrace to be struck."[85]

The consciousness of kind among pirates manifested itself in an elaborate social code. Through rule, custom, and symbol, the code prescribed specific behavioral standards intended to preserve the social world that pirates had creatively built for themselves. As the examples of revenge reveal, royal officials recognized the threat of the pirates' alternative order. Some authorities feared that pirates might "set up a sort of Commonwealth"[86] – and they were precisely correct in their designation – in uninhabited regions, since "no Power in those Parts of the World could have been able to dispute it with them."[87] But the consciousness of kind never took national shape, and piracy was soon suppressed.

Contemporary observers usually attributed the rise of piracy to the demobilization of the Royal Navy at the end of the War of the Spanish Succession. A group of Virginia merchants, for instance, wrote to the Admiralty in 1713, setting forth "the apprehensions they have of Pyrates molesting their trade in the time of Peace."[88] The navy plunged from 49,860 men at the end of the war to 13,475 just two years later, and only by 1740

[84] Gov. Hamilton to CTP, *Cal. St. Papers*, vol. XXXII, 165.

[85] Boyer, ed., *Political State*, vol. XXVIII, 153. For similar vows and actual attempts, see *Tryals of Bonnet*, 18; Defoe, *History of the Pyrates*, 143, 241, 245, 298, 317; *Cal. St. Papers*, vol. XXXII, 168; Dow and Edmonds, *Pirates of New England*, 239, 292; Watson, *Annals of Philadelphia*, 227; Hayward, ed., *Remarkable Criminals*, 296–7; Atkins, *Voyage*, 12; Jameson, ed., *Privateering and Piracy*, 315; Arthur L. Cooke, "British Newspaper Accounts of Blackbeard's Death," *VMHB* 56 (1953), 305–6; *American Weekly Mercury*, June 16–23, 1720; *Tryals of Thirty-Six*, 9; Spotswood to Board of Trade, CO 5/1318 (Dec. 22, 1718).

[86] Cotton Mather, *Instructions to the Living, From the Condition of the Dead: A Brief Relation of Remarkables in the Shipwreck of above One Hundred Pirates . . .* (Boston, 1717), 4; meeting of Apr. 1, 1717, in H. C. Maxwell Lyte, ed., *Journal of the Commissioners for Trade and Plantations . . .* (London, 1924), vol. III, 359.

[87] Defoe, *History of the Pyrates*, 7.

[88] Virginia Merchants to Admiralty, CO 389/42 (1713).

did it increase to as many as 30,000 again.[89] At the same time, the expiration of privateering licenses – bills of marque – added to the number of seamen loose and looking for work in the port cities of the empire. Such underemployment contributed significantly to the rise of piracy,[90] but it is not a sufficient explanation, since, as already noted, the vast majority of those who became pirates were working in the merchant service at the moment of their joining.

The surplus of labor at the end of the war had extensive, sometimes jarring social and economic effects. It produced an immediate contraction of wages; merchant seamen who made 45–55s. per month in 1707 made only half that amount in 1713. It provoked greater competition for seafaring jobs, which favored the hiring of older, more experienced seamen. And over time, it affected the social conditions and relations of life at sea, cutting back material benefits and hardening discipline.[91] War years, despite their deadly dangers, provided seafarers with tangible benefits. The Anglo-American seamen of 1713 had performed wartime labor for twenty of the previous twenty-five years and for eleven years consecutively.

Conditions did not worsen immediately after the war. As Ralph Davis explained, "the years 1713–1715 saw – as did immediate post-war years throughout the eighteenth century – the shifting of heaped-up surpluses of colonial goods, the movement of great quantities of English goods to colonial and other markets, and a general filling in of stocks of imported goods which had been allowed to run down."[92] This small-scale boom gave employment to some of the seamen who had been dropped from naval rolls. But by late 1715 a slump in trade began, to last into the 1730s. All of these difficulties were exacerbated by the intensification of maritime discipline over the course of the eighteenth century.[93] Many seamen knew that things had once been different and, for many, decisively better.

By 1726, the menace of piracy had been effectively suppressed by governmental action. Circumstantial factors such as

---

[89] Lloyd, *British Seaman*, 287, Table 3.
[90] Jameson, ed., *Privateering and Piracy*, 291; Pringle, *Jolly Roger*, 95; Lydon, *Pirates, Privateers, and Profits*, 17–20; Rankin, *Golden Age*, 23; Nellis M. Crouse, *The French Struggle for the West Indies* (New York, 1943), 310.
[91] Davis, *English Shipping*, 136–7; see Appendix C of the present book.
[92] Davis, *English Shipping*, 27.   [93] Ibid., 154.

the remobilization of the Royal Navy cannot account fully for its demise. The number of men in the navy increased from 6,298 in 1725 to 16,872 in 1726 and again to 20,697 in 1727, which had some bearing on the declining number of sea robbers. Yet some 20,000 sailors had been in the navy in 1719 and 1720, years when pirates were numerous.[94] In addition, seafaring wages only occasionally rose above 30s. per month between 1713 and the mid-1730s.[95] The conditions of life at sea did not change appreciably until war broke out in 1739.

The pardons offered to pirates in 1717 and 1718 failed to rid the sea of robbers. Since the graces specified that only crimes committed at certain times and in particular regions would be forgiven, many pirates saw enormous latitude for official trickery and refused to surrender. Moreover, accepting and abiding by the rules of the pardon would have meant for most men a return to the dismal conditions they had escaped. Their tactic failing, royal officials intensified the naval campaign against piracy – with great and gruesome effect. Corpses dangled in chains in British ports around the world "as a Spectacle for the Warning of others."[96] No fewer than 400, and probably 500–600 Anglo-American pirates were executed between 1716 and 1726. (See Figure 16.) The state also passed harsh legislation that criminalized all contact with pirates. Anyone who "truck[ed], barter[ed], exchange[d]" with pirates, furnished them with stores, or even consulted with them might be punished with death.[97]

---

[94] Lloyd, *British Seaman*, 287, Table 3; Davis, *English Shipping*, 27, 31.

[95] Davis, *English Shipping*, 136–7; Rediker, "Society and Culture," 318–28. See also Appendix C of the present book.

[96] Pringle, *Jolly Roger*, 266–7; Violet Barbour, "Privateers and Pirates of the West Indies," *AHR* 16 (1910–11), 566; Boyer, ed., *Political State*, vol. XXVIII, 152; Hayward, ed., *Remarkable Criminals*, 37; "A Scheme for Stationing Men of War in the West Indies for better Securing the Trade there from Pirates," CO 323/8 (1723); *Boston News-Letter*, July 7–14, 1726. Gary M. Walton, "Sources of Productivity Change in American Colonial Shipping, 1675–1775," *EHR* 20 (1967), 77, notes that the economic uncertainty occasioned by piracy declined after 1725. See Chapter 1 of this book.

[97] See "An Act for the more effectual Suppressing of Piracy" (8 George I, c. 24, 1721), in Sir Thomas Parker, *The Laws of Shipping and Insurance, with a Digest of Adjudged Cases* (London, 1775), republished in *British Maritime Cases* (Abingdon, Oxfordshire, 1978), vol. 24, 94–5. If the population range discussed previously is accurate, about one pirate in thirteen died on the gallows, which would have represented a vastly higher ratio than in any other period of piracy.

Figure 16. The hanging of pirate captain Stede Bonnet in Charleston, South Carolina, in 1719. Seamen looked on from the crow's nests of ships at anchor in Charleston's harbor.

The campaign to cleanse the seas was supported by clergy-men, royal officials, and publicists who sought through ser-mons, proclamations, pamphlets, and the newspaper press to create an image of the pirate that would legitimate his extermi-nation. Piracy had always depended in some measure on the rumors and tales of its successes, especially among seamen and dealers in stolen cargo. In 1722 and 1723, after a spate of hangings and a burst of propaganda, the pirate population began to decline. By 1726, only a handful of the fraternity remained.

Pirates themselves unwittingly took a hand in their own de-struction. From the outset, theirs had been a fragile social world. They produced nothing and had no secure place in the economic order. They had no nation, no home; they were widely dispersed; their community had virtually no geographic boundaries. Try as they might, they were unable to create reli-able mechanisms through which they could either replenish their ranks or mobilize their collective strength. These deficien-cies of social organization made them, in the long run, rela-tively easy prey.

The pirate was, perhaps above all else, an unremarkable man caught in harsh, often deadly circumstances. Wealth he surely desired, but a strong social logic informed both his moti-vation and his behavior. Emerging from working-class back-grounds and maritime employments, and loosed from familial bonds, pirates developed common symbols and standards of conduct. They forged spontaneous alliances, refused to fight each other, swore to avenge injury to their own kind, and even retired to pirate communities. They erected their own ideal of justice, insisted upon an egalitarian, if unstable, form of social organization, and defined themselves against other social groups and types. So, too, did they perceive many of their activi-ties as ethical and justified, not unlike the eighteenth-century crowds described by E. P. Thompson.[98] But pirates, experienced as cooperative seafaring laborers and no longer disciplined by law, were both familiar with the workings of an international

---

[98] E. P. Thompson, "The Moral Economy of the English Crowd in the Eigh-teenth Century," *P&P* 50 (1971), 76–136.

market economy and little affected by the uncertainties of economic change. Their experience as free wage laborers and as members of an uncontrolled, freewheeling subculture gave pirates the perspective and occasion to fight back against brutal and unjust authority and to construct a new social order where King Death would not reign supreme. Theirs was probably a contradictory pursuit. For many, piracy, as a strategy of survival, was ill-fated.

Piracy, in the end, offers us an extraordinary opportunity. Here we can see how a sizable group of Anglo-Americans – poor men in canvas jackets and tarred breeches – constructed a social world where they had "the choice in themselves."[99] The choice did not exist on the merchant ship or the man-of-war. The social order and practices established by pirates recalled several key features of ancient and medieval maritime life. They divided their money and goods into shares; they consulted collectively and democratically on matters of moment; they elected a quartermaster, who, like the medieval "consul," adjudicated the differences between captain and crew.[100]

Pirates constructed a culture of masterless men. They were as far removed from traditional authority as any men could be in the early eighteenth century. Beyond the church, beyond the family, beyond disciplinary labor, and using the sea to distance themselves from the powers of the state, they carried out a strange experiment. The social constellation of piracy, in particular the complex consciousness and egalitarian impulses that developed once the shackles were off, provides valuable clarification of more general social and cultural patterns among seamen in particular and the laboring poor in general. Here we can see aspirations and achievements that under normal circumstances were heavily muted, if not in many cases rendered imperceptible altogether, by the power relationships of everyday life.

The final word on piracy must belong to Barnaby Slush, the man who understood and gave poetic expression to so many aspects of the common seaman's life in the early eighteenth century:

---

[99] Hayward, ed., *Remarkable Criminals*, 37. See also Hill, *The World Turned Upside Down*.
[100] William McFee, *The Law of the Sea* (Philadelphia, 1951), 50, 54, 59, 72.

Pyrates and *Buccaneers,* are Princes to [Seamen], for there, as none are exempt from the General Toil and Danger; so if the Cheif have a Supream Share beyond his Comrades, 'tis because he's always the Leading Man in e'ry daring Enterprize; and yet as bold as he is in all other Attempts, he dares not offer to infringe the common laws of Equity; but every Associate has his due Quota ... thus these *Hostes Humani Generis* as great robbers as they are to all besides, are precisely just among themselves; without which they could no more Subsist than a Structure without a Foundation.[101]

Thus did pirates express the collectivistic ethos of life at sea by the egalitarian and comradely distribution of life chances, the refusal to grant privilege or exemption from danger, and the just allocation of shares. Their notion of justice – among themselves and in their dealings with their class enemies – was indeed the foundation of their enterprise. Equally, piracy itself was a "structure" formed upon a "foundation" of the culture and society of Anglo-American deep-sea sailors in the first half of the eighteenth century.

---

[101] Barnaby Slush, *The Navy Royal: Or a Sea-Cook Turn'd Projector* (London, 1709), viii.

CONCLUSION

The Seaman as Worker of the World

Ned Ward, an early-eighteenth-century Grub Street writer, had an eye for the telling detail that revealed a world of change. He observed that the common seaman considered his hands to be "his Bosom-Friends." The tar "generally carries them stopped within his Breast, or Pockets; not so much to keep his Heart, or his Money close within Board, but out of pure Moral Principle of not exposing his best Friends, they being the only two he has to trust to."[1] Barnaby Slush, a "Sea-Cook," expressed a similar sentiment and described the same social reality for those bereft of land, tools, and property. What, he wondered, was a man to expect when he had "but a pair of good Hands, and a Stout Heart to recommend him?"[2] Such was the condition of the seafaring proletarian. Slush's passionate question represented the working-class response, the necessary counter to the detached, impersonal discourse of Sir William Petty about the "Labour of Seamen" as a "Commodity."[3] Moral economy and political economy came face to face. They spoke in different voices about different and conflicting concerns.

By calling attention to the seaman's hands, the language employed by Ward and Slush reflected one of the dominant changes shaping early modern Britain and America. The term "hand," defined as a "person employed by another in any man-

---

[1] Ned Ward, *The Wooden World Dissected: In the Character of a Ship of War* (1708; reprint London, 1756), 73–4.

[2] Barnaby Slush, *The Navy Royal: Or a Sea-Cook Turn'd Projector* (London, 1709), 16.

[3] *The Economic Writings of Sir William Petty*, ed. Charles Henry Hull (Cambridge, 1899), 260. See also Chapter 1 of this book.

ual work; a workman or workwoman" or, more specifically, as "each of the sailors belonging to a ship's crew," came into use in the late seventeenth century, just as English capitalism was dramatically expanding, both nationally and internationally, and as more and more producers were divorced from the land and hence forced to work for wages to get a living.[4]

"Primitive accumulation," the process by which producers lost their ties to the land, was central to the creation of a maritime working class. Free-market and demographic forces did not produce free wage laborers at a pace fast enough to meet the challenges of an expanding capitalist system as defined by English rulers, who therefore resorted to impressment to stock the maritime labor market with mind and muscle. They then often relied upon economic pressure and a general lack of employment opportunity to move these naval conscripts into the merchant shipping industry. Violence, or the application of extraeconomic force, was thus crucial to the formative stage of capitalist development. When the merchant captain bellowed, "All hands on deck!" he unwittingly summed up both the wrenching process of social change that transformed labor power into a commodity and the new reality – of collective industrial labor – that pointed the way to the future.[5]

Merchant shipping, as we have seen, became a central site for collective industrial labor during the seventeenth and eighteenth centuries. A complex cluster of changes surrounded the

---

[4] See the *Oxford English Dictionary*, s.v., "hand." For general surveys of the changes in the British and Atlantic economies in the early modern period, see Rodney Hilton, ed., *The Transition from Feudalism to Capitalism* (London, 1976); Immanuel Wallerstein, *The Modern World-System: Capitalist Agriculture and the Origins of the European World-Economy in the Sixteenth Century* (New York, 1976); idem, *The Modern World-System II: Mercantilism and the Consolidation of the European World-Economy, 1600–1750* (New York, 1980); Ralph Davis, *The Rise of the Atlantic Economies* (Ithaca, N.Y., 1973); Maurice Dobb, *Studies in the Development of Capitalism* (New York, 1947); D. C. Coleman, *The Economy of England, 1450–1750* (Oxford, 1977); B. A. Holderness, *Pre-Industrial England: Economy and Society, 1500–1750* (London, 1976).

[5] James F. Shepherd and Gary M. Walton, *Shipping, Maritime Trade, and the Economic Development of Colonial North America* (Cambridge, 1972), 60, 81; Ralph Davis, *The Rise of the English Shipping Industry in the Seventeenth and the Eighteenth Centuries* (London, 1962), 72, 376; J. H. Parry, *Trade and Dominion: The European Overseas Empires in the Eighteenth Century* (New York, 1971), 206, 213; C. Ernest Fayle, *A Short History of the World's Shipping Industry* (London, 1933), 198; John Saville, "Primitive Accumulation and Early Industrialization in Britain," *Socialist Register* (1969), 247–71.

broad transition from luxury to bulk trade in transoceanic shipping as North America and the Caribbean evolved into primary
centers of production and consumption. Labor-intensive shipping developed as tobacco, sugar, slaves, and cloth began to
course through the arteries of the global trading system.
Traders increasingly institutionalized their practices. Credit
and bills of exchange multiplied; sailing schedules were regularized; the market chain grew more rational; capital accumulated in ever larger amounts through ever more orderly channels. As vessels fanned out across the Atlantic and beyond, both
capital and labor moved in increasingly international orbits.

Such capital necessarily set massive amounts of free wage labor in motion. In the mid-sixteenth century, between 3,000 and
5,000 Englishmen plied the waves. But by 1750, after two centuries of intensive development, their number had ballooned to
more than 60,000.[6] Merchant shipping mobilized huge masses
of men for shipboard labor. These workers entered new relationships both to capital – as one of the first generations of free
waged laborers – and to each other – as collective laborers. The
assembly and enclosure of wage laborers on the ship, an early
precursor of the factory, initiated a process by which labor was
carefully coordinated and synchronized. The hands, in precise
unison, loaded cargo, set sails, pulled the levers of the pump,
and steered the vessel. These cooperating hands did not own the
tools or materials of production, and consequently they sold
their skill and muscle in an international market for monetary
wages. They were an absolutely indispensable part of the rise
and growth of North Atlantic capitalism.

Once assembled on the ship, seamen turned the wooden
world to their own purposes, using it as the basis for a new type
of mobile community. Bonds among seamen arose from the
very conditions and relations of cooperative work, not least
from sailing a frail and isolated vessel that was surrounded by
the perils of the deep. Other perils originated from within the
ship, usually the captain's cabin. Hazards natural and unnat-

---

[6] C. H. Wilson, *England's Apprenticeship, 1603–1763* (London, 1965), 171. For
a longer discussion of the number of seamen in the various maritime enterprises, see Marcus Rediker, "Society and Culture among Anglo-American
Deep Sea Sailors, 1700–1750," Ph.D. diss., University of Pennsylvania, 1982,
41, 46–52.

ural, whether accidents, disease, or abusive mistreatment, made sailoring a dangerous calling. Caught between the devil and the deep blue sea, seamen used a many-sided process of negotiation and resistance to defend themselves and to protect and expand their privileges and rights. The irreconcilable conflict between the needs and imperatives of, on the one hand, an international market economy organized by merchant capitalists and, on the other, an international moral economy of common tars generated a collectivism of necessity among seamen. A specifically maritime occupational consciousness gradually moved toward class consciousness as seamen began to develop wider patterns of association, sympathy, and identification. The process was visible on land and at sea, in portside riots and in acts of collective resistance. When a band of seamen who had turned pirate captured a ship full of bound servants in 1717, they immediately ripped up the indentures and set the servants free.[7]

The tars' collectivism, as we have seen, took many forms. The hands, dispossessed and limp, that were assembled on board the ship slowly began to curl their fingers into a collective fist. The hand that turned the handspike in the windlass also downed it in a work stoppage. The hand that signed a wage contract drew up a mutinous Round Robin. The hand that mended white canvas sail emblazoned a black flag with the skull and crossbones. Seamen thus signaled in their actions a new dialectic whose power extended far beyond the world of maritime labor. As swelling numbers of men and women were reduced to the labor of their hands, they began to see the potential, even the necessity, of joining those hands in collective action and resistance.

Seafaring hands dealt with the aggregation of maritime labor in yet another way. They disaggregated it through desertion. They ran, individually and collectively, from port to port in search of a few shillings more a month, beer that did not stink, biscuit that did not move by itself, a safer ship, or a less brutal master. Footloose seamen, continually coalescing and dispersing, awarded great significance to an autonomous mobility that

---

[7] Richard B. Morris, *Government and Labor in Early America* (New York, 1946), 312–13. See also the *American Weekly Mercury*, March 17, 1720.

could be used to reduce exploitation and increase their chances of finding better employment. Standing by one another sometimes meant running alongside one another. The hands employed by the merchant captain were frequently last seen waving goodbye.[8]

The first half of the eighteenth century witnessed a cycle of seamen's struggle in which tactics shifted according to larger social and economic patterns and circumstances. During wartime and the ensuing postwar booms, when labor was scarce and wages high, seamen relied on desertion and perhaps "embezzlement" to improve their situation. The diversity of the maritime work force, brought about by the lifting of restrictions on the number of foreign seamen allowed in the merchant service in wartime, encouraged the use of such tactics. During periods of peace, when wages dropped, shipboard conditions grew harsher, and crews became more homogeneous, conflict tended to take different forms. Desertion, though less effective, continued. But mutinies multiplied and piracy, in many ways the most extreme form of resistance, erupted after the Treaty of Ryswick in 1697 and again after the Treaty of Utrecht in 1713. With the suppression of piracy in 1726, social conflict at sea did not abate, but was transformed into more personal acts of violence, sometimes murder, between officers and crew.[9] From the seaman's perspective, England's "era of political stability" was thus marked by the most extreme violence and terror.[10] After the Seven Years' War (1756–63), seamen increasingly resorted to the strike. The hands that set the sail learned to strike it.

The seaman's every innovation and concerted action faced enormous odds. The combined power of the state, the merchant, and the captain – hanging pirates, setting wages, and flogging seamen – was nothing short of extraordinary. Furthermore, the circumstances of early seafaring made it difficult for seamen to transmit from one generation to another the wisdom

---

[8] See Chapter 2 of this book.
[9] See Chapters 2, 5, and 6 of this book.
[10] Speaking of Robert Walpole and the stability of the 1720s and 1730s, E. P. Thompson has observed that "stability, no less than revolution, may have its own kind of terror" [*Whigs and Hunters: The Origin of the Black Act* (New York, 1975), 258].

they acquired in contest with such concentrated authority. High rates of mortality and disability obstructed the flow of experience from old to young.[11] Craft traditions, which often provided continuity in the transmission of experience, were weak among common seamen. Unstable employment, low status, and miserable conditions made seafaring an occupation of last resort – and early exit, if at all possible. Seafaring was, in short, a great gamble, a dance with doom. Jack Cremer went to sea "Neck or Nothing": "if I lived, all would be well, and if I were knocked on the head, thereair would be one short in the Family."[12] As a man told Ned Ward, "merchants are a pack of sharpers, masters of ships a parcel of arrant knaves, a vessel but a doubtful confidant, and the sea a mere lottery."[13] Men who had better options normally sought to avoid a lottery that left many of its losers maimed or dead.

But for all of its problems and risks, the seaman's work experience pointed the way to the future. Maritime workers were concentrated on the ship in much the same way that other laborers were assembled in ever larger numbers in manufactories or on plantations. They toiled under a watchful supervisory regime armed with violent disciplinary power, which was used to ensure their cooperation for the sake of profit. They rambled from port to port, selling their muscle for a monetary wage. Cotton Mather, disturbed by the social breakdown he associated with footloose seafarers, wrote in his diary in 1718, "And now, if I begin with Seafaring, Oh, what an horrible Spectacle have I before me! A wicked, stupid, abominable Generation; every Year growing rather worse."[14] Most seamen, be

---

[11] See John Rule, *The Experience of Labour in Eighteenth-Century English Industry* (New York, 1981), chap. 3, for an excellent discussion of work and health. See also Robert Malcolmson, *Life and Labour in England, 1700–1780* (New York, 1981), 77.

[12] *Ramblin' Jack: The Journal of Captain John Cremer*, ed. R. Reynall Bellamy (London, 1936), 38. Jonathan Press analyzed the petitions of Bristol seamen for hospital relief and found that the merchant seaman "could only rarely prolong his career into middle age, for his way of life made him peculiarly susceptible to rheumatic, arthritic, and consumptive complaints as well as to tropical disease." See *The Merchant Seamen of Bristol, 1747–1789* (Bristol, 1976), 15.

[13] Ned Ward, *The London Spy: The Vanities and Vices of the Town Exposed to View*, ed. Arthur L. Hayward (1698; reprint London, 1927), 270.

[14] Quoted in Carl Bridenbaugh, *Cities in the Wilderness: The First Century of Urban Life in America, 1625–1742* (Oxford, 1938), 226.

it noted, would no doubt have found the priggish, pompous Mather every bit as unbearable as he found them. But Mather was right to suggest that wage labor, with all of its corrosive effects, was increasing over time. More and more wage workers toiled upon the sea, as well as in other areas of the economy. Wage labor was used less in America than in England, but the overarching direction of change on both sides of the Atlantic was toward its ever greater employment. Seamen thus symbolized the advancing structural transformation in relations between capital and labor.

Seamen were also instrumental in the formation and extension of plebeian culture. They influenced both the form and the content of plebeian protest by their militant presence in seaport crowds. They manifested and contributed to the antiauthoritarian and egalitarian traditions within early working-class culture. Perhaps more crucially still, seamen used their mobility, specifically desertion, both to better their own lot within a context of labor scarcity and to create links with other working people. Their "labor movement" helped to define and extend the community and culture of working people in England and America. As Christopher Hill has demonstrated in another context, a mobile worker, whether itinerant craftsman, soldier, seaman, or escaped apprentice, was both a carrier of information and ideas between different groups of laboring people and someone who, by way of new experiences, was sometimes able to generate new ideas and practices.[15] The culture of free labor was, in fact, the only cross-regional culture of working people in the transatlantic English-speaking world. Mobile workers, whose strategic position in the social division of labor brought them into contact with many other working people, served as a medium for the exchange of experience and information within a more broadly defined culture of the laboring poor. As the most numerous of such mobile workers in early modern England and America, seamen were crucial to the cultural dimensions of class formation.[16]

[15] Christopher Hill, *The World Turned Upside Down: Radical Ideas in the English Revolution* (New York, 1972), chaps. 3–4.
[16] See Marcus Rediker, "Good Hands, Stout Heart, and Fast Feet: The History and Culture of Working People in Early America," *Labour/Le Travailleur* 10 (1982), 139–42.

The position of the seaman was not identical in England and America. Indeed, differences in the rate and character of capitalist development on each side of the Atlantic structured the lives of the seamen in different ways. Capitalism developed first and more quickly in England, and by 1750 nearly half of the English population worked for wages. Seamen were not only more numerous in England than in America, their role was more central to the economy, especially given its imperial and international organization.[17] As prospects for independent subsistence declined and dependence upon wage labor advanced among English working people, seamanship became more of a lifetime calling. Although many seamen did temporary stints of casual labor on land, usually along the waterfront, most found it difficult to take permanent leave of the seas.[18] By the mid-eighteenth century, seamen born in the United Kingdom tended to be older than those born in America, which suggests longer terms of employment in Britain.[19] Further, upward mobility in the British merchant service seems to have declined as the industry's growth slowed in the first half of the eighteenth century and as merchant captains increasingly secured their positions by kinship and other connections to merchants, rather than by promotion through the ranks.[20]

In America, greater opportunities for the acquisition of land, and hence for an independent life, retarded the development of both free wage and maritime labor. Between 80 and 90 percent of the American population worked in agriculture throughout the eighteenth century.[21] Some seamen retained

---

[17] Rule, *Experience of Labour*, 95; Malcolmson, *Life and Labour*, 144–6; E. P. Thompson, "Patrician Society, Plebeian Culture," *Journal of Social History* 7 (1974), 382.

[18] Christopher Lloyd, *The British Seaman, 1200–1860: A Social Survey* (Rutherford, N.J., 1970), 56; Davis, *English Shipping Industry*, 116.

[19] Jesse Lemisch reports that the average age of "foreign-born" seamen (mostly English, Scottish, and Irish) in New York between 1755 and 1764 was 27.8 years. For American-born seamen, the average was 24.3 years. See Lemisch, "Jack Tar vs. John Bull: The Role of New York's Seamen in Precipitating the Revolution," Ph.D. diss., Yale University, 1962, 2.

[20] This matter of upward mobility needs further study, but see Davis, *English Shipping Industry*, 118, 121–2, 126, 128. Mobility also slowed in the Royal Navy of the eighteenth century; see Lloyd, *British Seaman*, 76.

[21] Richard B. Sheridan, "The Domestic Economy," *Colonial British America: Essays in the New History of the Early Modern Era*, ed. Jack P. Greene and J. R. Pole (Baltimore, 1984), 43; John J. McCusker and Russell R. Menard, *The Economy of British America, 1607–1789* (Chapel Hill, N.C., 1985), 248.

the option of retiring from the wage labor market until the 1740s and 1750s, when land became more difficult to acquire.[22] Further, the general scarcity of labor in the colonies resulted in higher wages and enhanced the seaman's ability to change jobs, while the growth of the American merchant service offered opportunities for advancement.[23] American seamen, therefore, seem to have been less permanent members of the brotherhood of the deep. Ira Dye has shown that in the late eighteenth century the average American merchant seaman served between 6.6 and 7.5 years. Some seamen moved on to become farmers, whereas others continued to work for wages, but in less dangerous occupations. Many seamen, despite their short terms of service, never left the sea; they were instead buried in it.[24]

But free wage labor and laissez-faire tendencies were clearly growing in eighteenth-century America, especially after 1750. A downturn in the colonial labor market in the 1740s and an increasing scarcity of land pushed many into more difficult circumstances. As many as one in five worked for wages by 1775.[25] Moreover, American seamen began to develop a collective identity of their own. The social distance between American seamen and their merchant captains was growing, as evidenced by the masters' establishment of marine societies and fellowship clubs beginning in the 1740s and 1750s.[26]

---

[22] Jesse Lemisch, "Jack Tar in the Streets: Merchant Seamen in the Politics of Revolutionary America," *WMQ* 25 (1968), 376; Daniel F. Vickers, "Maritime Labor in Colonial Massachusetts: A Case Study of the Essex County Cod Fishery and the Whaling Industry of Nantucket," Ph.D. diss., Princeton University, 1981, 322; McCusker and Menard, *Economy of British America,* 239, 245.

[23] Morris, *Government and Labor,* 268; Lemisch, "Jack Tar vs. John Bull," 3.

[24] Ira Dye, "Early American Merchant Seafarers," *Proceedings of the American Philosophical Society* 20 (1976), 338–9. The problem of opportunity and occupational persistence needs additional study. Daniel Vickers, who has begun to address this important issue, has shown that New England fishermen retired early from the sea even when they had difficulty finding a second career. See "Maritime Labor," 221–6.

[25] Rediker, "Good Hands, Stout Heart, and Fast Feet," 137–8; Morris, *Government and Labor,* 152, 523–4; James T. Lemon, "Spatial Order: Households in Local Communities and Regions," *Colonial British America,* 102; Richard S. Dunn, "Servants and Slaves: The Recruitment and Employment of Labor," *Colonial British America,* 182; McCusker and Menard, *Economy of British America,* 246; Gary B. Nash, "Up from the Bottom in Franklin's Philadelphia," *Past and Present* 77 (1979), 70.

[26] Morris, *Government and Labor,* 199. On the development of the American seaman's collective identity during the Revolution, see Jesse Lemisch, "List-

The differences in the position of the seaman in England and America in the eighteenth century were important, but it would be wrong to overemphasize them. The seamen who roamed the empire's port towns, especially in America, were English *and* American, as well as West Indian, African, and even Indian. The social and cultural practices of these men, as almost everyone who saw them agreed, were quite similar. They possessed a common fund of experience. Both English and American seamen were witnessing the same basic social and economic processes, even if changes were taking place at different rates. The polarization of capital and labor, the ascent of the money wage, and the decline of paternalistic authority characterized the development of merchant shipping on both sides of the Atlantic. Seamen from both the Old World and the New were part of a developing class.

The class character of seafaring left little room for belief in the "dignity of labor." As Christopher Hill has observed of early English attitudes toward wage labor, "[t]he antithesis of freedom was the stultifying drudgery of those who had become cogs in someone else's machine."[27] The seaman found himself in precisely this position. The "stultifying drudgery" was the difficult, closely supervised labor at sea, the "someone else" was the merchant-ship owner, and the "machine" was the ship. Freedom had to be fought for and won. Jack Tar was often, though not always, equal to the task.

Samuel Eliot Morison maintained that "[t]he sea is no wet-nurse to democracy. Authority and privilege are her twin foster-children. Instant and unquestioning obedience to the master is the rule of the sea; and the typical sea-captain would make it the rule of the land if he could."[28] Morison's is, of course, only one point of view. It is the extremely one-sided perspective of capital, the latter-day version of the merchant's and the captain's tale. It contains an element of truth. Yet at

ening to the 'Inarticulate': William Widger's Dream and the Loyalties of American Revolutionary Seamen in British Prisons," *Journal of Social History* 3 (1969–70), 1–29.

[27] Christopher Hill, "Pottage for Freeborn Englishmen: Attitudes to Wage Labour," *Change and Continuity in Seventeenth-Century England* (Cambridge, Mass., 1975), 237.

[28] Samuel Eliot Morison, *The Maritime History of Massachusetts, 1783–1860* (Boston, 1921), 24.

the same time, the sea *was* a "wet-nurse to democracy" because maritime commerce mobilized thousands of men who spent much of their lives – and in many cases, all of their lives – battling "authority and privilege." Obedience was indeed a rule of the sea, but it was continually contested, as were the limits of authority. Jesse Lemisch has shown how the seaman's struggle against authority paralleled and contributed to a broader political struggle against absolutism and kingly authority in the American Revolution.[29] But matters did not end there. When the sea captain, in the later guise of the factory master, sought to make "authority and obedience" the "rule of the land," he confronted Jack Tar's heirs, the weavers, the Wobblies, the industrial workers, who continued the fight for democracy and freedom.

[29] Lemisch, "Jack Tar vs. John Bull"; idem, "Jack Tar in the Streets," 371–407; idem, "Listening to the 'Inarticulate,'" 1–29.

APPENDIX A

Age Distribution among Deep-Sea Sailors, 1700–1750

Tables A.1–A.3 are based on the ages of seafarers as given in depositions in the records of the High Court of Admiralty, HCA 1/15, 1/16, 1/17, 1/18, 1/19, 1/29, 1/30, 1/31, 1/53, 1/54, 1/55, 1/56, 1/99, 1/100, 15/43, and 15/45, and in the vice-admiralty records of Massachusetts, New York, North Carolina, Pennsylvania, and South Carolina.

Table A.1. *Age Distribution among Common Seamen (Foremastmen)*

Age Group	N	Percentage	Cumulative Percentage
15–19	21	10.6	10.6
20–29	118	59.6	70.2
30–39	37	18.7	88.9
40–49	18	9.1	98.0
50–59	4	2.0	100.0
	198	100.0	

Mean: 27.6   Median: 25   Range: 17–56

Table A.2. *Age Distribution among Officers and Skilled Workers*

Age Group	N	Percentage	Cumulative Percentage
15–19	0	00.0	00.0
20–29	39	43.3	43.3
30–39	36	40.0	83.3
40–49	11	12.2	95.5
50–59	3	3.3	98.8
60–69	1	1.1	99.9
	90	99.9	

Mean: 32.4

Table A.3. *Age Distribution among Unskilled Workers (including those of unknown occupation)*

Age Group	N	Percentage	Cumulative Percentage
10–19	35	10.9	10.9
20–29	164	51.3	62.2
30–39	79	24.7	86.9
40–49	35	10.9	97.8
50–59	7	2.2	100.0
	320	100.0	

Mean: 28.5

APPENDIX B

English Trade, 1650–1750

Although commercial statistics for the early modern period are notoriously fragmentary and difficult to interpret, the overall patterns in the growth of English trade are fairly clear. Most historians agree that the century between 1650 and 1750 saw "trade transformed."[1] A system of trade that combined local and regional commerce with long-distance trade in luxuries gave way to an expansive, regularized, increasingly global pattern of shipping that depended primarily on the movement of bulk goods.

English trade experienced an initial surge in the 1630s, propelled by successes in the fisheries and the Mediterranean. But the greatest expansion occurred in the second half of the seventeenth century under the influence of the Navigation Acts.[2] Ralph Davis, the finest historian of English shipping, showed that the tonnage carried by English vessels between 1660 and 1689 expanded at the extraordinary rate of 2 to 3 percent per year. The growth depended upon the colonies' large-scale production of new commodities such as sugar and tobacco and upon the expansion of the slave trade.[3] The proportion of English tonnage involved in foreign trade increased from 26.1 percent in 1660 to 45.9 percent in 1702, and further to 52.3

---

[1] D. C. Coleman, *The Economy of England, 1450–1750* (Oxford, 1977), 137.
[2] Ralph Davis, *The Rise of the English Shipping Industry in the Seventeenth and Eighteenth Centuries* (London, 1962), 10; B. A. Holderness, *Pre-Industrial England: Economy and Society, 1500–1750* (London, 1976), 117; Coleman, *Economy of England*, 134.
[3] Davis, *English Shipping*, 20, 23; Coleman, *Economy of England*, 135.

Table B.1. *English Tonnage, 1629–1773 (000 tons)*

Year	Davis	Lloyd	Harper	Usher
1629	115	–	–	–
1660	–	–	162	–
1686	340	–	–	–
1700	–	273	–	(331)
1701	–	–	–	261
1702	323	–	267	–
1711	–	–	–	(324)
1715	–	–	–	(426)
1723	–	–	–	(420)
1728	–	–	–	(456)
1736–8 (average)	–	–	–	(502)
1739–41 (average)	–	–	–	(471)
1749–51 (average)	–	–	–	(661)
1750	–	609	–	–
1751	421	–	–	–
1752	449	–	–	–
1753	468	–	–	–
1754	458	–	–	–
1755	473	–	–	473
1773	581	–	581	–

percent in 1773.[4] Thus, by the beginning of the eighteenth century, England's markets and sources of supply had suddenly shifted from the nearby ports of Europe to distant parts – Africa, North America, and the Caribbean.[5] In 1669, only 14.4 percent of English imports had originated in the colonies. But a century later, in 1773, the figure had jumped two and a half times to 36.5 percent.[6] The period 1650 to 1700 was crucial to the consolidation of England's maritime power.

The years 1700–50 constituted a period of moderate expansion in commerce. Trade leveled off to a "high, undulating plateau"[7] as the overall growth rate slowed to about 0.33 percent per year. Table B.1 gives the best available estimates of the trends.[8] These data indicate that English trade expanded dramatically in the late seventeenth century and at a more moderate pace, although with many oscillations, thereafter. The drop in shipping tonnage in 1739–41 was undoubtedly the effect of the War of the Austrian Succession. The increase between 1749 and 1751 represented the trade boom that commonly followed a lengthy international war.

[4] Adapted from Lawrence Harper, *The English Navigation Laws: A Seventeenth-Century Experiment in Social Engineering* (New York, 1939), 337.

[5] Murdo J. McLeod, *Spanish Central America: A Socioeconomic History* (Berkeley, 1973), 368.

[6] Harper, *Navigation Laws*, 271; Davis, *English Shipping*, 23; Charles Henry Wilson, *England's Apprenticeship, 1603–1763* (London, 1965), 162, 376.

[7] Holderness, *Pre-Industrial England*, 117; Davis, *English Shipping*, 31.

[8] The figures in Table B.1 are taken from Davis, *English Shipping*, 15, 20, 26, 27; Christopher Lloyd, *The British Seaman, 1200–1860: A Social Survey* (Rutherford, N.J., 1970), 285; Harper, *Navigation Laws*, 329; Abbott Payson Usher, "The Growth of English Shipping, 1572–1922," *Quarterly Journal of Economics* 42 (1928), 467, 469. Usher's figures, based on customs records, are given as foreign tonnage, whereas in fact they appear to be more plausible as estimates of total tonnage. Hence their inclusion here.

APPENDIX C

Wages in the Merchant Shipping Industry,
1700–1750

Table C.1. *Common Seamen's Wages, 1700–50 (£ Sterling)*

Year	N	Low	High	Median	Mean
1700	34	0.60	2.50	1.23	1.32
1701	16	1.15	2.50	1.95	1.87
1702	19	1.00	3.00	2.25	2.15
1703	26	1.25	3.13	2.75	2.60
1704	22	1.25	3.00	2.50	2.44
1705	34	1.50	4.00	2.75	2.67
1706	7	1.50	2.50	2.50	2.29
1707	23	1.50	2.75	2.50	2.35
1708	18	1.35	2.75	2.50	2.21
1709	18	1.50	2.50	1.88	1.91
1710	34	1.50	4.00	2.25	2.06
1711	17	1.50	2.50	2.00	1.98
1712	15	1.15	2.25	1.20	1.50
1713	21	1.05	2.25	1.20	1.24
1714	34	0.90	1.25	1.15	1.14
1715	134	1.00	3.00	1.30	1.39
1716	79	1.00	2.50	1.30	1.31
1717	70	0.90	2.25	1.30	1.35
1718	65	0.90	2.10	1.40	1.47
1719	74	1.15	4.00	1.75	1.68
1720	98	1.00	2.25	1.50	1.47
1721	50	0.90	3.50	1.28	1.49
1722	42	1.10	1.75	1.25	1.42
1723	39	1.15	3.25	1.28	1.53
1724	39	1.05	4.00	1.25	1.61
1725	46	1.20	1.75	1.30	1.37
1726	45	1.10	4.25	1.50	1.60
1727	20	1.15	2.10	1.60	1.51
1728	41	1.15	2.25	1.40	1.47

Table C.1. *(cont.)*

Year	N	Low	High	Median	Mean
1729	86	1.10	1.50	1.25	1.32
1730	37	1.00	2.00	1.30	1.39
1731	46	1.20	2.00	1.30	1.39
1732	38	0.90	2.25	1.25	1.27
1733	30	0.88	2.50	1.40	1.43
1734	34	1.10	2.63	1.75	1.74
1735	86	0.90	2.75	2.00	1.88
1736	31	1.00	2.40	1.28	1.47
1737	43	1.25	1.75	1.25	1.31
1738	37	1.25	1.75	1.50	1.43
1739	26	1.30	2.50	1.50	1.72
1740	51	1.25	2.75	2.25	2.08
1741	32	1.75	3.00	2.50	2.31
1742	30	1.00	2.75	2.00	2.01
1743	28	1.50	3.50	2.50	2.45
1744	33	1.50	3.00	2.50	2.39
1745	28	1.50	3.00	2.50	2.33
1746	33	1.50	3.50	2.75	2.56
1747	24	1.50	4.00	2.50	2.61
1748	21	1.25	3.00	2.25	1.99
1749	13	1.25	1.25	1.25	1.25
1750	33	1.00	2.00	1.25	1.33
	2000				1.66

War: $N = 554$; Mean = 2.20.   Peace: $N = 1446$; Mean = 1.46.

Source: HCA 24/127–24/139 and HCA 15/40–15/44.

Table C.2. *Wages of Officers and Men in War and Peace, 1700–50 (£ Sterling)*

	War			Peace			Total		
	N	Total Wages	Mean	N	Total Wages	Mean	N	Total Wages	Mean
Officers									
Captain	33	214	6.48	72	423	5.88	105	637	6.07
Mate	102	447	4.38	210	686	3.27	312	1133	3.63
Second Mate	63	218	3.46	74	189	2.55	137	407	2.97
Carpenter	87	356	4.09	157	483	3.08	244	839	3.44
Boatswain	89	285	3.20	135	278	2.06	224	563	2.51
Gunner	56	179	3.20	50	105	2.10	106	284	2.68
Surgeon	25	102	4.08	34	104	3.06	59	206	3.49
Total	455	1801	3.96	732	2268	3.10	1187	4069	3.43

Change (peace to war) = 27.74%

	War			Peace			Total		
Men									
Cook	50	120	2.40	91	147	1.62	141	267	1.89
Quartermaster	24	62	2.58	30	49	1.63	54	111	2.06
Seaman	554	1221	2.20	1446	2108	1.46	2000	3329	1.66
Total	628	1403	2.23	1567	2304	1.47	2195	3707	1.69

Change (peace to war) = 51.70%

Source: HCA 24/127–24/139 and HCA 15/40–15/44.

APPENDIX D

Literacy in the Merchant Shipping Industry, 1700–1750

Table D.1 is based on signed and marked depositions in the High Court of Admiralty Papers, HCA 1/15, 1/16, 1/17, 1/18, 1/19, 1/29, 1/30, 1/31, 1/53, 1/54, 1/55, 1/56, 1/99, 1/100, 15/43, and 15/45, and in the vice-admiralty records of Massachusetts, New York, North Carolina, Pennsylvania, and South Carolina. It has been assumed that the ability to sign one's name indicates a minimal and functional degree of literacy.

Table D.1. *Occupational Literacy among Seafaring Men, 1700–50*

Rank or Occupation	*N*	Number Literate	Percentage Literate
Captain	30	30	100.0
Chief mate	19	19	100.0
Second and third mates	11	11	100.0
Surgeon	10	10	100.0
Boatswain, gunner	6	5	83.3
Carpenter, cooper	15	12	80.0
Total (officers and skilled workers)	91	87	95.6
Cook	6	6	100.0
Quartermaster	5	5	100.0
Officers' mate	5	4	80.0
Apprentice	8	5	62.5
Common seaman (foremastman)	185	125	67.6
Occupation Unknown[a]	94	65	69.1
Total (unskilled workers)	303	210	69.3
Total (merchant shipping industry)	394	297	75.4

[a] Most men in this category were probably common seamen.

APPENDIX E

Mutiny at Sea, 1700–1750

Table E.1 has been constructed from a variety of sources to indicate the incidence of mutiny during the first half of the eighteenth century. The cases listed below represent an unknown (perhaps only a minor) portion of the mutinies that actually took place.

Table E.1. *Selected Information on Mutinies aboard Anglo-American Vessels, 1700–50*

No.	Year	Ship's Name	Ship Type[a]	Route	Piracy?
1.	1700	*Happy Return*	mv	Mediterranean	No
2.	1702	*Carlisle*	mv	East Indies	Yes
3.	1703	*Charles*	pv	–	Yes
4.	1704	*Susanna*	mv	East Indies	No
5.	1712	*Hamilton*	mv	Mediterranean	No
6.	1713	*Eagle*	mv	East Indies	No
7.	1715	?	mv	?	No
8.	1715	*Anglesea*	mv	?	Yes
9.	1716	?	mv	West Indies	No
10.	1716	*Wakefield*	mv	South Carolina	No
11.	1716	*St. Quentin*(?)	mv	Chesapeake	No
12.	1718	*Cumberland*	mv	?	No
13.	1718	*Horkenhull*	mv	?	No
14.	1718	?	pv	–	Yes
15.	1718	?	mv	West Indies	Yes
16.	1718	?	mv	Philadelphia	Yes
17.	1718	*Amen*	mv	?	No
18.	1719	*Buck*	mv	West Indies	Yes
19.	1719	*Hanover Succession*	mv	South Carolina	No
20.	1719	*Abington*	mv	Africa-W.I.	No
21.	1720	?	mv	?	No

Table E.1. *(cont.)*

No.	Year	Ship's Name	Ship Type[a]	Route	Piracy?
22.	1720	*Speedwell*	pv	–	No
23.	1720	*Duke of York*	mv	West Indies	No
24.	1720	*Stromboleen*	mv	Mediterranean	No
25.	1721	?	mv	Africa-W.I.	Yes
26.	1721	*Gambia Castle*	mv	Africa-W.I.	Yes
27.	1721	*Mary*	mv	Mediterranean	Yes
28.	1721	*Zant*	mv	West Indies	No
29.	1722	?	mv	West Indies	Yes
30.	1723	?	mv	Newfoundland	Yes
31.	1723	*Baylor*	mv	Africa	Yes
32.	1723	*Duke of York*	mv	East Indies	No
33.	1725	*Fame*	mv	Massachusetts	No
34.	1725	*Mary-Woodley*	mv	Rhode Island	Yes
35.	1725	*George*	mv	Mediterranean	Yes
36.	1726	*Elizabeth*	mv	Africa	Yes
37.	1726	*Trial*	mv	Boston	Yes
38.	1726	*Joseph and Ann*	mv	West Indies	No
39.	1727	*Young Lawrence*	mv	West Indies	Yes
40.	1729	*Loyal George*	mv	South Carolina	No
41.	1729	*John and Elizabeth*	mv	Chesapeake	No
42.	1730	*Mahon*	mv	?	No
43.	1731	*Georgia*	mv	Massachusetts	No
44.	1731	?	mv	?	No
45.	1731	*Hunter*	mv	?	No
46.	1731	*Duke*	mv	?	No
47.	1731	*Port*	mv	Mediterranean	No
48.	1732	*Duke of Cumberland*	mv	Mediterranean	No
49.	1734	*Levant*	mv	Africa	No
50.	1734	*Brixton*	mv	West Indies	Yes
51.	1735	*Haswell*	mv	Chesapeake	No
52.	1735	*St. John*	mv	?	No
53.	1736	*Pearl*	mv	Africa	No
54.	1736	*Dove*	mv	Mediterranean	No
55.	1737	*Tewkesbury*	mv	Africa	No
56.	1743	*Thomas and Diana*	mv	Mediterranean	No
57.	1743	*Prince of Denmark*	mv	West Indies	No
58.	1747	*Dreadnought*	pv	–	No
59.	1748	*Antelope*	mv	Africa	No
60.	1750	*Duke of Argyle*	mv	Africa	No

[a] mv = merchant vessel; pv = privateering vessel.

Sources (the numbers correspond to numbers in left column):
 1. Morgan v. Man, HCA 24/127 (1700).
 2. Information of Joseph Jennings, HCA 1/53 (1703), f. 134.
 3. "At a Court of Admiralty in Boston," HCA 49/106 (1704).
 4. Wright v. Ingledew, HCA 24/128 (1706).
 5. *The Voyages and Travels of Captain Nathaniel Uring,* ed. Alfred Dewar (1726; reprint London, 1928), 176–8.
 6. Wise v. Beekman, HCA 24/131 (1716).
 7. Depositions of William Pricklove, Jesse Standard, and Argentine Besleigh, HCA 1/19 (1715), f. 21.
 8. Information of James Turner, HCA 1/54 (1716), f. 36–7; Examinations of John Clark, Robert Tipping, Andrew Frazier, Thomas Peacock, HCA 1/30, (1716), f. 37.
 9. Information of Hockenhull Short, HCA 1/54 (1718), f. 71–2.
 10. Beck v. Seamen, Minutes of the Vice-Admiralty Court of South Carolina (1716), f. 32–47.
 11. Pim v. Goodloe, HCA 24/131 (1717).
 12. Cumberland v. Seamen, Records of the Court of Admiralty of the Province of Massachusetts Bay (1719), f. 9.
 13. Stanhope to HCA, HCA 1/17 (1719).
 14. "Memoriall of the Merchants of London Trading to Africa," ADM 1/3810 (1720).
 15. Examination of Richard Capper, HCA 1/55 (1718), f. 88–90.
 16. Daniel Defoe [as Captain Charles Johnson], *A General History of the Pyrates,* ed. Manuel Schonhorn (1724, 1728; reprint Columbia, S.C., 1972), 296.
 17. Astell v. Seamen, Massachusetts Admiralty (1718), f. 2.
 18. Examination of Walter Cannady, HCA 1/54 (1721), f. 121–2.
 19. Clipperton v. Seamen, South Carolina Admiralty (1719), f. 10.
 20. *The Tryals of Captain John Rackam and Other Pirates* (Jamaica, 1721), in CO 137/14, 29.
 21. *American Weekly Mercury,* November 1720.
 22. George Shelvocke, *A Voyage Round the World by Way of the Great South Sea* (London, 1726).
 23. Fleming v. Sanders, HCA 24/133 (1720).
 24. Lester v. King, HCA 24/134 (1723).
 25. Defoe, *History of the Pyrates,* 371.
 26. Information of Alexander Thompson, HCA 1/55 (1723), f. 23–4.
 27. Defoe, *History of the Pyrates,* 373.
 28. Gouldin v. Sanders, HCA 24/133 (1721).
 29. Defoe, *History of the Pyrates,* 319.
 30. Defoe, *History of the Pyrates,* 341–2.
 31. Elizabeth Donnan, ed., *Documents Illustrative of the History of the Slave Trade to America* (Washington, D.C., 1930), vol. 4, 185.
 32. Murray v. Hyde, HCA 24/135 (1726).
 33. Booker v. Grey, Massachusetts Admiralty (1725), f. 199.
 34. *Boston News-Leader,* Apr. 29–May 6, 1725.
 35. Examinations of James Williams, James Belbin, Peter Rollison, John Peterson, and Robert Read, HCA 1/55 (1725), f. 103–4, 107, 108, 116, 132.

36. *The Tryals of Sixteen Persons for Piracy &c* (Boston, 1726), 61.
37. *The Tryals of Five Persons for Piracy, Felony, and Robbery* (Boston, 1726), 59.
38. Doyle v. Holland, HCA 24/135 (1728) and HCA 24/136 (1729).
39. Examination of John Ashley, HCA 1/56 (1727), f. 14–9.
40. Seamen v. Alloyn, South Carolina Admiralty (1730), f. 784, 788.
41. "Proceedings of a Court of Admiralty" (Virginia), HCA 1/99 (1729), f. 1–4.
42. Information of William Yerbury, HCA 1/56 (1732), f. 50–1.
43. Pitcher v. Seamen, Massachusetts Admiralty (1731), f. 224.
44. Information of Christopher Bell, HCA 1/56 (1731), f. 42–3.
45. Information of James Tindall, HCA 1/56 (1732), f. 63.
46. Information of John Wilson, HCA 1/56 (1732), f. 58–60.
47. "Proceedings of the Court of Admiralty" (Philadelphia), HCA 1/99 (1731), f. 7–9.
48. Tatum v. Wilson, HCA 24/137 (1732).
49. "Proceedings of the Court of Admiralty" (Africa), HCA 1/99 (1734), f. 2.
50. Information of James Robinson, HCA 1/56 (1734), f. 87–9.
51. Governor Gooch to Secretary of State, CO 5/1337 (1735), f. 176–7.
52. Examination of Richard Coyle, HCA 1/56 (1736), f. 99–101.
53. Powell v. Hardwicke, HCA 24/139 (1738).
54. Information of Richard Walker and William O'Mara, HCA 1/57 (1737), f. 1, 8.
55. "Proceedings of a Court of Admiralty" (Africa), HCA 1/99 (1737), f. 2.
56. Case of Andrew Fletcher, HCA 24/176 (1743).
57. Information of John Allen, HCA 1/57 (1743), f. 82–3.
58. Information of William Gillings, HCA 1/57 (1748), f. 106–7.
59. Information of Thomas Sanderson, HCA 1/58 (1749), f. 2–4.
60. John Newton, "Journal kept on board the Duke of Argyle," Manuscript Department, National Maritime Museum, f. 36.

APPENDIX F

The Courts of Admiralty and Their Records

Admiralty jurisdiction in seventeenth-century England was intimately bound up with the raging conflicts between king and Parliament and between civil law and common law. Civil law courts, including the High Court of Admiralty, were closely identified with the king's prerogative. In the aftermath of the English Revolution and the Revolution of 1688, the powers of civil law courts were firmly curtailed and the High Court of Admiralty was stripped of much of its authority.[1]

Yet the High Court presided over a commercial domain characterized by surging growth and increasing complexity. After the revolutionary settlement of the late seventeenth century, king and Parliament decided to decentralize admiralty jurisdiction by establishing vice-admiralty courts around the rim of the English North Atlantic. The courts were empowered to confront four problems central to the empire and its economic development: the adjudication of prizes taken by American and English privateers; the trial of pirates (so that the crown got its share of the booty); the prosecution of violations of the Acts of Trade; and the organization of the maritime labor market, which entailed the effort to resolve disputes between capital and labor.[2] The establishment of the vice-admiralty courts

---

[1] Carl Ubbelohde, *The Vice-Admiralty Courts and the American Revolution* (Chapel Hill, N.C., 1960), 18; Charles M. Andrews, *The Colonial Period in American History* (New Haven, Conn., 1938), vol. IV, 225; idem, "Vice-Admiralty Courts in the Colonies," *Records of the Vice-Admiralty Court of Rhode Island*, ed. Dorothy Towle (Washington, D.C., 1936), 2, 3; Joseph Doty, *The British Admiralty Board as a Factor in Colonial Administration* (Philadelphia, 1930), 14.

[2] Ubbelohde, *Vice-Admiralty Courts*, 12; Andrews, *Colonial Period*, vol. IV, 230; idem, "Vice-Admiralty Courts," 24–78; Helen J. Crump, *Colonial Admiralty*

was crucial to the consolidation and extension of imperial power.

Although some admiralty matters had been tried in colonial courts in the early seventeenth century, London remained the locus of maritime authority until 1689. But as the theater of war expanded across the Atlantic, merchants and governmental officials pressed for the establishment of a mechanism that would allow quick and efficient condemnation of prizes taken by privateers. Vice-admiralty courts were perfectly suited to the task, and jurisdictions were proposed for Massachusetts, Rhode Island/New Hampshire, New York, Connecticut/East Jersey, Pennsylvania/West Jersey, Virginia, Carolina/Bahamas, Bermuda, Jamaica, Barbados, and the Leeward Islands. The courts were to issue letters of marque, or licenses, to privateers who wanted to prey on the commerce of the crown's wartime enemies.[3]

By the 1690s piracy had begun to worry imperial planners, especially since the benefits of accumulation through robbery at sea had shifted from the mother country to the colonies. Colonial merchants, fences for stolen goods, retailers in need of hard currency, and common people – all dealt with pirates. Indeed, many of New York's greatest fortunes were built upon concourse with pirates in Madagascar. Colonial officials were reluctant to apprehend pirates, and colonial courts and juries were not eager to convict them. Vice-admiralty courts – courts without juries – sought to destroy the colonists' reluctance and complicity. Royal officials Edward Randolph and Francis Nicholson saw that an independent vice-admiralty court system would serve as the legal machinery for the trial and eventual eradication of pirates.[4]

Jurisdiction in the Seventeenth Century (London, 1931), 27, 94; L. Kinvin Wroth, "The Massachusetts Vice-Admiralty," *Law and Authority in Colonial America,* ed. George Athan Billias (Barre, Mass., 1965), 44; Michael Craton, "The Role of the Caribbean Vice-Admiralty Court in British Imperialism" *Caribbean Studies* 11 (1971), 6.

[3] Doty, *British Admiralty Board,* 29; Andrews, "Vice-Admiralty Courts," 35–41.
[4] In addition to the excellent discussion of the evolution of Admiralty law, see the analysis of the changing relationship between piracy and the English state in Robert C. Ritchie, *Captain Kidd and the War against the Pirates* (Cambridge, Mass., 1986), 140–54, 10–16, 138–43. See also Ian K. Steele, *Politics of Colonial Policy: The Board of Trade in Colonial Administration, 1696–1720* (Oxford, 1968), 15, 50–8; Lawrence A. Harper, *The English Navigation Laws:*

The courts were established to limit another major source of accumulation in the colonies: smuggling. Vice-admiralty judges were charged with the strict enforcement of the Navigation Acts. Colonial products had always been central to illicit trade, but a boom in such traffic in the 1680s moved royal officials to implement further controls. Juryless trials promised the king's justice for both smugglers and pirates who flourished at the poorly policed edges of empire.[5]

The architects of maritime empire also sought to mediate the often ferocious disputes among merchants, captains, and seamen. In fact one of the earliest courts for admiralty affairs in the New World was proposed in 1615 for Newfoundland, "where disorders among fishermen were very common." Conflicts centered on wages, provisions, discipline, mutiny, salvage, desertion, custom, and rights. The swift expansion of overseas trade in the late seventeenth century gave new urgency to such problems, and the gravitation of trade to the New World meant that disputes could not easily be referred back to London.[6]

The establishment of the vice-admiralty courts, although formally a decentralization of jurisdiction and a transfer of administration from the metropolis to the colonies, actually represented a consolidation of metropolitan power within the empire. The shift was reflected in the cool and, in some cases, decidedly hostile reaction of various colonists to the new court system. Many elites in proprietary and corporate colonies saw the vice-admiralty scheme as a huge infringement upon rights granted in their colonies' charters. Where English rulers saw organization, many colonists saw interference. Resistance to the courts in Rhode Island, Pennsylvania, Connecticut, and South Carolina prevented the further consolidation of impe-

Footnote 4 (*cont.*):

A Seventeenth-Century Experiment in Social Engineering (New York, 1939), 176; Andrews, *Colonial Period,* vol. IV, 226; Crump, *Admiralty Jurisdiction,* 1; Doty, *British Admiralty Board,* 70. For examples of the leniency of colonial juries and the difficulties officials had in securing convictions, see "King's Letter to the Gov[erno]r of Virg[inia] concerning Wrecks," CO 5/1357 (1687); Edward Vernon to Josiah Burchett, Edward Vernon Letterbook, BL, Add. Ms. 40812 (Apr. 24, 1720); Robert Quary to Francis Nicholson, CO 5/1310 (June 2, 1699), ff. 58–60.

[5] Ubbelohde, *Vice-Admiralty Courts,* 12; Andrews, "Vice-Admiralty Courts," 11, 42–53.

[6] Crump, *Admiralty Jurisdiction,* 27; Andrews, "Vice-Admiralty Courts," 25–33. On wage disputes, see Chapter 3 of this book.

rial power until 1713 and after. But gradually the courts gained acceptance and power on the western side of the Atlantic. Although frequently a source of tension, they served as a foundation of eighteenth-century imperial rule.[7]

The records produced by the admiralty courts – documents on more than 2,200 cases between 1700 and 1750 – have served as a foundation for this study. The complexity of trade and the vastness of the admiralty's juridical domain made for liberalized rules of evidence in maritime cases. The courts accumulated reams of evidence, including multiple depositions with diverse perspectives on any given issue. Deponents – cabin boys, common tars, captains – frequently offered penetrating insights into social life, especially when they discussed the appearance and escalation of shipboard conflict. They carefully described both insubordination and punishment, the twin poles of the shipboard economy of discipline. Occasionally they related, word for word, an entire conversation between a captain and a seaman in conflict, showing how a mutiny might begin with a few deliberately disrespectful words. Admiralty records also provide a close look at many other aspects of the seaman's life, such as work, food, custom, wages, and desertion. Such sources contain ethnographic information and details utterly indispensable to understanding social life at sea.

Admiralty records do, however, suffer from problems and inconsistencies. A corollary to the flexibility of rules of evidence was the slowness and often – to the historian – the incoherence of the decision-making process in admiralty courts. The judge's final ruling on many cases is often unknown because decisions could be reversed as new evidence was submitted. Further, certain cases, for which voluminous evidence survives, have no recorded decisions because the contending parties settled out of court in order to avoid long delays. The historian therefore does not always have the advantage of knowing how judges weighed the evidence they heard. Such knowledge, even when available, does not, of course, always reflect the truth of the case. Judges rendered numerous verdicts that supported the interests of merchants and captains even when the evidence and the law stood firmly on the side of the common tar.

---

[7] Doty, *British Admiralty Board*, 28, 31, 34; Steele, *Politics of Colonial Policy*, 48; Ubbelohde, *Vice-Admiralty Courts*, 12; Andrews, "Vice-Admiralty Courts," 63, 66, 72, 76, 78.

It is important to note that the conflicts described in court records were not isolated incidents. Such conflicts appeared in almost all contemporaneous documents, whether produced by the state, the well-to-do, or the humble. Social tensions found reflection in merchants' and governmental correspondence, pamphlets, accounts of voyages, ships' logs, diaries and journals, state documents, folk songs, broadsides, newspapers, account books, and many other sources. Further, court records frequently add detail and context to processes and events that are independently verifiable in other sources. Moreover, there probably never existed a time, either before 1700 or after 1750, when the events described in the admiralty courts were so typical of those beyond the court's purview. After all, the admiralty court system was part of a general design to rationalize the imperial trading network, and a major part of this project was to confine social conflict to legal channels. Extralegal forms of protest were still popular among seamen, and court records may consequently understate the amount and intensity of shipboard conflict. In any case, the very efforts of the admiralty courts to mediate disputes between capital and labor resulted in an invaluable record of life at sea. When used in conjunction with a wide variety of other sources, the annals of the admiralty provide an unparalleled glimpse into the rough and rowdy world of the deep-sea sailor.

INDEX

vice-admiralty courts, 167, 212–3, 241
  and contract disputes, 140
  development of, 119, 312–15
  purposes of, 75, 119–21, 313–15
  records of, 315–16
  and wage disputes, 119–20, 314
  see also High Court of Admiralty
vice-admiralty judges, 56, 65, 67, 70, 241, 273–4
victuals (of seamen), 29, 93, 116, 117, 134, 212
  dispensation of, 222–4, 247, 251
  nature of, 126–30, 143, 159, 161, 258
  seamen's complaints regarding, 99, 101, 126–8, 151, 228, 232, 239
Virginia, 137, 281
  description of, 51–5
  pirates and, 254, 274, 277
  slave trade to, 220
  tobacco trade of, 43, 50–3
  see also Chesapeake; tobacco

wage labor, 21, 75, 116, 158, 207, 243
  abolition of, 107, 108, 146, 264
  development of, 16, 17, 77–8, 80, 114, 149–51, 199–200, 289–90, 293–4
  in England and America, 295–7
  pirates and, 107, 264, 286
  see also work; working class
wage labor markets, 31, 52, 61, 77, 104–5, 136, 140
wages (of seamen)
  and advance system, 125–6
  and contract, 117–18, 138–42, 158, 208, 210
  and culture, 168
  and custom, 126–7, 130
  docked by merchants, 143–5
  in East Indian trade, 40–1
  form of, 118–19, 131–3, 136–8
  and impressment, 145
  by rates, 121–4, 304–6
  and vice-admiralty courts, 119–21
  in West Indian trade, 104–5
  see also embezzlement
Wapping, 11, 24–7, 190
war
  and mutiny, 227–8
  and pirates, 272n52
  and Royal Navy, 31, 206

and trade, 20–1, 32–5, 61, 80
and wages, 121–4, 135, 151
working conditions for seamen during, 32–4, 79, 83, 97, 102–3, 200, 214–15, 282, 292
see also France; Holland; impressment; Royal Navy; Spain
War of Jenkins' Ear, 32, 63
War of the Austrian Succession (King George's War), 32
War of the League of Augsburg (King William's War), 32
War of the Spanish Succession (Queen Anne's War), 32, 34, 79, 117, 135, 281
Ward, Ned, 11, 59, 64, 96, 155, 165, 170, 171, 179, 250, 252, 288, 293
Weeden, William, 7
West Indies (British)
  economic development of, 58–9, 290
  piracy in, 56–8, 134, 257, 260
  population of, 81, 146
  seamen from, 80, 156
  trade in, 24, 45, 55, 62, 63, 66, 69, 79, 86, 139
  see also Jamaica; smuggling; sugar; trade
Whitefield, Reverend George, 64, 153, 167, 171n56
Woolman, John, 170, 171n56, 192, 203n142
work
  collective, 111, 112–13, 289–92
  and culture, 11–12, 154, 155–6, 158–9, 161, 198–201, 250
  and division of labor, 83–7
  and irreligion, 174–5
  and knowledge, 87–8, 95–6
  and language, 162–4
  nature of, 83, 88–94, 113–15
  and productivity, 75, 111–12
  stoppage, 97, 99, 106, 140, 291
  see also authority; collectivism; desertion; discipline; labor process; wage labor; wage labor markets; wages
working class, 31, 76, 77–8, 145, 205–6
  development of, 289, 294
  self-activity of, 152, 251, 253
  and speech, 167–8
Wycherly, William, 153